MIGRATING FAITH

MIGRATING

Pentecostalism in the United States and

DANIEL RAMÍREZ

FAITH

Mexico in the Twentieth Century

This book was published with the assistance of the Authors Fund of the University of North Carolina and the University of Michigan Office of Research.

© 2015 The University of North Carolina Press

Designed and set in Merlo by Rebecca Evans. Manufactured in the United States of America.

Cover illustration: believers en route to the 1928 convention of the Iglesia de la Fe Apostólica Pentecostés in Indio, California. From the Jose Ortega Photograph Collection; courtesy of Benjamin R. Ortega.

Title page illustration: members of Iglesia de la Fe Apostólica Pentecostés congregation in Colonia Zaragoza, Baja California, Mexico, 1928. From the Jose Ortega Photograph Collection, courtesy of Benjamin R. Ortega.

An earlier version of sections of Chapters 1, 2, 3, and 4 was originally published as "Borderlands Praxis: The Immigrant Experience in Latino Pentecostal Churches," *Journal of the American Academy of Religion* 67 (1999): 573–96.

An earlier version of sections of Chapter 1 was originally published as "Antonio Castañeda Nava: Charisma, Culture and *Caudillismo*," in *Portraits of a Generation: Early Pentecostal Leaders*, ed. Phillip Goff and Grant Wacker (Fayetteville: University of Arkansas Press, 2002)

An earlier version of sections of Chapter 6 was originally published as "Alabaré a Mi Señor: Hymnody as Ideology in Latino Protestantism," in *Singing the Lord's Song in a Strange Land: Hymnody in the History of North American Protestantism*, ed. Edith Blumhofer and Mark Noll (Tuscaloosa: University of Alabama Press, 2004).

An earlier version of sections of Chapter 3 was originally published as "'No Me Olvides'/ 'Forget Me Not': Pentecostal Praxis and Solidarity in Xenophobic Times," *PentecoStudies* 12 (2013): 8–35.

Library of Congress Cataloging-in-Publication Data
Ramirez, Daniel, 1958–
Migrating faith : Pentecostalism in the United States and Mexico, 1906–1966 / Daniel Ramirez.
pages cm
Based on the author's thesis (Ph. D.)—Duke University, 2005, entitled Migrating faiths.
Includes bibliographical references and index.
ISBN 978-1-4696-2406-8 (pbk   )
ISBN 978-1-4696-2407-5 (ebook : alk. paper)
1. Pentecostalism—United States—History—20th century. 2. Pentecostalism—Mexico—History—20th century. 3. Mexican-American Border Region—Religious life and customs—20th century. 4. Pentecostal converts—History—20th century. I. Title.
BR1644.5.U6R36 2015   277.08′2—dc23
2015002753

This book was digitally printed.

This book is dedicated to the memory of

LUIS, ELISEO, TOMÁS, *and* ROBERTO RAMÍREZ

CONTENTS

FIGURES, MAPS, AND TABLES

Figures

Maps

Tables

Many first books have their origins in doctoral dissertations. This one began well before that point. It received an early impetus in Guadalajara, Mexico. That incident bears relating here.

> *November 1993*—The first question from the floor was directed to the U.S. and Canadian members of the roundtable, all leading lights of the Society for Pentecostal Studies [SPS]: "¿Cual es su opinión sobre los peligros del neoliberalismo para el bienestar de la membresía de nuestras iglesias latinoamericanas, y qué pueden hacer la iglesias norteamericanas para frenar su expansión?" Moderator Manuel Gaxiola, a professional academic text translator, ably communicated the challenge: "What is your opinion of the dangers that neoliberalism poses for the well-being of our church members in Latin America, and what can the North American churches do to slow its expansion?" From the response, it was obvious that something more than expert translation was needed: "We should be wary of all currents of liberalism that can sway the church. Perhaps we in North America can do a better job of publishing materials to help the church in Latin America mature theologically and be on her guard."

While my recollection of the exact phrasing of the reply may not be precise, it does capture the gist of the exchange. I do recall clearly the looks of astonishment in the faces of the several Latin American and Latino scholars and church leaders, Gaxiola's awkward embarrassment, and my own bemusement at yet another squandered opportunity for dialogue between the global North and South. For the Society's twenty-ninth annual meeting, SPS regulars had gathered to compare notes with an unprecedented number of Latin American peers. The separate siting of parallel language tracks, however, made for little meaningful dialogue. The English-language sessions were held in the conference hotel and the Spanish ones at a Congregational church in another part of the city—hence, the heightened importance of the roundtable. But even in the bilingual setting of the plenary, vastly different optics and meanings were at play.

Why the urgency of the matter? At that moment, further south in Mexico, a revolt was smoldering, threatening to smudge the ink on the still-drying North American Free Trade Agreement (NAFTA). The interrogation proved prescient. On January 1, 1994, the very day of NAFTA's implementation, indigenous and mestizo rebels rose up in armed protest against late capitalism's exclusionary new paradigm and wrapped their struggle in the agrarian mantle of Emiliano Zapata, the revolutionary champion of land redistribution. President Carlos Salinas de Gortari dispatched the federal army and state and local police. The armed skirmishes provoked a global chorus of criticism against the NAFTA accord, one of economic neoliberalism's charter documents. In the face of the looming economic onslaught, Mexican church leaders and scholars pondered with deep concern the consequences for their flock, especially in the vulnerable countryside. The erasure of protectionist arrangements (owing to NAFTA's rules), the flood of heavily subsidized corn from the United States (in contravention of NAFTA's rules), and the dismantling of the agrarian communities inspired by Zapata (a parallel neoliberal reform of President Salinas) threatened to overwhelm and uproot subsistence farmers into a transnational pool of cheap labor. "Free trade" between a Goliath and a David did not ensure *fair* trade.

Clearly, a more prophetic challenge could not have been put forth to coreligionists from the North. Indeed, in the NAFTA period, rural migration, especially from southern Mexico and Central America, intensified. Among the desperate peasantry-turned-migrating-proletariat were thousands of Pentecostals. Lacking the social and economic capital of more elite countrymen—the advocates and beneficiaries of NAFTA and neoliberalism—and given the tiny legal funnel, their entry into the U.S. labor force took place by irregular means via channels set in place over many decades—as described in this book. Once in the United States, they replenished and reinvigorated Pentecostal congregations, especially Latino ones and including many in the flagship denominations like the Assemblies of God and the United Pentecostal Church International. From their comfortable perch, however, the global North scholars could only imagine that the danger being alluded to in Guadalajara in 1993 was coming from an as-yet-unknown (to them) theological current swirling somewhere in the hemisphere. A second-generation liberation theology perhaps? More important, who was minding orthodoxy's store? And what could be done to arrest the allure of heterodoxy? The incommensurabilities stretched further than mere lexical differences. They also included differences in loci of enunciation and epistemic-experiential prisms. The Pentecostal South, whose theological reflection and religious practice, like that of the liberationists, were shaped by economic exigencies, was decrying inequitable arrangements in the production and consumption of food. In earnest response, the Pentecostal North pledged to produce better food for thought. This book begins with a similar instance of crossed meaning and signification in Los Angeles nearly nine decades before the Guadalajara one.

Readers will detect my familiarity with the story chronicled in *Migrating Faith*. Students in my "Latino/a Religions and Cultures" course invariably hear stories about my maternal and paternal grandmothers, Cipriana Gonzalez and María Ramírez, the first a devout *guadalupana* and the second a devout *aleluya*. My connection to the aleluya story begins with María. When, as a single mother in 1924, María Mendoza boarded a train from Pénjamo, Guanajuato, for Ciudad Juárez, she was unaware that the offer of marriage she was taking up (it had arrived through the post) came with an unfortunate condition. Her countryman, Hilario Ramírez, a longtime resident of Del Mar, California, drank heavily. After a decade of troubled domestic life and instances of near death by his inebriated hand, María found in conversion (first with Presbyterians and then with Pentecostals) and *evangélico* music the means to "reform the machismo" of her spouse (I borrow from Elizabeth Brusco's celebrated phrase). As a result, my cousins and I knew only the sweetest and jolliest of grandfathers, Tata Layo. Nana María surely cradled me during my infancy, but our lives overlapped by only two years. I got to know her through her four sons, Eliseo, Tomás, Luis, and Roberto. Tomás and Roberto later served as prominent pastors and bishops in the apostolic movement; Eliseo and Luis, my father, as prominent laymen. The boys that trembled while singing "Yo Me Rindo a El" (I Surrender All) around their mother's protective skirt went on to become the legendary Hermanos Ramírez quartet that graced many a church conclave in the 1960s.

Such bona fides have certainly facilitated access to many of the "fugitive sources" analyzed in *Migrating Faith*. Manuel Gaxiola, José Ortega, Isaac Cota, José Avalos, and others entrusted much material into my hands. I lament their passing and hope that I have honored their trust. The establishment (December 2013) of the Apostolic Archives of the Americas at Fuller Seminary's Hubbard Library—anchored by the Manuel Gaxiola, Manuel Vizcarra, and Egla Montero Collections—preserves their legacy for scholars and posterity and relieves me of their charge to me. The historical work done by Manuel Gaxiola, Kenneth Gill, Felipe Gaxiola, Maclovio Gaxiola, José Ortega, Felipe and Nellie Rangel, Ernesto Cantú, and Samuel López has been foundational to *Migrating Faith*. Nevertheless, "insiders" will scour the book in vain for many familiar names and terms. This is decidedly not a denominational history but rather a social and cultural one of a broader religious movement. I have decided, therefore, not to include a roster of leading characters.

As a historian of religion, I bracket off the question of divine or suprahuman causality and seek to understand religious history, practice, and identity in social, historical, economic, and political contexts, especially charged, contingent, and precarious ones. When and where *Migrating Faith* peers through the thicket of congregational and other conflicts, it does so with the larger question of subaltern agency in mind. The examination of intra-Pentecostal tussles helps to guard against a romanticizing of the subaltern. So, too, does a critical optic concerning gender, ideology, official narratives, and dissent. I have sought to apply this optic to the *Migrating Faith* story. To riff on Grant Wacker's wonderful line about being a pilgrim with one leg still stuck in the Pentecostal tent, I, too, scampered in and out of an *aleluya carpa* as a child, literally. At one moment, I was part of the crowd watching evangelist Gilbert Muñoz praying over supplicants for healing (he famously kept trophy jars of extracted tumors); the next I was watching a roast pig being extracted from a pit. (The prolonged *campaña* planted a church in Arlington, California; there are photos of my father carving and grading the earth with his backhoe tractor.) What bound the whole glossolalic, healing, singing, and eating event together was the hospitality shown to saint and sinner alike. My critical gaze, then, is tempered by a belief that the sensory and social side of the story should be included.

The critical optic can also be used to reflect back the academic gaze. *Migrating Faith* poses new questions about, for example, a predilection for text-centric approaches to American religious history and our understanding and expectations for political engagement among the religiously mobilized. In the case of *Apostólicos* and other *Pentecostales*, that engagement perforce had to unfold in the legal shadows, owing to the high percentage of noncitizens in the pews and pulpits, and its traces must be sought in sonic and other corporeal spheres. This precarious residency, like that of the anonymous "saints in Caesar's household" whose salutations Paul relayed discreetly to the church in Philippi (Philippians 4:22), necessitated crouching as far below officialdom's (and academics') radar as possible. As a result, decades after the period studied here, many Pentecostal congregations were prepared intuitively to offer a deep and meaningful "sanctuary" to scores of thousands of Central Americans fleeing war and calamity in the 1980s. Although the storied movement of that name garnered media and academic attention (and left a voluminous paper trail), it ultimately did not embrace the sojourners as intimately as did Pentecostal congregations. The few refugees who came through did not remain in the sanctuary congregations; indeed, that was never the purpose of the cause. "Sanctuary" served as a proxy for the more important battle being waged against Ronald Reagan's foreign policy on the front pages of the *New York Times* and *Washington Post* and in front of the Supreme Court. Yet, accompaniment and hospitality mattered as much as vigorous and savvy advocacy. It is small wonder, then, that many of the Central American children fleeing gang violence today are arriving to familial embraces in Pentecostal congregations with long histories as places of respite. The plight of those children reminds me of that of José Avalos and the scores of thousands of other children uprooted during the Great Repatriation of the 1930s (Chapter 3). I laud the long-overdue apology issued in February 2012 by the Board of Supervisors for Los Angeles County's role in that nefarious calamity. I also note the steep social and economic opportunity cost of shortsighted scapegoating and indifference, costs we continue to incur today. Yet, as the repatriate Apostolic story chronicled in *Migrating Faith* and the ancient one about Joseph and his brothers remind us, actions meant for harm can rebound in unexpected and lifegiving ways.

ACKNOWLEDGMENTS

The seeds of *Migrating Faith* gestated initially in the orbit of the Society for Pentecostal Studies. I owe this community of scholars a debt of thanks. The SPS also introduced me to the light of my academic life, Grant Wacker, who insisted that I leave administrative work at Stanford University, his undergraduate alma mater, in order to study American religious history with him in Duke University's Graduate Program in Religion. The deep faculty bench there and down the road at the University of North Carolina at Chapel Hill only enhanced that wonderful experience. Walter Mignolo, Laurie Maffley-Kipp, Russ Richey, Bruce Lawrence, David Steinmetz, Liz Clark, and Tom Tweed modeled exemplary pedagogy and scholarship. Their excellence was matched by that of the hearty band of Wackerites, who still meet for fellowship and sarsaparilla years after leaving Durham. The Program's unique setting also made for invigorating exchanges with faculty and students in the Duke Divinity School. I am particularly indebted to Willie Jennings's sagacity and to Dean Greg Jones's generosity.

I also was blessed with the support of the Pew Trusts–supported Hispanic Theological Initiative (HTI). The brainchild of historian Justo Gonzalez, *un gran visionario*, this doctoral network linked me to a valued mentor, Luis Rivera Pagán, who, in turn, introduced me to philosopher Enrique Dussel. The HTI *hermandad*, including my subsequent HTI mentees Erica Ramírez and Francisco Peláez-Díaz, continue to be a source of inspiration in the many venues where it meets. I thank them by thanking the directors who have helmed the Initiative: Daisy Machado, Zaida Maldonado, and Joanne Rodríguez. As the *Migrating Faith* project developed, it benefited from the guidance and encouragement of Rudy Busto, the late Otto Maduro, Luis León, Paul Barton, Juan Martínez, Edwin Aponte, Jesse Miranda, Efraín Agosto, Elizabeth Conde-Frazier, Carlos Cardoza, Carmelo Alvarez, Anthea Butler, David Daniels, David Reed, A. G. Miller, Sammy Alfaro, Mel Robeck, David Bundy, Domingo Torres, Ismael Martin del Campo, and Amos Yong. Now that this book joins those by Arlene Sanchez-Walsh and Gastón Espinosa, two supportive colleagues, perhaps our tiny guild can relax our rule about never boarding the same air flight together.

I have previewed different sections of this project with colleagues in Mexico, beginning with the Red de Investigadores del Fenómeno Religioso en México (RIFREM) and its leaders and members. These include Cristina Gutiérrez, Rodolfo Morán, Carlos Garma, Alberto Hernández, Renee de la Torre, Genaro Zalpa, Patricia Fortuny, Antonio Higueras, Felipe Vásquez, Olga Odgers, Liliana Rivera, María Eugenia Patiño, Daessy Jael de la Luz García, Ramiro Jaimes, Gabriela Robledo, Ariel Corpus, Gustavo López, and Raúl Méndez. Bob Wright, Alberto Pulido, Timothy Matovina, and the other members of the U.S. chapter of the Comisión para la Historia de la Iglesia en Latinoamerica (CEHILA) have also accompanied this project. My RIFREM and CEHILA colleagues' several institutions have welcomed presentations of the *Migrating Faith* story: El Colegio de Jalisco, El Colegio de la Frontera Norte, the Instituto de Investigaciones Históricas at the Universidad Autónoma de Baja California, the Universidad Autónoma de Quintana Roo, and the Universidad Iberoamericana. *Mil gracias, muy estimados colegas.*

I appreciate the wise and generous collegiality of Joel Gereboff and members of the Religious Studies Department of Arizona State University, my second academic home. As it neared completion, the *Migrating Faith* manuscript benefited enormously from review by Allan Anderson and Mark Noll. I am grateful for the invitation extended to them by the University of Michigan Department of History and Department of American Culture. Colleagues at the University of Michigan Institute for the Humanities and at the Louisville Institute also weighed in with helpful suggestions. Sylvia Pedraza and Yeidi Rivero have also been generous in their moral support, as has Bob Roth, University of Michigan Wesley Foundation chaplain.

My editor at the University of North Carolina Press, Elaine Maisner, merits special praise as an expert and patient book midwife. I express my deep appreciation to her and to the Press's external reviewers. The project would not have been brought home without the Microsoft Word expertise of my brother Louis; the generous contributions of Benjamín Ortega (photos), Maricela Maffey Luján (photos), Milca Montañez (photos), Michael Cota (maps), Herminia "Minnie" Martínez (genealogy), and Moses Gutiérrez Jr. (genealogy); and the help and encouragement of Felipe Agredano, Jorge Montes, Armando Razo, and Abraham Ruiz. The book's many flaws are entirely mine to own, however.

I have often remarked that if I could be half the mentor for someone that Grant Wacker was for me, I will have accomplished a great thing.

Lloyd Barba arrived to the University of Michigan American Culture doctoral program to put me to the test. More than a student, Lloyd has turned out to be a colleague and teacher. The field awaits his important findings on the untold Pentecostal Okie and *bracero* stories. His insights will prompt new interrogations of John Steinbeck and Dorothea Lange's iconic oeuvre.

The theme of hospitality runs throughout *Migrating Faith*. I have received copious amounts of this from the families of Manuel and Gloria Gaxiola (Mexico City), Apolinar and Elena Muro (Zapopan), Absalón and Febe Avalos (Guadalajara), and Celerino and Bernarda Ríos (Oaxaca). Finally, I have learned to rest on the unconditional support of my siblings Margie (*QEPD*), Mary Anne, Louise (*QEPD*), Louis, Joseph, Stella, and Jonathan. This sibling love is a testament to our late parents, Luis and Margarita. My siblings, in turn, shared with me an affectionate brood of nephews and nieces, who now generously keep the next generation connected to Tío Danny. For this I am grateful.

MIGRATING FAITH

Introduction

En esta vida esperamos la victoria	In this life we await the victory
La que el Señor él mismo nos dará	Which the Lord himself will give us
Despues iremos a estar con él	Then we shall go to be with him
en gloria	in glory
Donde se goza de plena libertad	There to enjoy full liberty
Aleluya, aleluya, aleluya	Hallelujah, hallelujah, hallelujah
Aleluya, aleluya al Señor	Hallelujah, hallelujah to the Lord
Aleluya, aleluya, aleluya	Hallelujah, hallelujah, hallelujah
Él nos libra del tentador	He frees us from the tempter

This hymn by one of early Latino Pentecostalism's most prolific composers offers up, upon first hearing, some of the themes that one would expect in a musical artifact of early twentieth-century Evangelicalism: sanctification in the present life, salvation in the next, and familiar liturgical phrasing, all carried along by an upbeat 4/4 rhythm.[1] The song also marks the emergence of a robust original Spanish-language hymnodic repertoire—lyrical, rhythmic, and instrumental—that began to loosen the seams of the corpus of translated Protestant hymnody. The new spirit-infused wine required pliable wineskins. It also required dedicated husbandry. Marcial de la Cruz (b. 1885) was reported often to emerge, guitar in hand, from the pup tent in which he prayed and fasted, with a newly inspired song to debut before preaching.[2] Listeners along his evangelistic circuit in California, Arizona, and New Mexico thrilled to the sound of the familiar instrument and poetic cadence with which he heralded a new Pentecost. The minutes of early borderlands Pentecostal conclaves offer traces of the composer's fecundity. The "active and pious apostolic" minister's folkloric style even enchanted more upscale Methodists, Presbyterians, and Baptists. His valedictory "Aleluya al Señor" takes on an additional layer of significance, however, when we consider the circumstances of its composition: De la Cruz's deathbed in Tijuana, Baja California. Tuberculosis had provoked the evangelist's expulsion from California during the protracted period of anti-Mexican xenophobia known as the Great Repatriation. His final months were marked by penury. His remains were quickly buried in an unmarked pauper's grave in Tijuana's Second Municipal Cemetery, mere yards away from the country to which he had migrated over twenty years earlier.[3] Unable even to sing his new song at the end, De la Cruz left the last verse for his daughter Beatriz to finish. Thus, in addition to the hymn's soteriological and eschatological themes, we must also consider the compositional context of voluntary, forced, and circular migration; calamitous and fortuitous macroevents and microresponses to these; and even religious remittances (De la Cruz's music preceded him back to Mexico, carried along by repatriated migrants and new hymnal compilations.) The song's enunciation of abundant life in the here and now offers a poignant counterdiscourse against the zero-sum Malthusian one of restricted citizenship and exclusionary scapegoating. It echoes Mary's Magnificat (Luke 1:46–55) and promises a future cosmic comeuppance. Notably, the chorus embraces the popular epithet hurled at early Pentecostals. The song endured well beyond the composer's short life. His music lived on to thrill and encourage coreligionists through the following decades, including those decades beset by perennial xenophobic fevers in the body politic. Clearly, Tijuana was more than a barren and exilic periphery. If the hundreds of Pentecostal congregations in its metropolitan region today (including San Diego) are an index, then it is worth investigating the early history of such peripheries for historical and cultural clues to the impressive religious demographic change afoot in Latino USA and in Latin America today. *Migrating Faith* proposes such an expedition.

Pentecostalismo

Students of modern religious history are now generally aware, at a century's distance, of the importance of the Azusa Street Revival that erupted in 1906 in Los Angeles, California. The spiritual tremors that shook the decidedly downscale venue (derided as a "tumble-down shack" by the city's taste-arbitrating *Daily Times*), together with distant ones in South India, Wales, and elsewhere, set off a global pneumatic tsunami that swept Evangelical Christianity during the first quarter of the twentieth century. The preexisting topographies, however, shaped the particular outcomes of revivalism in each region. When the initial wave partially receded in the United States, the newly configured religious archipelago still reflected the racialized topography of Jim Crow America. Several of those islets were populated by glossolalia and Spanish-speaking enthusiasts claiming healing and other gifts. Few scholars, however, charted that change.

By contrast, the flood of Pentecostal and Pentecostal-like revivalism in the Spanish- and Portuguese-speaking Americas in the last quarter of the twentieth century—a later pneumatic-driven wave—captured the attention of sociologists, anthropologists, political scientists, and philanthropic foundations. Some heralded the democratic promise of heated Wesleyan piety. Others lamented the extinguishing of liberation theology's flame or the "mutation" of historic Protestantism. All noted the growth.[4]

Migrating Faith proposes to chart the flow of one early Pentecostal current between these two points and periods. Like the hydrological basin that shapes the course of the river known on its northern bank as the Rio Grande and on its southern bank as the Rio Bravo, early borderlands Pentecostalism can provide clues about patterns and flows downstream and in other regions. In particular, the history of its immediately subsequent transnational flow, with salient features of migration, mobility, and musicality, can help us chart more precisely the seemingly muddled waters of contemporary global Pentecostal effervescence. This historical expedition seeks to return to fountainheads and prime tributaries that shaped the force and flow of modern Pentecostalism.

To switch metaphors, this book seeks to fill in the middle between the above chronological brackets (early and late twentieth century) and also to illumine the underappreciated chromaticity of the front-end bracket. Until now, the story of early U.S. Pentecostalism has been rendered largely in black and white. Early protagonists variously straddled, reinforced, or ignored the racial divides of Jim Crow America. Yet all who contemporaneously recorded or retrospectively reconstructed the revival's events and interpreted its meanings did so in English. This redaction skewed the arc of the story early on. This study seeks to recover the oft-ignored diacritics of the grammar of Azusa Street, in order to hear the other (non-English) voices that were present at the movement's genesis and that were as constitutive of early Pentecostalism's sound (or cacophony) as English ones—in other words, to paraphrase Gayatri Spivak's celebrated argument, to hear the subaltern speak in her or his own tongue(s).[5] In line with the restored inflection, this cultural history examines the sonic, lyrical, corporeal, and migratory dimensions of early Latino Pentecostalism (and invites new semiotic approaches), in order to understand the broader movement's still considerable proselytizing charms.

Like brackets, borders both exclude and include. Mexicans and Chicanos (Mexican Americans) are all too aware of this, even today. *Migrating Faith*, however, inverts the standard approach and makes central the previously peripheral. The analytical point of departure begins with the outsider as insider. This locus allows us to hear the enunciation of solidarity and view its practice by liminal subjects caught (or moving) between nation-states and to perceive patterns and templates that prefigure features of the contemporary transnational revival of such great academic interest.

To begin, let us consider two citations about and by indigenous Mexican Pentecostals that roughly bracket the time period under study. The following is drawn from the first issue of the Azusa Street mission's *Apostolic Faith* magazine. The report of an event four months into the revival teases us with an intriguing description of Azusa Street's extraordinary polyglot, multiracial, and gendered mix:

> On August 11th, a man from the central part of Mexico, an Indian, was present in the meeting and heard a German sister speaking in his tongue which the Lord had given her. He understood, and through the message that God gave him through her, he was most happily converted so that he could hardly contain his joy. All the English he knew was Jesus Christ and Hallelujah. He testified in his native language, which was interpreted by a man who had been among that tribe of Indians. This rough Indian, under the power of the Spirit was led to go and lay his hands on a woman in the congregation who was suffering from consumption, and she was instantly healed and arose and testified.[6]

Anticipating the skeptics and seekers, the editors included the following testimonial as confirmation:

> Los Angeles, Aug. 12th, 1906. This will certify that my daughter, Mrs. S. P. Knapp, of Avenue 56 and Alameda street, was healed of consumption by God on the above date, God's Spirit working in answer to prayer and through a poor Mexican Indian. For particulars, inquire of Frank Gail, with Troy Laundry, corner 14th and Main, Los Angeles.[7]

For the editors, the proof of the new Pentecost—heralded in the banner title of the *Apostolic Faith*'s second issue—lay precisely in the Spirit baptisms among "God's humble people." While the characterization of the Mexican Indian convert helped to flesh out a picture of downscale revivalism, however, it also unwittingly echoed the racial ideology of the era and replicated its practice of erasure. Notice how the transcription of the healing event severely redacted the healer's discourse. The definitive textual record—the datum necessary for later historical research—included only those words that were intelligible to the editors: "Jesus Christ" and "Hallelujah." The editors, thus, excluded his testimony, thereby rendering the discursive unit inaccessible to historians seeking to reconstruct more fully the dimensions of the revival. We can only safely surmise that our near phantom had migrated from central Mexico to Los Angeles at the turn of the century. We are left to wonder whether he testified in Nahuatl, Otomí, Purépecha-Tarasco, Totonaco, or any other of the many languages of central Mexico. More important, we are left to wonder whether he returned to modern Mesoamerica to plant the seeds watered and harvested later by pioneer evangelists and missionaries like Andrés Ornelas and Axel Anderson, whose movements realized early inroads into Otomí-speaking populations.[8] We can marvel at the linguistic abilities of the well-traveled translator but also must lament the sociolinguistic captivity of the revival's leaders.

The ideological blinders also muffled the sound and meaning of subaltern languages. This prevented the leaders from appreciating the irony of their redaction against the backdrop of celebratory claims concerning xenolalia.[9] By contrast, the editors did publish the bilingual testimony of "Spanish" evangelists Abundio and Rosa López, replicating, as a result, the racialized social hierarchies of New Spain and Mexico and glossing over the divide between subordinated indigenous groups and more centrally situated mestizos in "greater Mexico."

To be fair, the *Apostolic Faith*'s editors also did not include more information on German speakers. They did include them, however, in an interesting couplet that reiterated the trope of a democratic Pentecost:

> It is noticeable how free all nationalities feel. If a Mexican or German cannot speak English, he gets up and speaks in his own tongue and feels quite at home for the Spirit interprets through the face and people say amen. No instrument that God can use is rejected on account of color or dress or lack of education. That is why God has so built up the work.[10]

We can safely surmise that the status of a German American or immigrant differed radically, as did that of lighter-skinned Mexican Americans, from that of an indigenous Mexican immigrant in turn-of-the-century California. Methodist and Lutheran polities still included important German-speaking jurisdictions throughout the country, while Mexicans were being thrust into what sociologist Tomás Almaguer has characterized as California's "racial fault lines." [11] Thus, the editors and letter contributor could deploy adjectives like "poor" and "rough" in the case of the Mexican Indian and none whatsoever in the case of the German woman, without giving the difference in description a second thought. That difference is telling, in that it reveals the continued incommensurabilities that were to persist and haunt the new Pentecost. The divides were more than racial.

Now to a contrasting example. Over a half century later, the May 30, 1957, issue of the *Exégeta*, the periodical of Mexico's Iglesia Apostólica de la Fe en Cristo Jesús (one of that country's flagship Pentecostal denominations), carried a prodigal's story in its "Testimonio" section. The following truncated narrative of labor and spiritual migration (this excerpt skips over description of boat travel within Mexico from Acapulco to Ensenada and movement from there to Tijuana and Mexicali) contrasts sharply with the brief cameo granted the "rough Indian" in the *Apostolic Faith* report of five decades earlier:

Testimony

I was born in the city of Oaxaca, Oaxaca, and while yet young was orphaned, which left a younger brother and me in the care of my mother. After several years, some relatives of my mother invited her to go live in the port city of Acapulco, Guerrero; she accepted the offer. . . . I wrote to my mother to let her know that I was fine and was working. I anxiously awaited her reply. After she replied, I decided to leave that place [Ensenada], wishing to explore the state capital, Mexicali. I passed through the city of Tijuana, and since it was late, I looked for a place to pass the night. I came across an older man, who happened to be a Christian from the Apostolic Church. He recommended that I go to that church where they would put me up. Sure enough, I was greeted warmly and given a place to stay. They even helped me with my luggage and other unmerited favors.

The brother of the place where I lodged began to talk to me about the things of the Lord. What impressed me the most and touched my heart were the following words: "Look, young man, if you desire happiness, and wish to find peace in one place, accept the Lord in your heart, and you'll be happy." It seemed that the man knew my condition. It was none other than the Lord at work. I spent a happy night with that talk that refreshed my soul.

I found work the following day after arriving in Mexicali. It was

October, and there was work in the cotton harvest. I went to live in Colonia Zaragoza, about ten kilometers outside the city, and although there is an Apostolic temple there, I never felt the desire to visit it. One day as I was looking for some friends, I wandered off my path, and passed by a house with a large corral and lots of cattle. A cowboy was curing a cow, and while I conversed with him, a woman came up to us and asked me, "Young man, where are you headed?" "I'm looking for some friends," I replied, "Are you in a hurry?" "No, M'am." "Well then, why don't you come inside to eat with us?"

I accepted the invitation [in Mexicali], and as I sat at the table and heard the blessing, I realized that they were the same type of "Aleluyas" I had met in Tijuana. As I ate, they plied me with questions about my religion, and offered me sound advice. Finally, they invited me to work there, and I stayed with them three days.

On Wednesday I observed that they began early to arrange the house, because that night they were going to celebrate a service. Many brothers arrived, and I saw them sing and pray very fervently. The preaching of the Word of God finally filled my heart. It was February of 1955. . . . I continued to work with those brothers, whose names are Ramón and Gregoria Sandes. On Sundays they would take me to the church in Colonia Zaragoza; thus, little by little I began liking the Word of God. I am very grateful for these brothers and their work on behalf of my salvation. I ask God to bless them. After three months of visiting the church, I began to sing with the youth choir, and although I was not baptized, I felt great joy being with them. I even got into strenuous arguments with some people, defending the brothers and the Word of God. . . . On July 7 there was a tarrying service, and the Lord sealed me with his Holy Spirit. It was a most glorious experience to feel the divine joy and to glorify God in other tongues. On the tenth day of the same month the pastor, Bro. Faustino Mendoza baptized me in Jesus' Name for the forgiveness of my sins. . . . I am now writing to my mother, and I am giving her the testimony of my salvation, and of my happiness, since I am now a new creature in Christ. She is very happy that I have been rescued from my lost life. I ask prayers for her so that she may be saved as well. May the Lord grant me one day to go and give my testimony of His power to the lost souls in that city of Acapulco, in which there is much perdition. I have no doubt that there are evangélicos there, but it seems as if they have hidden the light—Urías Rodríguez Alavez. [12]

The juxtaposed passages prompt several questions: How do we understand the transition in representation from incoherent other to articulate historical subject? From joyful ineffability to deliberate speech acts? What larger social, cultural, and economic processes made this possible? This project seeks to chart the transition over five decades from the barest of sketches about a xenolalic other (albeit with thaumaturgic gifts) to a fully fleshed-out portrait of purposeful solidarity. Rodríguez's story, which could stand in for thousands of such stories in earlier and later decades, exposes the emotional and cultural underpinnings that underlie the process of religious change in *las Américas*. Migration due to economic exigencies or opportunities or vicissitudes leads to human uprootedness, mobility, and liminality, which, in turn, often shake loose traditional or received ways and beliefs. Migrating and converted agents often turn to culture, especially musical culture, to express nostalgia, melancholy, hope, and power. These affects are reinforced in congregational spheres or webs of hospitable solidarity and transmitted through wider, often transnational circuits of fellowship. The evangelistic imperative often prompts return migration or the dispatching of religious remittances: songs, testimonies, pamphlets, Bibles, periodicals, offerings, instructions, and so on. The reception of these ranges from the eager to the indifferent to the hostile and often sets religious fields in flux. Rodríguez's testimony (read in myriad corners of Mexico, the United States, and Central and South America) and entreating correspondence with his mother reflect the above dimensions, as well as the important one of gender (maternity and filial concern).

In order to understand this process, this book traces the evolution of a major tributary of Mexican/Chicano Pentecostalism, Apostolicism,[13] through the first six decades of growth and examines the construction of transnational circuits and webs that bolstered subaltern responses to macroevents and prejudicial actions of nation-states and dominant cultures. The project proposes to map (and sound out) the early history of the movement through a focused study of religious genealogies (congregational, regional, and individual) that spread and took root along the borderlands swath stretching from the Pacific coast to the Texas–Tamaulipas border and deeper into both countries. This study proffers analytical templates for understanding Pentecostalism's explosive success in later decades throughout farther-flung regions in the hemisphere. Its historical contextualization introduces notions of linkages and genealogies to discussions of contemporary *evangélico* growth among U.S. Latinos and in Latin America and underscores Pentecostalism's continuities and discontinuities with prior mainline Protestant expansion in the late nineteenth and early twentieth centuries.

In Mexico and the U.S. Southwest, as elsewhere in Latin America, Pentecostal and Pentecostal-like religious practices migrated more easily than others because they required less institutional support and management. Consequently, they emerged as prime carriers of popular culture, flowing along the fissures created by the large-scale economic, political, and social transformations of the twentieth century. A vibrant religious musical culture tied these expanding transnational communities as much as did more material elements. Accordingly, this primarily social historical study plumbs through ethnomusicological method the movement's expressive culture, in order to understand Pentecostalism's profound emotive dimensions. Such an understanding minimizes, of course, zero-sum assimilationist models of psychological and material deprivation that may seek to explain U.S. Latino conversion to Protestantism; such models simply do not apply in deep Mexico and other regions of Catholic hegemony. Religious conversion—its language about newness notwithstanding—does not represent necessarily the erasure of one essentialized identity in favor of another essentialized one; rather, in Pentecostalism we can see an intensified process of religious cultural hybridity and flux.

This book focuses on heterodox (non-Trinitarian) actors, movements, and cultures, reading mainline and orthodox sources against the grain and combing through Mexican officialdom's records for traces of Pentecostal agency and interreligious competition. It tracks transborder or transnational circuits and highlights cultural elements of the story, thereby blurring the American religious history guild's traditional geopolitical and disciplinary boundaries. In addition to interrogating mainstream U.S. Pentecostal history, *Migrating Faith* also posits a view of Latino USA as the northernmost Latin American country.

This study's close attention to a specific ethno-religious group and zone tugs at the sweeping hypotheses offered by scholars such as sociologist David Martin. The renowned theorist of dissimilar secularizations extended worldwide his hopeful Wesleyan renewal metaphor concerning Latin American evangelicalism and extolled the promise of democratic reform for and by the "culturally despised," new traders of religious cultural goods.[14] Pentecostalism, for Martin, is like Islam; it is globalizing and continually revitalizes itself. But unlike Islam (in Martin's view), Pentecostalism is neither inherently political nor violent but rather personal and cultural—a religion tailor-made for a rapidly globalizing moment.[15] Such sanguinity invites testing on the ground, and the U.S.–Mexico borderlands represent a promising zone for this. There, at great distances from hegemonic arbiters of orthodoxy (religious, aesthetic, and political) in both countries and in a period before those surveyed by Martin, subaltern Pentecostal actors widened social and political crevasses in order to make room for new religious options. Often in that process, the orthodox ramparts engineered by mainline missionaries proved too tenuous to withstand the breaching by heterodox converts and agents. Also, in their utilitarian approach to geopolitical boundaries and labor opportunities, the Pentecostals studied here prefigured much of the transnational reverse-missions movement of African and Asian Pentecostal migrants to Europe and North America later in the twentieth century.[16]

Pentecostalismo as Protest

As in the case of its mainline precursors, especially Methodism, the growth of early Mexican/Chicano Pentecostalism transcended national borders. Indeed, the original revival in its initial charismatic phase blurred and transgressed several boundary lines segmenting the southern California borderlands of the era. The revival flowed freely back and forth across the U.S.–Mexico border and tested Jim Crow sensibilities by "wash[ing] away in the blood" the new century's "color line."[17] It eschewed Victorian propriety in favor of ecstatic worship, the multiracial embrace of bodies, and female leadership.

In more material terms, the historian Robert Mapes Anderson argued that early U.S. Pentecostalism represented a protest of "the disinherited" against the strictures of an expansive capitalism. For Anderson, enterprising members of the uprooted rural and urban working and middling classes achieved through religious activism and leadership some measure of self-respectability, while leaving intact and uninterrogated the inequities of the U.S. economic system.[18]

The inevitable institutionalization of the movement streamlined the religious anarchy into the more recognizable parameters of the status quo of early and mid-twentieth-century America. The historian Grant Wacker ascribed this to the movement's twin thrusts, primitivism and pragmatism, which moved at times in tension and at other times in imbalance.[19]

Pentecostals could both proclaim an eschatological denouement to history—the end-times—and embrace modernity's technological advances in communication and transportation. They could both trade music across racial lines and acquiesce to Jim Crow arrangements. They could both trust the Holy Spirit to communicate immediate direction to believers and marshal impressive periodical resources to disseminate that communication. The contradiction or synthesis lay in the eye of the beholder.

In terms of gender, the sociologist Margaret Poloma demonstrated how denominational maturation diminished women's clerical options over time (Wacker reinforced this point).[20] Thus, while in the revival's first two decades women such as Florence Crawford and Aimee Semple McPherson shared equal billing with male leaders, by the time of World War II, the number of women on ministerial rosters had shrunk considerably. Institutionalization reflected and bolstered male privilege.

Behind Anderson's, Wacker's, and Paloma's analyses lay, of course, Weberian notions of sect-to-church evolution and routinization of charisma. Although only Anderson included Latinos in his study (albeit minimally), these approaches illumine important features of early *pentecostalismo*.[21] Still, *Migrating Faith* attempts to understand a sui generis ethnic religious movement on its own shifting ground and in its own contingent context. Such an approach necessarily brackets several long-standing arguments in American Pentecostal history, for example, whether the roots are more Wesleyan, Reform, or African American.[22] In the case of Latino and Latin American Pentecostalism, these also include proto-evangélico, Catholic, indigenous, and Afro Latino strains.

In contrast to Weberian models, the Chicano/Mexican variant of the revival magnified dimensions of cultural and social protest throughout its institutionalization in the early twentieth century. Different sectors of the "disinherited" appropriated revivalism in very different ways. Pentecostal conversion did not entail necessarily a step up the social ladder, as has been assumed for conversion to mainline Protestantism. In the case of borderlands Apostolics, ecclesial consolidation reinforced ethnic autonomy and transnational solidarity, in response to chaos and drift in the social and political periphery. The growing transborder consciousness solidified just in time to help Apostolics withstand immediately subsequent periods of scapegoating and persecution in both countries as well as internal schism. That consciousness then allowed them to profit from the renewed uprooting forced on them by external events.

Apostolicism in Greater Mexico

Uneven and competing surveys and absent (in the United States) and imprecise (in Mexico) census data about religion continue to hamper research on Pentecostalism in Mexico and among Mexican-origin populations in the United States. Nevertheless, some reports detect general and important trends. For example, the 2007 Pew Research report "Changing Faiths: Latinos and the Transformation of American Religion" presents a national snapshot that can be parsed by national origin. Much of the disparity between the 19.6 percent representation for Protestant (Evangelical plus mainline) U.S. Latinos versus 16 percent for Mexican-origin Latinos can be explained by the vastly higher representation among Puerto Rican and Central American–origin respondents: 36 and 25 percent, respectively. Of course, the sheer size of Mexican-origin populations mitigates the 3.6-point difference (19.6 versus 16 percent). However, the disparate intra-Latino Evangelical numbers (where Pentecostals would be included) clue us in to the outsize role of Puerto Ricans—and increasingly Central Americans—within U.S. Latino Pentecostalism: Puerto Rican, 27 percent; Central American, 22 percent; Mexican, 12 percent. Another way to view this is in terms of the Catholic percentage in each national-origin group: Puerto Rican, 49 percent; Central American, 60 percent; Mexican, 74 percent.[23] In other words, Catholicism has demonstrated considerable staying power within Mexican-origin Latinos. This is congruent with the picture in Mexico, where the 2010 census reported 89.3 percent of the population above five years of age to be Catholic and 5 percent evangélico. Of the 8,386,207 evangélicos, nearly 10 percent (820,744) belonged to the "historic" or mainline denominations and 23 percent (1,970,347) to official Pentecostal ones. Arguably, Pentecostals, Charismatics, and other pneumatic types would have comprised at least half of the remaining 5,595,116 Protestants (the typologies fail to capture *evangelicalismo*'s broad Pentecostal inflection).[24] This clearer view of religion in "greater" Mexico helps us to understand Apostolicism's significance in Mexican and Chicano evangelicalismo and religion generally, especially in light of the following.

Some reports about and from two flagship denominations can serve as tentative indices of growth (and decline). Outside researcher María Valenzuela reported a conservative adult baptized membership of 82,799 for the Iglesia Apostólica in 1996.[25] In 2000, the Iglesia Apostólica reported

1,174 congregations and 110,047 baptized members in Mexico; the 2010 figures were 1,527 and 184,332, respectively.[26] Throughout their shared history, the membership figure of the U.S. Apostolic Assembly has lagged slightly behind that of the Iglesia Apostólica of Mexico. This renders a conservative estimate of overall baptized membership of 300,000 in both countries in the first decade of the twenty-first century. Using this as a base and employing church growth methods, we can estimate the overall community (adherents, sympathizers, and children of both denominations) to number over one-half million in both countries. This estimate does not include the membership of both groups in the other's national territory (a growing constituency), the membership in mission fields in Central and South America (the Assembly reported 31,000 baptized adult members there in 2004[27]), and the several now-autonomous denominations established by the two churches in Central America. Also, if we add early excisions, such as the Iglesia Cristiana Evangélica Espiritual, the Luz del Mundo (Light of the World), and several long-separated sibling movements, and later ones, such as Efraím Valverde's Church of Jesus Christ in the Americas, the Oneness stream would more than double in size. This helps us appreciate Apostolicism's relatively high profile within Mexican and Chicano Protestantism. Small wonder, then, that the academic study of Pentecostalism in Mexico has paid fuller attention to this heterodox variant—especially the outlying Luz del Mundo with its 188,326 adherents over the age of five years reported in the 2010 census—than has the general study of Pentecostalism in the United States and elsewhere in the world.[28] (Columbia and Nicaragua have also been exceptional cases in this regard, due to the equally high profile in those countries of the Iglesia Pentecostal Unida and the Iglesia Apostólica, respectively.) Apostolicism remains an important cultural tributary within the much larger Pentecostal river. And as we shall see, musical cultural samples extracted downstream show clear, albeit diluted *apostólico* traces.

Yet institutional growth represents only a small part of the larger picture of religious change, much of which occurs in spite and outside of institutions. When these calcify or seek to contain the ebullience, new fissures appear to remind us of Protestantism's perennial schismatic tendencies. Pentecostalism's genius is also part of its problem. Believers and their goods migrate as the spiritual winds blow (or currents flow). Although tied through spiritual genealogy, they may grow apart institutionally or completely outside institutions.

Chapter Outline

Mexicans and Mexican Americans witnessed the very first perforation of Azusa Street's revivalism well in Los Angeles in 1906 (we return to our hydrological metaphor), eagerly joined the Apostolic Faith Mission, and soon thereafter carried a heterodox (non-Trinitarian) variant of Pentecostalism to border zones and agricultural valleys (Imperial, Coachella, San Joaquin, Ventura, Salinas, Maricopa, etc.) and mining towns in California, Arizona, New Mexico, and Baja California. Chapter 1 sets the early growth of this self-denominated Apostolic movement against the backdrop of mainline precursors (mostly Methodist), Pentecostal competitors (mostly Assemblies of God missionaries), and distant African American sponsors (Pentecostal Assemblies of the World). The minutes of pioneering conclaves (1925–27) in southern California and Baja California reveal a developing self-understanding in terms of doctrine and social and gendered practice, including a sanctified machismo. On the Mexican side, the movement's practices provoked governmental alarm over charlatanism, public health, and transgressive behavior between sexes. The Archivo General de la Nación (Mexico's national archive) has yielded valuable sources—such as correspondence up and down the chain between municipal, state, and federal authorities—that document Pentecostals' resolute insistence on constitutional rights and prerogatives and Mexican officialdom's suspicion of undesirable "gringo" and "negro" influences in this evangélico upstart.

Chapter 2 traces Pentecostal growth in central northern Mexico and southern Texas from 1914 to 1930. Like chapter 1, it appraises the pioneering role of women as well as an ambivalent proto-evangélico identity open to Pentecostal seduction. Missionary retreat in the face of revolution and clumsiness in the face of nationalistic sensibilities also facilitated Pentecostal advance. That advance began to register in governmental and academic sources in the late 1920s. Manuel Gamio's pioneering study of Mexican migration captured traces of social and elite opprobrium evident in epithets and monikers like "Aleluya." The loosening of anchoring ties to historic orthodoxy also facilitated a deep drift into heterodoxy and heteropraxis. By 1930, Apostolicism in Mexico had split into three distinct variants. The most sui generis one, the Luz del Mundo, leveraged founder Eusebio Joaquin's (the apostle Aaron) military connections in the governing regime to carve out an important niche in Guadalajara's Catholic-dominated ecology. The more institutional variant, the Iglesia Apostólica, clung fast to its U.S. counterpart, the Apostolic Assembly. This fraternal arrangement provides a useful frame for the ensuing analysis in the following chapters.

Pentecostalism began to acquire institutional and transnational form at a moment of great vulnerability: heightened xenophobia in the United States and renewed church-state conflicts in Mexico. The Great Repatriation of the 1930s leveraged almost a half million Mexicans and Mexican Americans out of the United States, and the delayed but forceful enforcement in 1926 of the harsh anticlerical clauses of the 1917 constitution precipitated armed conflict between Catholic partisans and the consolidating revolutionary regime. Chapter 3 recovers the life histories of repatriated Pentecostals, whose memories of this wrenching experience are imbedded in generally positive accounts of long ministerial careers. This remarkable resilience and creativity brought about an unexpected outcome, namely, Pentecostalism's expansion into new regions in western (Nayarit, Jalisco, Sinaloa, Sonora) and northern (Chihuahua) Mexico, the strengthening of transnational ties, and missionary expansion throughout the hemisphere and into Europe. The Cristero War caught many evangélicos in the middle, and the hardened anticlericalism worked to their detriment as they sought approval from local authorities to open or reopen temples (legally deemed federal property) or simply to change pastors. Rather than acquiescing as subdued scapegoats, though, many repatriates recovered prerogatives of citizenship, inserting themselves into and assuming leadership in agrarian *ejidos* (the Revolution's chief program) and vigorously contesting the custody of temples. Taken individually and in concert, Pentecostal subaltern responsive tactics carried strategic implications and yielded important results over time.

The subaltern Pentecostal response to macro events represents a prescient case of "transnationalism from below." In 1945, within a decade and a half of their forced return, the repatriates joined their U.S. counterparts in ratifying charter documents (a Constitution and Treaty of Unification) that bound the two emerging flagship denominations, the Iglesia Apostólica of Mexico and the Apostolic Assembly of the United States, tightly together. The transnational consolidation coincided with the start of the Bracero guest worker program. The intensifying labor migration flow— including an undocumented one—and the structure codified by the accords grew Apostolicism in both countries and provided a mechanism for confronting perennial episodes of renewed xenophobia (e.g., Operation Wetback, 1954). The retrieved records of bracero evangelism and borderlands hospitality cast midcentury studies of the bracero experience and proselytism in a different and brighter light. For example, letters of recommendation carried by migrants from their home congregations to others in their places of destination allow us not only to trace individual and family migratory trajectories but also to parse succinct discourse units about hospitality and accountability. Chapter 4 also takes stock of the repatriates' impressive musical fecundity, including that of the Hermanos Alvarado, a trio of U.S.-born brothers who, although exiled as children, returned to Los Angeles in adulthood and, through a fortuitous encounter with a cluster of Hollywood evangelical actors, achieved prominence in the 1960s as the hemisphere's most widely heard evangélico musical group.

Chapter 5 examines the movement's periodical record in order to texturize our understanding of subaltern religious life during the time period of the Bracero program (1942–64). This optic, however, foregoes the usual data for the study of Pentecostalism—healing, conversion, and tongues speaking—in favor of reports that reflect taken-for-granted contexts of migration and transnational life. This perspective places in sharper relief practices of fellowship, hospitality, healing, evangelism, and bereavement that spanned the border and reached deeply into both countries and beyond, as well as the centrifugal pressures (e.g., strongman *caudillismo*) that stymied these. The periodical and hymnodic record also reveals a pattern of Pentecostal pugilism in the face of residual cristero-inspired intolerance and in defense of the tentative turf previously carved out by evangélicos, liberals, and Masons. Finally, the chapter flips over Mainline and Catholic critiques of Pentecostal methods in order to test the argument for Pentecostal success.

Pentecostalism did not migrate quietly. It was often a noisy affair. The new revivalism burst through at a moment when *evangelicalismo* was moving through adolescence. Early Pentecostals avidly deployed the musical resources of their proletarian and peasant cultures and sacralized instruments and musical genres that Protestant missionaries and their spiritual progeny had marked as profane. The new approach finally allowed *evangelicalismo* to burrow deeply into the subsoil of Catholic popular religiosity. It also introduced new sonic, corporeal, and emotional elements into the sacred space to replace the visual ones banished by iconoclastic Protestantism. Chapter 6 plunges into the musical archive in order to trace the continuities and discontinuities between the missionary repertoire and its robust Pentecostal competitor. The historical study borrows from ethnomusicology in order to understand Pentecostalism's bricolage, creativity, and emotive core, as well as its overflow into Catholic and mainline Protestant spheres. The dynamic globalized marketplace of contemporary Christian worship can be better understood in light of this earlier hybridity and fecundity.

The concluding chapter argues for a rethinking of rubrics and genealogies. It joins the current theoretical deconstruction of the notion of apolitical Pentecostals and rural-to-urban migrants on "social strike" in urban religious haciendas. The recovered data from the early to mid-twentieth century suggests that folks can remain at once both Pentecostal and socially engaged or migratory and politically active—and politically active in unexpected ways. This historical awareness can help nuance the study of religion and politics in Latin America and Latino U.S.A. In terms of culture and viewed through theoretical lenses of habitus and everyday practice, the Pentecostal subaltern now appears to have been busily working—adapting, poaching, and reassembling *evangelicalismo*'s offerings—and speaking in the first six decades of the twentieth century. A more ambitious work could well have begun, though, in the mid-sixteenth century, when religious dissidents uprooted themselves from Iberia. These templates of religious and cultural mobility can be seen in later periods, especially in intensely globalizing ones like our present one.[29]

Chicano/Latino Studies and Religious History

Latino Catholic historiography continues to outpace its Protestant counterpart. Historians have turned their earlier concern for tensions between institutional and popular actors to more localized studies that also recognize important theological developments. The works run the gamut from comparative and interdisciplinary treatments of ethnic origin groups to regional, local, and organizational histories to biographies to documentary histories and histories of devotional (*guadalupano* and Penitente) traditions.[30] Recent (and long overdue and still too few) critical studies of Latino mainline Protestant traditions await comparable work on Pentecostalism among the same population.[31]

The field saw a watershed moment with the 2005 publication of Rudy Busto's *King Tiger*, a hermeneutical biography of New Mexican land-grant activist Reies López Tijerina.[32] Tijerina, one of the "four horsemen of the Chicano Apocalypse," enjoyed a period of notoriety for his leadership of the Alianza Federal de Mercedes Reales and for this group's armed take-over of the Tierra Amarilla County courthouse in 1967.[33] Most biographies of Tijerina, however, had focused on and allowed this undeniably important event in Chicano history to eclipse his formative years in Pentecostal ministry (he studied at the Assemblies of God Latin American Bible Institute in Texas).[34] More important, authoritative histories of the Chicano movement, especially Rudolfo Acuña's ever-evolving *Occupied America* (the opus underwent several editions from 1972 to 2007), gradually pushed the erratic, charismatic leader to the margins, owing to, among other things, his jarring apocalyptic discourse.[35] Busto rightfully took Chicano studies to task for this and provided an exemplary corrective by recovering and according coherence to Tijerina's story (in a similar vein to what Carlo Ginzburg accomplished with his unforgettable Menocchio and the sixteenth-century Italian Inquisition).[36] Dusting off the heretofore neglected or heavily redacted (by others) texts of Tijerina's creation—sermons, memoirs, interviews—Busto applied a fuller hermeneutic worthy of the larger-than-life activist, one that took seriously Tijerina's preaching, visions, and dreams. As he filled in the gaps, Busto laid bare a great lacuna in Chicano history: revivalistic religion. I strongly suspect that we will look back on Busto's contribution and wonder how the bias was tolerated for so long. If I may offer a parallel with a contemporary of Tijerina, it would be as if historians tried to understand the March on Washington, D.C., without consulting Martin Luther King Jr.'s doctoral dissertation at Boston University, his "Letter from a Birmingham Jail," his numerous sermons, or, for that matter, the black church.[37] Yet this is what Chicano history and well-meaning journalism—pre-Busto—wrought with Tijerina.[38]

The thin presence of religion in Chicano historical and social scientific scholarship is ironic, given the variable's ubiquity in a foundational text of the early twentieth century. Manuel Gamio's landmark 1926–1927 study of Mexican immigration, commissioned by the U.S. Social Science Research Council and published by the University of Chicago, systematically queried informants about religious belief and practice.[39] In his first volume (*Mexican Immigration to the United States: A Study of Human Migration and Adjustment* [1930]), Gamio undertook a sociological analysis of Mexican immigrant life—including religious life—in the United States. Mexico's foremost anthropologist (a student of Franz Boas of Columbia University) marshaled an impressive array of statistics obtained from official and extraofficial sources in both countries. The data included points of origin, residency, time of residency, remittances to Mexico, return to Mexico, occupational status, labor history, cultural practice, and English-language facility. Gamio's second volume (*The Mexican Immigrant: His Life*

Story [1931]) proffered a gold mine of immigrant life histories, transcribed at some length, with introductory discussions of each chapter and each case study. The religion vein was especially rich. Respondents claimed a balanced religiosity ("soy católico pero no fanático"), described folk healing arts and midwifery, and claimed *santero* (wood carved saints) artisanship, among many other indices of religiosity. Gamio's research team followed his field guide on the matter. Five questions asked about the type of churches attended by the immigrants (compared with those in Mexico), icons, images, offerings, scapulars, necklaces, medals, and saints. In addition, researchers also inquired after ceremonies and rituals, birth control, vices and criminality, Mexican patriotism, and exogamous marriage. They posed even more questions on religion to Mexican American respondents, including several concerning Masonic lodges and Protestant churches. An additional set of questions for Mexican Americans was clustered under the heading "Superstitions."[40]

Gamio included the life histories of one Baptist and two Methodist preachers or lay leaders in the second volume's chapter, "Intellectuals." Also in that chapter, San Antonio–based journalist Manuel Márquez (listed pseudonymously as "Alonso Galván") complained strenuously about the "greatest headway" that a certain Pentecostal sect, "*los apostólicos*" or "*aleluyas*," was making among his gullible countrymen in Texas.[41] In spite of such concern, Gamio opined in his analytical volume that, generally, the Mexican immigrant was "unable to respond to the cold, intellectual, moralistic quality of Protestantism, and lack of color and artistic impression."[42] Gamio's description, while possibly true of the mainline churches, seems less applicable to the more emotional (and noisy) Pentecostal ones, where cultural and liturgical production was booming and where aural stimuli were replacing the visual (Catholic) ones banished by iconoclastic Protestant missionaries. A survey—especially an acoustic one—of the "*aleluya*" churches then springing up throughout the U.S. Southwest and Midwest, could have led Gamio to more prescient and nuanced conclusions. Although his field guide instructed researchers to query respondents about their musical tastes ("American or Mexican or both?"), this was not asked in tandem with the religious identity and practice questions. Of the thirty musical compositions gathered by team researcher Luis Recinos, only thirteen were included in the analytical volume's chapter, "The Songs of the Immigrants." The compilation, inserted by Gamio's translator and editor, Margaret Park Redfield, received minimal analysis.[43]

Still other clues about the upstart religious movement eluded Gamio.

For instance, a team researcher's intriguing note—archived and never published—that up to 15 percent of the 150 Mexican parishioners of Chicago's St. Mark's (Presbyterian) Church had "moved away" or been lost "to the Pentecostal evangelistic campaign" in late 1929 prompts questions about the impact of repatriation and migration (an issue that engaged Gamio) and the success in midwestern cities of Pentecostal evangelists such as Mexican immigrant Francisco Olazábal (an issue that escaped Gamio's attention).[44] Perhaps Gamio's reliance on mainline Protestant social agencies (settlement houses and vocational schools) and Masonic lodges skewed his vision of the non-Catholic universe. Certainly, the hindsight afforded by seven decades allows for a fuller appraisal of a growing religious pluralism on the ground in that period and of an infant Pentecostalism's ability to attract many Mexicans on the move. Also, as literary critic José Saldivar has noted, Gamio's centralizing vision—at once nostalgic and progressive—of Mexican society and its prodigals may have prevented him from conceding the latter agency in their decision to carve out and creatively inhabit an alternative homeland.[45] Still, although religion was but one of the variables considered by Gamio, its inclusion in his groundbreaking scholarship is significant, especially in view of the variable's slight presence—with a few notable exceptions—in Chicano historiography and social science during the following decades.[46]

Gamio's work remains a fountainhead of scholarship on Mexican American life in the early twentieth century.[47] Historian George Sánchez framed his *Becoming Mexican American* (1993) with a narrative about a successful funeral home operator, Zeferino Ramírez (Gamio's pseudonymous "Anastacio Cortés"). The East Los Angeles, California, community leader and his family provided a ready template to illustrate the transition from immigrant to ethnic identity in the 1920s. I have also encountered Ramírez in dispatches in the *Evangelista Mexicano*, a contemporaneous periodical of Mexican and Mexican American southern Methodism. The active lay leader was converted through Methodist outreach in Los Angeles's Plaza. The Chihuahua City–based periodical lauded Ramírez's leadership of the Sunday school of the Belvedere MECS (Methodist Episcopal Church, South) church and reported on the impact a birthday commemoration service Ramírez sponsored for his late father had on the community surrounding La Trinidad church (due to its novelty).[48] The April 1928 dispatch also lamented that only one-third of southern Methodists who had migrated to Los Angeles, California, from Jalisco, Nayarit, Sinaloa, Sonora, Arizona, New Mexico, Texas, Chihuahua, Durango, Coahuila,

Nuevo León, San Luis Potosí, and other places had found their way into MECS fellowship. The remainder were gathering under northern auspices (Methodist Episcopal Church) and in other Protestant and, especially, Pentecostal churches. Clearly, the early twentieth-century migration and cultural processes studied by Sánchez and others included an important religious dimension. But whereas Sánchez dedicated a chapter to the topic in his monograph, other historians largely overlooked it.

Chicano historians also have generally turned a deaf ear to the cadences of religious musical culture (the Penitente tradition of New Mexico is the exception). While the postcolonial template set in place three decades ago has evolved in favor of studies of cultural change and adaptation,[49] the guild's early disciplinary formation and ideological commitments prevented—except for Richard Griswold del Castillo and Richard Garcia's 1995 biography of labor leader César Chávez and George Sanchez's work—the benign consideration of religious culture, especially its enthusiastic evangelical variants.[50] Yet a datum about the important impact of noisy Pentecostal liturgy on a novice community organizer has lain embedded in César Chávez's autobiographical narrative since 1975. The events described took place in the wake of Operation Wetback, roughly about the time of Urías Rodríguez's encounter with Apostolics in Tijuana and Mexicali. Chávez's account even parallels Rodríguez's in its descriptive elements of music, hospitality, and solidarity:

> I didn't know it then, but I was in for a special education in Madera [California]. One of the first cases I had was a Pentacostal [sic] preacher who was having trouble getting his papers in order. He'd paid a lot of money to many people who handle paperwork for a fee, coyotes we call them, to get his green card from the Immigration Service. He still didn't have it. Both he and his wife needed the green card, which gives them permanent residence status, before they could become citizens. They also had a daughter who was born here but was stuck in Mexico. Immigration wouldn't let her return because she couldn't prove her birth here.
>
> When I went to their home, which was very, very humble, we talked and ate. Then he excused himself to conduct services. "I'll be back in about an hour," he said. "Can you wait for me?" He went into a little room—it hadn't occurred to me that it was a church— I thought it was just a living room.
>
> After they started their service, I asked if I could join them.

In those days there was a lot of separation between Protestants and Catholics; in San Jose I was one of the few Catholics who attended Protestant services. When we first came to Sal Si Puedes, Protestants were the ones who gave us lodging and food and invited my mother to go to the service. She wasn't afraid of them.

So in that little Madera church, I observed everything going on about me that could be useful in organizing. Although there were no more than twelve men and women, there was more spirit there than when I went to a mass where there were two hundred. Everybody was happy. They all were singing. These people were really committed in their beliefs, and this made them sing and clap and participate. I liked that. I think that's where I got the idea of singing at the meetings. That was one of the first things we did when I started the Union. And it was hard for me because I can't carry a tune.

I went to this Pentacostal preacher's home regularly to go over his records, and he would schedule services. We were organizing each other. At the end of the services, it would turn into a house meeting. Eventually the preacher got everybody in his congregation to join CSO [Community Service Organization].[51]

The band of apostolic farmworkers pastored by Mariano Marín (who had been mentored by Tulare, California, pastor Epifanio Cota) facilitated Chávez's introduction to other coreligionists. This new constituency, grateful for his advocacy on their behalf, reciprocated by providing Chávez with the support he needed when the local CSO board, composed of a Catholic priest and several established Mexican American leaders, sought to expel him from town as a suspected Communist. The Apostolics and other evangélicos of Madera ousted his adversaries and handed Chávez his first victory (Marín's daughter Sallie Torres served as Chavez's first secretary in the Madera CSO chapter):

> This time we elected nothing but farm workers, and we came up with an all Protestant board. Most of them didn't know how to speak English. Then we started moving. That was one of the best CSOs we had. I radicalized that chapter more than any other chapter, I guess, in that short period of time. They weren't afraid to take on the police or the immigration service. They weren't afraid to fight for their rights.
>
> It turned out to be a very good experience, but it was a very frightening one at the time. People were scared, but not the farm

workers, not the poor. It was those guys who have little jobs, who protected their little self-interest. That taught me the best lesson, a good lesson about self-interest. From then on, I had a rule: There would be no more middle-class Chicanos in the leadership.[52]

I will return to the question of Pentecostal social engagement in my concluding discussion. It is important to note that this story of proletarian religious praxis and sensibilities predates by nearly a decade the arrival of mainline Protestant support for Chávez's cause (the National Council of Churches Migrant Ministry). Its description of musical enchantment and inspiration also reminds us of the important cultural sphere that can accompany mobilization. That sphere includes gut-level affect. As Mamie Till's dogged insistence on publicly mourning her murdered son Emmet in her south Chicago Pentecostal church (Roberts Temple Church of God in Christ) emboldened Methodist Rosa Parks to follow through on her challenge to Jim Crow in Montgomery, Alabama, and inspire a young Baptist preacher of that city, so, too, did apostolic songs, tongues speaking, and affect steel a novice prophet of labor justice—already steeped in Catholic social doctrine—for his long road ahead.

This sonic feature surely also attended another foundational Chicano story. But even Rudy Busto's pathbreaking *King Tiger* was tinged with a Baptist bias (Reies Tijerina first converted as a child in a Baptist ministry among *tejano* migrant workers in the Midwest), as evidenced by its focus on texts and its silence concerning the telltale spheres of Pentecostal religiosity, namely, the sonic and corporeal ones. Thus, we are left bereft of information about the songs that accompanied Tijerina's sermons, that were sung during his itinerating ministry, and that resounded in his utopian desert community, Valle de Paz. The only rhythm we hear is that of the preacher's thunderous cadence. But of other voluble, singing, moving, gesticulating, hand-clapping bodies? Practically nothing. Put simply, Busto's *frontera quemada* is too quiet.

Borderlands Theory and Religious History

Rudy Busto's term for the heavily evangelized border region cleverly appropriates Whitney Cross's for the regional impact of the Second Great Awakening.[53] The term can be translated variously as burnt-over borderline, frontier, or borderlands. The last, especially, reminds us of the debt owed to Gloria Anzaldúa, who, beginning with the "unnaturally" bifurcated region she inhabited, moved out from there to speak of the mestiza Chicana's several border crossings: psychological, sexual, and spiritual.[54] Her discussion of precocious *pocha* (Anglicized Spanish) tongues in need of taming by language orthodoxies (English and Spanish) also resonates with the case of our phantom Mexican at Azusa Street, whose discourse was occluded from Pentecostalism's early record. Anzaldúa's "borderlands" concept has carried over into many disciplines, areas of inquiry, and world regions. Its elasticity allows us to consider the far-flung spaces occupied by migrants as part of a broad social and epistemic swath. The expansive idea has also overlapped with contemporaneous ones of transnationalism, globalization, and diasporic life and movement. *Migrating Faith* benefits from this confluence. The *apostólico* story traced in *Migrating Faith* began as a subaltern labor diaspora in tentative borderlands settings. Impinging hegemonic forces then threatened to intensify displacement, whereupon its protagonists carved out and inhabited, through expressive culture and religious practice, a deterritorialized, imagined space that transcended the nation-state (hymns and *coritos* often heralded an alternative homeland). In a sense, Apostolics occupied a middle position between diasporic and settled borderlander communities. We can see examples of both in the story of Urías Rodríguez Alavez. His travel and settlement throughout and in "Oaxacalifornia" exemplify the term coined by his activist countrymen and women of a later time period to refer to that geographic and labor diasporic expanse that runs from the Isthmus of Tehuantepec to Baja and U.S. California. The new subaltern geopolitical coinage entails, of course, as much a state of mind and soul as an elastic description of geography traversed. It also presses and stretches older borderlands paradigms.

Migrating Faith has been informed by sober, ground-level histories of specific sites and regions in the U.S.–Mexico borderlands. For example, Anthony Mora and Omar Valerio-Jiménez have drawn in sharp relief the local contestations over identity between contiguous populations and towns in the southern regions of New Mexico and Texas, respectively.[55] The tensions, whether owing to cartographic adjustments in the case of Mesillas, New Mexico (through the 1854 Gadsden purchase), or to racialized legal and family law regimes in the case of south Texas, reflected borderlanders' studied opportunism. Mora and Valerio-Jiménez provide, thus, a cautionary note about long-standing intraethnic differences among settled borderlanders.

Borderlands Pentecostalism, however, could not boast of such longevity. The newness and tentativeness of Pentecostal gatherings—around farm labor campfires, under tents, and in the legal shadows—prevented a long, deep settlement for many. With lower geopolitical stakes and frequent uprooting, the Pentecostal zone resembled more the Sonora–Arizona copper borderlands studied by Samuel Truett. There, the success of mineral extraction depended, ultimately, on the whims of a floating labor population that could just as easily settle as return home as seek opportunities elsewhere. There, as in the case of the carefully engineered missionary enterprises noted in Chapters 1 and 2, "the best-laid plans of states, entrepreneurs, and corporations repeatedly ran aground in fugitive landscapes of subaltern power."[56] Importantly, Truett notes the need for a nuanced view of the region—peopled and traversed by Yaquis, Chinese, Mexicans, Mormons, and so on—as a "shifting palimpsest of spaces, each with its own circuits and borders."[57] In his ethnobiography of the same region, anthropologist Carlos Vélez-Ibáñez traced the historical demographic and cultural "bumping" of perennial population waves from the south.[58] In like manner, bracero and other migration waves stymied unilinear assimilation trends in Mexican American Pentecostal congregations. *Migrating Faith*, by definition then, surveys a broader transnational cartography, with middle (border) nodes and farther-flung endpoints. Like Timothy Matovina and David Badillo's historical studies of local Catholicism in Texas, *Migrating Faith* takes into account the impact of migration and external macroevents (e.g., the Mexican Revolution, Cristero War, etc.). Matovina and Badillo, however, generally keep taut their units of analysis: a cathedral in San Antonio and the city of Houston, respectively. Lacking such long-standing sites, especially sacred ones, borderlands Pentecostalism alighted where it could, namely, in close proximity to the workplace of a migrating peasantry and proletariat. This does not discount the deep roots Pentecostalism set into older communities nor the prominence of U.S.-born and settled movement pioneers of Apostolicism; however, even they were compelled by economic exigencies and/or evangelistic imperatives to move about along the same circuits guiding their Mexican coreligionists. Mexican/Chicano Pentecostalism, perforce, thrived in and perpetuated a liminality par excellence. This study, nevertheless, awaits fruitful comparison with more localized sites of deep rooting in both countries: congregations, families, individuals, towns, and even migrant labor camps, including those inhabited by Pentecostal Dust Bowl refugees.

Americano Religious History

Until recently, standard surveys of religious history in North America have given short shrift to Latino Protestantism (even shorter shrift to Latino Pentecostalism) and have forced most Latino religious history into the flow of events westward from Plymouth Rock or northward from New Spain.[59] Most mainstream religious history has treated religious experience and identity in the U.S.–Mexico borderlands as additive (the narrative begins with missionary agency and convert adaptation) and illustrative of a new pluralism. Rarely is it examined as constitutive of—or contestatory to—mainstream religious history, whether U.S. Protestant or Spanish/Mexican Catholic. Chicano history of the last thirty years reciprocated the favor, tacking on religious data as secondary variables to the larger story of inner colonial resistance and leaving the recovery of—mostly female—religious traditions to poets and graphic artists. In 1997, Thomas Tweed and others called for a retelling of U.S. religious history based on such factors as gender, body, and region. This study moves in this direction. Its vantage point at the interstices of two countries and in the social crevices deep within both countries allows for new mappings and soundings of a religious cartography that reflects people's experience and movement through spaces both real and imagined and, thus, that captures many of the features summed up as "crossing" and "dwelling" by Tweed in his more theoretical opus.[60]

The Pentecostal zone entails dimensions that are at once geographic, religious, cultural, and epistemic and that stretch beyond geographically adjacent places. They encompass the back-and-forth migration or movement of people and material and symbolic goods. This movement, in turn, affects migrants' notion of themselves (imagined identities) as individuals belonging to transnational communities in flux and as creators and practitioners of religious culture.

The story of *Migrating Faith*, however, represents more than a long overdue ethnic appendix to U.S. religious history (the chapters that Sidney Ahlstrom forgot to include in his *Religious History of the American People*). To be sure, many lacunae persist in the textbooks that replaced that magisterial 1973 opus. U.S. religious history always stands in need of perspectival shifts. So, too, does Mexican religious history. The previously marginalized can be brought into sharper relief through attention to borderlands loci, transnational movements from below, subaltern agency and culture.

American religious historians must also remember that not all religious agents inhabit epistolary cultures nor do they enjoy easy access to the written word. But they do sing and move. And the music they sing travels; it carries the word. The implications of this are important. Church and religious historians can no longer argue from silence or allow that subaltern oral cultures lacking deep archival or epistolary records remain relegated, as in the case of the "poor, rough" Mexican Indian in the Azusa Street report or the tuberculosis-ridden Marcial de la Cruz languishing in Tijuana, to the derivative periphery (vs. the constitutive center). To limit the narrative to the available standard textual evidence is to privilege certain strands. We know from those texts—especially those of its elite detractors—that the Pentecostal movement generated considerable noise and emotion. The moniker "*aleluya*," established through repetition by the movement's detractors, alerts us to this. Our research tools must be attuned to this remarkable feature. *Migrating Faith* offers a cartography that relies on careful soundings as well as on mappings of dynamic sound and sacroscapes.

Proto-*Evangelicalismo*

The above-mentioned case of Reies Tijerina also presents us squarely with the problem of confessional ascription and slippery religious folk. What do we make of a historical subject who refuses to stand still long enough to be counted under conventional sociological and theological rubrics? A moving target, Tijerina eluded even Busto's careful sightings. Busto's explication of his purpose was clear: "the exposition of [Tijerina's] ideas and their origins in a particular theological mindset."[61] In his attempt to "expose and explore the framework of sources and ideas that support idiosyncratic worlds,"[62] Busto repeatedly referenced Tijerina's mastery of biblical texts, his voracious reading of colonial documents, treaties, and legislation, and his masterful deployment of these in revindication of Hispano land-grant rights. We would expect such text-centric strategies from a Baptist leader. Yet Busto also faithfully recorded the invigorating and compelling dreams, visions, and signs that guided Tijerina's actions as much as scripture did. Good Baptists, however, do not generally or easily inhabit such magical worlds; bad Baptists do. So do Pentecostals and many Catholics. This common experiential and epistemic substrate shared by Pentecostals, vernacular Catholics, and heterodox Baptists makes for fuzzy boundaries and even for difficult sequencing of individuals' religious change and transformation. If Tijerina never withdrew from this dreamscape—whether as a child holding Jesus's hand and a red wagon handle; or as a young man flying over dark pine forests, viewing graveyards full of frozen horses, and conversing with angels of justice and judgment; or as a political prisoner experiencing space travel—then where exactly do we situate him confessionally? Busto argued that Mexican American Evangelicals, unlike Catholics, try to keep their dreams and visions tethered to scriptural referents (texts). Pentecostal testimonial tradition, however, allows the line tethering dreams to texts and to commonsense experience to stretch quite far, indeed, as far as the credulity of the believer and community will permit. The continuity in Tijerina's lifelong dream discourse evidences no rupture in this area of practice and epistemology—once a dreamer, always a dreamer. This Pentecostal practice represented not so much a break from as a recovery or affirmation of older sensibilities. Such sensibilities resist disciplining along denominational and confessional lines.

This fluid religiosity was necessary in contexts of hegemonic Catholicism. In such situations, a proto-evangelicalismo united Protestants of many stripes and has stretched at times to include even heterodox Oneness Pentecostals and Seventh-Day Adventists. This process is very distinct from the well-known saga of liberal–conservative divides in U.S. Protestantism, a particular struggle that has bequeathed a particular nomenclature (Liberal, Fundamentalist, Evangelical) that ill fits the Protestant story in Latin America and among U.S. Latinos. "Evangélico" and "proto-evangelicalismo" refer, then, to a common experience of religious dissent and marginalization vis-à-vis hegemonic Catholicism, an experience that stretches from the sixteenth to the twenty-first century.

A recognition of the longer history of evangelicalismo helps to guard against the notion of Pentecostalism as a tabula rasa. Projects of religious dissent date back to proto-evangélico antecedents such as the sixteenth-century Bible translators Juan Enzinas, Casiodoro de Reina, and Cipriano de Valera. Although it had to await the loosening of the *cordon sanitaire* (e.g., the Inquisition's *Indice Expurgatorio*) thrown around Spanish realms, the long-dormant *Reina y Valera* Bible (1569, 1602) emerged anew from the presses of British and American Bible societies. Agency colporteurs such as James "Diego" Thompson spread the texts on the ground tilled by Liberals and Masons intent on cracking the Catholic Church's political and religious monopoly in the new republics. The dissidents included priests like José Mora, the father of Mexican Liberalism. Other clerics forswore allegiance to Rome and formed incipient proto-Anglican societies such as the

Iglesia de Jesús in Mexico. The floodgates of Protestant incursion opened fully in the wake of constitutional and legislative reforms by Liberal presidents and leaders such as Mexico's Benito Juárez and Miguel Lerdo de Tejada.[63] The arrival of missionaries in the last quarter of the nineteenth century, together with that of supportive foreign consuls, industrialists, managers, and workers, overwhelmed the nascent proto-evangélico nuclei. This set the course for Protestant growth. By 1910, evangélicos had established significant beachheads in education and carved out important spaces of Liberal dissent, spaces in which revolutionary thought and activism were incubated.[64]

An urge for autonomy, though, was evident from evangelicalismo's earliest days. The Iglesia de Jesús waged a bitter debate with Methodists over the former's claim to an organic genealogy and the latter's subordination to U.S. bishops.[65] Other proto-evangélico scissions in Mexico, the U.S. Southwest, and Chile discarded confessional labels altogether (e.g., the Iglesia Evangélica Independiente). The often clumsy unilateral implementation of comity agreements (between mission boards), the growing tensions between liberal and fundamentalist camps in U.S. denominations and missionary agencies, the drastic interruption of war, and protracted church–state conflicts made for uneven maturation and even resentment. As evangelicalismo entered into adolescence, the catalyst for future growth arrived, borne in the burning hearts of Pentecostal migrants and missionaries. The infusion would trigger metastasis in the already fissiparous evangélico DNA.

Religious Remittances

Migration scholars Douglas Massey and Emilio Parrado's instructive study (1994) of *migradollars* and the impact of monetary remittances in the microeconomies of communities of origin prompted me to think in terms of *religious remittances* and of the need to explore their catalytic and supportive role in expanding religious pluralism in Mexico.[66] (Financial remittances represent one of the three pillars of Mexico's economy—the two others are petroleum and tourism—and a critical one in several states and regions.) I understand *remesas religiosas* to mean those symbolic goods sent or brought home by migrants to prompt or maintain their relatives' and friends' conversion and new religious identity. Financial resources sent to shore up ministries and congregations or to pay for religious events (e.g., a *quinceañera* [female rite of passage] celebration) clearly fall within the categories explored by Massey and Parrado. Conversely, so, too, do migrants' proscriptions against certain expenditures of financial remittances (e.g., financing patron saint festivals or repairing Catholic temples). Thus, while material remittances have often served to maintain hometown traditions, in other instances the circulation of material and symbolic goods has often proven catalytic and provocative.[67] One of the more relevant points to keep in mind about remittances—both financial and symbolic—is that they flow within networks, and their disbursement and expenditure (or saving) is determined by complex processes at play in kinship and communal webs. Thus, even ostensibly nonsymbolic, material remittances can acquire a symbolic significance and affect cultural practices.[68]

Migration as Social Process

Since 1982, researchers in the binational Mexican Migration Project (MMP), employing both sociological and ethnographic methods, have focused on the complex social processes of the migration phenomenon and the knitting of ties between "sending" communities in western Mexico and "receiving" communities in the United States.[69] Rather than viewing Mexican migration to the United States in terms of old tropes ("escape valve," "melting pot" acculturation, etc.), researchers have explored the assimilation of migration itself into communities' ways of life during many decades.[70] Researchers interview returned migrants in places of origin and settled migrants in sites of destination. Queries concern family and community networks, identity formation, border crossing lore and border crossing as male rite of passage, use of remittances, and so forth.[71] The scholarly output has been considerable.[72] Researchers, however, did not pose explicitly religious questions to respondents until 1999, when the MMP initial questionnaire was adjusted to query, "In your trips to the United States, have you belonged to a social/religious association?" Previously, researchers had asked, "In your last trip to the United States, did you belong to any social associations?"

It is not that the religion variable is unimportant to the researchers. Principal investigators Jorge Durand and Douglas Massey's catalogue of migrant ex-voto *retablos* collected from shrines throughout Mexico augured a thematic shift in this valuable research enterprise. The medieval tradition took root and continues to thrive by means of the ex-voto retablo practice. These rectangular tin sheets, on which are painted scenes recollecting calamities and interventions along with the representations of the interceding saint or virgin, are left in rooms set aside for their collection in basilicas and churches throughout Mexico.[73] Though less tangible than ex-voto retablos, the traces left by songs, songwriters, and singers provide an evidentiary and more mobile record of Pentecostals' border crossing and transnational vision. That record merits retrieval.

Life Histories

A final caveat about these "fugitive sources" is in order. The study of life histories presents, of course, methodological challenges. Among these: What to make of the testimonial and memoir? Of their construction of coherence, their reversal of chronology, and their claim for respectability? As much as the search for respectability or dignity, another motive at work in the telling of life stories is the search for coherence. As explicated by Charlotte Linde in her work with elderly Jewish Americans, social respectability requires "a coherent, acceptable, and constantly revised life story."[74] Since these (life stories) are transmitted over time and in separate "discontinuous unit(s)," the coherence entails taking the units in toto and in relation to one another. Fact-checking, per se, is a secondary concern for Linde. Thus, when seeking to ascertain the subject's notions of causality and continuity, the historian balances an interest in the material catalyst for action with an interest in how the subject narrates the sequence of events. Linde proposes the following common repertoire: (1) character; (2) richness of account; (3) accident; and (4) strategies of apparent break (conversion testimonials would probably fit best here), temporary discontinuity, self-distancing, and sequence ("one thing leads to another"). In the cases of micromovement in response to macroevents and forces, migratory Pentecostals often reported the catalytic agent to be God or the Holy Spirit, an absent factor, of course, in Linde's schematic. In fact, for most, divine agency worked in tandem with any or all of the Linde elements.

In the case of the life stories of repatriated Pentecostals (Chapter 3), the protagonists did not foreground the migrant experience. This renders each discursive unit all the more plausible as a datum in the study of religion and migration. That is, the lack of migrant self-consciousness means that the life histories were not skewed to a particular argument about migration and religion. (We are bracketing, of course, the teleological interpretation rendered by the teller.) Thus, in the same way that historians derive great insights from antagonistic contemporaneous accounts (e.g., Inquisition trial transcripts), we are able to scrub migrant life histories at a different angle than that intended by the subaltern authors and fore-ground taken-for-granted features of import.

Borderlands Headwaters and Transnational Streams

From its very beginnings, modern Pentecostalism displayed many of the features discussed above: interstitial location between cultures and nation-states; polyphonic voice; robust expressive culture; fluid confessional identity; hybrid practice; ethnic revindication and autonomy; and migratory movement. Let us now follow this heterodox Pentecostal stream as it coursed its way from borderlands headwaters into increasingly larger hemispheric flows and emptied into global basins of pneumatic effervescence. We will see how this dilution renders problematic a strictly borderlands approach. Like moving water, religion is hard to dam up and contain. As we have learned to rethink the connecting role of oceanic basins, so, too, must we consider carefully the expansive flow of revivalistic religion.

CHAPTER 1

Pentecostal Origins in the Borderlands

Vida eternal Él prometió,	Eternal life He promised,
Él prometió	He promised
Al que en Él, al que en Él	To the one who, To the one who
Quisiere creer.	In Him chooses to believe.
Y estará allá con Él;	And such will dwell there with him;
Porque así fué el anuncio que dió	For thus was the announcement given
//Ven a la luz que te da Jesús//	//Come to the light that Jesus gives you//
Y vivirás allá con él	And you shall live there with him
Y para siempre tú no morirás	Never more to die

Marcial de la Cruz's well-traveled "Ven a la Luz" provided early *Pentecostales* with an attractive tool for evangelistic enchantment. Framed, like "Aleluya al Señor," in an upbeat 4/4 rhythm and easily strummed on guitar, mandolin, or banjo, the hymn cast its invitation in the soteriological and eschatological terms broadly shared by postmillennial evangélicos.[1] The song would have been welcomed by the far-flung recipients of J. P. Cragin's 1933 *Melodías Evangélicas* hymnal, which included it and two others of De la Cruz's authorship. The first musical scoring of De la Cruz's music occurred posthumously (1952), under Church of God missionary auspices.[2] The imprimatur by a flagship denomination ensured even wider dissemination of the troubadour's song. However, its title and chorus hint that the spiritual illumination claimed by certain Pentecostals was also leading them down long-obscured pathways. This chapter charts that expedition into heterodox terrain. It also explores other border crossings, namely, cultural and aesthetic ones.

Although he remained monolingual in Spanish, De la Cruz was an avid student of the music he encountered in fellowship with black congregations and with African American members of Latino Apostolic churches. Pioneer Antonio Nava, who took up the mandolin to create a duet with De la Cruz, recalled his colleague's immediate recall of rhythms and chords he heard in such settings.[3] The antiphonal opening lines of the verses of "Ven a la Luz" suggest a borrowing of the call and response of early black gospel music. In performance of the song, however, Apostolics favored the collective singing of both call and response; the repetition is marked only with a comma in early nonscored hymnals. The flattening out of this distinctive feature of African American religious music can be seen, or heard, as an adaptive broadening of a shared musical tradition. It also reminds us that the cradle of Latino Pentecostalism was rocked by African American hands, music, and affects.

Borderlands Pentecostalism

While modern Pentecostalism bubbled and flowed out of several originary points in Wales, South India, and the United States, its course through Los Angeles (via Topeka, Kansas, and Houston, Texas) took it from that northern point of "greater Mexico" to proximate regions. The locus of the Azusa Street Revival of 1906 ensured a spillover onto the contiguous "Sonoratown," a section immediately north of downtown Los Angeles populated by Mexicans and Mexican Americans and anchored by the city's historic plaza.[4] Mexicans may have been present, though, at the very first perforation of Azusa's revivalism well. The first reported spirit baptisms at the Azusa Street site occurred on April 13 or 14 among construction workers brought in to clean up the abandoned (and arson-damaged) building that had served first as the African Methodist Episcopal Church and later as a horse stable. The employees of the McNeil Construction Company—a racially mixed crew—were met by women of the Bonnie Brae Street group (the revival began in a home there, in what is today the mid-Wilshire area). According to McNeil foreman Arthur Osterberg, the Catholic workers' spirit baptisms were instantaneous. If "Catholic" is code for "Mexican," then we can assume that Latinos were among the first to taste Azusa's spiritual waters.[5] It is important to note that the praying hands that dug the spiritual well—and that were laid on the unsuspecting laborers—belonged mostly to African American women.[6]

Polyglot Los Angeles and borderlands society eagerly packed itself into the Azusa Street venue. In the first issue of the five-month-old mission's *Apostolic Faith* magazine (September 1906), a leading layman of the city's First Methodist Church celebrated the downscale revivalism: "I bless God that it did not start in any church in this city, but in a barn, so that we might all come and take part in it. If it had started in a fine church, poor colored people and Spanish people would not have got it, but praise God it started here."[7]

The periodical's second issue (October) carried the Spanish and (awkwardly) translated testimony of Abundio and Rosa López, who had begun preaching about their new experience. The couple had visited the mission on May 29 and dated their Holy Spirit baptism to June 5 in the plaza.[8] The third issue (November) included an update on the evangelists, who were "being used of God in street meetings and in helping Mexicans at the altar at Azusa street" and whose efforts in Los Angeles were being complemented by those of young Brígido Pérez' (another Azusa convert) in San Diego (where the couple joined him by year's end).[9] Longtime Los Angeles resident Juan Navarro also found his way to the meetings.[10] His ties to William Seymour's coworkers link the Apostólico movement to the revival.

Ultimately, however, Azusa's multicultural and multilingual promise proved illusory.[11] Frank Bartleman obliquely decried the disenfranchisement of "some poor illiterate Mexicans" from the "old" Azusa mission in late 1909. The eyewitness historian likened the expulsion to "murdering the Spirit of God."[12] Bartleman's dispiritedness proved premature, however, at least in terms of prospects for growth among that population (we should not discount his lament concerning the loss of racial harmony and doctrinal sufferance). By that time in Otay–San Diego, Luis López had been baptized in Jesus's name.[13] Construction job opportunities in that growing region—the site of Pérez's and Abundio and Rosa López's earlier work—had attracted several believers from Los Angeles. Both before and after his brief stint in 1912 as pastor of Margaret Mitchell Hallquist's Star of Bethlehem Spanish Mission in Los Angeles, Juan Navarro evangelized in San Diego and the Riverside–San Bernardino area. In 1912, in the former city, he baptized a young immigrant from Acapulco, Mexico, Francisco Llorente. In turn, two years later, Llorente baptized his countryman Marcial de la Cruz, who hailed from Torreón, a robust industrial city in the northern Mexican state of Coahuila.[14] In 1916, De la Cruz converted Antonio C. Nava. Meanwhile, the longer-lived pastorate of Genaro Valenzuela at 627 Alpine Street anchored the embryonic movement in Los Angeles.[15]

Born October 4, 1892, to Simón and Roberta Nava of Nazas, Durango, Antonio Nava sought to enlist in the insurrectionary forces at the start of the Mexican Revolution. His father's firm opposition and the restive youth's desire to save face with peers prompted Nava to seek a paternal blessing in 1915 for travel northward instead. He secured employment in Riverside, California, and the surrounding Imperial Valley, where he met De la Cruz and, with the latter's persistence, finally relented to visit Los Angeles.

At this point, Robert Anderson's characterization of early U.S. Pentecostal leaders bears reiteration:

> The composite picture of the Pentecostal leader that emerges from our analysis is that of a comparatively young man of humble rural-agrarian origins. Often a victim of physical as well as cultural and economic deprivation, he nevertheless managed to secure a smattering of advanced education of relatively low quality. Peculiarly subject to the loss or estrangement of those closest to him, his primary relationships deeply tinged with melancholy, cut loose from his roots in the soil, highly mobile and unstable in residence, occupation and religious affiliation, hovering uncertainly between working class and middle class life, he sought a resolution of the anxieties stemming from his social experiences, not by clinging to the faith of his fathers but by the intensification of the pietistic, emotional, and world-rejecting elements of that faith.[16]

I do not take issue here with Anderson's description of uprootedness and marginality. Indeed, revolutionary upheaval in Mexico uprooted Antonio Nava and one million of his compatriots in the early twentieth century. Also, an expansive imperial and capitalist project carried laborer Juan Lugo, the future "apostle of Pentecost to Puerto Rico," from one newly acquired territory (Puerto Rico) to another (Hawaii) at the turn of the twentieth century. There, he joined the proletarian mix of Chinese, Japanese, Filipinos, and natives on the island's plantations.[17] Anderson's template seems, however, inadequate for cases of radical conversion to a faith not of one's fathers and mothers. These historical subjects claimed distinct, additional motives, and they did so in poetic ways. Take, for instance, Nava's accounts of his conversion, which reportedly occurred (on a weekday) in an empty church in Los Angeles:

> I refused to enter the temple, but at his [De la Cruz's] insistence I relented, and, much to my surprise, as I entered the place I felt touched by the power of the Lord, and after ten minutes or so I was filled with the power of the Holy Spirit, speaking in other tongues as the Spirit gave me to speak. In all my prior life I had never felt such a thing.... Oh, unforgettable moment when I experienced the Power of God manifested in my being! By means of the warmth of the Holy Spirit, that immediately subdued my passions, I felt a new life in all my being. This change was effected through the love of the Lord

who controlled my soul. My heart was enlightened to love others with the perfect love that is God's. When we left to go home it seemed that Nature had been transformed, and when I heard music in the streets, my heart was saddened, for I wished that all could feel what I was feeling.[18]

Nava did not remain in a state of ineffable rapture—not for this intrepid prophet the hushed blush of romantic religion. Nava's subsequent vocational vision arrived wrapped in motifs possibly lifted from the Mexican Revolution. The young would-be insurgent was once again summoned to battle, albeit in a different corps. The 1918 episode began with Nava in prayer and meditation:

A vision came upon me in which I was taken by a power away from that place. I felt my body to be the same, but since I was praying, I could not tell if my body was able to react until that power carried me to a very different place, where a sun shone—not like the sun we know, but similar to the moon—and sat me upon on a rock that seemed beautiful to me. At that point a great thirst came over me, and I had no way to slake it. Then I saw to the side of the rock a well in which the water was visible about three meters down. I felt a desire to move and drink that water, but I had no abilities to do so. Then there appeared to me two men in military dress, who asked me if I was thirsty. I responded that I was. They lifted me, and I went to drink the water, as there was a way to descend into the well. The water I drank was truly very sweet.

Afterwards they transported me to a white building and carried me inside where a man was seated in a chair (I was unable to see his face as my faculties were very weak). He asked me, "Did you drink the water?" I answered, "Yes, I drank." "Now go and preach the gospel, and do not fear, for I will be with you."[19]

The epiphany left Nava in a state of anxiety for the next several days as he tended to his tasks as the ranch's sole hand and delivered tracts in the nearby town during his spare time. Marcial de la Cruz brought along a (white) minister to confirm De la Cruz's ready interpretation of Nava's calling. The visitor had inquired after Nava, to whom he was supposed to relay—in quintessential Pentecostal fashion—an urgent commission: "I have come with the purpose to deliver the message the Lord gave me for you. He has called you to preach His Word and to preach it right away.

I have now fulfilled my mission, and may the Lord bless you and may you obey that which the Lord has commanded."[20] The messenger and De la Cruz conducted Nava's ordination the following Sunday. (Francisco Llorente ratified—by repeating—Nava's ordination in September 1919.)

Although subsequent denominational history glossed over it, Nava's may be the first account of ministerial calling in the United States wherein the celestial messengers were garbed in military dress. Eusebio Joaquín González, founder of the (also Oneness) Luz del Mundo church in Mexico reported a similar experience in Nuevo León—a decade after Nava's—at the moment of rupture with his erstwhile patrons, the prophets Saulo and Silas (see discussion below).[21] The former soldier's narrative immediately took up a restorationist discourse (in which God rechristened him as the prophet Aarón and called him to restore the faith after twenty centuries of divine silence and religious apostasy) and passed into church folklore. Nava's story remained private for several decades but nevertheless seems to have catalyzed his vocational commitment from that day forward.

We cannot discount the deep sympathies that existed ever since Benito Juárez and Miguel Lerdo de Tejada's mid-nineteenth-century *Reforma* between military leaders, soldiers, and families, on the one hand, and liberal and evangélico belief and practice, on the other. The sympathies owed as much to a common foe (Catholicism and conservatism) as it did to a shared ethos. As a leader, Nava displayed some of the characteristics of the military *caudillos* (chieftains) he had admired as a youth. At once benevolent and authoritarian, Mexico's revolutionary strongmen (e.g., Pancho Villa, Emiliano Zapata, Venustiano Carranza) commanded deep personal loyalty from their troops and compatriots. Nava exemplified the first attribute. Also, an early record of healings solidified his status as a charismatic leader.

Returning to Anderson's template, it is notable that our historical subjects—migrant laborers in agricultural fields—possessed the insouciance to believe that their words and deeds carried cosmic significance. Though the exigencies of civil war at home and an expansive agricultural capitalism may have pushed and pulled him to *el Norte*, for Nava the leading of the Holy Spirit prompted him to imagine and carve out an expansive religious ethnoscape, one that transcended geopolitical borders.[22] His subsequent mobility represented more than that of a pliable unit of proletarian labor, and it mirrored his theological creativity. It was chiefly Nava's and his fellows' authority as preachers, mystics, healers, and troubadours that won their following. When they preached and sang, contemporary accounts allege, folks listened and followed, even into heterodox terrain. Finally, the commissioning visions of Nava and Joaquin provided a charismatic end-run around denominational clerical systems. Taking the kingdom of Heaven quickly by force called for Pentecostal caudillos, much as the subduing of the early nineteenth-century U.S. frontier required intrepid Methodist circuit riders.

But why would the subaltern resort to glossolalic speech? Perhaps it was as much a question of power as it was a matter of theological insight. Recent immigrants and native minorities enmeshed in the net of labor discipline lacked meaningful access to the written (and publicly spoken) word employed by English-speaking elites. Language was part and parcel of the project of the creation of pliable subjects in the newly acquired Southwest. Small wonder, then, that a sector of the "disinherited" of American and global society opted to upend the rules of the social linguistic game and to speak in the tongues of angels instead. In this, they joined a long tradition of babblers and mystics. For the heirs of the Enlightenment, glossolalia may have represented nothing more than psycholinguistic babble and noise (morphemes wildly tossed together in syntactical disarray). But for many subalterns it signified a discourse about transcendental goodness, human connectedness, and power relations set aright (especially when that discourse was wedded to material solidarity among the poor). Such semiotic dimensions eluded the analysis of Robert Anderson. The spectral backdrop of language suppression and dominance and the linguistic discipline of the Enlightenment haunt the story of the origins of modern Pentecostalism.

Borderlands Evangelism

In 1919, Nava and Ramón Ocampo, a young convert from Zacatecas, Mexico, left Riverside to evangelize in Yuma, Arizona, where Nava's sister lived. Her reported healing from cancer brought several families from the Mexican Methodist and Baptist churches into the apostolic fold in early 1920, including Baptist elders Bernardo Hernández and Jesús Torres. Nava and Ocampo left Yuma in May of 1920 to establish a church in Calexico, California, on the U.S.–Mexico border. The first recruits were members of the Mexican Methodist Church, including the Luis and Maria Herrera family. From this base the evangelists planted two churches on the Mexican side of the border in 1921, in Mexicali and Colonia Zaragoza, an outlying settlement earmarked by the territorial government to placate land redistribution demands.[23] These were joined later that year by a third one in Santa Rosalía (midway down the peninsula in Baja California Sur territory on the Sea of Cortez coast), a result mainly of Ocampo and Gregorio Domínguez's efforts.[24] Ensconced in the liminal zone of the California–Baja California border, Nava settled in for a prolonged period of pastoral work. In spite of difficult travel conditions, Nava, Llorente, De la Cruz, and others sustained an active and growing network of congregations throughout California, Arizona, and New Mexico.

Although the precursor mainline missions had broken ground and planted seeds there, Pentecostals reaped the religious harvests in California's inland valleys. In 1911, the Methodist Episcopal Church (MEC) was forced to turn over its Mexican mission church in the inland town of Redlands to a Korean congregation, owing to the disappearance of the mission's members. Redlands had served as the original hub of MEC Mexican work in southern California. In 1903 it had reported seventy-six members, drawn from the surrounding inland towns of Riverside, San Bernardino, Colton, and Ontario. In the aftermath of the Azusa Street Revival, the MEC appeared to have ceded temporarily the towns and valleys of interior southern California to aggressive Pentecostal evangelists, including Azusa Street participants Juan Navarro and Susie Valdez.[25] Except for a nonsupplied mission in Rancho Cucamonga, California (near Ontario), in 1919, the MEC Conference reported no work in this interior region through 1927. Vernon McCombs, a returned MEC missionary from the Andes region, arrived in time to buttress the sole remaining Mexican mission in Pasadena, California, which was soon joined by strong ones in Los Angeles and Santa Ana. However, even his sanguine progress reports (for example, 549 full members in 1919, 697 in 1920; twenty-two circuits in 1921) were leavened with the sobering news of "painful losses" (240 in 1916, 160 in 1918, 55 in 1919).[26] Given the abundance of testimonial narratives in the broad swath of the U.S. Latino borderlands (from California to Texas to Puerto Rico) describing the journey from Catholicism to Methodism to Pentecostalism, it is probable that a high percentage of the defections were to the daughter movement. Azusa Street pioneers Abundio and Rosa López would have been included, according to historian Cecil Robeck, in that number.[27] So, too, would have Adolph Rosa, a key member of the MEC's Spanish and Portuguese work in Northern California. The *Apostolic Faith* October 1906 issue carried his testimony (in English) about his spirit baptism in Oakland, California.[28]

Roberto Domínguez listed eight Methodist-trained pioneers of Pentecostal work in Puerto Rico in his hagiographic 1971 history, *Pioneros de Pentecostés.*[29] We also can add the Methodist-turned-Pentecostal San Antonio preacher Arnulfo López to the transition roster. The Assemblies of God's *Evangel* offered its readers regular updates on López, whom it had first introduced as an obstinate Methodist minister softened by the "lovely [singing] voice of a female convert" (note the role of music).[30] In early 1917, the periodical lauded López for forsaking a secure Methodist appointment for a financially tenuous Pentecostal ministry and offered López's own testimony about the change:

> Now I am happy, and I can see all things from my God, bless His name! Now I never think of the salary that I used to receive. My old church used to pay me with money, but the Lord's church pays me with the Holy Ghost, bless his sweet name, glory to God, Hallelujah, Amen! Now Lopez is going to live a free life, Hallelujah! The 250 members of my old church say to me, "You have not received any money since our church turned you out," but I say, "I have received the Holy Ghost, thanks be to God, and that is worth more than gold, bless His holy name, Hallelujah!"[31]

Five months later, readers read the distressing news of the sudden death of the evangelist's son: "I return back home and I found one of my dear son[s] going off from this world."[32] Such personal calamity, though, only steeled early Pentecostals' resolve. Sacrificial austerity served as a marker of apostolic calling.

Perhaps the greatest blow to the MEC work came with the loss of Pasadena, California, pastor Francisco Olazábal to the Assemblies of God (AG) during his tour of MEC Mexican churches in Northern California in 1917.[33] Olazábal, who had been trained in the Methodist Episcopal Church South (MECS) in central and northern Mexico, emerged as a leading pioneer builder of U.S. Latino Pentecostalism. His turbulent departure from the AG in 1923 marked a significant turning point in the history of Latino Pentecostalism.

Mainline Protestants were not the only ones bothered by the religious upstarts. Nava's evangelistic activities in Calexico and Mexicali also provoked the ire of the Caballeros de Colón. Mexico's Knights of Columbus, like several lay auxiliaries, had taken to the field against—in their view—a tyrannical regime bent, with the connivance of Masons and Protestants, on the de-Catholicization of Mexico. The Caballeros were active in most points of the Mexican compass. Nava claimed to have received two anonymous letters from the Catholic auxiliary's local group demanding the cessation of the noisy services in the Herrera household (two doors down from a Catholic church). The letters' ultimatum ("we will remove you from this world") troubled the young preacher but only temporarily. An unexpected visit from a parishioner couple during a Sunday school benediction resulted in the man's reported healing from blindness and steeled Nava's resolve.[34] Notably, many local and territorial officials made no confessional distinctions while implementing anticlerical policies. Aggressive evangélico proselytism, especially public preaching and singing, invited official censure. Stints in the Mexicali jail (with songwriter Elvira Herrera, one of the converted Methodists) merely provided Nava with more opportunities for evangelism.

Renewed Heterodoxy

Pentecostal orthodoxy provided a third source of opposition, owing mostly to Apostolics' extreme embrace of Protestantism's *sola scriptura* dictum. In line with the primitivist streak discussed by Grant Wacker, a significant minority of early U.S. Pentecostals, eschewing creedal traditions, rejected historical Trinitarianism in favor of a proto-Modalist or economic Trinitarian stance. Apostolics understood Jesus Christ as the full representation of the Godhead; and Father, Son, and Holy Spirit as manifestations of the Godhead and not ontological persons—hence, the water baptismal formula "in the Name of Jesus Christ" (Acts 2:38) as the apostles' understanding and fulfillment of the Great Commission passage in Matthew 28:19. The recovery of this practice was heralded by Canadian evangelist R. E. McAlister and John G. Schaepe at the Worldwide Pentecostal Camp Meeting held in Arroyo Seco (between Los Angeles and Pasadena) in April 1913. The soteriological implications were then mulled over by Azusa pioneer Frank Ewart for twelve months, before he opted for rebaptism in April 1914.

While documentation exists of Jesus's name baptism since Charles Parham's early ministry, we can surmise that the alternative baptismal formula would not have provoked a strong reaction had the reforming party not insisted on the rebaptism of believers previously baptized under the Trinitarian formula. And once the classic understanding of the Trinity—one God in three coequal, cosubstantial, and coeternal persons—was placed up for grabs, all hell and heaven broke loose. The "New Issue" ruptured the Finished Work (truncated Wesleyanism) camp of U.S. Pentecostalism. Pentecostal pioneers Howard Goss (a Charles Parham disciple), Frank

Ewart, and Frank Bartleman (Azusa's eyewitness historian) embraced the return to an Apostolic paradigm. With looming heterodoxy threatening to overtake its ranks, the nascent AG disavowed its original disavowal of creeds and adopted a comprehensive Trinitarian one. Importantly, the new Apostolicism took even deeper root in African American and Latino spiritual soils. Key to this process were the persuasive pen, hymnody, and pulpit of Garfield T. Haywood of Christ Temple in Indianapolis, Indiana.[35]

Equally key was the agency of restive borderlanders. Historical sequence matters here. In addition to the pre-1914 Jesus's name water baptisms of pioneers Luis López, Juan Navarro, and Francisco Llorente, the robust Oneness Pentecostal doctrine carried by Romana Valenzuela to her native Chihuahua in 1914 (and preserved by the derivative movements in Mexico; see chapter 2) also argues for a ratcheting down of the Arroyo Seco event—and Frank Ewart's retroactive interpretation of this—as the singular watershed event of Oneness Pentecostal history. This entails, of course, a de-privileging of the dominant narrative of AG rupture.[36]

Apostolics' zeal for the "Jesus's name revelation" soon drew missionary ire. This is understandable. By 1920, most of the Latino Pentecostal movement in Arizona and southern California may have embraced the heterodox belief in radical monotheism and Jesus's name baptism. Or so it seemed at least to one key antagonist, AG missionary Alice Luce, whose dispatches on the AG's "Mexican work" (carried in that denomination's *Pentecostal Evangel*) lamented the wholesale defection being fomented by "many false teachers."[37] Luce established her base in California in 1917 after a stunted sojourn in Monterrey, Mexico.[38] The move shored up orthodoxy. Her April 1918 plea underscored the high stakes at play as she understood them:

> Dear helpers-together-by-prayer, if ever we needed your help in
> prevailing intercession it is now. False teachers have been among
> the flock in these parts, and they have been tossed and torn by many
> winds of doctrine, so that it is hard to find any who are standing
> together in unity.[39]

Luce's 1920 application for license renewal with the denomination—sent from Los Angeles—stressed the orthodoxy of her recent converts: "All our converts have been immersed according to Matt. 28:19. The 'new issue' error is the greatest difficulty here. They are trying to steal away our flock all the time."[40]

Luce's alarm may have been justified. For example, Nava's efforts seem to have eclipsed AG pastor M[ack] M. Pinson's work among Mexicans in Calexico, on which the *Evangel* reported in late 1919.[41] Pinson, formerly of Phoenix, Arizona, and a key AG pioneer, had moved to Los Angeles to study Spanish and then to San Antonio, Texas, in 1916 to minister as colleague to H. C. Ball (the Assemblies' new leader of Spanish-language work).[42] He and his wife arrived in Brawley, California, with plans to "construct a church" in the fall of 1918.[43] The following year, the *Evangel* lamented his distance of 150 miles from any other AG work but noted that Pinson had closed his tent meetings in Calexico, California, in order to hold nightly services in a "Christian colored church." The periodical's concern for a chapel to "properly care for the work" proved prescient.[44] The chapel in question seems to have been the very one purchased in 1924 by Nava's group.[45] With no periodical or white coreligionists to sponsor them, each of the families of the Calexico–Mexicali Apostolic congregation contributed $25 apiece for their movement's first temple on U.S. soil.[46]

Distance, convert ambivalence, and stubborn Catholicism rendered difficult Luce's task. She offered a candid snapshot of her field of operations to *Evangel* readers in September 1923:

> The brethren of these northern [California] Missions go out into the fruit ranches for the whole summer, as fruit picking, cutting, drying and canning form their livelihood for the whole year. So after visiting them and encouraging them to remain faithful to the Lord, sister [Florence] Murcutt and I felt led to come back to Los Angeles for the summer where we are working up in a Mission in a suburb called Belvedere. . . . These poor, dark souls. . . . Yes, "'dark'" indeed, for they have not the Light of the glorious Gospel of Christ who is the image of God—bound by chains of idolatry and superstition, bowing down to images of the virgin, saints or angel.[47]

Luce's appeal echoed long-standing Protestant views of Roman Catholic belief and practice (as well as more recent mainline missionary frustration over converts' labor mobility). But even the Full Gospel light required refraction through orthodox lenses. The spread of heterodoxy among Latinos prompted the *Evangel* to warn its readers about the contested and ever-shifting turf in the Southwest:

> In Arizona the work has had more to hinder its growth than in Texas, New Mexico or Colorado. In Texas thus far we have had no new-

issue whatsoever, but not so for Arizona. And it seems that after they have entered and split up an assembly that they and the outsiders become so hardened to the gospel appeal as to not be touched. We only have in Arizona one mission, in Pirtleville. Bro. Floyd Howard is in charge. He is a good, capable worker. Bro. Howard also works among the Mexicans in Bisbee and Douglas in Arizona and in Agua Prieta, Sonora, Mexico.[48]

A gifted educator and former missionary with the Anglican Church Missionary Society in India, Luce deemed the best defense against heresy (and spiritism, the other impediment to church growth) to be sound biblical pedagogy and Anglo supervision.[49] After a series of Bible conferences—the first was held in Rosenberg, Texas, in July 1920—she and Ball pursued a more institutional strategy: Bible institutes.[50]

In May 1920, AG general chairman J. W. Welch toured most of the denomination's Latino congregations in Texas and reported to *Evangel* readers the following statistics: 500 members, thirteen assemblies, ten pastors, and four buildings. He noted that plans were afoot for a Bible training school to serve the Assemblies' growing (white) constituency in Texas and suggested that a Mexican department could be administered under its auspices. Speaking of the "fine young Mexicans" he had encountered, he opined that their necessary tutelage would not be an extended affair: "Supervision by Americans will always be helpful, if not necessary however."[51]

Ball had expressed similar concerns three years earlier to the readers of the *Evangel*: "We need more American missionaries. I have, in the past two years, trained several Mexican workers, but while they are excellent workers, they need American oversight. Let us unite in prayer and faith that we shall see several more missionaries here on the field."[52]

Given his prior training and pastoral ministry in Methodism, no leader seemed as well equipped as Francisco Olazábal for the educational enterprise. Since his ordination in the AG in 1917,[53] Olazábal had conducted successful healing and evangelistic campaigns throughout California and Texas.[54] The *Evangel* likened Olazábal's turn from Methodism to the conversion of Saul of Tarsus on the Damascus Road and lauded his main speaking role at the Assemblies' second Mexican work convention, in San Antonio in October 1918.[55] The following year, Olazábal began fruitful work in El Paso, Texas, where Baptists, Presbyterians, and Roman Catholics were drawn to his healing services. Once converted, many were carried away in the migratory flow toward California and the return flow toward

Mexico.[56] In September 1922, Olazábal reported successful church extensions across the border in Ciudad Juárez, Chihuahua; Hipólito, Coahuila; and a Texas town twenty miles from El Paso. Importantly, he noted the need for a Bible school for "my boys."[57]

Olazábal's pedagogical aspirations foundered, however, on the shoals of white paternalism. Three months later (December 15–16), he was summoned to a meeting in Springfield, Missouri, with Welch, Ball, Luce, and George Blaisdell to discuss, among other matters, the problem of El Paso's distance from the bulk of the Mexican works. The *Evangel* reported the outcome in January 1923: Olazábal would stick to evangelism, and Ball would assume responsibility for ministerial training under the auspices of the General Council's Missionary Committee.[58] Ball and Luce laid plans for the founding of two institutes in October 1926, the Latin American Bible Institute (LABI) in Texas, under Ball's direction, and the Berean Bible Institute in San Diego, California, under Luce's.[59] The conspicuous absence of one of early Latino Pentecostalism's most notable leaders from the Texas LABI's first faculty roster was partially compensated by the inclusion of Ramón López as music instructor.[60] Theological pedagogy would remain the province of missionaries, while converts would be encouraged to develop their virtuosity in musical performance.

Unbeknownst to most *Evangel* readers, Ball had brought the matter of leadership to a head in the fall of 1922 when he informed restive Mexican pastors at a meeting in Victoria, Texas, of an official veto of their plans to form a separate district, presumably with Olazábal at the helm. Olazábal, Demetrio Bazán, Arnulfo López, Isabel Flores, and others severed their ties with the AG one week after the *Evangel*'s January 1923 dispatch. In March they formed the Concilio Mexicano Interdenominacional de las Iglesias Cristianas (Pentecostales).[61]

Olazábal's conflict with the AG revolved around issues of autonomy and not doctrine; his movement remained Trinitarian. "El Azteca" may have simply tired of ecclesial bureaucracies that required him to run repeatedly and redundantly through the education hoops or that checked his pedagogical ambitions. In California the MEC assigned him a training curriculum that was redundant with his prior course of study with the MECS in central and northern Mexico. The final hurdle reflected an unwillingness by the AG to entrust even seasoned Latino ministers (Olazábal was Ball's senior by at least one decade) with theological leadership; the thinking was that they were best deployed on the evangelistic and pastoral circuit.

In his later account of Ball's final meeting with the restive Latino ministers, Miguel Guillén celebrated his predecessor's defection as emancipation from Ball's and the AG's heavy-handed paternalism:

> Rev. Ball responded to them that the minutes forbade their action [formation of a free-standing district council] for four years and that for many reasons they [i.e., the Assemblies' leadership] believed that the Mexican people were not equipped to organize themselves in a district council. . . . Not having reached any agreement with the one who would be chief, they proceeded with plans to form a council exclusively for the Spanish-speaking.[62]

Ironically, the break with the AG brought Olazábal full circle. In June 1908, the star student of the Colegio Wesleyano in San Luis Potosí accompanied MECS missionary Frank Onderdonk on a fund-raising tour (for Wesleyano) of prominent Texas Methodist churches. There, Olazábal took a temporary appointment to help organize a small Mexican congregation in Bridgeport, Texas, near Fort Worth. The following month he weighed in with a caustic letter to the MECS periodical *El Evangelista Mexicano*, denouncing an erroneous report of a missed meeting (to discuss a circulating missionary board statement) in that town between missionary David Carter and a leader of the Iglesia Evangélica Independiente (IEI). The IEI's organ, *México Evangélico*, was engaged at that time in a polemical exchange with the *Evangelista* over the question of autonomy, identity, and ideology. Olazábal insisted that the board document in question had not come up in conversation and that, contrary to the IEI's account, Carter had not fled on a train to skip the appointment (the flooded tracks had prevented him from leaving for three additional days). Methodism's young champion wondered with rhetorical flourish whether "independence was full of such little things [lies]!"[63]

The IEI's prescient critique would resonate fourteen years later in Olazábal's own career and two decades later within a nationalizing Mexican Methodism. It certainly resonated widely within missionary ranks. In 1916, delegates to the Panama Congress on Christian Work in Latin America were informed that San Antonio's "immense" IEI had effectively "depopulated" that city's denominational churches. Given such a "strong nationalistic spirit," the Congress's Commission on Cooperation and Unity counseled greater sensitivity toward native clergy and converts throughout the hemisphere.[64]

Ultimately, ecclesial autonomy freed Olazábal to move more widely in the U.S. mainland and Puerto Rico and even beyond Latino constituencies.

The group's rechristening in 1932 as the Concilio Latinoamericano de Iglesias Cristianas (CLADIC) reflected Olazábal's impact on Puerto Rican and other Latino communities in New York and Chicago through a decade of independent work.[65] By the time of his unexpected death (by car accident) in 1937, Olazábal's was arguably the largest and most pan-Latino Pentecostal movement in the United States. It stood on the brink of merger with A. J. Tomlinson's Church of God of Prophecy. (A decade earlier, Olazábal had rejected evangelist Aimee Semple McPherson's overtures to consolidate his movement with her Foursquare Gospel Church.)[66] Without the charismatic glue of its leader, however, the movement shattered into many regional or ethnic-specific denominations.[67]

The cases of Francisco Olazábal, Juan Lugo, David Ruesga, Abundio López,[68] and Antonio Nava merit deeper, comparative study for patterns of subaltern religious agency. Lugo, founder of the Iglesia de Dios Pentecostal, Puerto Rico's largest Protestant denomination (with significant mainland membership), ultimately broke or, rather, never fully consolidated with the Assemblies of God, significantly setting back that group's efforts on the island.[69] David Ruesga, pastor of the AG's largest church in Mexico City, split off to found the Iglesia de Dios en la República Mexicana and later repeated the action with the Church of God.[70] In both cases, Ruesga successfully garnered governmental support by invoking the anticlerical articles of the 1917 constitution, provisions aimed originally at foreign Catholic clergy.[71] Certainly, personality differences and idiosyncrasies exacerbated the various situations. So, too, did male Latino discomfiture with Anglo female leadership.

Antonio Nava, of course, never enjoyed or sought Assemblies patronage, owing to obvious doctrinal incommensurabilities. Yet his subsequent complaints over *gringo* indifference suggest experiences common to several movement builders: marginalization, subordination, and, frankly, disrespect.[72] Like their mainline predecessors, white Pentecostal leaders—Trinitarian and Oneness and, in the case of Oneness, black and white—erred in their estimation of Latinos' confessional sensibilities, denominational loyalties, and patience.[73]

Persistent Heterodoxy

By 1919, the growing band of apostolic preachers had established congregations in six California towns and cities: Watts, Oxnard, El Rio, San Bernardino, Colton, and Riverside; along with older ones in Los Angeles,

San Francisco, and San Diego. They also set up preaching points in several other Mexican American communities. During the following six years, churches and preaching points emerged in seventeen additional locations. The preponderance of agricultural towns, especially in the California Coachella, Imperial, Ventura, Salinas, and San Joaquin valleys, reflected the rural nature of the movement, a factor in its growth among immigrant farm workers. By 1925, the year of the first convention of the Iglesia de la Fe Apostólica Pentecostés (IFAP), churches in Phoenix, Arizona, and the New Mexico mining and railroad towns of Lordsburg, Santa Rita, Hurley, Hatch, Deming, and Las Cruces, had been added to the roster (Map 1). But numbers did not necessarily translate into coherence.

By 1925, the AG churches under Ball's and Luce's supervision had celebrated at least six conventions, all in Texas (Kingsville, San Antonio, El Paso, and Houston) or northern Mexico (Múzquiz, Coahuila, 1923) and at least two regional gatherings in Los Angeles for the California assemblies. In spite of their numerical success in California, Arizona, and northern Mexico, Apostolics lagged behind organizationally. The recent conversion from Catholicism of most apostolic ministers and laypersons or their brief interludes in mainline Protestantism help to explain the lack of familiarity with Protestant organizational imperatives. Equally significant, Francisco Llorente's strong reticence to move beyond a loose fellowship structure represented a persistent current of antiorganizational sentiment within primitive Pentecostalism: come-outism, a fear of replicating the captivity of denominational structures and a trust in the Spirit's leading.

Borderlands Conclaves

Llorente, Nava, and fellow ministers carried credentials issued by E. W. Doak, Garfield T. Haywood, and Thomas C. Davis, leaders of the (by now Oneness) Pentecostal Assemblies of the World (PAW). The PAW viewed them from afar as their "Mexican representatives."[74] This arrangement sufficed for the bilingual Llorente. Nava, however, fretted about theological ambiguity. He credited a vision with compelling him to seek greater harmony among his colleagues. A phrase in red ink, "United you shall triumph, divided you shall fail," superimposed itself on the text he was studying (Acts 1). Troubled, he originally thought the warning applied to his local pastorate in Calexico, California; the larger implications became apparent to him soon thereafter. He canvassed his colleagues throughout California to gauge their interest in a first-ever gathering. The flow

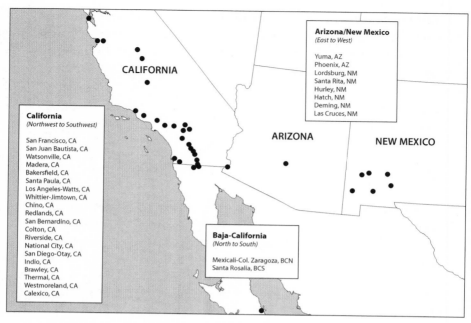

Arizona/New Mexico
(East to West)

Yuma, AZ
Phoenix, AZ
Lordsburg, NM
Santa Rita, NM
Hurley, NM
Hatch, NM
Deming, NM
Las Cruces, NM

CALIFORNIA

ARIZONA

NEW MEXICO

California
(Northwest to Southwest)

San Francisco, CA
San Juan Bautista, CA
Watsonville, CA
Madera, CA
Bakersfield, CA
Santa Paula, CA
Los Angeles-Watts, CA
Whittier-Jimtown, CA
Chino, CA
Redlands, CA
San Bernardino, CA
Colton, CA
Riverside, CA
National City, CA
San Diego-Otay, CA
Indio, CA
Brawley, CA
Thermal, CA
Westmoreland, CA
Calexico, CA

Baja-California
(North to South)

Mexicali-Col. Zaragoza, BCN
Santa Rosalía, BCS

MAP 1 Iglesia de la Fé Apostólica Pentecostés Congregations, 1925–1927. (Map by Michael Cota)

of correspondence and affirmative responses strengthened Nava's hand with Llorente. Meanwhile, the recalcitrant leader suffered a devastating personal blow with the death from tuberculosis of his young wife, Delfin, six months before the conference scheduled for December in San Bernardino. Still, Nava had to wait until September for Llorente's assurances that he would attend.[75]

Ultimately, Llorente presided over the convention, a meeting marked by a tone of reconciliation and a search for doctrinal cohesion. The conclave drew thirty-three ministers and 178 laypersons. In spite of his earlier misgivings, the ministers ratified Llorente's de facto leadership, electing him pastor general and Antonio Nava the second-in-command *anciano ejecutivo*.[76]

Bernardo Hernández's minutes of the business meetings provide a glimpse into the issues deemed most pressing by the leaders and their colleagues. Clearly, primitivist urges prevailed. In the first session (December 1), Marcial de la Cruz called for unity of doctrine for the sake of an improved (external) testimony, and Nava pled for communion in all matters. Llorente followed up with several points of his own, necessary prologues to any discussion of doctrine: (1) reconciliation; (2) forgiveness; (3) fraternal love; (4) mutual respect; and (5) unity.[77] In Hernández's account, Llorente's exegetical skills (he preached on John 15) and the attendees' search for harmony resulted in a virtual love fest:

> With these conditions approved by all present, the meeting proceeded on to reconciliation, the result of which was a tidal wave of phrases, of brotherly love and teachings dictated by the Holy Spirit.
>
> This Spirit stirred mightily in all the hearts of His servants, causing joy with tears and sacred songs offered before the select throne of God.[78]

The delayed arrival of several ministers prompted Nava to reiterate Llorente's five-point exhortation during the second day's business session. Again, Hernández's record emphasized the heightened emotive state of the meeting and referenced the sonic dimension:

> The cry born from the Christian heart is the expression of the soul toward Christ. This is what occurred in those solemn moments.
>
> Our exquisite Christ made his sweet voice heard, as he did among his disciples, when he entered where they were gathered and said to them, "Peace be unto you." Sweet peace, celestial music that moves the Christian soul.[79]

Hernández described late arrival José Martínez's lapse into an ineffable state: "Bro. José Martínez spoke next, and with few words told of what his heart was feeling in that moment; but unable to speak any longer, due to the emotion that was overcoming him, his silence spoke louder, letting his love for Jesus shine forth."[80]

The group did not take up doctrinal points until the end of the third day's business session. They returned to the matter after elections on the fourth day (recall Grant Wacker's pragmatist urge). They reached or reiterated consensus on Jesus's name water baptism and Holy Spirit baptism. During the final three sessions, the assembly took up an extensive list of questions submitted by De la Cruz, Martínez, and others. These included such apostolic distinctives as (1) a woman's head covering; (2) a holy kiss (upon greeting a fellow believer of the same sex); (3) foot washing (of the same sex); (4) the inadmissibility of personal revelation as dogma; (5) the primacy of preaching over manifestations of the Spirit; (6) the office of deaconess reserved for older, spiritually experienced women only; and (7) affirmation of male authority in the church.

More conventions followed. A second, held in Indio, California, in November 1926, saw the participation of ministers from the New Mexico and Baja California churches. The convention took up and affirmed twenty doctrinal points but first declared the Pentecost event in Acts 2 as the pneumatic starting point: "And the true Christians have always felt the Holy Spirit as comforter; the Holy Spirit as guide; the Holy Spirit as sanctifier; the Holy spirit as seal; the Holy Spirit as baptism; the Holy Spirit as power; and the Holy Spirit as witness."[81] The pneumatic thrust complicates, of course, the generally accepted fourfold Christology of U.S. Pentecostalism: Christ as Savior, Baptizer, Healer, and Coming King.[82]

A third conclave, during Christmas of 1927, further cemented ties with the Baja California churches. Given the strong revival in the sister border towns of Calexico and Mexicali, the convention was held in the new temple in Colonia Zaragoza (the first for the future Iglesia Apostólica of Mexico). Apostolics from the United States crossed over to confirm revival reports on (for them still familiar) Mexican soil.

As migrant religious gatherings, the 1925 and 1926 conventions deserve closer scrutiny. Bernardo Hernández's rosters noted places of ministry and ministerial office. Other sources allow us to collate his roster with birthplace or place of origin. Of the forty-three ministerial attendees with identifiable places of origin, only a handful were U.S.-born. The same holds true for the thirty additional Apostolic pastors and evangelists known to have converted and to have been in or on the threshold of active ministry in the 1920s. Clearly, migratory experience shaped the ecclesial table. The developing polity would reflect this. And while some leaders, such as Epifanio Cota and Arturo Hermosillo, were U.S.-born, they never stopped rubbing elbows with Mexico-born colleagues at that table or, for that matter, in the workplace and barrio.

The respect accorded Miguel García in the 1925 gathering demonstrates an awareness of transborder origins and religious genealogies—all leading back to Los Angeles—among the cadre of apostolic ministers. García, the nephew of Romana Carbajal de Valenzuela, Apostolicism's missionary to Mexico (see Chapter 2), had arrived on the scene from Torreón, Coahuila, three years earlier with his widowed mother, Nicolasa. His pastorate in the California Imperial Valley town of Westmoreland neighbored that of Antonio Nava. In his salutation to the 1925 convention's second business session (the day of his arrival), José Martinez introduced Bakersfield, California, pastor Juan Rodríguez as a "son in the Lord" of Miguel García.[83] The latter had baptized Rodríguez in 1918 in Torreón. When García opted for migration to California, Rodríguez followed not far behind.[84] Juan's brother Aurelio—another García convert—stayed behind and was serving at the time of this convention as the Torreón pastor of the Iglesia Evangélica Espiritual del Pentecostés.[85] Another García disciple from Torreón, Isabel Sánchez, attended the 1926 convention from his base in the Ciudad Juárez–El Paso basin. For early Apostolics, bona fides mattered; these later would take the form of letters of recommendation as the movement codified its practice.

Body, Gender, and Healing

The topics taken up in the final three sessions of the 1925 meeting reflected concerns common to many Pentecostal groups wrestling with the challenge of balance, of subjecting the spirit to prophets. They also fleshed out the tactile dimensions of Christian sociability, demarcating proper dimensions for corporeal contact. Victorian sensibilities would be assuaged by limiting this to the same sex. The first and final two distinctives (women's head covering and deaconesses subject to male authority), though, were deemed necessary, in order to set Latino Apostolic practice apart from that of its black and white counterparts. The ministerial prerogatives assumed by women transgressed traditional mores. The use of head coverings and the absence of women from the pulpit would eliminate at least two potential barriers to evangelism among Catholics.

The documentary evidence on women's ordination is compelling and intriguing. The PAW ministerial credential certificates for "Elder" Antonio Nava and "Missionary" Marcial de la Cruz allowed an important caveat: "Women workers are permitted to officiate in Marriage, Funeral, Baptismal Services and Lord's Supper in cases of emergency."[86] After the IFAP's independent incorporation in California as the Apostolic Assembly in 1930, the language about exceptional circumstances was simply bleached out of the otherwise exact replicas of the older PAW license. Yet, although the discussion of men's authority and women's head covering may appear at first glance a reiteration of male privilege, it also asserted Mexican cultural norms over black and white ecclesial cultures. The sanctified machismo undergirding the cultural resistance also came bundled with an acknowledgment of female healing and spiritual powers and, of course, filial affect, somewhat akin to or continuous with popular Catholic practice and *guadalupanismo*. As primitivists, Apostolics defended their practice with Pauline prohibitions (1 Timothy 2:11–12). As pragmatists, they grounded their machismo on familiar cultural turf. An important question, though, lingers over the office of deaconess and the status accorded the older women, mostly widows, who held it. These included Miguel García's mother, Nicolasa García, whose sister Romana Carbajal de Valenzuela was credited with initiating Apostolicism in Mexico (see Chapter 2); Dolores Gonzalez, mother of pastor Rodolfo González; María Zapata; and Ruperta Chacon, of Mexicali and one of Antonio Nava's first converts. As late as 1939, Antonio Nava, Arturo Hermosillo, and Bernardo Hernández issued a license, with a new format, to Nicolasa García. The revered pioneer was licensed to "Preach the gospel, Baptize and officiate Funeral Ceremony."[87] Clearly, the office could not be eliminated while its occupants remained alive and active; its disappearance had to await their demise. The pioneer deaconesses were simply not replaced. Ultimately, the existence and eclipse of the office were excised from later official Apostolic Assembly history. Sanctified machismo won out and served to demarcate ethnic difference. Still, as women's and subaltern studies have reminded us, it remains to be seen how much of that process reflected strictly male prerogatives and how much involved female assent, complicity, and subterfuge. The photo documentary record also suggests a pliable acquiescence in the case of the head covering, which over the course of many decades was transformed by enterprising women from an ostensibly male-imposed symbol of female piety to a bustling import–export cottage industry that provided veils as aesthetically pleasing accessories.

The Disciplining State

The retrospective denominational history (written four decades later) cast the initial conclaves in Southern and Baja California in positive light. This should not surprise us. The description of the 1927 gathering in Colonia Zaragoza celebrated multiple healings. This set the pattern for many such gatherings—regional, national, and international conventions—in the ensuing decades; attendees expected and reported numerous healings and water and spirit baptisms. Pentecostalism arrived to compete with (or replace) the storied healers of the borderlands, moving the thaumaturgical spectacle out of the private and into the collective space.[88] The terrain had begun to shift, though, with the long-delayed legislative implementation under President Plutarco Calles of the 1917 constitution's anticlerical clauses. The press of tuberculosis victims seeking healing at the 1927 convention and at the Mexicali church soon thereafter provoked official alarm. On February 9, 1928, municipal authorities ordered Mexicali pastor Pedro Ceniceros to shutter the Apostolic temple in the Nuevo Pueblo neighborhood, owing to public health concerns. One month later, they refused final permission to the Colonia Zaragoza church to open, rescinding an earlier (April 23, 1927) construction permit (thus, the December 1927 convention there may have been held prematurely). The ensuing four-year exchange of appeals and denials all the way up to the federal presidency and Interior Ministry (spanning three administrations) left a trail of official discourse about modernity and morality and religious counterdiscourse about culture and citizenship.[89] The original charges were laid out for territorial governor Abelardo Rodríguez by the municipal president:

> The religious practices to which the adepts of the "Fé Apostólica de Pentecostés," as this Sect is called, give themselves consist of repugnant fanatical acts, contrary to the most elemental requirements for hygiene, since, prisoners of a type of spasmodic fervor, they affect contortions and roll about many times, men and women together; and as such individuals are not known for their cleanliness or sobriety, their meetings become true sources of infection, with nothing edifying [to commend them].[90]

The Interior Ministry instructed Rodríguez (a close military ally of President Calles) to ratify the denial, characterizing the religious practices as "act[s] of immorality which should not be tolerated under any circumstances."[91]

In a petition to the Interior Ministry dated July 1, 1928, Ceniceros and fifty-nine church members reiterated his March 24 refutation of the municipality's charges: "The Religion [Cristiana de Pentecostés] is practiced in the United States of North America and in other civilized nations, among these, our Mexican Republic; there are thousands of persons who practice that religion, which has as its base faith and morality. . . . There is no lack of persons with scant scruples for respecting others' Religion, who have tagged us with the epithet '"Aleluya."' The petitioners tagged on a final coda for the interior minister: "We hold our services inside the temple [a constitutional requirement]; our religion has as its base morality and order, through which we have always stayed within the precepts of the law; thus, the order to close our temple has curbed the right granted us by article 24 of the Constitution."[92] In spite of Ceniceros's offer to keep the temple disinfected and off-limits for sick persons, the interior minister denied the appeal.

The following April, pastor Encarnación Meza and twenty-six church members, anticipating a softer anticlericalism (in light of the impending modus vivendi accords between the federal government and the Catholic hierarchy), petitioned new president Emilio Portes Gil for permission to reopen the Colonia Zaragoza temple. To rebut the "completely absurd calumny" of immorality, they pointed to a temperament "innate in every Mexican," which would never permit such a thing.[93] Portes, who had served as Calles's interior minister, continued the ban. On June 23, 1931, Pedro Ceniceros appealed to the "spirit of tolerance and goodwill" of Portes's successor, Pascual Ortiz Rubio.[94] In response to the Interior Ministry's query, Governor Carlos Trejo reaffirmed the standing charges and layered on a new one: the "sect" in question was "of Negro origin . . . brought to the national territory by North Americans."[95]

Trejo's observation was partially correct. Aberlardo Rodríguez and other revolutionary leaders were familiar with the interracial dynamics of the neighboring society; Rodríguez spent six years of his youth in Los Angeles, from 1906 to 1912. Whether through intuition or direct experience, Mexican officialdom noted something different about this evangélico variant. Apostolicism arrived steeped in African American influences and carried by Mexican Americans. Let us consider, then, an instance of the unexpected impact of religious remittances in the transcultural settings of the borderlands. In this case, Indianapolis, Indiana, served as the unlikely place of origin and Calexico, California, as the equally unlikely place of reception and reworking.

Religious Remittances in Black and Brown

The laity's clamor for instruction in Oneness doctrine led Antonio Nava to search for popular catechetical tools; the ministerial meetings were generally closed affairs. He encountered a valuable resource in *The Bridegroom's Songs*, a hymnal of ninety-four songs compiled by PAW leader G. T. Haywood and sent to his far-flung network of correspondents, including Francisco Llorente. Nava welcomed pianist Luis Herrera's rendition of Haywood's 1914 composition, "Baptized into the Body"—the booklet's hymns were musically scored. Within a few days the young pastor returned with a freely translated hymn to teach his receptive flock.[96] Its wide dissemination through the ensuing decades transformed "El Nombre del Mesías" (The Name of the Messiah) into a doctrinal anthem of Latino Apostolicism. This was not Haywood's doing, however. A textual comparison between the two versions reveals Nava's creativity; he was not a theological parrot. His poetic reworking forced Haywood's interrogatory into a more declarative and catechetical form for ready repetition and memorization. It also hewed more closely to scriptural text. In doing so, it softened the sectarian edge to Haywood's pointed soteriological challenge (to Trinitarian Pentecostals) and rendered a hymn that, save for the chorus's final line, could be sung in any evangélico setting. The redaction of that line allowed for the increasingly popular hymn's inclusion in J. Paul Cragin's *Melodías Evangélicas* and H. C. Ball's *Himnos de Gloria* (see Chapter 6). The orthodox missionaries simply replaced the baptismal imperative with the more obtuse "[his name] for all eternity," thereby blurring the Apostolic distinctive concerning water baptism in Jesus's name.

A deeper ethnomusicological analysis would also reveal Nava's reworkings. He left Haywood's melody intact but slowed down considerably its quick 4/4 tempo. Nava's lyrics also hewed to Spanish-language rhyme conventions. In short, Nava used Haywood's creation to create, in turn, a sui generis Oneness Pentecostal creed wrapped in *mexicano* musical form.

We may surmise that Nava's appropriation of Haywood's music mirrored their relationship, under which the PAW provided loose sponsorship in the form of licenses and literature but left its "Mexican representatives" free to organize as they saw fit. Haywood's stature as one of the preeminent apologists for Oneness Pentecostalism and his assumption of leadership of the PAW had placed Indianapolis at the center of the multiracial dissident movement (the Oneness movement splintered over race, ultimately).[97] Although neither Llorente nor Nava ever traveled to Indianapolis or any other Oneness stronghold outside of the Southwest, Haywood affirmed their connection in at least one swing through southern California.[98]

Whatever their formal arrangements with the PAW, for at least the first decade and a half of growth, Latino Apostolics negotiated their place as newcomers on the half-century-old Latino evangélico block by forging strategic alliances with other groups on the religious and social periphery. Put differently, in this instance of the power and significance of circulating symbolic goods, Nava transformed Haywood's heterodox hymn into (to borrow a Gramscian notion) a pliable "defensive, counter-ideological, symbolic expression"[99] to deploy on behalf of his community's identity, continuity, and autonomy. This autonomy bred creativity.

That such black–Latino contacts and influences flowed in reciprocal directions is hinted at by the continued interracial fellowship between

Baptized into the Body
(Author: G. T. Haywood)

1. Have you been baptized into the Body?
Baptized with the Holy Ghost?
There is but one way to enter in it,
just as they did on Pentecost.

[Chorus] Are you in the Church triumphant?
Are you in the Savior's Bride?
Come and be baptized into the Body,
and forevermore abide.

2. There is but one Church, Bride or Body
and into it we're all baptized.
The one, true, promised Holy Spirit,
tho' by the world we're all despised.

3. Every creed has claim'd to be the Body
But the "plumb-line" proved untrue;
All their dreams by God determined
To bring His Son's True Bride to view.

4. Many thought they were in the Body;
'Till the Holy Ghost had come.
When the Word of God opened to them
they entered in, and yet there's room.

these two groups through the 1920s and 1930s (e.g., in the Watts, California, Apostolic congregation). Other borderlands reports confirm this. H. C. Ball reported to *Evangel* readers on African American enthusiasm for Mexican worship in the Jim Crow setting of South Texas in mid-1922:

> The brethren worship in a large room in a private house, perhaps some thirty gathering there, and in the back part the colored people gather. These colored people are anxious to hear Pentecost preached in their own language, but a white man could hardly preach to them in this part of the country. Yet, these colored people have learned to sing the Spanish songs with the Mexicans, even though they know very little Spanish. I hope that some colored Pentecostal preacher will go to Edna sometime and hold a meeting among them.[100]

El Nombre del Mesías	The Name of the Messiah
(Antonio C. Nava)	(My translation of Nava lyrics)

La señal que fue desde el principio	The sign that has since the beginning
dada a la humanidad;	to humankind been given;
Príncipe de Paz será su nombre	he shall be called Prince of Peace
por toda la eternidad.	for all eternity.
Es el nombre que era oculto,	'Tis the name that was hidden,
que no era revelado	that was not revealed.
Jesucristo, éste es su nombre.	Jesus Christ, this is his name
En él debeís ser bautizado.	into which you must be baptized.
Fué Mesías grande y verdadero	He was the great and true Messiah
que a la tierra decendió.	who descended to earth.
Trajo a las gentes luz y vida,	He brought light and life to the nations,
mas el mundo no creyó.	but the world did not believe.
Hay un solo nombre dado al mundo	There's but one name given to the world
Por el cual se salvará.	by which it may be saved
Ese nombre da virtud y gracia;	That name gives power and grace;
Y él que cree salvo será.	and he who believes shall be saved.
O, hermano, sabes tú que Cristo	Oh, brother, do you know that Christ
te podrá salvar a ti.	is able to save you?
Ven a Él, renaciendo de nuevo	Come to Him and be born again,
y pondrá su Espíritu en ti.	and He will place his Spirit within you.

Three months later, AG minister George Blaisdell, whose early ministry spanned the Sonora–Arizona border, depicted even more complex religious cultural interactions that he observed during a visit to the work pastored by Floyd and Chonita Howard:

> On Sunday we crossed the boundary to help the brethren in Pirtleville and we had a wonderful day. Even the Hawaiian Islands could not give one a more cosmopolitan crowd. There were Americans, Mexicans, Negros, one Yaqui Indian, one half breed Chinese. The Spirit was present in power and we had a wonderful time. Praise God![101]

Given its novelty and utility, Nava's song soon assumed prominence throughout the movement in both countries and later in missionary areas in Central and South America and Italy. Its circulation via performance and hymnal compilation represents multiple instances of religious remittances. The song's performance thousands of times over in the ensuing decades, from Alaska to Tierra del Fuego, replicated Nava's attempt to claim and demarcate theological and ecclesial turf. Such fecund agency, of course, is eclipsed by larger forces in the analysis of Robert Anderson. And it remains largely absent in the studies of the Imperial Valley's agribusiness, irrigation, and labor histories.

Geographic turf and doctrinal turf are often coterminous. At first glance, the Imperial–Mexicali Valley seems an unlikely battleground for renewed debates of the pre-Nicene era. Clearly, the area was peripheral to both U.S. Protestantism and Mexican Catholicism. Yet it was precisely the periphery's inconsequence and resultant freedom that allowed heterodoxy to take root, flourish, and flow out in new forms and in several directions from this "rim of Christendom."[102] Herein lies much of the power of the Apostólico story. In order to understand how this heterodox variant looms larger within Chicano/Mexican Pentecostalism than its white counterpart does within U.S. Pentecostalism, we must employ interpretive lenses that take into account the mutually constitutive force of religion, marginality, and mobility. With this in mind, we can now turn, after a brief excursus about Azusa's music traveling to the Southern Cone, to the development of Apostolicism in Mexico and southern Texas.

CHAPTER 2

Pentecostal Origins in Northern Mexico and Southern Texas

Cuando Dios a las huestes de Israel	When God sent the hosts of Israel
Los sacó al desierto a peregrinar	Into the desert to roam
Fueron guiados todos por Aquel	They were all guided by the One
Que les ayudó a llegar	Who helped them to arrive
En el fuego de noche fue	It was in the fire by night
En la nube de día está	It is in the cloud by day
El Señor que los libró	The Lord who freed them
De la cruel esclavitud	From cruel slavery
Devolviendo la libertad	Restoring liberty
A su pueblo que escogió	To his chosen people
A la voz del gran Libertador	At the voice of the great Liberator
Venció sin ningún temor	They conquered without fear

Abundio and Rosa López, two of Azusa's Latino preachers, surely carried with them the hymnodic repertoire of reheated Wesleyanism. For example, the revival's emblematic song, "The Comforter Has Come," represented an intensification of a popular Holiness hymn. Its in situ performance, in English and in Spanish ("El Fiel Consolador," translated by Methodist Vicente Mendoza), signified the new understanding of a "third blessing" (spirit baptism) after Wesleyan sanctification. Abundio López tried his translating hand at C. Austin Miles's 1900 composition, "The Cloud and Fire."[1] The song, set in a martial frame, heralded Jehovah's salvific action and theophanic presence in the Exodus story. López's "La Nube de Fuego" (The Cloud of Fire) hewed closely to the emancipatory theme (the part about freedom from cruel slavery and restored liberty are absent in the English-language original) and to Miles's maritime one:

Como barco en una tempestad	Like a ship in a storm
Caminaron sin ningún compás	They wandered without a compass
Pero Dios les mostró su gran bondad	But God showed them his great goodness
No dejándoles jamás	Never abandoning them

Like its metaphor of a vessel seeking harbor, the song was carried to unexpected places, probably through missionary circuits.[2] Its reception and performance in far-off Chile left an imprint on the story of Pentecostal origins in that Southern Cone country. The narrative of the birth of Chilean Pentecostalism centers around MEC missionaries Willis and Mary Hoover. Touched in 1907 by reports of revival in South India, they corresponded extensively with other points of the new global Pentecostal map. The ensuing revival and backlash resulted in the formation of the Iglesia Metodista Pentecostal and its successor variants. Nellie "Elena" Laidlaw, a new prophetess, is credited with carrying the Pentecostal message from Valparaiso, Hoover's center of operation, to Santiago's Methodist churches. She found great receptivity there but also clerical resistance, owing, in part to her problematic preconversion past. Pressured by Presbyterians and others, exasperated missionary William Rice called on police authorities to spirit the irrepressible messenger away,[3] whereupon a majority of the congregants accompanied Laidlaw to jail, defiantly singing López's lyrics about the wandering hosts of Israel.[4] Thus, a migrating musical artifact forged in the pietistic setting of Philadelphia Methodism and stamped in the revivalistic borderlands of Los Angeles served to mark Chilean Pentecostals' exit from missionary structures on September 12, 1909. The in situ performance transformed Miles's invigorating tune and López's emancipatory lyrics into an anthem of what sociologist Miguel Mansillas has called "spiritual nomadism."[5] This chapter explores the parallel process in northern Mexico and concludes with an examination of the encounters of and solidarity between Pentecostal nomads making new spiritual and social homes.

Migrating Bodies: Pentecostalism in Northern Mexico and Southern Texas

Among the Mexican Pentecostals gathered in house churches in Los Angeles in the wake of the Azusa Street Revival was a woman from Villa Aldama, Chihuahua, Romana Carbajal de Valenzuela. Several accounts of the origins of Mexican Oneness Pentecostalism trace its roots to her return to her hometown in late 1914 and to the reported Holy Spirit baptisms experienced by twelve of her family members—including her sister Nicolasa and nephew Miguel García—in November of that year.[6]

Valenzuela's initiative is notable in light of the revolutionary storm clouds over northern Mexico. By this point, the Mexican Revolution had devolved into its second, more violent phase. After the initial deposition of Mexican dictator Porfirio Díaz and the subsequent assassination of consensus president Francisco Madero, the Revolution's various military chieftains rallied successfully against usurper Victoriano Huerta. Mutually wary regional strongmen such as Pancho Villa in northern Mexico and Emiliano Zapata in southern Mexico then jousted with the stronger *constituciónalista* leaders such as Venustiano Carranza and Álvaro Obregon for supremacy and influence in the consolidating revolutionary regime.[7] The Chihuahua into which Valenzuela ventured had witnessed minor and major skirmishes between the contending villista and huertista forces in 1913.[8] Pancho Villa's Division del Norte had stormed Torreón, Coahuila, from its Chihuahua stronghold several months before Valenzuela's return, and the several factions were jockeying for power at the Constitutionalist convention held in Mexico City and Aguascalientes from October 10 through November 9. The U.S. military occupation of the port city of Veracruz also preceded Valenzuela's evangelistic trip by several months. Apart from those of U.S. emissaries and troops, Valenzuela's journey was an exception to the massive northbound exodus precipitated by the protracted conflict. Importantly, Valenzuela did not assay her missionary trip alone. She was accompanied initially by Carmelita Fraijot, a Trinitarian convert from the Azusa Street Revival, and Fraijot's husband. Upon assessing the danger of travel in tumultuous Chihuahua, the Fraijots returned from El Paso, Texas, to Arizona, leaving the new mission field to Valenzuela's heterodox version of Pentecostalism. The Fraijots later took up residency in Tijuana, where they eventually befriended Apostolic evangelist Jesús Arballo and embraced Apostolicism.[9]

To be sure, Valenzuela's was not the only instance of cross-border evangelism in that period. In 1916, José Guzmán, a recent émigré convert, traveled from California to Gómez Palacio, Durango, to evangelize. The former textile factory owner, who had moved to the United States in search of medical succor for his wounded feet (from working foot-pedaled looms), had been healed earlier that same year in Fresno, California. In Gómez Palacio, Guzmán, in turn, laid healing hands on Natalia Rodríguez, a young member of a Baptist family. Her reported healing from tuberculosis led to the conversion of her brother-in-law, Inocencio Guevara. This opened doors for the novice preacher in Gómez Palacio, Torreón, and Matamoros, Tamaulipas, along the border.[10] Unlike Alice Luce and Florence Murcutt, returning migrants such as Romana Valenzuela and José

Guzmán moved under the radar of and against the flow directed by U.S. consular authorities.

The Arizona-Sonora and Texas-Tamaulipas borders also provided ready conduits for Pentecostal transmission, much as they had for prior mainline efforts. In the first region, Carrie and George Montgomery's interest in evangelism paralleled more material concerns; they owned copper mines in Nacozari, Sonora.[11] H. C. Ball and others saw the borderlands as a point of entry—and training—for lands farther south. Given the revolutionary tumult, however, they found themselves limited to Mexican border communities immediately proximate to Texas or Arizona towns: Matamoros, Tamaulipas, and Nogales and Agua Prieta, Sonora. The AG finally began its first significant thrust into Mexico in the early 1920s with the arrival of Cesáreo Burciaga to Múzquiz, Coahuila; of David Ruesga to Mexico City in 1921 (joining Ann Sanders, who arrived there in 1920); and of returned migrant Rodolfo Orozco to Monterrey, Nuevo León, in 1922.[12] Múzquiz, the site of the Assemblies' first temple in Mexico, hosted the group's convention in 1923.[13]

The contrast between the missionary models bears noting. It is one thing for missionary strategists to plan and carry out incursions into foreign territory. It is quite another for highly motivated immigrants to dash home with good news. Often, many such latter types enable the former's programs. Historians are challenged to weigh carefully the sometimes complementary and sometimes competing efforts. Viewed through a De Certeauian lens, Valenzuela's and Guzmán's excursions into Mexico represent more a tactic of religious subalterns than a strategy implemented by missionary hegemons.[14] And as seen from her subsequent activity, Valenzuela undermined the strategies carefully set in place by mainline missionaries. Guzmán, too, undermined the Assemblies of God's efforts in northern Mexico.

Valenzuela was observant of Apostolic gender norms. In 1916, she sought out Rubén Ortega, the sole remaining Methodist (MECS) minister in Ciudad Chihuahua, for her flock's water baptisms. A Chihuahua church member's spirit baptism won the recalcitrant preacher over. After Ortega's spirit baptism, Valenzuela escorted the minister to El Paso—the refuge for most of Chihuahua's Protestant missionary force—for his own rebaptism in Jesus's name at the hands of an African American minister in that city.[15] After their water baptism in the Junta River, the small Villa Aldama flock dug in for a protracted season of persecution, adding few converts to their dissident band.

In late 1916, Valenzuela ventured southward to the twin cities Gómez Palacio, Durango, and Torreón, Coahuila, to spread the word of Pentecost in evangélico churches. She spent one year in the Lagunera region. The Inocencio Guevara family solidified their fluid confessional identity with the arrival first of Valenzuela and later (in 1918) of her nephew Miguel García. Valenzuela's testimony—delivered first in Gómez Palacios's Baptist church and then on that church's porch when her heterodoxy became apparent—swayed Pánfila, Inocencio's wife, into Apostolicism. The Guevara home served as the first gathering site for *Lagunera* Apostolics.[16] From this base, García befriended and converted Isabel Sánchez, an evangélico pastor in neighboring Torreón. By this time, Mexican Apostolicism's matriarch had passed on the mantle to her nephew. She died within two months of her return from Torreón in late 1917.[17]

Missionary Retreat and Pentecostal Advance

Valenzuela's ability to gain initial entry into beleaguered Protestant circles, including Ortega's church in Chihuahua City, suggests a confessionally malleable identity. It also highlights the importance of female agency, especially in a vacuum of male (and foreign) leadership. And it demonstrates the power of music. To aid her in her extraordinary work, the intrepid evangelist counted on a fine singing voice and expert mandolin playing skills. Like many pioneers, she heralded Pentecost in song.[18]

Ortega's conversion also reminds us of the transient nature of religious networks. These are not sustained by still souls and bodies. First, Nicolasa García and her sister Romana had already assumed an evangélico identity before Valenzuela's initial departure from Villa Aldama.[19] This placed the family in the same evangélico zone as Rubén Ortega, who served a pastorate thirty miles away in Chihuahua City. Lacking Ortega's formal training within the MECS, the Garcías' and Valenzuela's would have been more of a proto-evangélico identity, flitting between Methodist and Congregationalist rubrics and open to further transformation.

But what do we make of the preacher's conversion? Historical theologian Kenneth Gill suggested that Ortega's probable resentment of the proposed transfer of Chihuahua's Protestant churches to Congregational auspices under the 1914 Cincinnati Plan made him receptive—after six years of ministry and four years in the pulpit—to Valenzuela's more independent approach.[20] The evidence for this is decidedly mixed but gets to the heart of proto-evangélico ambivalence.

Disappointed over the exclusion of Latin America from the agenda of the 1910 Edinburgh World Missions Conference, U.S. and British missionaries created the Committee for Cooperation in Latin America (CCLA).[21] The Cincinnati, Ohio, meeting, held June 30 to July 1, 1914, took advantage of the emergency exit of missionaries from Mexico. Its comity accords sought to avoid redundancies and seek efficiencies between the Protestant mission boards operating in that country. Cincinnati also led to the consolidation of the CCLA. Together with a similar arrangement for Puerto Rico (1902), Cincinnati set the table for congresses convened by the CCLA: Panama (1916), Montevideo (1925), and Havana (1929). Cincinnati, however, included no Mexican participants. Neither did preparatory meetings in Mexico.[22]

Clearly, the missionary strategists stumbled in their well-meant deliberations and actions. Yet, they could also draw from deep wells of trust. According to the Panama Congress's Committee on Cooperation, Rubén Ortega offered to take himself out of the denominational equation entirely, if doing so would facilitate a maximum outcome for comity in Chihuahua:

> There will doubtless be grave problems in the division of territory. But in Chihuahua, Mexico, the Mexican pastor of the Methodist Episcopal Church, South (which denomination was to leave that field in case of the proposed change going into effect) offered even to leave the ministry entirely if that were necessary in order to effect the withdrawal of his Church, so much did he believe in the proposed plan of dividing the territory so as to occupy the field adequately.[23]

The gesture, probably communicated in a field report solicited by the commission prior to Panama, doubtless served to assuage missionary anxiety. Ultimately, the offer was rendered moot. The American Board of Commissioners for Foreign Missions (ABCFM) accepted the Pacific coast swath from Colima through Hermosillo, Sonora, and accepted Guadalajara from the MECS in exchange for the ABCFM's exit from Chihuahua.[24] The shift widened proto-evangélico crevices in the Pacific coast states of Nayarit, Sinaloa, and Sonora, leaving fertile niches for encroaching Pentecostal shoots (see Chapter 3).

Other factors also may have propelled Ortega's confessional mobility. One of these was revivalism. Prior to the Revolution, missionaries and Mexican leaders in general, influenced by the writings of evangelist

Reuben A. Torrey, primed evangélicos for revival, in order to reverse the "spiritual crisis" that held the several denominations "prostrate under the narcotic of a profound sleep."[25] An executive committee (chartered in July 1908 in Torreón at the Convención Nacional Evangélica) began to lay out an ambitious "Upper Room" effort to be held in tandem with annual interdenominational youth and Sunday school conventions. The *Evangelista* laid out the hopes for a

> great revival that reaches back to the glorious day of Pentecost, in which the people of God are raised from the lowest levels of spiritual poverty, to higher places that place them nearer to the Divine Christ, more in communion with the great God of holiness and purity; a revival of this nature, we say, is absolutely necessary for our evangélico field. The most pious men, the most spiritual men cherished in the churches, have felt this.[26]

In this, Mexican evangelicalismo shared much of the same expectancy gripping Protestants across the globe. It is worth noting, though, a difference between the Anglo-American and the Latino/Latin American Pentecostal experience. While Methodist and Holiness orbits pulsed, as did their North American counterparts, with revival expectations and yearning for a "higher life," these impulses—save for the experiences of some missionaries—did not reflect generally an exasperation with an institutionalizing Protestantism. With some notable exceptions, there were simply too few evangélico institutions to renew or "come out of." Rather, *Pentecostalismo* arrived as a younger sibling religiosity and buttressed evangelicalismo's viability in the Catholic-dominated ecologies of Latin America. Early Pentecostales gathered up and energized scattered nuclei of proto-evangélico believers and reached deeply into the proletarian and peasant niches missed by historic Protestantism. Unlike the United States, Wales, India, Chile, and other places, however, the thirst for revival in Mexico would not be slaked immediately. The Revolution—which caught most of the missionary establishment by surprise in its protraction and scale of violence—dashed the strategists' plans. Revival waters flowed in through more improvised channels, many of them dug out by migrating believers.

Ultimately, migration and mobility proved more determinative for Rubén Ortega, albeit in an unexpected way. Chihuahua's wartime conditions affected dramatically the Methodist Church and Colegio Palmore, half of whose members and students had fled—along with all American personnel and Chihuahua elites—by late 1914 to El Paso.[27] In 1913, the Board of Missions reported that Ortega remained as "the only Protestant Christian worker" in that city and that he, too, had sent his family (wife and infant child) out of harm's way to El Paso, the site of his earlier service (1910–1911) as a junior minister.[28]

The incendiary situation in Mexico prompted vigorous consular activity during 1914–1915. At certain moments of acute conflict, the U.S. State Department instructed consuls to extract all U.S. citizens and foreigners from the combat zones.[29] By 1915, matters had taken a turn for the worse for Protestant missions in central and northern Mexico. As early as 1911, three Chihuahua-based Congregational pastors reported to their mission board that among the thousands of revolutionary troops occupying Ciudad Juárez under Pascual Orozco's command could be found 300 Protestants. They also noted with ironic relief that had the insurrectionary forces not prevailed, Protestantism would have been wiped off the map.[30] (Raised a Congregationalist, Orozco led early military victories for Francisco Madero against Porfirio Díaz.) Four years later, L. B. Newberry, presiding elder of the Central Mexico Conference's Guadalajara District (MECS), lamented from his Texas exile that "many of the male members of our Church have joined the [Constitutionalist] army." He ascribed practical motives to the enlistments: "Some, no doubt, have done this in order to keep the wolf from the door, as there was no other alternative."[31]

In other places, the exodus of missionary personnel merely represented the aging of a veteran missionary force. Take, for example, Tennessee native John Corbin (b. 1849), who began his work in Laredo, Texas, in 1882, and continued on to Saltillo, Coahuila, in 1884.[32] After two decades of service, he accepted the pastorate in Torreón, a relatively new Methodist outpost (begun in 1902).[33] In 1907, the Board of Missions requested prayers for Corbin owing to his "increasing physical debility."[34] One year earlier, the Board had presciently noted the strategic importance of the Lagunera region. It informed MECS readers that the tri-city area, with its trolley line and up to 50,000 souls, seemed very promising: "There is no field in all Mexico riper for the harvest than this." Under his stewardship, Corbin had the "most flourishing district in this rapidly developing country, waiting to see what Protestant Christianity is willing to do and to spend for a people in the transit from the darkness and slavery of religious superstition to that which shall prove itself light or to a denser night of skepticism and infidelity!"[35] In 1915, halfway through the Revolution, the Board reported that its work of eleven years in Torreón was "badly organized," with the failure of the appointed preacher to arrive there. A year earlier, the Board reported the Monterrey District, save for Saltillo and Monterrey, to be "for the present blotted off the Methodist map."[36] By this time, Corbin had served for a half decade in Phoenix–Tempe, Arizona, as presiding elder for the Northwest Mexican Mission Conference's Sonora District. As would be the case soon afterward in the Imperial Valley and other regions of southern California, the temporary evacuation of missionary structures in the states of Chihuahua, Coahuila, and Durango presented brief but wide windows of opportunity for religious dissident movements borne entirely on native shoulders. Against all reason (economic, political, social, etc.), Romana Valenzuela rushed in where and when missionaries feared to remain.

Proto-Evangélico Ties That Bind

Rubén Ortega's earlier ministerial trajectory also reminds us of the durability and elasticity of religious networks. The San Luis Potosí Colegio Wesleyano student's name first surfaced in a report by missionary Frank Onderdonk, the institution's director, to the 1904 annual conference of the MECS Central Mexican Conference. The missionary included Ortega in a list of his invaluable assistants ("inmejorables ayudantes").[37] Five years later, the MECS Northwest Mexican Mission Conference report of 1909 recorded his admission "on trial." One year later, he was listed as junior preacher in El Paso, Texas. Ortega was admitted to full connection as an ordained deacon in 1911 and assigned to the Chihuahua City Mexican congregation. His name continued on the roster in several capacities until 1917.

Another novice minister appeared in church records at the same time: Juan N. Pascoe, scion of one of Mexican Methodism's most prominent families.[38] The young Palmore student was designated to supply the Mexican MECS work in Torreón in 1907. He and Palmore instructor S. Y. Esquivel visited a circuit that included Meoqui, Labor Nueva, and Julimez during that year. Pascoe served in the Central Mexican Conference thereafter but returned for a short teaching stint at Colegio Palmore in 1914. Upon its nationalization in 1930, the Iglesia Metodista Mexicana elected him its first bishop. Prior to that, he had acquired prominence as one of Mexican Methodism's most ubiquitous faces and voices at denominational conclaves in the United States and elsewhere.

Equally important, Francisco Olazábal joined Ortega's conference in 1910 as a transfer from the MECS's Central Mexican Conference. The Board of Missions report from that year listed Ortega and Olazábal as still "on trial" in the Northwest Mexican Mission Conference. In 1911, the Board reported on Olazábal's work as assistant pastor in Durango, with responsibility also for Guanacevi. He was assigned that year to replace Ortega in El Paso. He was admitted to full connection and ordained a deacon in 1912.

The binding ties thicken even further. The 1910 minutes of the MECS's Central Mexico Conference, which listed Olazábal as a trial admission (apparently, prior to his transfer northward), also listed Juan Pascoe as still "on trial." Finally, in 1914, the MECS Board reported on "our young brother" Henry C. Ball's successful work in Kingsville and Ricardo, Texas, a circuit of the Mexican Border Mission Conference.[39] (By then, the more seasoned Olazábal had transferred to assume the MEC pastorate in Pasadena, California.)

This excursus underscores an often glossed-over feature of early Pentecostalism and adolescent Methodism: many key protagonists knew and constantly encountered one another in their religious peregrinations. As they bartered and exchanged religious goods and identities, they often traded (or tussled) with familiar partners. This feature helps to correct inaccurate notions of tabulae rasae and imprecise ones of unidirectional movement between religious identities, say, from Roman Catholicism or Methodism to Pentecostalism. Rubén Ortega ultimately surrendered his credentials in the Northwest Mexican Mission Conference in 1917.[40] After a short-lived Apostolic pastorate in Chihuahua City's Pacífico neighborhood, he disappeared from the Apostolic movement's record, leaving a small nucleus of believers in the capital city to await rescue by Antonio Nava in 1929, nearly a decade later.[41] The peripatetic preacher resurfaced, however, in Methodist orbits, first in El Paso and later in Austin. From this base, he dedicated his many remaining years (d. 1968) to tuberculosis education and eradication in Texas's Spanish-speaking communities and to evangelistic preaching.[42]

Torreón: Cradle of Mexican Apostolicism

When Villa Aldama finally grew too inhospitable, the small Apostolic group followed Miguel García and his mother southward to the more tolerant climes of the Lagunera region. By all accounts, García's stature grew throughout the region and elsewhere in northern Mexico during the following four years. This facilitated his transition into a new setting in his aunt's adopted land in 1922.

The proto-evangélicos gathered in Isabel Sánchez's "Iglesia del Faro" (Lighthouse Church—the Iglesia Metodista Libre's nickname was owing to its location in the preacher's grocery store of the same name) in Torreón, provided García's ministry with a fresh breakthrough after the aridity of Villa Aldama. The congregation's profile reinforces our sketch of proto-evangélico identity, an identity that can also be examined through the prism of socioeconomic class and migration. One family, the Rivas, arrived to Torreón from Silao, Guanajuato, in 1908. Originally from San Pedro Piedra Gorda, Zacatecas, Rafael and Guadalupe Rivas had sought economic opportunity in Silao. There, Guadalupe secured work as a domestic for the Liceaga family, members of the Methodist Church. The association resulted in the Rivas family's conversion and in son Felipe's early education (evangélico children were barred from that city's public schools). *Cristero* antipathies caused them to seek out a more hospitable environment in Torreón.[43] Unfortunately, their coreligionists did not allow their sympathies to meaningfully bridge class lines. After a season in the Methodist Church, the family sought out humbler fellowship with Isabel Sánchez. By this time, another downscale preacher, Miguel García, had had an impact on the Methodist Church with his preaching and healing of a paralytic. Ultimately, status and propriety carried the day in Torreón's Methodist Church. Others drawn to Sánchez's Iglesia Metodista Libre and/or led there by Miguel García included the Rodríguez family, whose son, Aurelio, showed promising signs of Methodist ministry. Another son, Juan (the Bakersfield pastor mentioned earlier), was among the first to be baptized in the new work. The consolidation at "El Faro" also attracted the nucleus of Apostolic believers in neighboring Gómez Palacio, across the state line.

In 1920, García christened his movement: Iglesia Evangélica Espiritual del Pentecostés (IEEP). Documentary photo evidence from 1921 shows a respectable number of adult members (fifty-five) and children (thirty-five), with García at the head.[44] By the time of his departure in 1922, García counted congregations in Torreón, Gómez Palacios, San Pedro de las Colonias (a nearby town), Monterrey (Nuevo León), Tampico (Tamaulipas), and La Dulce Grande (San Luis Potosí) within his circuit. (Gregorio and Gonzalo Mendoza, two converts baptized in Gómez Palacio in 1921, established the last, southernmost point.[45]) Thereafter, the movement spread to other points in northern Mexico and, importantly, southern Texas.

García's departure for California, however, left his and his aunt's legacy in a precarious state. As the Apostolic movement in northern Mexico splintered in his absence, the story of its female founder retreated into obscurity. Two successor variants, the Luz del Mundo church and the Consejo Espiritual Mexicano–IEEP, disavowed a matrilineal lineage, while the Iglesia Apostólica placed restrictions on women's ministry.[46] Two decades after his interview with Nicolasa García (in Westmoreland, California), Maclovio Gaxiola restored the Valenzuela legacy in his diamond jubilee history of the Iglesia Apostólica (1964). The narrative about a matrilineal heritage allowed the Iglesia Apostólica to lay claim to roots in the Azusa Street Revival and its immediate aftermath. When the United Nations Educational, Scientific, and Cultural Organization proclaimed 1975 as the Year of the Woman, the Iglesia commemorated its founding matriarch in that month's issue of the *Exégeta* periodical.[47]

The case of Valenzuela and her sister and nephew illumines key points of juncture in the larger story. These points argue against treating Chicano and Mexican Pentecostalisms as two discrete movements. First, Antonio Nava's ready acceptance of Miguel García's ministry in neighboring Westmoreland (a half decade before Nava's own trip to the seat of Mexican Apostolicism) suggests the acknowledgment of a spiritual pedigree. So, too, does the collegial affirmation of Bakersfield, California, pastor Juan Rodríguez as García's disciple at the 1925 convention (San Bernardino, California) of the Iglesia de la Fe Apostólica Pentecostés as well as the reception of García disciple Isabel Sánchez at the IFAP's 1926 meeting (Indio, California). Francisco Llorente's 1924 trip from San Francisco, California, to El Paso, Texas, to tend to a summons from Sánchez[48] (who transplanted to Ciudad Juárez from Torreón in 1922), also demonstrates the organic growth of a binational network.[49] As we shall see in the following chapters, these networks served to move the migrating faithful between both countries.

Heterodox Headway

As Valenzuela, García, and others joined the current of human migration back and forth across the border, their persistent proselytizing often drew the ire of official Catholicism and anticlerical officialdom. Their liturgical practice also drew the derisive scorn of Mexican and Mexican American Catholics. As noted by Mexicali pastor Pedro Ceniceros in his appeal to reopen that city's temple, the expression "aleluya" (heard emanating from the noisy temples and houses where the Pentecostals worshipped) served detractors as a common epithet to hurl at this particularly troublesome brand of evangélico.

That Apostolics met with considerable success is evident from Manuel Gamio's referenced study on Mexican immigrants. Gamio reported one respondent's alarm:

> INTERVIEWER: What is the religion which has the most followers in the cities where there are Mexicans, that is to say, what is the principal religion among the Mexicans in the places in Texas which you have visited?
>
> GALVAN: I would say that the majority are Catholic, but it would be better to say those who are half-educated belong to that religion while the others, the majority, don't have any religion, for they are very ignorant. I have noticed that the majority of our countrymen are allowing themselves to be guided by the Protestants, by any religious sect. One of the sects which has made the greatest headway is that of the so-called Apostolicals, which the Mexicans call the Aleluyas. The preachers of that sect say that they are the sons of Christ and they heal by means of prayer. They are the ones that exploit the Mexicans the most, for the Mexicans think that these preachers have special faculties and that they will be healed by means of prayer.[50]

As discussed earlier, Gamio's imprecise assessment of Protestantism's appeal was probably owing to his reliance on mainline church relief agencies, which may have skewed his view of the religious landscape (and soundscape). In his own country, Gamio had also rubbed shoulders with Protestant elites—missionaries and native leaders—as seen in his contributions (since 1920) to the magazine *Nueva Democracia* (sponsored by the CCLA).[51] His was not a quarrel with the historic Reformation. After all, Protestants had demonstrated their value to Mexico's renewed liberalism and revolutionary regime. However, the pseudonymous "Galván," an elite in his own context,[52] included Pentecostal charlatanism as one of the twin evils—Catholic obscurantism was the other—afflicting his gullible countrymen. The complaint offers contemporaneous evidence of early Apostolicism's notable growth in northern Mexico and the southwestern United States.

Romana Valenzuela's conversion of Rubén Ortega and of several Methodist, Presbyterian, and Baptist families in the Lagunera region emblematized Pentecostals' penchant for replowing and watering older evangélico seedbeds. Still, Pentecostals found the vast majority of their converts among Catholic peasants, laborers, artisans, and small vendors. The class location of the new believers brightened Protestantism's prospects for growth. In a sense, Pentecostalism represented as much a movement of labor and migration as of religious belief and practice. When economic and political macroevents uprooted them, the Pentecostal proletariat and peasantry, like their Catholic counterparts, could travel light. They often, of course, attributed their mobility to divine and not economic or political forces or more frequently saw them working in tandem. Sometimes they felt the former pushing them against the latter, as in the case of the intrepid Valenzuela, whose return to revolutionary Mexico would have confounded the expectations of purely economic migration models.

Heterodoxy Unhinged

Romana Valenzuela's strand of Apostolicism was not the sole one in circulation in northern Mexico. Subsequent to her death and Miguel García's departure, a rival version disembarked in January 1924 in the northeastern port city of Tampico, Tamaulipas, in the person of Joseph Stewart. Of Northern Irish origin, Stewart had served with the Christian and Missionary Alliance (CMA) in Argentina. His expulsion was one of many effected by A. B. Simpson, as the CMA leader sought to hold Pentecostal excesses at bay in that Holiness denomination.[53]

After a decade in (and out of) southern California and deportation to his native country, the independent missionary arrived from Northern Ireland to northeastern Mexico. Like Valenzuela, Stewart found his first converts in established evangélico churches throughout the region's states. He also visited nascent Pentecostal ones, including the Torreón one now pastored by Aurelio Rodríguez. Stewart's unexpected death in Guadalajara in November 1926 did not curtail his influence, however. The confluence of the two streams nearly drowned Valenzuela and García's legacy.[54]

Stewart's movement sought out niches in Monterrey (Nuevo León), Matamoros (Coahuila), Tampico (Tamaulipas), and La Dulce Grande (San Luis Potosí), thus overlapping with sites and congregations established by Miguel García. Indeed (as in the case of Inocencio Guevara), some converts proved nimble in their alleged loyalties, displaying some of the same intrepidity as, say, Romana Valenzuela. García convert Francisco Borrego quickly assumed leadership of the Apostolic movement in Matamoros

(Stewart's spiritual progeny) and, in 1925, asserted this prerogative in the Torreón congregation served by Aurelio Rodríguez (Valenzuela and García's spiritual progeny). Among his innovations, Borrego rechristened the movement from Iglesia Evangélica Espiritual to Consejo Espiritual Mexicano (CEM).

Borrego and his close collaborator, Ireneo Rojas (a Stewart convert), who assumed positions as pastor general and secretario general of the CEM in 1927,[55] introduced even more radical changes. The insertion of self-styled prophets into the chaotic mix pushed the movement beyond recognizable boundaries. After their baptism in Nuevas Casas Grandes, Chihuahua, at the hands of Agapito Soto, Antonio Muñoz and Francisco Flores assumed a prophetic identity as Saulo and Silas, respectively, in La Dulce Grande (San Luis Potosí). Borrego met the duo in this southernmost outpost, brought them northward, and inserted them into the volatile settings of Torreón and elsewhere. Several innovations followed their assumption of authority: a disparagement of scripture in favor of prophetic edict and an outlawing of instrumental music and of such basic hygienic practices as bathing, shoe wearing, and shaving. The prophets' striking visage—long beards, tunics, and sandals—enhanced their charismatic authority as healers and seers. The pair traversed northeastern Mexico for two to three years, cutting Apostolicism loose from its original moorings. One of their converts, Eusebio Joaquín, a soldier quartered in San Pedro de las Colonias, in turn later assumed the helm of his own ecclesial ship, the Luz del Mundo church.

Discomfited by capricious authoritarianism, Miguel García's initial converts in Torreón—the Rivas and Rodríguez families, in particular—found themselves marginalized within their own congregation and movement. For a season, withdrawal seemed the only viable option. The movement prospered elsewhere in forms palatable to most Apostolics and Pentecostals. After its split with Felipe Rivas and Antonio Nava's budding binational movement, the Consejo Espiritual Mexicano continued growing in Durango, Nuevo León, and San Luis Potosí and in southern Texas. CEM preachers Alonso Ball, Fausto Alcalá, and Cayetano García evangelized in San Benito, Texas. Teófilo and Antonia Zuñiga, CEM adherents in Donna, Texas, won over Assemblies of God members Adela Sáenz and her daughter Tomasa.[56] José Guerra, an independent evangelist from Houston, Texas, arrived soon after to oversee the water baptism of Methodist convert Benjamín Cantú in 1931. Several of the Nuevo León and Texas-based

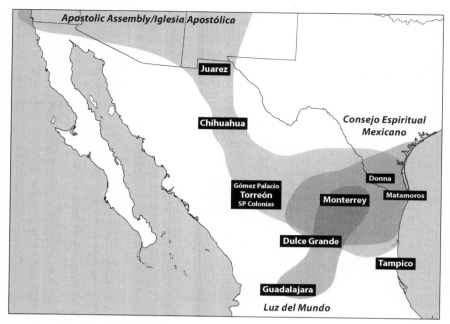

MAP 2 Early Apostolic Movements in Mexico and the United States, 1930. (Map by Michael Cota)

CEM preachers eventually sided with Felipe Rivas and José Ortega in their struggle with Borrego, Rojas, and the prophets. Apostolicism's spatiality assumed complex, overlapping dimensions (Map 2).

The conflictive half decade beginning in 1925 was a watershed for the several streams of Mexican Apostolicism that emerged from the ebullience of revival. Left to fend for themselves, Mexican Apostolics, like the insurrectionary forces of the previous decade, lined up behind several caudillos and their competing projects: the Consejo Espiritual Mexicano, led by Borrego and Rojas; the Asamblea (later Iglesia) Apostólica, led by Felipe Rivas, José Ortega, and Antonio Nava; and the Luz del Mundo, led by Eusebio Joaquín. Prior formation or experience in mainline Protestantism made a difference in that election. The institutional sobriety absorbed by Felipe Rivas and Benjamín Cantú among Methodists[57] and by Romana Valenzuela and Lorenzo Varela (see Chapter 3) among Congregationalists carried the day in favor of a more institutional Apostolicism. So, too, did the strategic intervention by Antonio Nava, the dogged dedication and ecumenical equanimity of José Ortega, and the influx of repatriated evangelists and laypersons from the United States. This is not to say that this was the only viable outcome; the three principal groups thrived into the twenty-first century. As early Mexican Apostolicism's small flotilla scattered (to return to a maritime metaphor), its several vessels followed different lodestars. The most innovative helmsman was the prophet Aarón.

La Luz del Mundo

Born in 1896 in the *cristero* town of Colotlán, Jalisco, Eusebio Joaquín González enlisted in Venustiano Carranza's Constitutionalist Army at the age of seventeen. The triumph of this wing of the Revolution placed him in good stead with ascendant military leaders Marcelino García Barragán and Paulino Navarro, under whose command he served (they were lieutenant colonels at the time).[58] Upon his conversion in 1926, he left the military to enlist as a disciple of Saulo and Silas, whom he followed to Monterrey. According to Luz del Mundo church tradition, on April 6 of that year he received his divine summons (see Chapter 1) to restore the primitive church. The "apostle of restoration" extricated himself from Saulo and Silas's control (near indentured servitude) and, together with his wife, Elisa, undertook an exodus or pilgrimage toward Guadalajara. The six-month trek by foot included numerous incidents of persecution, hunger, and deprivation. After a season of proselytism in Guadalajara's Congregational churches, he established Mexico's most idiosyncratic stream of Apostolicism, the Iglesia del Dios Vivo Columna y Apoyo de la Verdad, la Luz del Mundo (Church of the Living God and Pillar of the Truth, the Light of the World). Importantly, church lore established the date of his arrival to coincide exactly with that most Mexican and Catholic of dates: December 12, the feast day of the Virgin of Guadalupe. This coincidence presaged future antagonisms.

> While the city celebrated the greatest hoax that our country has received in believing that there exists in the heavens a woman of flesh and blood, and that that woman showed herself on the cloak of an Indian so that the image of the beast would be adored on that date of great meaning for humanity; such a loyal and Marian city joined herself to such a heresy.[59]

Joaquín's arrival in Jalisco also coincided with the outbreak of the Cristero War. Afterward, Joaquín secured the patronage of Marcelino García, who played a key role in suppressing cristero revolts in Jalisco and elsewhere and rose through the federal military ranks to the level of brigadier general and head of the Military College (1941–1943). The support of his former commander provided Joaquín's church with important leverage. The armed forces represented an important sector of the governing Partido de la Revolución Institucional (PRI); thus, García was tapped and elected to serve as governor of Jalisco from 1943 to 1947. (He later served President Gustavo Díaz Ordaz as secretary of defense, from 1964 to 1968.)[60] In 1954, the municipal government began facilitating the church's settlement of a new neighborhood in the eastern environs of Mexico's third largest city. The church reciprocated with loyal electoral support for officialdom's party. Its members took active membership in the Federación de Organizaciones Populares de Jalisco, an important component—like the military and workers and peasants' union—of the corporativist PRI.[61] The symbiosis allowed the Luz del Mundo church to thrive in a region where the Revolution continued to vie vigorously with a combative, conservative Catholic Church bent on recapturing the public square and on fostering a new cult of saints (the priests killed in the Cristero War).

By the time of Aarón's' death in 1964, the church's enclave, Hermosa Provincia (Beautiful Province), occupied an important niche in Guadalajara's otherwise very robust Catholic ecosystem. In 1983, his son and successor, Samuel Joaquín Flores, initiated the eight-year construction of a marble cathedral, the church's seat and destination for its pilgrims. By that point, the Luz del Mundo's trajectory had taken it far beyond the bounds of institutional Apostolicism. Although the Iglesia Apostólica and Luz del Mundo overlap in origins, doctrine, clans, and membership (defectors), the latter disavows connections to the former (especially the Iglesia's narrative of matrilineal origins). Given Mexico's dynamic religious landscape, it is in a good position to continue doing so. Its prominence in Guadalajara—embodied in the Hermosa Provincia district and temple and annual pilgrimage—accords the Luz del Mundo bragging rights to competitor status with the Catholic Church in the region. In this role, it has attracted inordinate attention from Catholic partisans, prelates, and academics, as well as from journalists.[62] Proof of this is the census agency's decision to assign a separate identification question in 2000 and 2010 to this denomination, the only evangélico church to be so treated.[63] The church's growth and corporativist and authoritarian features have also attracted the attention of Latin American religion scholars over the last two decades.[64]

Borderlands Contact and Solidarity

The 1927 convention of the Iglesia de la Fe Apostólica Pentecostés in Colonia Zaragoza, Baja California, reaffirmed Antonio Nava as anciano ejecutivo. He returned to Mexico, nevertheless, in early 1928 to proselytize his ailing parents in Nazas, Durango, and evangelize in his homeland. His father's healing made the first goal possible. In response to mailed entreaties from Felipe Rivas and others in Torreón, he also sought to reclaim Valenzuela and García's progeny, visiting Consejo Espiritual Mexicano churches in Torreón, Monterrey, Tampico, and other northern cities. A struggle between caudillos ensued. Nava reported an encounter where he took up a dare (with a barber companion) to cut and shave Saulo's and Silas's hair and beards. He emerged unscathed from the predicted celestial conflagration.[65] Rapprochement with Borrego and Rojas proved impossible, however. The CEM threatened with disfellowship the Rivas and Rodríguez families and any other would-be collaborators of the émigré preacher from *el Norte*. The lines between rival camps of *rivistas* and *rojistas* hardened further. Nava encouraged Rivas and others to endure their circumstances as best as possible; only unilateral excommunication from the CEM should trigger and justify a union with Apostolics in the United States. The eventual expulsion, in 1929 (after Nava's return to the United States), pushed Rivas into closer collaboration with Nava. Their personal bonds were soon fleshed out in more institutional ways.[66] The process of institutionalization helped to fend off (for Rivas and others) looming chaos.

While buttressing Rivas's position in Mexico, Nava received word to return to California to lead the demoralized IFAP upon Francisco Llorente's untimely demise in late 1928. The journey—in the company of his newly converted siblings Eladio and Cleofas—took several months and included a forced stay over in Chihuahua, where General Marcelo Caraveo was in rebellion against the consolidating regime.[67] The evangelist ascribed the train stoppages and derailments to a higher force:

> I tried to take maximum advantage of the time, since I was not sure how long my visit would last. As soon as the governmental problem was resolved, I would continue my journey. We had already arranged our immigration documents, but this revolution detained us, maybe since the Lord willed it so, and I (now) understand that the Lord wanted us to testify in that place."[68]

While marooned in Chihuahua City, Nava sought out the remnants of the flock left by Romana Valenzuela, Miguel García, and Ruben Ortega.

The remainder of the trip—through El Paso, Lordsburg, Phoenix, Yuma, and Calexico–Mexicali—allowed Nava to reacquaint himself with the troubled flock and provide nurture in the wake of three significant defections or schisms in California, those of José Martínez in Watsonville, Paz Lujan in Jimtown (Whittier), and José Guerrero in Los Angeles. (The last two later returned, chastened.)[69] Proposed tithing policies were also drawing strong resistance from Los Angeles pastor Guadalupe Lara and others.[70]

During his absence, regular correspondence had kept taut Nava's ties with the Imperial–Mexicali Valley flock. Florencio Urenda, Nava's replacement, faithfully shared Nava's dispatches and just as faithfully collected and relayed love offerings to Mexico (a case of circular material and symbolic remittances).[71] The regional congregations gathered at the Calexico train depot to receive the evangelist with a caudillo's welcome—complete with special hymnody—prepared by Urenda and Mexicali and Colonia Zaragoza pastors Pedro Ceniceros and Encarnación Meza.[72]

The IFAP ministers elected Antonio Nava president at year's end of 1929, in the fifth convention, held in Indio, California. Nava then persuaded his colleagues that the extremely loose alliance with the splintered and once again predominantly African American Pentecostal Assemblies of the World in Indianapolis was inadequate for the needs of their growing movement.[73] In 1930, he incorporated the IFAP in California as the Apostolic Assembly of the Faith in Christ Jesus. Soon afterward, he directed secretary Bernardo Hernandez to dispatch credentials and notarized letters of deputation to Rivas and Rivas's new assistant, Jose A. Ortega, a Nava protégé who had returned to Mexico several months before.

The incorporation rescued the fledgling movement. Widower Francisco Llorente's growing ambivalence in his cultural and confessional loyalties—evident in his new marriage to Methodist Juanita Peach—alarmed his colleagues. (A delegation sent to Yuma to deliver an ultimatum arrived to the news of Llorente's sudden death.) Nava's monolingual leadership and close ties to colleagues in Mexico halted the drift and stamped the movement with a sectarian ethnic imprint for the next two decades. (In eight decades of U.S. residency, Nava's duties and itinerary permitted little time for learning English, this in spite of several autodidactic attempts.) The revitalized ethnicity reinforced ecclesial autonomy. As noted, Llorente distrusted denominational development and had only reluctantly acceded to his colleagues' moves in that direction. Upon his assumption of the ecclesial helm, Nava's vision for institutional growth and maturation prevailed. The change provided symbolic, legal, and material resources to deal with developments in the larger political and economic spheres: first, the Great Depression and its political fallout in the United States; and second, residual cristero movements and sentiments and official anticlerical antipathies in Mexico. The value of transborder alliances soon became apparent, although the primitivist-pragmatist tension would occasionally intensify and tear at unity.

CHAPTER 3

Persecution and Expansion: *Repatriado* Histories

El tiempo está cerca	The time is near
De Dios la palabra cumpliéndose está	The word of God is being fulfilled
No vagues errante, que Cristo amante	Do not stray, the loving Christ
Llamando y esperando está	Is calling and waiting
Hoy es el día de salud	Today is the day of redemption
El tiempo de salvación	The time of salvation
No tardes, perdido,	Do not tarry, lost one,
ven a Jesús	come to Jesus
Que Él te dará su perdón	For he will give you his pardon

The rise of premillennial dispensationalism within U.S. Protestantism in the early twentieth century is a well-known story. Fundamentalists and Pentecostals generally assented to the scheme proposed by John Nelson Darby of the Plymouth Brethren: a sudden rapture of the church and its return with Christ after an interim tribulation period on earth. The devastation of global conflicts and epidemics, the rise of fascism and communism, the Zionist question, and economic depression heightened the expectancy. Cyrus Scofield's new study Bible, published by Oxford University Press in 1909 and 1917, offered a precise hermeneutic for previously opaque prophecies. The new eschatological magisterium gripped many, including missionaries supported through Scofield's Central America Mission, one of a growing global network of independent faith missions.

In the case of Mexicans and Mexican Americans Pentecostals, we also could fold into the eschatological mix xenophobic persecution; this lent even more urgency to the evangelistic task. Fidel García's "El Día Está Cerca," set in a melancholic *vals* frame (6/8 rhythm), surely brought the message home to uprooted souls in search of assured salvation. Indeed, the composer himself was one such individual, as we shall see.

García's composition represented, in fact, an extremely loose adaptation of G. T. Haywood's 1919 "The Day of Redemption." Along with his considerable hymnody, the multifaceted leader of the Pentecostal Assemblies of the World also produced an impressive corpus of prophecy charts, which rendered visually accessible Darby and Scofield's ideas about God's dispensational calendar. Whether these were as readily available to the PAW's "Mexican representatives" as Haywood's music is not clear. What is clear is that such resources had to pass through an existential filter. Once "The Day of Redemption" was uprooted and planted into a different social and cultural milieu, its postmillennial thrust was redirected in favor of a more immediate soteriological one, as seen by comparing Haywood's original text with García's:

The nations are breaking,	The day of redemption is near,
And Israel's awaking,	Men's hearts are failing for fear
The signs in the Bible foretold;	Be filled with the Spirit,
The Gentile days numbered,	Your lamps trim'd and clear
With horrors encumbered;	Look up! Your redemption is near.
Eternity soon will unfold.	

Fidel García's aggressive redaction and translation is understandable, in light of the unavailability of the Scofield Bible in Spanish (it was not published until 1987) and, more important, García's target audience: Mexican Catholics. Although these may have shared a general apocalyptic foreboding, they would not have been familiar with the premillennial schemes emerging out of British and American Evangelicalism. Thus, Haywood's end-times warning would not have registered among them as deeply as it would have among errant prodigals of U.S. Evangelical homes.

As mentioned, García experienced in person the effects of xenophobia-driven dislocation. But rather than settling for passivity as social flotsam, the preacher fashioned a salvation vessel to maximize the opportunities opened up by forced displacement. The following excerpt from an oral history of that period gives us a glimpse of his intrepidity:

During the trip we would meet in the caboose, and Bro. García's company made the trip seem short to us. He was a great consolation to us, and in the end he gave us his guitar. He would talk for hours with Francisco and Secundino. The three would meet apart from the family. I believe that he gave them much advice about the work of God, since he had much experience in the ministry; and he encouraged them greatly, saying that they were the instruments that God would use in the state of Nayarit and that they should make great effort to the best of their ability for the blessed work of God. In two and a half days as travel companions they became good friends and promised to write each other in order to stay informed about the work of God and to share experiences to come.[1]

In this account, José Avalos, an orphaned child in the care of his married brother Francisco, recalls how the trauma of deportation eased somewhat when his two older brothers, Francisco and Secundino, encountered García among the hundreds of train passengers being carried back to Mexico. The pastor of the Apostolic Church in Corona, California, was headed to his native Jalisco and the Avalos brothers to Nayarit. The repatriates knew each other through fellowship in the Apostolic churches of Southern and Baja California. Given that Pentecostal ministers came from the same proletarian and peasant classes as their flock, it should not surprise us to find them among the deportees. What is notable about this case, though, is that the very same rails ferrying the train of migrant failure southward also facilitated a mobile makeshift seminary and musical training workshop. Francisco, who had been active in the California–Mexico borderlands Apostolic churches for about a half decade, boarded the iron machine as a frustrated migrant; this was his third repatriation. But when he alighted in Nayarit, his new course as an apostle had been set. With the passing of time, the unintended effect of U.S. xenophobia became evident: it expanded the territorial reach of Mexican and Mexican American Pentecostalism to dimensions unimagined even by the nascent movement's leaders and faithful. It also facilitated the diffusion of that movement's cultural offerings. García's insistent hymn appears in the record of Apostolic expansion a decade later in the Pacific coast state of Sinaloa. Evangelist Filiberto López recollected its role, along with that of two other hymns, in the conversion of the Uriarte clan of Dos Arroyos, Sinaloa, in 1943.[2]

Trouble in the Borderlands: The Great Repatriation

The history of the massive repatriation of Mexicans from the United States during the decade of the 1930s is not well known among American religious historians. Mexicans had already served as convenient and deportable targets of the previous decade's "Red Scare"[*] but subsequently had filled—at numbers reaching to 500,000 in the 1920s by one estimate—the labor vacuum caused by the 1917 and 1924 Immigration Acts.[3] The country's renewed economic vicissitudes prompted a new hunt for ready scapegoats. Federal, state, county, and local authorities, as well as civic elites, joined efforts to expel "unwanted" Mexicans. Several dramatic and well-publicized raids—with accompanying newspaper photos of deportee trainloads—provided the impetus for a large-scale "voluntary" exodus. According to Abraham Hoffman, the number repatriated totaled 458,039, including many children born in the United States.[4] Francisco Balderrama and Raymond Rodríguez, citing official and journalistic sources, calculated a much higher, albeit, according to them, still conservative number of one million.[5] Hoffman's lower estimate represents, nevertheless, a considerable demographic loss of about 35 percent, since the census of 1930 counted 1.3 million Mexicans in the United States. In other words, the massive exodus uprooted one out of every three Mexicans.[6] It also uprooted one out of three Pentecostals. The dimensions of the calamity were even greater in the smaller and more tenuous midwestern Mexican communities of Detroit, Chicago, and Gary, Indiana. Since blood ties spanned legal categories, entire families (including scores of thousands of U.S.-born children) were effectively leveraged out of the United States. U.S. agencies underwrote rail transportation and secured Mexican government waivers of duty tariffs for household items and automobiles; thus, the majority of *repatriados* returned by automobile.

The social and political ramifications of such forced movement are incalculable. The heavy blow stymied the political and social maturation of the Mexican American community; nearly a generation—two decades—of momentum was lost. Those who remained hunkered below officialdom's radar when necessary and continued to negotiate their place in America when possible. It took the return of hundreds of thousands of soldiers from World War II—and the sacrifice of their fallen comrades—to invigorate a civil and educational rights agenda through such organizations as the GI Forum and the League of United Latin American Citizens. Scores of thousands of the repatriated children later returned to the land of their birth upon reaching adulthood. But with a disrupted educational trajectory, most returned to occupy lower rungs in the economic ladder, thereby exacerbating the opportunity cost of American xenophobia.

In Mexico, the unexpected windfall of skilled labor seemed at first to augur favorably for the Revolution's agrarian program. Primed by his prescient study of Mexican immigrants in the United States, Manuel Gamio advised President Lázaro Cardenas to match the new farming techniques brought by the repatriates with land, implements, and irrigation.[7] Like many such projects, however, the record was decidedly uneven, owing to official incompetence, competing unions and farmer associations, anti-*agrarista* violence, and migrants' restiveness.[8]

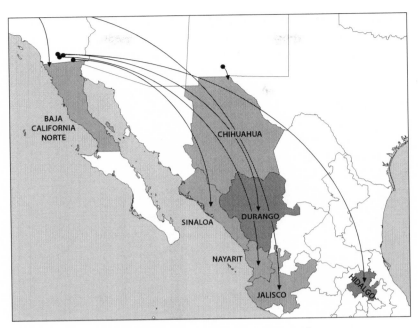

MAP 3 Repatriado Return Trajectories. (Map by Michael Cota)

Subaltern Responses

By contrast, Mexico's still-embryonic Pentecostal movement derived enormous benefit from the influx of repatriates, who carried their proselytizing zeal to their places of origin in such states as Nayarit, Sinaloa, Sonora, Durango, Coahuila, México, and Chihuahua. Map 3 depicts the return of several of the repatriados.

Guadalupe García, one of the most prominent of the repatriados (in terms of future ministerial trajectory), had labored as a cotton worker in California's Imperial and San Joaquin Valleys. With the blessing of Epifanio Cota, their mentor/pastor/labor contractor (note the conflated vocations), he and his brother Vicente loaded up their families and two truckloads of household possessions and set off to evangelize the state of Durango and the Sierra Madre mountain range.[9] García later served as bishop of Durango in the Iglesia Apostólica of Mexico. Several repatriados from southern California's Coachella Valley—Ignacio Mariscal, Reyes Ruelas, Gil Valencia, Tiburcio Santos, and Antonio Arias, among others— returned to begin or bolster the Apostolic work in Sinaloa and Durango, serving there later as prominent evangelists, pastors, and presbyters in

José Ortega Boarding Train in Torreón, Coahuila, en route to Pachuca, Hidaldo, 1929. Photo courtesy of Benjamín Ortega; José Ortega Photograph Collection.

the Iglesia Apostólica.[10] The somewhat younger José Ortega returned to the state of Hildago and concluded his repatriate trajectory in Torreón, Coahuila, where he helped Felipe Rivas helm the nascent Iglesia Apostólica. Child repatriates Ysidro Pérez and (U.S.-born) Efraím Valverde eventually served as presidents of the Iglesia Apostólica and Apostolic Assembly, respectively.

We are faced here with the problem of sorting out motivations. The original religious impulse prompting return migration sometimes predated or was reinforced by an economic or even filial one. For example, José Ortega returned initially to central Mexico in obedience to maternal entreaties. Upon discovering her eldest son's clandestine Bible reading and subsequent conversion in California, Isidra Aguilar determined to return with her family to Mexico and promised to respect José's new religious beliefs in order to secure his agreement to accompany them. Her intolerance, however, prompted him to take his painful leave and return northward. After several years in the mentoring shadow of pioneers Epifanio Cota, Antonio Nava, Jesús Torres, and others, Ortega relented to his mother's wish that he return to her (now ailing) side in Pachuca, Hidalgo. He believed her infirmity would present an opportunity for his witness.

Nava presided over a requisite train-side farewell service in Calexico in late October 1929. A three-day stopover in Torreón allowed for an introduction to Felipe Rivas and his troubled flock. Isidra's obdurate intolerance once again propelled her son northward. Rivas's glad reception during a stopover and the beleaguered preacher's insistence that Ortega assist him convinced the émigré to let his U.S. visa lapse. While Ortega may have been oblivious to the growing repatriate stream around him at that time (October 1930), he averred a clarity concerning his new calling (note the emotive tone of the Torreón train photo).[11]

Ties That Bind

The confidence displayed by repatriates as they inserted themselves into the religious fields of their homeland was hardly the type of behavior one would expect from subdued scapegoats. That insertion often required the recovery of Mexican citizenship prerogatives and the leveraging of resources from coreligionists north of the border. Religious genealogies help to explain this. Agustín Cerros and José Montellano had served as assistants to pioneer Miguel García in Westmoreland, California, before returning to the Lagunera region, the site of García's initial labor.[12] Repatriates Ignacio Mariscal, Reyes Ruelas, and Gil Valencia were mentored by pioneer Jesús Torres in Indio and Thermal, California.[13] Tiburcio Santos was baptized by Miguel García in Westmoreland in 1924; he left for Sinaloa in 1930. Antonio Nava presided over the 1929 departure from Calexico of his protégé José Ortega.

Religious genealogies can also be viewed in terms of subsequent trajectories. On the eve of repatriation, Macario Martínez was commissioned to return from California to Sinaloa, where he recruited members of the numerous Gaxiola clan in Los Mochis.[14] (Tiburcio Santos collaborated in the project.) He also gathered up abandoned Adventists, Congregationalists, and Free Methodists in La Union. One prodigiously talented Gaxiola family member, Maclovio, in turn, converted Methodists in 1936 in Tameapa, whose congregation, founded at the turn of the century, had been decimated by the Revolution. To follow the genealogy, Gaxiola convert Filiberto López won the sizeable Sidonio and Manuela Uriarte clan of Dos Arroyos, Atotonilco, Badiraguato, Sinaloa. Eldest son Domingo, a grocery store owner, had assumed a proto-evangélico identity since 1925 through avid Bible reading. He held fast to that identity in spite of proselytism by Baptists and Jehovah's Witnesses in the rural settlement. A chance

November 1943 encounter with López and others seeking nourishment on their way to El Zapote de los Quezada, Durango, resulted in the formation of an Apostolic congregation. Within six months, forty converts had been baptized.[15] The Uriarte family later provided key ministerial leadership in Sinaloa (son Tito served as bishop of this district) and Arizona. (Filiberto López was also mentored by repatriates Ignacio Mariscal and Tiburcio Santos.)

Maclovio Gaxiola quickly rose to national and international prominence in the movement. His appearance at the 1935 convention in Torreón linked the Pacific states of Sinaloa, Nayarit, and Jalisco to the Iglesia's main compass points: Torreón, Mexicali, and Monterrey. After serving as the first *anciano* (elder) and bishop of the Pacific region, he succeeded Felipe Rivas as presiding bishop of the Iglesia Apostólica in 1958.[16] A notable hymn writer, Gaxiola also launched the Iglesia's periodical and hymnal, *El Exégeta* and *Suprema Alabanza*; established the Instituto Teológico Apostólico Internacional (ITAI) in Mexico City; and undertook the first exploratory missionary forays on behalf of both the Iglesia and Apostolic Assembly into Central America and the Southern Cone. Finally, among Gil Valencia's converts (and Macario Martínez's mentees) in Sinaloa was his nephew Valentín Nieblas, who served later as the Iglesia's missionary in Nicaragua.[17]

The rapid multiplication and mentoring of converts renders the Great Repatriation story in vastly brighter shades than the bleak ones usually proffered by historians. Political and social calamity pulled loose the very threads with which the converting peasantry and proletariat could reweave a sacred canopy. The converging trajectories underscore the importance of religious genealogies, networks, circuits, and symbolic remittances. Such resources provided leverage against two obstacles blocking the repatriados' reinsertion into their society of origin: religious intolerance and anticlericalism.

Religious Intolerance

Like many areas of the country, the Sierra Madre region resisted some of the Revolution's programs, including religious pluralism. Religious dissidents often found themselves bereft of any official protection from Catholic intolerance in lightly garrisoned communities and had to survive through their own wits or higher interventions. The Cristero conflict of 1926–1929, although brought to an uneasy close by the modus vivendi accords between the Catholic hierarchy and the federal government, still smoldered in far-flung regions and was easily restoked by local clerics or lay leaders.[18] Conversely, mayors and other officials often proved obdurate in their militant opposition to religious meetings and temple construction projects—of any group. (Temples were deemed federal property under constitutional and legislative provisions.) To counter this anticlericalism, Pentecostals appealed up the chain of command, to the country's president, if necessary. One year after Felipe Coronado's appeal to church leaders for succor in Ciudad Juárez, Gil Valencia sent in by proxy a similar appeal for church intervention with governmental authorities in Sinaloa.[19] Also, repatriates and others who acquired plots in communal *ejidos* shared the vulnerability of these against cristero attacks. Thus, they pressed leaders at the Iglesia's 1934, 1935, 1936, and 1939 conventions for scriptural guidance on *agrarista* participation and leadership; these were deemed legitimate, except in the bearing of arms to fight counterrevolutionary opponents. (That Apostolics would mount a vigorous defense of religious liberty while some imbedded themselves in the revolutionary agrarian reform project interrogates, of course, notions of apolitical passivity.) The reasons for persecution proved more complex than this, however, as seen in the itinerant ministry of Ignacio Mariscal.

IGNACIO "NACHITO" MARISCAL

Ignacio Mariscal was born in 1900 in La Ventena, Durango, a locality bereft of any schooling opportunities. In 1922, he crossed from Mazatlán, Sinaloa, over the Sea of Cortez to work in Santa Rosalía, Baja California. The following year he arrived in El Centro, California. Mariscal's brief but valuable memoirs relate his encounter with an Apostolic woman and subsequent life course. From these, we can glean elements of a common template that shapes many Pentecostal testimonies: migration and movement, labor, hardscrabble life, divinely appointed encounter, conversion, religious genealogy, and intrepid (often female) agency oblivious to impinging macroforces:

> There was in the apostolic church of El Centro a sister named Valeria [Lucio] de Garcia. As I was working in the field near her house I approached to ask for water, as I was very thirsty. She was waiting for me, since the Lord had spoken to her and indicated that a young man would come asking for water, which she was to give

him and then speak to him about the water of life. That is how it happened, and Sis. Garcia spoke to me about Christ. I began to attend the services, and after fifteen days made my profession of faith.

I was baptized in the name of Jesus Christ, and soon I received from God a great inspiration and began to testify to everyone I encountered. I felt a desire to testify about Christ in Mexico, and crossed the border to live for a time in Mexicali and Colonia Zaragoza. After a while I returned to California to the church in Canoga Park [San Fernando Valley] pastored by Bro. Miguel Garcia, nephew of Sis. Romanita de Valenzuela [note the invocation of a spiritual pedigree]. Afterwards I was in Los Angeles, and purposed with a brother to move ourselves to the state of Sinaloa. That was in 1932. Once in that state, we found out that a work had commenced in the Gaxiola household, in Guamuchil [the result of Macario Martínez's earlier effort]. I went to visit the brethren, and began to work with them.[20]

From this base, Mariscal ventured into the Sierra Madre mountain range that spans the states of Sinaloa, Sonora, Durango, and Chihuahua. In the last state's town of Atascaderos, he and José Peña found themselves enmeshed in land disputes, struggles fueled by the Lázaro Cardenas administration's vigorous land redistribution policies. Initially, several healings among the town's poorer residents prompted the town's leading families to pressure the authorities to expel the evangelists with death threats. The preachers took refuge in the outlying marginal neighborhoods, where the healings continued apace. Soon, the residents took up the evangelists' cause with the authorities, who were forced to relent:[21] "At the same time [in Atascaderos] God manifested in signs and miracles which were known to all, and we befriended the *agraristas*, who were opposed to the rich landowners. We counseled them against violence, and thereby won many people, and a numerous church was formed, which is still standing today."[22]

While Mariscal may have found grace in the eyes of agrarian peasants and mill workers, the same cannot be said of his encounters with the miners and foundry workers of the Sierra Madre. In Las Bocas, Durango, the conversion of the town's most fetching young women triggered a violent episode at the hands of angry men who felt robbed of their marital prospects (and machista prerogatives). On another occasion, in Quebrada Honda, Durango, an enraged, drunken horseman, forgetful of his prior consent, stormed an outdoor baptismal service as Mariscal was about to initiate the man's wife into the faith. The quick-thinking convert grabbed the reins to allow the preacher a chance to escape her husband's machete blows. The notorious and other episodes are celebrated in a *corrido* ballad, "Los Cuatro de a Caballo," that is still sung in the region:

The Four on Horseback

They had been following him
They had already planned their evil
They hated the man
Who came to preach to them
They were four on horseback
The worst ones of that place
They harbored the dark intent
Of killing the preacher

In a clearing on that mountain
One of them shouted
Stop, and raise your hands
You've met your end, preacher
The moon was a mute witness
Of what happened there

Since you're going to kill me anyways
Give me an opportunity
I wish to make a prayer
To my Heavenly Father
Father who art in Heaven
Please forgive them
This that they do to me
They do not knowing your love

When he had finished praying
A surprise awaited him
The four were kneeling
He prayed with them
There the four accepted
Christ in their hearts
Each one of the four
Is now a preacher

Natividad Torres's lyrical legend of "Nachito" Mariscal rests on a historical legacy (the song presents a composite of several of his close escapes). Mariscal's ministry yielded impressive results. By 1942, he counted twenty-two preaching collaborators in the region (he first attended an Iglesia Apostólica convention in Torreón in 1940).[23] His early successes in Durango included fifty-two water baptisms in Pie de la Cuesta and thirty-five in Quebrada Honda. The latter baptisms occurred among the several believers gathered under Pedro Pérez's ministry (see the section on Ysidro Pérez below). His fellow repatriate had sought Mariscal's pastoral accompaniment in the face of certain martyrdom:

> One day Bro. Pedro Pérez wrote me asking me to go to Quebrada Honda, as a new wave of persecution had begun and an ultimatum had been given for his death. I took Bro. José Peña as a companion and we went to Quebrada Honda, arriving there one day before the end of the time period given for Bro. Pérez's death, as we wanted to either aid him or watch him die. We arrived at a barrio called El Calvario, where the enemies of the gospel were. Although it was early, we began a service and preached all day into the night. The next day we met again, and instead of killing Bro. Pérez, as they had promised, thirty-five persons were baptized![24]

Still, economic and social circumstances proved harsh. Several of the families won by Mariscal in Quebrada Honda sought out more tolerant climes. Over time they proved instrumental to church growth and maturation in Sinaloa (Culiacán), Jalisco (Guadalajara), the Lagunera region, the Ciudad Juárez–El Paso basin, and, importantly, the midwestern United States. Two sons of the Luciano and Graciela Montes family, whose trajectory took them from Quebrada Honda to Torreón in 1947, to Ciudad Juárez in 1950, and to Chicago, Illinois, in 1967, were elevated into the episcopate of the Apostolic Assembly at century's end.[25] Ignacio Mariscal and Tiburcio Santos's mobile ministries demonstrate, thus, the binding ties of a transnational religious genealogy that spans a century, connecting as it did their spiritual progeny of the mid- to late twentieth century and early twenty-first century to their mentor, Miguel García and, through Miguel García, to Romana Valenzuela, the migratory matriarch of Mexican Apostolicism.

Ysidro Pérez's family began as the common-law union between Soledad Cota and Plácido Galaviz, both Vainoral, Sinaloa, natives. In June of 1923, two months after the birth of Ysidro, the family boarded a boat from To-polobampo, Sinaloa, over to Baja California, where they worked in the Mexicali Valley cotton fields. After the harvest, Plácido insisted on return-ing home and Soledad on staying near the border (her mother had immi-grated from Chicorato, Sinaloa, to Los Angeles, California). The couple separated, and Soledad took up an offer of marriage to Pedro Pérez. By decade's end, the family had crossed the border and secured work in the citrus and nut orchards of San Fernando, Santa Paula, Saticoy, and Ojai, towns northwest of Los Angeles. Young Ysidro was enrolled in primary school. The family's labor in the last three towns placed them within the orbit of Pentecostal ministers Eduardo Rodríguez, Honorato Jiménez, and José Carrasco.[26] Their conversion coincided with the ascendancy of Francisco Olazábal's ministry; the evangelist conducted several tent revivals in the area.

The family's new religious ties influenced their choice of destination in the repatriation process and subsequent movement. They arrived in Chihuahua City by rail in June 1934. Four months later, they moved to the Sierra Madre town of Arianeña in the Durango municipality of Guanaceví. Their subsequent migration within the same state took them in January 1935 to San Pedro, in October to Metates, and finally in February 1936 to Quebrada Honda. While employment opportunities shaped their trajec-tory, they opted to settle in the last town owing to references concerning and the hospitality of several families there. While still in Metates, Pedro Pérez's piety impressed Quebrada Honda resident Diodoro Montenegro. The latter insisted that the family take lodging in Quebrada Honda with Petra Aguilera, a member of the Rios clan.[27] Thus, both economic and religious variables impinged on proletarian decision making.

As in other places, prior missionary work (in this case, Methodist col-porteurs) had left several abandoned Bibles and hymnals scattered in its wake. These were stored in various homes, including that of Apolonia Silva. With these and the "rudimentary knowledge of the Gospel" left by evangélico predecessors, Pedro Pérez began to hold services on a thatched porch in Rosaura Rios's home.[28] He soon counted fifty baptized members. Soon thereafter, Ignacio Mariscal arrived to usher the group into Oneness doctrine. For the Pérez family, the force of earlier warnings in California about "orphans" and "half-truth" movements had dissipated.[29] Distance from orthodox tutelage allowed for an easier embrace of heterodoxy. So, too, did proximate persecution. As it turned out, Apostolicism already had arrived to the mountains through Consejo Espiritual Mexicano–affiliated families.

The search for labor opportunities often dovetailed with a concern for religious solidarity; the two motivations operated in tandem. In February 1937, when Pedro and Ysidro sought work in a mercury mine in the El Cuarenta settlement of Durango's María del Oro municipality, they secured lodging with a Pentecostal family. The four-day trek and hard labor proved fatal to Pedro, who died within two months. The tragedy left fourteen-year-old Ysidro alone to rely on his wits and the support of a fellow miner, an inactive Methodist preacher surnamed Reyes. Reyes and the community's other evangélicos assisted in the burial. Given the region's sketchy communications systems, word of Pedro's death did not reach Soledad for several months. In response to Ysidro's summons, his widowed mother and siblings joined him in the fall of that year.[30]

In the interim, Ysidro took accommodations and employment with the Rosalío Martínez family, foundry owners and members of the Consejo Espiritual Mexicano. The Pérez family's arrival allowed for the formation of a CEM church, although the congregation proved short-lived, as the foundry closed and families dispersed throughout the region. While some opted for return to Quebrada Honda, the Pérez family chose San Francisco del Oro, since the town was rumored to have mine work available and fellow believers in residence ("que allí había hermanos").[31]

Now well into his teens, Ysidro decided to undergo water baptism. His earlier disenchantment with Rosalío Martínez (whom Ysidro claimed defrauded him of his earnings) and the CEM (where ill was spoken of Ignacio Mariscal and Felipe Rivas) led him to seek out Mariscal in Quebrada Honda. Together with José Robles, whom he had befriended in El Cuarenta, he set out on a four-day journey. The baptism was followed by several weeks of itinerant evangelism with Mariscal throughout the region.[32]

As noted, economic exigencies and the heat of persecution eventually pushed the Quebrada Honda flock in several directions. While several families headed to points west and east of the Sierra Madre, the Pérez family aspired to return to California. The onset of World War II augured renewed migration and, with Ysidro's command of English, improved labor prospects. By this time, however, the young repatriate's religious motivations prevailed over more material ones. In 1940, the family relented to his wishes to settle in Torreón, the seat of the Iglesia Apostólica. There, the newly arrived pastor (from the United States), Leonardo Sepulveda, lodged them with the Zeferino and Juana Reza family, who worked as clothes and newspaper vendors.[33] While his mother and sisters took employment as domestics, Ysidro joined the Rezas as a food vendor.[34] The Pérez family's calamity-propelled migration came to an end of sorts when they settled in Mexican Apostolicism's "Jerusalem." Pentecostalism served them as a migratory safety net and softened the landing.

Ysidro's proclivities soon became evident. In 1946, he followed Sepulveda to Mexico City. Sepulveda had been dispatched to serve the capital's First Church and study in and help administer the Iglesia Apostólica's new ITAI.[35] Ysidro's bilingual skills—first acquired in a California primary school—proved useful to the church; he served as the ITAI's English instructor.[36] After graduation In November 1947, he took up an offer from the newly formed United Pentecostal Church (UPC) to attend its General Conference in Dallas, Texas, and to study at the Apostolic Bible College in Tulsa, Oklahoma.[37] His stay in Tulsa proved key for later Apostolic expansion and consolidation in Central America. When asked to translate letters sent to Tulsa by long-isolated Apostolics in Nicaragua, Pérez also sent copies to Iglesia Apostólica leaders, thereby providing the contacts for Maclovio Gaxiola's exploratory foray to the isthmus. Thus, the lad deemed expendable by one nation-state and barely noticed by another transcended the restrictive visions of both as he helped to engineer his movement's hemispheric expansion.

FRANCISCO AVALOS

Let us return to the story of Francisco Avalos. It, too, is a story marked by calamity but shaped ultimately by resoluteness. A native of Soyatlán del Oro, Jalisco, Avalos moved with his siblings to southern Nayarit after the death by lightning of his stepmother, Matilde, and the subsequent death by grief of his father, Odilón. Secundino, the eldest son, had married and established his new home in the Palo Herrado settlement of Nayarit's Compostela municipality months before. He took in his orphaned siblings. When the burden of supporting the brood, especially the three young children of the second marriage, became too heavy (José, the youngest, was four years old at the death of his parents), the eldest bachelor siblings opted to migrate northward, basing their decision on

Francisco, Esther, José, and Benito Avalos, San Diego, California, late 1926 or early 1927. Photo courtesy of Maricela Guzmán.

their mother's (Odilón's first wife) description of life in the United States.[38] Nineteen-year-old Isidro began the process, returning within the year to recruit his brother Francisco, who was still in his late teens. (Both were proficient musicians.) That second stint allowed them to return for the latter's marriage to Esther Valenzuela Haro of Palo Herrado. Shortly, in 1926, the newly formed nuclear family of Francisco, Esther, and young José set out for Mexicali, Calipatria, and San Diego, where the couple took work in the lemon harvest and lodging with a friend of Francisco's.

Misfortune soon struck in the form of a workplace raid by immigration authorities. After a month in custody, the couple was deported to Tijuana, whereupon the friend delivered his young emergency charge, José, into their hands. Francisco then secured work in Rosarito, preparing adobe bricks for hotel construction (probably telephone impresario Manuel Barbachano's Rosarito Beach Hotel). Isidro caught up with the family there, and after a month's labor they once again crossed the border to work in Calipatria. Their joint labor soon made possible the purchase of a late-model Ford. Unfortunately, this material achievement soon became a point of strong fraternal discord, prompting Isidro to leave for Los Angeles. He found work and lodging in Jimtown (Whittier, California). After a season of interaction with an Apostolic family, he assumed a new religious identity, a significant step for someone who had sought out a priest for confession before his last departure from Nayarit.

In the interim, Francisco had moved his family to the coastal town of Oceanside, California. From here, and at his wife's bidding, he drove to Los Angeles in search of his brother. They happened upon one another at an intersection; the reconciliation was instantaneous. Isidro acceded to Francisco's insistence that he join them in Oceanside, and Francisco gradually succumbed to Secundino's persistent proselytism. In quintessential evangélico fashion, Francisco forswore alcohol, secured civil marriage with Esther, and absorbed a new musical repertoire, which he and Secundino performed in the region's Apostolic churches. The new ties of spiritual kinship did not completely replace biological ones, however, as is evident from José's memoirs:

> Every once in a while Isidro would say to Francisco: "Brother, go to Mexico to preach the gospel of salvation to our family, while I stay working here in the United States and help you economically. You've already received the Holy Spirit, as has your wife." But Francisco would say to him: "I will never return to Mexico; too much poverty, too many plagues and diseases and no doctors. We're fine here; I already have my house and car, which I am paying in installments. Why would I wish to beg over there?" Ysidro would say to him: "Look, Secundino, our eldest, lives without God and without hope." Francisco would say to him: "You go; you have nothing to hold you down. I have to support my family (his first son Benito had been born by this time), and José needs to study; he's already nine years old. Why should I expose this family [to risk] by going to Mexico?"[39]

Though recollected from a distance of many decades (by José Avalos), the above dialogue represents thousands of similar conversions and conversations. Torn between religious motivation, filial affection, and economic opportunity, migrating religious agents often hesitate until external events precipitate renewed movement or return. In the case of Francisco Avalos, the nearby jail escape of a dangerous prisoner with the same name provoked the next crisis, one that uprooted him suddenly in February 1930 from his comfortable circumstances. When police and immigration agents descended on the carrot field where he was laboring, Avalos's first instinct was to proselytize them. As a result, he found himself thrown into the El Centro, California, jail while the matter of mistaken identity was sorted out. Esther, newly expectant, was deported to Mexicali with her two U.S.-born children; young José was entrusted to the care of the J. Guadalupe Banda family. During the following months, Isidro, movement leader Antonio Nava, and others regularly visited Francisco in jail and Esther in Mexicali. Nava appealed Avalos's case to the authorities.

Like Paul in Philippi (Acts 16) and Rome, the prisoner transformed his constricted misfortune into purposeful sojourn. He memorized vast amounts of scripture and aggressively evangelized his fellow inmates. Many of these sought baptism in the region's churches upon their release. He also accepted the inevitable repossession of his prized house and vehicle by his creditors. Finally, with macroevents swirling around them, the hapless family was cast into the swelling current of repatriation. Francisco was officially pardoned on the condition that he accept transport by boat to Manzanillo, Colima. Esther's appeal to the U.S. consul, based on her midstage pregnancy, secured a closer destination, Mazatlán, Sinaloa. On the appointed day of embarkment, a five-car caravan, including Isidro and José, set out to the San Pedro port to see Francisco off with gifts and offerings. José's tender recollections paint a disconsolate tableau:

> Many brethren, friends of Francisco Avalos went from Brawley, California. . . . It was a delegation of about five automobiles. The plan was to give him a fraternal farewell, so that Francisco could see that he had brethren and friends who loved him with all their hearts. However, upon arriving to San Pedro port, [we saw that] the boat carrying Francisco had left its berth and was about fifty meters away from the pier. Francisco went to the rear of the boat and with a handkerchief in his right hand waved goodbye to his friends and brothers. We, the delegation members, bade him farewell, some with their right hands raised; others of us began to cry, and between sobs I heard the voice of Brother J. Guadalupe Banda say, "I will not see my brother again until the coming of the Lord"; and in truth they did not meet again, as Brother Banda died a few years after. The whole delegation kept looking at the horizon until the boat disappeared in the distance. We all returned to Brawley, California, a little sad. Some had taken gifts, others money, but it was impossible to give these to him, and we had no address where we could send them.[40]

Avalos and two fellow prisoners were transferred to Mexican government custody in Mazatlán harbor and immediately given their freedom, whereupon they headed out to wait for the first northbound train—a case of perennial migrant chutzpah. The news that this would be preceded by a southbound one prompted Francisco to recall Ysidro's earlier charge to reach their eldest brother. Francisco arrived in Yago, Nayarit, to find Secundino gravely ill in bed.[41] The outcome of the story is, of course, an expected one.

Even with the conversion of his brother Secundino and others, Francisco continued to worry about his nuclear family and, especially, his wife's pregnancy:

> After much thought, he prayed to the Lord to illumine his thinking on how to proceed, since time was fleeting and Esther was due to give birth soon. The next day he visited the family, and told them of the reasons why he needed to return to Mexicali, BC. For they wished him to remain. In the end, they were convinced. The next night he prayed to God asking for direction. In the end, he decided to sell the violin he had brought from the United States as well as most of the clothing he had, and Secundino sold his house. Everything was cheap. They counted the money, and it was not enough for four tickets. María sold her chickens, and slaughtered the rest in order to have something to eat on the way.[42]

It is noteworthy that Francisco's familial band (now including his sister Angela; Secundino and his wife, María; and the couple's two small children) moved counter to the general repatriation flow, probably on a train that was returning from carrying hundreds southward to Jalisco. Francisco arrived to Esther's side in Mexicali in late October 1930, in time for—in fact, on the very night of—the birth of their third child, Dalila. Once there, he had every intention of remaining in Mexicali in order to provide for his young family. Within three months of their arrival, Angela, Secundino, and María were baptized by Mexicali pastor Ascensión Meza. Together with Isidro (still living in Brawley) and Secundino, Francisco began constructing a home in the Loma Linda *colonia*. Francisco and Secundino secured *ejido* land plots on the outskirts of town and began plowing. All the while, persistent pleas for spiritual succor continued to arrive in letters mailed by Francisco's converts in Nayarit. These, combined with the government's failure to deliver on promises of irrigation, prompted the brothers finally to forswear their ejido rights and return to Nayarit in December 1931.[43] For this trip, they availed themselves of the U.S. and Mexican governments' standing offer of free rail transportation for repatriates from Calexico to Nogales and, from there, to points southward.

The melancholic requisite farewell service took place under the thatched roof of the Loma Linda church:

> Pastor Ascensión Meza invited us to pass to the front of the small congregation, and both the pastor and the church prayed for us with great fervor, as some spoke in tongues as the Spirit gave them to speak and others cried. Clearly we were wrapped up in that glorious environment, as all the family joined in the church's crying. In the year and months we fellowshipped with that congregation we had won the love and affection of the brethren. It was very sad to abandon brothers in the faith whom we esteemed greatly.[44]

To be sure, Pentecostal repatriates were not the only ones shedding tears. One of Francisco Balderrama and Raymond Rodríguez's informants offered the following description of the emotions on display on a repatriation rail trip that began in Orange County and passed through El Paso:

> At the station in Santa Ana, hundreds of Mexicans came and there was quite a lot of crying. The men were pensive and the majority of the children and mothers crying.
>
> When they arrived in Los Angeles, the repatriates were calmed a bit because they were in Los Angeles. . . . From Los Angeles to El Paso, some sang with guitars trying to forget their sadness and others cried. Hill [Mexican Consul Rafael de la Colina] spoke very little, was very sad . . . the crying and the singing. No one had any desire to speak. Varela [an Orange County Department of Charities employee] tried to lift spirits and tried to converse.
>
> The train did not arrive at the station in El Paso but rather at the border. There was a terrible outcry. . . . Many did not want to cross the border because they had daughters and sons who had stayed . . . married to others here who did not want to return to Mexico. [It was] a disaster because the majority of the families were separated. There was no way for anyone to try to leave the train or run or complete their desire to return to the United States.[45]

The Avalos family surely drank from the same emotive cup as other repatriates during the day and overnight trip to Nogales, Sonora. The cup was sweetened, however, upon their recognition of a fellow émigré traveling in another rail car: Corona, California, pastor Fidel García. Recently widowed, the minister had saved up money to move to Guadalajara to preach. His presence, singing, guitar playing, and gift of the instrument reassured the deportees, especially Francisco and Secundino, that their new trajectory carried heavenly import.

Indeed, Francisco Avalos's final return to Nayarit proved catalytic for Pentecostal growth in that state.[46] By 1940, Nayarit counted fourteen congregations and an equal number of preaching points. The full conversion of Congregationalist minister Francisco Gándara was secured by a visit by Iglesia leader Felipe Rivas and enhanced by musical enchantment:

> After several months, during the first days of the month of June of the year 1935, Brother Felipe Rivas H., President of the Apostolic Church of the Faith in Christ Jesus in our country, arrived to the city in which I found myself. Our afore-mentioned brother explained things sufficiently to me, in such a manner that I remained even more convinced that what the brethren had told me was true. They then came into my house to hold a service, and after singing the first hymn, which was Number 10 of the Consolación hymnal, I felt a great blessing and wept like a child. When she saw me in that state, my wife, who was more suspicious than I, grew afraid, thinking that I was going to die at that moment. But such was not the case. When I came out of my ecstasy under which I fell, I urgently asked to be baptized in the name of Jesus Christ, and together with twelve brethren, I was allowed to descend into the baptismal waters. From that day forward I remained as helper to Brother Francisco Avalos Virgen.[47]

While in Nayarit, Francisco Avalos continued to look northward for guidance (especially from Antonio Nava, who ordained him by correspondence) and liturgical referents (note Gándara's reference to the Apostolic Assembly hymnal). More material help arrived in modest postal orders that José Rosas, a lay member of the Mexicali congregation, and brother Isidro (still in Brawley) inserted in quarterly letters of support. Through Nava, Avalos kept apprised of developments in Torreón. Thus, the repatriate's vision expanded beyond his limited sphere. Although unable to attend, he and the Santiago Ixcuintla congregation sent in an offering ($6.50) for the 1937 Iglesia Apostólica convention in Torreón (only one of eight churches so credited in the minutes). His attendance at the 1939 and 1940 conclaves allowed him to join in the deliberations over pacifism

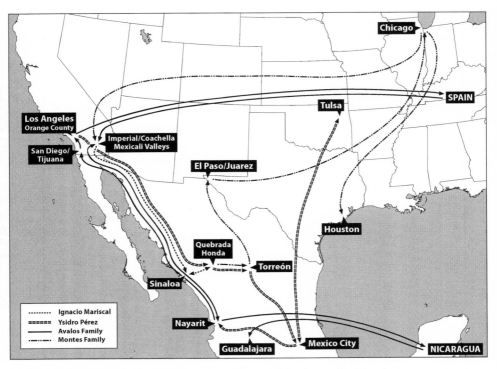

MAP 4 Transnational Repatriado Trajectories. (Map by Michael Cota)

and persistent anticlericalism. The latter presented an acute problem in Nayarit.[48] All the while, Francisco and Secundino farmed plots assigned to them by the agrarian *ejiditarios* of Santiago Ixcuintla.[49]

Ultimately, Francisco Avalos did not rise in the hierarchy of the Iglesia Apostólica, possibly owing to his rudimentary literacy. He did mentor many ministers and future leaders, however. His younger brother, José (our memoirist), became the bishop of Nayarit, when the state finally counted enough churches, and later served as missionary to Central America.[50] Isidro eventually took up a pastorate; in 1947, he established Tijuana's fifth Iglesia Apostólica congregation.[51] Several sons-in-law and grandsons of Francisco later served as bishops, pastors, and missionaries (including to Spain) in the Apostolic Assembly of the United States.

The outcome of the Avalos saga can be overlaid on to the Mariscal and Pérez trajectories to yield a picture of Apostolicism's thickening transnational density. By also tracing the trajectory of just one family among Mariscal's spiritual progeny, the Montes family of Quebrada Honda, Durango, we can appreciate the complexity of the transnational cartography set in place by early Pentecostalism.[52]

THE VARELA BROTHERS

While connecting with Felipe Rivas and others, Francisco Avalos sought out the repatriates and other believers left by Fidel García in the neighboring state of Jalisco, several of whom had been arrested for conducting water baptisms in a gully. Initially, Avalos was able to leverage legal recognition as a Protestant minister in Nayarit in favor of similar recognition for Apostolics in Jalisco. Avalos turned down, however, the government's offer of a confiscated Catholic temple for his movement.[53] The vigorous opposition by Catholic partisans to such transfers in Jalisco and his own experience with intolerance in Nayarit undoubtedly led him to pursue a less confrontational path than that taken by other *jaliscense* Protestants.[54] Meanwhile, Eusebio Joaquín and Joseph Stewart's competing streams of Apostolicism had also taken root in Jalisco. Avalos countered what he considered their extremism by appealing to the denominational sobriety that Apostolic converts like Lorenzo Varela had learned in their prior formation and identity as Congregationalists.

The trajectory of Lorenzo Varela and his siblings rounds out the repatriation story in terms of western Mexico. The Jalisco native, a Congregationalist at the time of his migration to the United States, was baptized in April 1930 in the Apostolic church in Ventura, California, a town within the orbit of Epifanio Cota's ministry.[55] After stints in Idaho, Varela returned to Guadalajara from Oceano, California, in 1931. His brother Moisés returned from Bisbee, Arizona, flush with earnings from work in the copper mines and on the railroad, which allowed him to build a shoe business in Guadalajara. Another brother, Isaac, remained in Guadalupe (near Oceano). Together with Mariano Rizo and fellow repatriate Merced Huerta, the Varela brothers helped consolidate Apostolicism in Guadalajara.[56] Moisés, whose Apostolic maid had encouraged his Catholic wife to convert after five miscarriages, provided financing for the construction of the Iglesia Apostólica's first temple, beginning in 1935. The commitment incurred heavy financial loss for the businessman, who moved permanently with his family to California in 1954 in order to save face.[57] His involvement in a church ownership dispute involving the Consejo Espiritual Mexicano may have also had something to do with his remigration.[58] While Moisés also may have flirted briefly with the Luz del Mundo, only brother Jacobo opted to join this Apostolic variant.[59] Lorenzo Varela also was instrumental in the conversion of his cousin, the aforementioned Francisco Gándara of La Atarjea, Nayarit.

The Luz del Mundo's historical narrative offers an intriguing glimpse into the Varelas's prized status: "In the company of Bro. Rodolfo Garibay and Sis. Guadalupe Fuentes he [Aarón] visited the home of the Varela family on Chilares Street toward the Algodonal; they had the doctrine of the Congregational church, and upon converting to the Lord Jesus Christ, some of the members of said family held meetings in that place occasionally."[60]

As one more iteration of proto-evangélico ambivalence, the case of disputed origins in Guadalajara is instructive, although it extends beyond the immediate period under study here. The Luz del Mundo faulted Ezequiel Ballesteros and Mariano Rizo for seducing away twenty-two of Aarón's followers to form the First Apostolic Church in Guadalajara's Colonia Libertad in 1933.[61] Apostolic church historian José Ortega, however, described Rizo as a founding Iglesia Apostólica member and Ballesteros as a long-suffering pastor enduring persecution in 1937 from both the Luz del Mundo and the Consejo Espiritual Mexicano.[62] Finally, church historian Manuel Gaxiola charged Ballesteros and Moisés Varela with engineering CEM leader Ireneo Rojas's ten-month takeover of the Guadalajara Iglesia Apostólico temple in 1946, a reprise of Rojas's and Francisco Borrego's actions in Torreón two decades earlier.[63] Ortega concurred in his oblique reference to Varela as a discontented prominent member who provided the financial means to undertake the legal maneuver.[64] From this distance, it is now possible to glean from officialdom's records a clearer and disinterested understanding of the protracted conflict.

The final leg of his inaugural supervisory trip to the Pacific coast states brought Iglesia Apostólica president Felipe Rivas to Guadalajara in August of 1935. The flock entrusted to Francisco Avalos by Fidel García required closer shepherding. Rivas designated repatriates Merced Huerta and Lorenzo Varela as interim pastor and secretary, respectively, and Mariano Rizo as evangelist. Two years later, Varela and Julio Ramos purchased a house and lot from widow María Jesús Valenzuela for construction of a temple. The seven-year project garnered governmental approval for worship in September 1943 and nationalization of the temple in February 1948.

The tangible outcome, however, precipitated a conflict over control of the property. The struggle exposed Apostolicism's growing fault lines in full view of municipal, state, and federal authorities. The Varela brothers helped to widen the rifts. On the evening of September 29, 1948, a group led by Moisés Varela, Rizo, and Ezequiel Ballesteros, claiming originary membership and the authority of a neighborhood committee (*junta vecinal*), interrupted the evening service and unceremoniously ushered out Iglesia pastor Manuel Retes and other church members. The intra-evangélico tussle drew in municipal police. Iglesia vice president Maclovio Gaxiola's October 1 protest prompted the Interior Ministry to demand of governor Jesús González a "cessation of the state of agitation" in the temple.[65]

The competing claims flummoxed municipal authorities, as these reported on the affair to state and federal authorities during the next thirty-four months. Gaxiola's protest listed Moisés Varela, Rizo, and Ballesteros among fifty-five "expelled" members (as of May 1946). On November 4 and 11, the dissident group presented their claims to the Guadalajara mayor and state office of the federal Secretariat of National Properties and Administrative Inspection, respectively. Their first notice listed Idelfonso Suárez as pastor-designate and included a detailed inventory of the building's contents, as required under federal law for pastoral changes. The governor's office included the particulars in its November 26 report to the Interior Ministry. The dissidents also alleged denominational caprice and sufferance toward clerical turpitude. Iglesia pastor Manuel Retes submitted a report concerning a pastoral change (Manuel Ramírez) and requisite inventory to the mayor and Interior Ministry on January 24 and 26, 1949, respectively. The federal decision in favor of the Iglesia was communicated to the governor on March 30, citing a district court's finding two weeks earlier against Moisés Varela and others for crimes against federal property. Judge Diodoro Bremauntz, however, noted the defendants' disadvantaged class position ("scant education" and poor economic conditions as "workers, shoe peddlers, and bakers") and sincere religious motivation and suspended the ten-month prison sentences and fifty-peso fines for this first-time infraction. He did levy 1,000-peso bonds.

The lack of clarity allowed the dissident group to secure a reversal of the Interior Ministry's prior decision on August 23, 1950. Mariano Rizo took possession of the temple as pastor on September 11. Maclovio Gaxiola promptly denounced the Iglesia Apostólica's longtime antagonist Ireneo Rojas of the Iglesia Cristiana Espiritual Mexicana (formerly Consejo Espiritual Mexicano) as the mastermind behind the whole affair. As proof, he submitted a copy of the ICEM's periodical, *Testigo de la Fé Apostólica*. He also reminded the Interior Ministry of the pending criminal charges.

The addition of Rizo's name to the list of defendants provided the final impetus for the federal government to adjudicate the matter in favor of the Iglesia Apostólica and pastor Manuel Ramírez. The property of the nation could not be entrusted to a convicted usurper.

The struggle over real estate and sacred space exemplifies the agency asserted by repatriates, including the warring Varela brothers. Clearly, they hit their native ground running, exercising prerogatives of original citizenship and deploying constitutional and regulatory mechanisms to their advantage. For example, the dissident group led by Moisés insisted on subjecting denominational dictates (emitted in far-away Sinaloa, Torreón, or Mexico City) to local consent via the *junta vecinal*. Thus, an anticlerical provision ostensibly aimed at Roman Catholic clergy and foreign prelates provided evangélicos with a weapon for their own internecine struggles. Conversely, Lorenzo, formed in Congregationalism before his migration and conversion, championed the connectional ties and legal claims of an emerging denomination with strong binational ties.

Pentecostals addressed their competing claims to important regional and national elites of the institutionalizing revolutionary regime. Jesús González Gallo had served as personal secretary to President Avila Camacho (1941–1946) before assuming the Jalisco governorship. His own chief of staff, Carlos Guzmán, the signatory or addressee of most of the intergovernmental missives, served as interim governor during González's absence in 1949. While most of the federal appeals were meant for President Miguel Alemán Valdes, they were addressed to his interior minister, Adolfo Ruiz Cortines, who succeeded Alemán in the presidency (1953–1958).

The official archival record also reveals other dimensions of early Pentecostalism, notably, the class position of the upstart movement. Judge Bremauntz's benign denigration of "workers, shoe peddlers, and bakers" was quoted directly in intergovernmental correspondence. We can also see from the inventory lists submitted to the mayor's office some of the musical aesthetic shift occurring in evangelicalismo. The piano, guitar, mandolin, and banjo represented a wider and more popular ensemble than those found in similar inventories submitted by mainline congregations. For example, the inventory submitted by Congregational pastor Joel Zambrano, to Tepic, Nayarit, mayor Felipe Ibarra as part of a July 1953 pastoral change, listed only an organ with the furniture and other items. That same year saw the dedication of the Apostolic temple in Tepic's Heriberto Casas ejido. The Interior Ministry required petitioners Rafael

Muro and thirty-one other ejidatarios to secure approval from the federal Agrarian Department.[66] The contrasting locations in the same municipality bespeak evangélicos' class divide at midcentury. While Congregationalists occupied a centrally located temple (a mere three blocks from the principal plaza) purchased decades earlier with missionary funds, Pentecostal peasants erected theirs in peripheral agricultural settlements set up by the revolutionary regime.

Repatriada Pathways

This discussion of returned migrant proselytism in western Mexico is not exhaustive, of course. The case of repatriate widow María Zapata, who returned in 1930 from San Bernardino, California, to Fresnillo, Zacatecas, and donated land for temple construction (Felipe Rivas visited her in 1932), underscores the multiple dimensions—lay, female, economic—of the Apostolic repatriation story.[67] Similarly, the later return (mid-1940s) to Guadalajara of Paula Bonilla de Orozco and her active sponsorship of evangelists in Jalisco through remitted earnings from her four sons' trucking business in Los Angeles, California, reminds us of the leveraging potential of religious remittances, both material and symbolic.[68] Importantly, Zapata's *diaconisa* status (accorded her in California) continued during her repatriation; Bonilla de Orozco's actions amounted to a de facto supervision of young male ministers. As in the case of Romana Valenzuela, a weak institutional presence allowed for greater female agency in leadership.

Repatriate Pathways

The several repatriate trajectories discussed here exemplify processes whereby (1) initial migration away from places of strong traditional belief exposes individuals and groups to new ways of thinking; (2) subsequent travel reinforces attachments to new belief systems and networks, creating new migrant cartographies and imagined communities; and (3) return and circular migration stretches religious networks and even spins off new ones through the exchange of symbolic and material resources. The subsequent trajectories of the adult and child repatriados, along with those of their biological and spiritual progeny, give us a sense of Apostolicism's early transnational dimensions.

The geographic and vocational expanse of the repatriado stories is by no means exceptional. Such a religious genealogy (broadened to include converts, disciples, and congregations) can be replicated for scores and hundreds of Pentecostalized clans. Our tentative mapping can only hint at the complexity. The genealogical tracing begs a methodology to match early Pentecostalism's mobility and religious cultural texture. A key to understanding pneumatic Christianity's vitality, mutation, and movement in other places and later periods, then, may lie in a more accurate measurement of its original phenomenal DNA and in a multilayered mapping of its dynamic cartography and topography. Importantly, this will also require perspectival shifts away from U.S.-centric histories and toward multiple, often overlapping histories of transnational human movement and religious encounter. By the time of their jarring uprooting and expulsion from the United States, the repatriados could count on tenuous but binding ties with aleluyas who remained in *el Norte*. Their trajectories, unlike that of our anonymous Indian of the Azusa Street Revival, can be traced, fleshed out, and studied. The following chapter will follow the story of the repatriados and their religious kin in this broader transnational setting and will weigh the institutional outcomes.

CHAPTER 4

Borderlands Solidarity

Somos un cuerpo en Cristo	We are one body in Christ
Con diferente don	With different gifts
Diáconos y ministros	Deacons and ministers
Y la congregación	And the congregation
Y si en acuerdo vamos	And if we go forth in accord
Crece la caridad	Love will increase
Solos no nos quedamos	We will not remain alone
Jehovah nos ayudará	The Lord will help us
Todos en uno amados	All together in one, beloved
Todos en comunión	All united in communion
Siendo regocijados	Relishing the joy of this salvation
Por esta salvación	

Marcial de la Cruz's spontaneous compositions endeared the evangelist to his listeners and won him an audience beyond Apostolic circles. As noted, several of his songs traveled the Spanish-speaking Americas via hymnal compilations, albeit often with anonymous attribution. The lore surrounding "La Iglesia el Cuerpo de Cristo" (The Church, the Body of Christ), helps us understand how the songwriter's music could register so deeply in the evangélico heart. In one especially heated moment of ministerial discord that threatened to sunder the fragile Apostolic movement, the poet withdrew into pained prayer. He returned with a poignant rhapsody about unity, a musicalization of the Pauline passage (1 Corinthians 12) about complementary gifts and deep empathy:

2. In this body is found the distribution of gifts
Some are healing, others exhorting
Others gifts of tongues, others interpretation
To others prophecy, and to others teaching

3. Although this body has distinct members
Still all are together, with different action
One helps the other to be able to labor
So that one or the other can evangelize.

6. We are a single body in the Lord Jesus
Dead to the world, living in his light
Participants in the resurrection
We will enter Zion triumphantly
Singing praises to Christ

The tender *vals* frame brought home the message about self-effacement and restored fraternal affect in a wave of tears and embraces. For their movement to hold together, Pentecostals would need many such moments in the following decades. They would also need to tend to the matter of institutionalization, in order to guard against atomizing macroforces but in such a way so as not to smother the original charismatic flame.

Consolidation and Coherence

My discussion of Pentecostal growth in the United States and Mexico has explored social, cultural, and geographical dimensions of that history, underscoring the mutual constitutiveness of migratory and religious experience at the personal and collective level. It has also sought to frame Pentecostal origins in the longer and broader context of prior evangélico history, missionary programs, and ethnic and nationalist restlessness. Early Latino Pentecostalism did not emerge in a vacuum; neither did its daughter Charismatic movement (nor, for that matter, did its granddaughter Neo-Pentecostal movement). Depending on one's point of view, this most mobile of Christianities succeeded because it was parasitic, opportunistic, reactionary, or creative. My focus on the migratory dimensions tends to favor the last characterization. These dimensions matter, for they allow us to see the emergence of a religiously inspired transnationalism *from below*. In the case of the several repatriated evangelists and their spiritual and biological progeny, we can detect the early articulation of transnational consciousness. The consolidation of Mexican/Chicano Apostolicism in the early to mid-twentieth century, viewed against the backdrop of the Great Depression, the Great Repatriation, global war, macro labor flows, and perennial xenophobia, represented a subaltern response to hegemonic forces as much as it did a Weberian process (from sect to church). In this response, religion and religious impulses—even self-effacing ones— served as weapons of the weak.

Transnational Solidarity

The arrival of notarized deputizing credentials from Antonio Nava and Bernardo Hernández (dated March 20, 1931) provided Felipe Rivas and José Ortega (Nava's mentee) with the impetus to convene an inaugural convention of the Asamblea Apostólica de la Fe en Cristo Jesús in December 1931 in Torreón. The attendees included twelve ministers and forty-eight lay members representing seven congregations within the Lagunera region. With divisions between *rivistas*, *rojistas*, and *aaronistas* still sundering infant Apostolicism, the meeting yielded few results beyond the recognition of Rivas and Ortega's de facto leadership among disfellowshipped Consejo Espiritual Mexicano believers. Ecclesial consensus would have to await a doctrinal one. The duo set about preparing doctrinal studies for the following year. At the same time, they began an outreach to the scattered Apostolic diaspora, seeking out repatriado evangelists in northern and western Mexico and sounding out fellow CEM dissidents in northeastern Mexico and southern Texas.

An August 1932 convention attracted eleven ministers, including one each from Monterrey and Nuevo Laredo. The ministers recognized Rivas as pastor general and Ortega as secretario general. Before attending to the weighty agenda items (doctrinal cohesion, clerical and lay discipline, Lord's Supper liturgy, recommendation protocol, children's ministry, and tithing), the delegates held an initial session on reconciliation and consensus.[1] The tumult of the prior half decade had sorely tested the movement's unity.[2]

In September 1932, Rivas dispatched Ortega to Monterrey, Nuevo León, to present their program to Apostolics chafing under Ireneo Rojas and Francisco Borrego's capricious extremism. Ortega's mandolin and hymnodic repertoire attracted considerable attention both among restive CEM adherents (the CEM had forbidden instruments) and potential converts. In the meantime, Rivas visited congregations in the states of San Luis Potosí, Zacatecas, Tamaulipas, and Coahuila. In early 1933, Rivas took up an invitation from Canuto García and Benjamin Cantú to visit Texas's Rio Grande Valley. Encarnación Rangel, who had ordained the latter two, encouraged their union with the Torreón-based church. García and Cantú, in turn, attended the Iglesia's convention in October 1933.

Originally scheduled for December, the convention was moved up two months in order to allow Rivas and Ortega to attend the Apostolic Assembly's long-awaited seventh convention in Tulare, California, in December of that year.[3] The arduous trek through Texas, New Mexico, Arizona (they gradually picked up fellow believers in all three states), and California propelled the narrative's insertion into Apostolic lore.[4]

Upon receiving Nava's commission to retrieve the Mexican visitors in El Paso, Texas, New Mexico anciano (elder) Pablo García Chávez purchased a worn Ford truck and outfitted its rear platform with a protective shell and wooden benches. His initial passengers also included Ortega's new bride, Esther Rivas, and new Ciudad Juárez pastor Felipe Coronado (a repatriado). By the time the rickety *Fordcito* (little Ford truck) lumbered into Arizona, six New Mexico pastors and laypersons had climbed aboard. When the vehicle broke down in Silver City, forty miles shy of Lordsburg, Ortega recruited the nonmechanics to join him in the town, Bibles and hymnals in hand, for a public serenade. Passersby warmed to the engaging repertoire ("Ya se Acerca el Tiempo de Pruebas" [The Time of Trials Is at Hand] and "El Tren del Evangelio" [The Gospel Train]) and Ortega's guitar playing. They responded generously to his brief sermon and appeal for help. The modest collection ($4.00) supplied the group with food and the vehicle with gas and oil for the next leg.

Two young women joined the group in Lordsburg, where pastor Pablo Soto rescued loaves of days-old bread to nourish the travelers. The band of thirteen became fourteen with the addition of pioneer Arturo Hermosillo in Tucson, Arizona. A gift of spark plugs from Santos Bracamontes in Phoenix, Arizona, helped to revive the sputtering vehicle; increasingly greater amounts of available food the farther west they traveled likewise strengthened the pilgrims. Finally, thirteen days after departing El Paso, the weary pilgrims arrived to the relieved and hearty embrace of their hosts in Tulare, California. Young eyewitness and recent convert María Luisa Curiel summed up the joyful reception:

> Seeing the brothers [arrive] was like seeing angels. To see how the laborers of God were held in such esteem, respect, and love. And the brethren would embrace and cry and cry and cry and speak in tongues. It was something new for me, but it pleased me so much, since I was not familiar with this. I saw how much they loved each other, how content they all were, "Brother so-and-so arrived. Look!" And the news would travel, "Look, the brother arrived!" The sisters making tortillas, making food, would get caught up speaking in tongues over here, with the pan in hand. How beautiful![5]

The assembled ministers and laity welcomed the Mexican delegates' participation, especially their sermons and songs—a case of religious remittances come full circle. To Rivas was entrusted the task of baptizing the more than sixty candidates who presented themselves for water baptism—a gesture of considerable import.[6] The conventioneers also heard (and remembered afterward) Marcial de la Cruz debut one of his final (and prescient) compositions, "Allá a lo Lejos" (In the Great Beyond).[7]

The arrival of his allies strengthened Antonio Nava's hand at a critical juncture, as the Apostolic Assembly continued to wrestle with the perennial issue of tithing for institutional growth. Although they had left the matter pending at their October convention in Torreón, Rivas and Ortega supported Nava's pro-tithing stance in Tulare, thereby reciprocating Nava's earlier intervention on Rivas's behalf in Mexico. The conclave's decision largely settled the matter but also precipitated the departure of important leaders, including Pedro Banderas, pioneer evangelist of Northern and Central California and New Mexico.[8] The pattern of transborder consultation and support would hold for the next half century; so, too, would the pattern of primitivist protest and exit.

The depth of trust reached between the two groups is evident from the decisions concerning polity and territories: ecclesial supervision of the churches in Baja California was transferred in 1934 to the Iglesia, while three years later, the Iglesia reciprocated by entrusting its work in Texas to the Assembly. The exchange recognized the de jure status of national borders, and represented the first of many adjustments that Apostolics would make in the face of weighty geopolitical realities throughout the following decades. The Apostolic Assembly began to cast its eyes eastward toward Texas's Rio Grande Valley and the Iglesia Apostólica westward toward Baja California.

Before returning to Torreón in January 1934, Rivas and Ortega undertook their maiden supervisory tour of the Baja California churches. Nava accompanied them and solemnly formalized the transfer of jurisdiction to Iglesia auspices in Tijuana, Colonia Zaragoza, and Mexicali.[9] The visit to the Mexicali–Imperial Valley represented a homecoming of sorts for Ortega. Ironically, his 1929 return to Mexico had resulted in, over the span of almost a half decade, a vastly enhanced status both within the valley region and throughout the Southwest United States. Similarly, their participation in the Tulare conclave greatly enhanced Rivas and Ortega's stature among their counterparts in Mexico.[10] Upon their return through Ciudad Juárez, they persuaded repatriates Ventura Salas and Felipe Coronado to return with them to Torreón.

Later that same year, Nava returned once again to Torreón, this time for the Mexican Iglesia's convention and with freshly imprinted credentials and stamping machine in hand. In Ortega's recollections of the visit, Nava's advice proved timely; the pioneer's vision clearly transcended national boundaries:

> [Nava's] visit was very comforting, as he gave broad orientation to all the convention ministers. We depended upon Bro. Nava as the person to consult with and for counsel, since at that time there were no other men of God equipped to do so, or if there were, we did not know about them, since the confidence born in our hearts toward him drew us in search of his advice. That is why between him and us there grew a friendship of companions and friends.[11]

During his summer 1935 inaugural tour of western Mexico, Felipe Rivas issued a vigorous summons to that year's convention (December) in Torreón. This helped ensure the long-awaited participation of even more repatriates and their growing spiritual progeny. The thirty-six new ministers, in addition to lay delegates, expanded the church's reach to thirteen states in northern and western Mexico as well as to the nation's capital.[12] José Ortega noted a key variable in that expansion:

> The attendance of all these delegates caused a pleasant surprise, which grew continually as each delegation presented itself, and which filled everyone with joy and blessing. The common denominator in the formation of these groups was that in the repatriation from the United States to Mexico, due to the economic depression, many ministers who had returned and re-established themselves in Mexico had testified to their families about the Jesus' name baptism and infilling of the Holy Spirit with the evidence of speaking in tongues, and thus had formed small and large Apostolic congregations. The Apostolic message had proliferated in all these states, in groups that now asked to be incorporated into the ranks of the Apostolic Church.[13]

Xenophobia's Unexpected Outcome

The minutes of the early Iglesia Apostólica organizing annual conclaves (1932–1940) in Torreón, Coahuila (the 1937 conference met in Monterrey, Nuevo León), record the active participation of repatriated ministers, beginning with Felipe Coronado, Agustín Cerros, and José Montellano in

1934. Coronado requested advice in countering official anticlericalism that prevented construction of a temple in Ciudad Juárez; Cerros requested a vote of confidence on the ministerial abilities and status of "those of us who come from the north"; and Montellano moved that the sister churches (Iglesia Apostólica in Mexico and the Apostolic Assembly in the United States) formalize the practice of commissioning delegates to each other's conventions, "so that there by a tightening of relations."[14] The determined activism of migrants and émigrés under political and economic duress underscores the resilience of fictive religious kinship ties. Passivity in the face of macroevents was not an option.

Given the protracted Depression, the Apostolic Assembly did not celebrate its eighth convention until 1937 in Los Angeles, California. Maclovio Gaxiola, now the Iglesia's Pacific coast overseer, joined Felipe Rivas and José Ortega as representatives of the Mexican church; Benjamín Cantú of Texas attended in his own right, this time as a minister of the U.S. church (he debuted his considerable talents as a translator of English-language hymnody). Echoing repatriate José Montellano and others' concerns, movement leaders began exploring more formal ties. Iglesia leaders reported on this at the 1939 and 1940 Torreón conclaves.[15] In the United States, the looming institutionalization propelled the departure of pioneers Guadalupe Lara (Los Angeles), Bautista Castro (Otay/San Diego, Solana Beach/Del Mar, and Tijuana), and others. The primitivists continued to dissent over the issue of tithing. Upon exiting the Assembly, they reclaimed Pentecostal Assemblies of the World auspices as the PAW's "Spanish Department."[16]

A final joint Constitution and Treaty of Unification were ready for ratification in 1944. The site of the Iglesia–Assembly accords' near-final redaction in April 1944 also suggests an apt metaphor. Santiago Rodríguez had expanded his San Ysidro, California, celery and cauliflower farm with buildings purchased from interned Japanese farmers.[17] Thus, several yards from the borderline at Tijuana, surrounded by bracero (temporary guest worker) laborers and meeting under the shelter of borrowed roofs and the shadow of war, ten leaders, all but three of Mexican birth, forged an ecclesial instrument of transnational solidarity, one that enshrined the "rights of hospitality." Each of the treaty's seven points reaffirmed the common goals signaled in the prologue:

> The goal of this Treaty is to conserve the ties of Christian fellowship that have been cultivated over the last several years between both

movements, and to establish the foundation within the rules of the Word of God (Romans 12:9, 10); and thereby to unite officially, with improved understanding, the ideals and sentiments that, within the doctrine of our Lord Jesus Christ and according to the apostolic order, we have been practicing in both countries.[18]

The treaty regulated (or eased) the exchange of clergy, members, and goods—both material and symbolic—across the border. Reference (or obedience) to relevant immigration law was omitted from the document:

> The rights shall be reciprocal, in order to recognize and respect one another in a ministerial category when visiting one another. Having right to make use of the word in the temples, to preach, teach and provoke one another to love and good works, in accordance with the doctrine we have approved (Hebrews 10:24). Suffering to visit the homes of our brothers and enjoy the rights of hospitality and other privileges that a worker of Christ deserves, up to the point permissible by circumstances.
>
> It is the obligation of the workers, upon visiting the churches outside the country to which they belong, whether carrying out a special commission, or responding to an invitation, or simply on a personal visit, to equip themselves with their ministerial credential and a letter of recommendation issued by their supervising authority. And also to display these documents to the authorities of the congregations they visit, respecting and laboring in accord with them; even when their ministerial category is superior (1 Peter 5:3).[19]

Essentially, Apostolic leaders formalized what Apostolic believers had been practicing for many years. For Apostolics, as for many other Mexicans and Mexican Americans, the southwestern United States and northern and western Mexico continued to constitute a "single cultural province," one in which people *migrated* (as opposed to immigrated) in search of better economic opportunities but not necessarily different social arrangements. Differences of citizenship were flattened in the name of an imagined fraternal community. When U.S. law capriciously raised barriers to divide a people, a higher law given concrete expression in the formal treaty and fleshed out in the daily praxis of the community called for a constant social ethic built on brother and sisterhood and charity toward the sojourner, with scant regard for de jure distinctions.

The churches refined their episcopal forms of polity with central governing boards (composed initially of six executives elected to four-year terms) and regional jurisdictions. Reflecting recent historical experience, the provision for exceptional replacement of a governing board member made explicit the possible causes of vacancy: death, moral lapse, or *emigration*.[20] Except where necessary to reflect relevant national laws and circumstances, the treaty bound both churches fast to each other and granted each veto power over treaty and constitutional amendments proposed by the other.[21] At this time, they also agreed to a clear differentiation in legal nomenclature, with the Mexican group adopting the name Iglesia Apostólica de la Fe en Cristo Jesús and the U.S. group retaining the original legal name (Apostolic Assembly of the Faith in Christ Jesus) adopted in 1930. The constitution also definitively established the practice of tithing for the churches' sustenance. In terms of doctrine, they reaffirmed a clear Oneness position in theology and a more ambivalent one in pneumatology and soteriology. Baptism in the Holy Spirit was strongly encouraged for members ("to seek the Promise") and made a sine qua non for ordination. The question of soteriology determined the extent of sectarian introversion. Many Apostolics did not link Holy Spirit baptism, evidenced by tongues speaking, to soteriology; however, the charter document urged the experience on all believers as ideal and normative.[22]

The constitution and treaty garnered approval by both denominations' general conventions in 1944, first on October 24 at the Iglesia's thirteenth general convention in Torreón and then on December 29 at the Assembly's sixteenth in Los Angeles, California. A final ratification vote—of changes approved in Los Angeles—was taken up in an extraordinary meeting at the Iglesia's tenth regional convention in Angostura, Sinaloa, on March 9, 1945 (the bulk of the attendees there—about one half of the Iglesia's ministers—had been absent from the Torreón conclave, owing to the distance). All three votes reached unanimity. The total number of 250 ministerial signees included 134 ministers in Mexico and 116 in the United States.[23] Viewed in light of the number (fifteen, two of these by proxy) of ministers who participated in the Iglesia's 1932 convention in Torreón, the roster presents a snapshot of vigorous growth and ecclesial maturation on both sides of the border. José Ortega's retrospective fills in the picture's emotive tones:

> I wish to emphasize that a fraternal spirit, respect and companionship always reigned during these accords. Pride and haughtiness [*soberbia*] did not appear since we applied the scriptural theme of

considering ourselves inferior each to the other. This was the spirit that ruled when we signed the two documents: the Constitution and the Treaty of Companionship. Mexico rendered its respects to Bro. Nava for his liberality and broad vision, recognizing him as their pastor and advisor, remembering the official documents [privileges] that he sent to Bro. Rivas in 1931 to propel the work of the Lord.[24]

Along with Ortega, Rivas, and Nava, the charter signees included such first-generation Apostolics as Iglesia treasurer Aurelio Rodríguez, who signed in Torreón; his brother Juan (Bakersfield, California, pastor), in Los Angeles, California; Marcelo Hernández, Cayetano Torres, Miguel Alvarez, and Juan Reta and his son Emeterio, in Torreón; and Ramón Ocampo, Rodolfo González, Cirilio Leyva, Jesús Valdez, Celso Moran, Juan Amaya, Pedro Nava, and Ramón Carrillo, in Los Angeles.[25]

Importantly, the charter also secured the imprimatur of the repatriados, whose prestige derived from their pioneer status (Table 1). These included Reyes Ruelas, anciano (supervising elder) of Sonora, and Guadalupe García, anciano of Durango, who signed in Torreón and Angostura; Felipe Coronado, anciano of Chihuahua, Lorenzo Varela, and Agustín Cerros, in Torreón; Ignacio Mariscal, anciano of Topia y Tepehuanes, Durango, in Angostura; and Fidel García in Los Angeles.[26] Young Ysidro Pérez signed in Torreón. The several Avalos siblings likewise affixed their signatures: Isidro in Los Angeles and Francisco and José in Angostura. So, too, did the numerous spiritual progeny and colleagues of the repatriates. In addition to the several Gaxiola clan members, Ramón Canales, an Avalos convert from Nayarit, and José Peña, Mariscal's close collaborator in Atascaderos, Chihuahua, signed in Torreón; Manuel Corrales, a Ruelas convert from Choix, Sinaloa, Pablo Rodríguez, Ysidro Pérez's companion from El Cuarenta and Quebrada Honda, Durango, and Armando, Domingo, and Francisco Uriarte, Filiberto López converts, signed in Angostura.[27]

It is important to note that Apostolics formalized their transnational alliance entirely free of missionary supervision. In this, they differed somewhat from Francisco Olazábal and the Concilio Latinamericano de Iglesias Cristianas, who two decades earlier had sought emancipation from missionary paternalism. Clearly, Apostolicism emerged from the political and religious persecution of the previous decade not only intact but also strengthened. Dismissed by one country and barely tolerated in another, the repatriados held fast to their coreligionists, in order to imagine and create a more transcendent one, thereby embodying a transnationalism

TABLE 1 Ecclesial Trajectories of Apostolic Repatriados

Name	Title	Denomination
Reyes Ruelas	Supervisor, Sonora	Iglesia Apostólica
Guadalupe García	Supervisor, Chihuahua	Iglesia Apostólica
Ignacio Mariscal	Supervisor, Topia y Tepehuanes	Iglesia Apostólica
José Ortega	General secretary	Iglesia Apostólica
José Avalos	Bishop, Nayarit	Iglesia Apostólica
	Missionary, Nicaragua	Iglesia Apostólica
Ysidro Pérez	President	Iglesia Apostólica
Marcelo Pacheco	Bishop, Baja California	Iglesia Apostólica
Efraím Valverde	President, Men's Auxiliary	Iglesia Apostólica
	Bishop, Northern California	Apostolic Assembly
	President	Apostolic Assembly
	Presider	Iglesia de Jesucristo en las Américas

from below, decades ahead of more contemporary case studies.[28] This suppleness positioned Apostolicism well for a reencounter with white Oneness Pentecostalism (the recently formed United Pentecostal Church) and new waves of labor migration and xenophobic reaction to these.[29]

Global Citizenship: From "Mexicans" to Missionaries

Early Apostolicism's chartering documents do not reflect sectarian introversion or social passivity. Rather, they cast a vision beyond the borderlands. The drafters were keenly aware of important macroevents; the published prologue alluded to global violence, crime, and hatred and, of course, their remedies: "Violence and crime are growing in the world, and as a consequence, the seed of hatred, which causes sorrow, will be sown. It is only through the Sacred Word of God that we can have victory over these problems; for this reason we believe that we, the Church of our Lord Jesus Christ, must work without ceasing, attempting to do all decently and in order."[30]

The constitutional revision of 1950 (December) addressed the acute pastoral challenge represented by the military drafts of World War II and Korea and reaffirmed and codified a pacifist tradition. A seventeenth article of belief was added to the original sixteen. Church members were forbidden to take human life in military service: "All its members are obligated to fulfill civic duties, but should not accept those in which it is necessary to kill another human being or do the things that the conscience of a faithful Christian does not allow."[31] The pacifist norm—dutiful noncombatant military service—held until the late twentieth century, decades after white Pentecostal denominations had shifted to a more pro-combatant or ambivalent footing.[32] As with other pacifist churches, though, the norm was often honored in the breach.

Military service also wrought an unexpected expansion of Apostolics' view of the world, as concern over the safety of soldiers evolved into a keen interest in the evangelism undertaken by those soldiers among, say, Spanish Civil War exiles in southern France and Filipinos in the Pacific. In his report of their May 1944 arrival to the twin border cities of Calexico and Mexicali, Maclovio Gaxiola shared with *Exégeta* readers the anxiety expressed to him, Felipe Rivas, and José Ortega by the León Morales family (their Calexico hosts) over the absence of soldier son Daniel.[33] Four months later, the *Exégeta* reported on Eduardo Najar's successful appeal, undergirded by five months of fervent maternal prayer, for conscientious objector status.[34] The December 1944 convention in Los Angeles (the conclave that ratified the constitution and treaty) was made possible, in part, by pooled wartime food rations. Along with coordinating the kitchen committees, many women sent up public prayer requests during the services on behalf of absent sons and husbands.[35] One of these, Air Force member Canuto García Jr., son of the Texas leader, sent in his testimony and a poem, "Conversión: La Oración de un Soldado" (Conversion: A Soldier's Prayer"), to be shared with the delegates.[36] The March 1945 issue of the *Exégeta* carried an update on Morales:

> From France, Europe. Some of the brethren, members of our Church, who in the carrying out of their duties as citizens of the U.S.A., find themselves in France, and have written that they have been favored by the hand of the Lord. In particular, our esteemed brother Daniel Morales, who has translated some very beautiful hymns into Spanish, which the churches sing with joy, has let us know that he has been able to preach the Gospel in the place he is

in, that many soldiers have been happy to accept it, and that they have improvised a prayer chapel where they meet to pray fervently. Let us pray for all our brethren who are in great danger, but who trust in the Lord."[37]

As World War II drew to a close, *Exégeta* readers eagerly awaited updates about Morales (in Spain with returned exiles) and others and about the periodical's distribution via soldiers and sailors to places in the Philippines and France and bases in the United States. The November 1945 issue explicitly stated that the Apostolic Assembly's new initiative in foreign missions merely awaited the return of the denomination's youth from military service.[38] Indeed, upon returning, Morales accompanied leaders of both churches in their early forays into the Central and South American mission fields. He also helped to broker relations with the United Pentecostal Church. That the bulk of the *Exégeta* readers were in Mexico, of course, demonstrates an expanding transnational vision as well as enduring cords of fraternal concern.

Borderlands Expansion and Contraction

The manpower demands of World War II precipitated a labor shortage in the country's agricultural industry and brought about a new receptivity toward Mexican labor. In 1942, the two governments instituted the Bracero program, in order to meet U.S. agriculture's demands for a plentiful—and pliable—work force. The availability of agricultural employment in the United States was widely advertised throughout Mexico. The program's conditions stipulated that would-be guest workers sign a contract with a grower's' representatives in Mexico and remain with the original employer for the duration of the employment term. Nearly two million Mexican men were thus contracted and brought into California alone (most without wives or children), under the program's auspices from 1942 to 1960.[39]

Early into the program, however, growers began to exploit its loose enforcement provisions, hiring former braceros who had "skipped" on their contracts (choosing not to return to Mexico once the original contract had expired) and had thereby entered the "illegal" work force. This practice further expanded the supply of available labor and, thus, depressed wages. On many farms, the work force consisted of three distinct groups—domestics, braceros, and "illegals"—all working side by side.

Initial governmental enforcement proved lax, probably by design. The Immigration and Naturalization Service averaged apprehensions of fewer than 10,000 per year for the several years leading up to 1943,[40] thereby signaling to laborers on both sides of the border that, one's immigration status notwithstanding, work was plentiful and available; they could arrive and stay with practical impunity. A scarcity of contract offices in Mexico also prompted many would-be braceros—enticed by the program's wide publicity—to forgo the formal contractual process altogether and head directly north.[41] The bottlenecks at designated contracting sites (e.g., Chihuahua and Durango cities and Empalme, Sonora) often presented host mayors and governors with volatile, transient populations of would-be braceros unable to return to homes in the countryside.[42]

In 1947, in response to domestic political pressures over an oversupply of Mexican labor and in anticipation of a recession, a newly emboldened Border Patrol began to clamp down on undocumented workers. A series of well-publicized raids throughout the Southwest netted a total of 193,657 apprehensions in 1947; 217,555 in 1948; leading up to 543,538 in 1952, the year in which Congress outlawed the willful or knowing concealment, harboring, shielding from detection, transporting, or encouragement of aliens illegally entering the United States. The felony carried a fine of $2,000 and a five-year prison sentence for each undocumented alien so aided. However, the law provided the following loophole for American business: "For the purposes of this section, employment, including the usual and normal practices incident to employment, shall not be deemed to constitute harboring."[43] The harshest crackdown took place in 1954. As part of the notorious "Operation Wetback," agents of federal, state, county, and municipal authorities were mobilized to assist the Border Patrol in repelling a Mexican "invasion." The pooled efforts netted 1,075,168 apprehensions of Mexican "illegals."[44]

The general feature of capricious and often harsh enforcement continued to characterize U.S. immigration policy throughout the following decades, a period that saw the passage of the Immigration and Naturalization Acts of 1964, 1976, and 1978 and the Immigration Reform and Control Act of 1986. The churches' ethos and praxis remained constant and stood in stark contrast to this fluctuation. Long-settled Apostolics were reminded—upon greeting or baptizing each new arrival—of their own time as sojourners.

Bracero Evangelism

The onset of the bracero era intensified the rate and pattern of Apostolicism's growth in both countries. As the migratory stream shifted northward again, Mexican Apostolics joined their countrymen in search of better economic opportunities. The church in Mexico did not suffer a corresponding loss in membership, however. As newly converted braceros returned home from their stints in the United States, they invigorated or established congregations in Mexico, often bringing their entire families into the new faith.

Once again, Apostolics along the border found themselves strategically situated for labor market–driven evangelism. Congregations served as islands in the streams of northern and circular migration. These served as social and religious oases where sojourners could enjoy a respite before pressing on (the metaphor may be more appropriate to inland travel through arid landscapes). The migrant flow increased so rapidly that, as part of its 1946 expansion, Tijuana's First Apostolic Church commissioned architectural blueprints for a second floor over the high sanctuary ceiling, in order to build a warren of rooms for northward-bound braceros—religious network as hostel and trampoline. When the city's structural engineers deemed the ceiling and frame too weak, the church shelved that innovative part of the project but continued the practice of hospitality in the temple and members' homes.[45] The new temple served thereafter as an important gathering site for borderlands Apostolicism.

The several residency categories proved as porous as occupational ones. Our analysis must take this complexity into account. For example, what should we make of the fact that many attendees to the 1943 Assembly convention in Phoenix, including Iglesia minister Miguel Gaxiola and his nephew Manuel, spent several days harvesting cauliflower after the conclave, in order to underwrite their continued travel?[46] Or that, in order to return to Texas, Benjamín Cantú and others had to do the same for three days in the cotton fields of Maricopa County after a convention in 1940 in the same city, the very meeting in which Cantú was ordained anciano of his home state?[47] Clearly, religious motivations weighed heavily. Economic ones came in at a close second, impinging on migrants' trajectories.

Manuel Gaxiola, at that time a young, unbaptized member of his Sinaloa clan, had accompanied his uncle Miguel to the 1943 Phoenix gathering, then traveled to Hermosillo, Sonora, to take up a brief mechanical apprenticeship. Soon thereafter, he traveled to Mexicali and tried his hand at carpentry, while hosted by Eduwiges Cazares, a minister from Sinaloa (and constitution signee in Angostura). In February 1944, he accepted Brawley, California, pastor Gilberto Muñoz's request to paint and prepare that congregation's temple for a regional convention of the Assembly's Southern California district. At that gathering, he met his countryman, Adolfo López, whose mother had served as the hometown midwife during Gaxiola's birth in Guamuchil, Sinaloa. López, a pioneering member of the church in Solana Beach (Del Mar, California), invited the youth to work in that area's avocado and strawberry harvests and as a golf course caddy in Rancho Santa Fe. The traveler finally made his calling sure in the company of Solana Beach's aleluyas. The experience of liminality ushered him over the threshold of religious and vocational identity (note the marked emotive contrast in his account of deportation to that of many such stories today):

> My stay in Eden Gardens [the Mexican *colonia* in Solana Beach] familiarized me with the way of life of a congregation of the Apostolic Assembly, our sister church in the United States, and at the same time I observed the way of life and adaptation of Mexicans in the U.S. system. Almost all the residents of the colonia came from the lowest classes of Mexico, and for them the most attractive part of the "American Dream" was that which included the use of alcohol, vices, sexual promiscuity and drugs. The brethren of the church, coming out of the same environment, literally shone like lights in the darkness.
>
> My attendance in the services and my relation with the brethren revived my inclinations toward the Gospel and what I had perceived since my childhood as a call to the ministry. My need for baptism grew more solid; to achieve this I had an experience of conversion. Thus, when in May of 1944 the Border Patrol found me and deported me to Tijuana, I left the United States ready to give my life in service to Jesus Christ.[48]

Hospitable arms were extended to outsiders as much as to sectarian insiders. Indeed, most hosting congregations imagined they were entertaining potential converts as well as possible angels. The enchantment of invitational music—including journeying and prodigal themes—performed in familiar musical genres, plucked many a homesick heartstring. Repatriate evangelists contributed heavily to this repertoire. Reyes Ruelas's "Ya No Te Detengas" (Hesitate No Longer), published in the Apostic Assembly's *Consolación* hymnal, is but one example of persistent proselytism by serenade:[49]

Ven a Cristo Jesús, es tu buen Salvador,	Come to Christ Jesus, he's your good Savior,
Hoy Él quiere librarte de la perdición;	He wishes to free you from perdition today;
Hoy es tiempo que puedas tener el perdón	Today is the time that you may have pardon
A tu alma dará Salvación	He will give Salvation to your soul
Ya no te detengas, ven al Salvador,	Hold back no longer, come to the Savior,
Para que recibas de Él la bendición;	So that you may receive from Him the blessing;
Sólo en Él encuentras hoy la vida eterna	Only in Him will you find eternal life
Y hallarás la salvación.	And you will find salvation.

The gathering in of bracero sheaves took place by many means. For example, the Solana Beach church sponsored a bus to fetch braceros from their camp in Escondido, California, for services and meals. Converts then circulated between that congregation and such places of origin as Mesillas, Zacatecas, and Mexico City, in tandem with their labor contracts.[50] As with the repatriados before them, braceros' mobility grew the movement, even in the face of, as in the case of Mesillas, religious intolerance.[51]

Such enterprise did not go unnoticed. Donald MacGavran gleaned from it elements with which to fashion his major missiological innovation: church growth theory. MacGavran underscored the contrast between Pentecostal bracero evangelism and general mainline indifference or cluelessness:

Some denominations have never found the *braceros*. One church in Mexico, located on the edge of one of the *bracero* shipping stations, in the midst of thousands of men milling around waiting for orders to move, has never distributed tracts, put on a movie to bring men in and preach the gospel to them afterward, or set up a social center where the men could find wholesome entertainment and the truth about Christ. But other denominations have sought out the *braceros*, both in Mexico and the United States. Pentecostal churches, being churches of the common man, have found much *bracero* responsiveness. They have communicated Christ to Mexican laborers in the United States, and they have won many people of the working classes in Mexico. . . . The leaven of the "America-returned" is widespread in Mexico. Men from both resistant sections and receptive sections return influenced—a few converted, some friendly to Evangelicals, some having read the New Testament, and some merely jarred a little in their age-long prejudices. This leaven is an important element in Evangelical growth.[52]

Given their long, shared history with coreligionists in Mexico, *tejano* Methodists were privy to ecclesial and political developments south of the border. During its first decade, the meetings of the newly organized Annual Mexican Conference of the Southwest (northern and southern Methodists reunited in 1939) saw the regular participation and even presiding leadership of fraternal delegates from the Iglesia Metodista de México (IMM), including the IMM's second bishop Eleazar Guerra. In 1941, Mexico's celebrated composer-translator, Vicente Mendoza, returned to the country of his earlier exile to conduct an evangelism campaign in the conference's southern district (Rio Grande Valley).[53] Two years later, the district reported an increase of 476 members, reversing the 1940–1941 loss of 270 members.[54] The opportunities and challenges portended by an impending flood of guest workers, however, caught many unaware. In his report to the October 1941 annual conference, northern district superintendent Frank Romo fretted presciently about *metodistas*' urban captivity: "The rural work is going forward, but there is too little of it. We should pay more attention to this labor, since thousands of Mexicans live in the fields and ranches. We do not have the means to reach these people as we should, but we want to underscore the opportunity for the churches and women's societies."[55]

The absent means would have included, of course, centers of hospitality and bracero evangelists. None of the latter could be found. Besides, other imperatives impinged upon metodista life. Foremost among these was the need to carve out jurisdictional space within a reuniting Methodism; thus, the Rio Grande Annual Conference, encompassing tejano and *nuevo mexicano* Methodists, was organized in 1949. This development, in turn, intensified a long-simmering resentment over lower salaries for Latino ministers. The resolution to this problem required improved training; the long-standing Wesleyan and Patterson Institutes of San Antonio and El

Paso, respectively, no longer sufficed.[56] Ironically, the professionalization of its clergy distanced borderlands Methodists from the bracero waves swirling around them.

In addition to evangelistic opportunities, Apostolics also insisted on pastoral accompaniment. As a result, church growth closely mirrored the settlement patterns of Mexican and Mexican American labor circuits. For example, the Sabás Ramírez family of Chicago, natives of Nuevo Laredo, Tamaulipas, joined with Conrado and Herminia Anaya of Michigan (who had arrived there from Weslaco, Texas, in 1944)[57] to pioneer Apostolicism in the Midwest. In 1952, they issued a call to the Apostolic Assembly for denominational help.[58] The Assembly's new president, Benjamín Cantú, arrived to take stock of the region's potential. He soon dispatched aid in the persons of Domingo Torres and Roberto Valverde, grandsons of repatriado Refugio Valverde.[59] Cantú did not arrive to meet strangers. The Ramírez and Anaya families had strong ties to ministers and laypersons in both churches. In addition, the Anayas and Cantú shared a joint baptismal lineage at the hands of José Guerra in Donna, Texas.[60] The Anaya family, in turn, sired a ministerial legacy that proved instrumental in the later growth of Apostolicism in Oaxaca and Chiapas, via Escondido, California.

Another model of pastoral accompaniment can be seen in Manuel Vizcarra's residence in a state-run labor camp in Westley, California, while pastoring in nearby Grayson. In 1967, Vizcarra was elected bishop of the Apostolic Assembly's Northern California district upon the previous bishop Efraím Valverde's election to the presidency. For the following two years, the site made famous three decades earlier by Dorothea Lange's ubiquitous camera boasted an episcopal residence, that is, the modest dwelling occupied by the family.[61] No longer farmworkers per se, the Vizcarras nevertheless exemplified the reason for the Pentecostal success noted by Donald MacGavran.

Hermanos Indocumentados

The migratory cycle had several features. Some braceros adhered to the strict letter of the law, returning home after the expiration of their contract (often at the end of harvest season), to await the following year's trip. Others chose to stay on in the United States after their contracts expired. Still others sent for, or returned to gather, their families to immigrate (legally and illegally) to the United States. Apostolics fell into all three categories. Some wiggled between categories.

In the case of braceros who arrived already converted from Mexico, one's status could lapse into "illegality" with the termination of the original bracero contract. The sanctions of the 1952 law notwithstanding, pressure to return home was seldom—if ever—applied by coreligionists. Indeed, in the case of lapsed braceros who quickly found alternative, albeit "illegal," employment, it behooved a pastor to retain such resolute wage earners—and tithers.

As more Apostolics slipped into "wetback" status, their percentage of the membership of the Apostolic Assembly increased significantly, up to 15–20 percent in the period from the mid-1950s to the early 1960s by one estimate.[62] (The percentage would have been higher, of course, in rural congregations.) As deportation pressures mounted in the period leading up to Operation Wetback, the churches again provided anonymity and protection from officialdom's capricious hand. They also effectively filled the social and emotive needs noted by sociologist Julian Samora:

> In a real sense the wetback lives "'half a life'"—never a participating part of the community or society (he can't vote, for example); always in a strange culture; seldom integrated into the life of the community; with little opportunity for roots and permanence, for example, marriage and establishing a family; and always living with the fear of being apprehended. Any individual with whom he is in contact can turn him in. Buying on credit, cashing checks at banks, *attending church*, any everyday normal activity is fraught with danger.[63] (emphasis mine)

Life in the legal shadows could be dark, indeed. Yet we are hard-pressed to find instances of disclosure to immigration authorities by Apostolic clergy and laity of the presence of so many undocumented immigrants within these easily identifiable communities. Conversely, the examples of sheltering, employing, feeding, and transporting of "illegal aliens" are legendary. During a period of frequent immigration raids, presiding bishop Benjamín Cantú reassured anxious members of his flock with a paraphrase of Jacob's epiphanal declaration: "This is not an immigration office; it's the house of God and the gateway to Heaven!"[64]

Against the backdrop of criminalizing official and media discourses concerning "wetbacks" and "illegals," compositions such as "La Biblia Es la Bandera" (The Bible Is the Banner), by Puerto Rican Pentecostal composer Juan Concepción, acquired a multivalent resonance. Juan Concepción, pioneer Juan Lugo's musical collaborator, penned his hearty *vals* in the midst of the Puerto Rican colonial and diasporic experience. Apostolic migration circuits carried the song southward by midcentury; it appeared in the hymnals of Mexican and Nicaraguan Apostolic churches.[65] The mobile composition never entered the canon of mainline hymnody, however. Its exclusion mirrors others: among these, the dismissal of Pentecostal congregations as sites of political empowerment and prophetic articulation. Yet the song strikes a dissonant note against a blind loyalty to the nation-state and its symbols. First, note the reworking of patently *norteamericano* symbols (a Mexican or Central American composer would not have employed stars and stripes). Concepción's second verse reinscribes supranational meanings on familiar patriotic elements; the metaphorical subversion is akin to the process by which slave spirituals acquired a double meaning on the eve of Emancipation. The third verse heralds a moment of universal reunion beyond terrestrial boundaries. Patriotism represents, thus, not only the last refuge of scoundrels but also an idolatrous impediment to God's universal design for humankind. In the charged context of Operation Wetback and similar episodes, noncitizens belted out the chorus's declaration of celestial and, hence, terrestrial dignity, all the while keeping an eye cocked for light-green *migra* vans. Viewed (and heard) in the social context of its performance, the song declares a view of the human condition that does not necessarily square with that held by elites and officialdom. Constrained by "bowels of compassion," borderlands Apostolics opted for solidarity and held at bay the patriotic civil religion engulfing Cold War–obsessed U.S. Evangelicals at midcentury.

1. The Bible is the banner of the celestial land
Its stripes, its stars speak to us of [his] love
City of the redeemed, refuge where my Christ
Purchased with his blood, expiation's price

[Chorus] I am a citizen of that eternal city
By faith I've been redeemed and am today a citizen
Christ is the governor of that glorious land
Whose floating banner announces redemption

2. The sixty and six stars upon the banner
Represent the books that in it you will find
Its stripes, which are twelve, its tribes represent
And the mast from which it waves the Paschal Lamb

3. From every people, race, tribe and tongue
A homeland shall be formed in the celestial Zion
And gathered together there under that banner
We will sing the glories of peace and redemption

Apostolics never recognized their activity as civil disobedience per se; they also lacked a social doctrine. Their practice was simply a matter of fidelity to a higher law of hospitality and to a vocation of solidarity in an imagined religious ethnoscape. To be sure, they could not ignore an increasingly vexed borderline and the impinging power of political and economic elites. Rather, in their tactical response to exclusionary legislation and enforcement, they heeded the ancient dictum that in the relationship between the law and humanity (e.g., Sabbath prohibitions), the former should serve the latter and not the reverse.

Migrant Empowerment

As rituals of welcome developed (including hymnodic elements), most congregations deemed the requisite letter of recommendation from the congregation of origin sufficient to confer full membership status with attendant rights and duties. This epistolary economy acquired greater importance in the absence of other social capital. The following information is drawn chiefly from a data set of letters of recommendation for sixty-three individuals and families, dated from June 1952 to June 1965, and addressed to the Apostolic Assembly church in Solana Beach/Del Mar, California, one of three original congregations in the San Diego–Tijuana region (Solana Beach/Del Mar and Tijuana were daughter congregations of the Otay/San Diego church) and a transit and destination point in the migratory flow.[66]

Over half (thirty-three) of the letters originated in Iglesia Apostólica churches in Mexico; twenty-eight of these originated in congregations in northern border cities, principally Tijuana (twenty-four). The remaining letters also frequently reflected migrant and bracero movement within the United States. Many pastors inserted into a space left blank for such purposes the reason for a member's travel, for example, "to seek a contract" (*con el fin de contratarse*) or "to work materially" (*con el fin de trabajar en lo material*). In most cases (about three out of four), the addressee was a particular pastor; in others involving stays at border contracting stations, the letters were addressed to "whom it may concern" (*A Quien Corresponda*). The most standard forms used Iglesia Apostólica letterhead, printed expressly for this purpose. Others were written on local church letterhead, while still others were written by hand. Later printed forms added allusions to customs of biblical hospitality: "I beg you to receive my recommendee as is the custom among us ('Do not forget to practice hospitality, for thus, some have entertained angels unaware. Hebrews 13:2'), that you extend him/her the right hand of fellowship, and that you help him/her with counsel and with the *orientation* that may be necessary" (emphasis mine).[67]

The ritual reading of a letter of recommendation in the congregation's hearing—and the expected public salutation by the individual—transformed the otherwise ordinary document into an empowering credential. Thus, an immigrant held in low esteem (and meagerly compensated) by a capitalist society during the day (or on the graveyard shift) regained a large measure of self-esteem when gathered with spiritual kin for spiritual fellowship and bread breaking. Newcomers were often entrusted with the congregation's various offices and projects; after careful monitoring, some congregants even entrusted their daughters or sons in marriage to the newcomers. When necessary, the band of pilgrims provided anonymity from the official surveillance described by Julian Samora.

The letters also provided a mechanism for accountability. Receiving congregations and pastors expected the documents; and often, a returning recommendee's dates of residency and behavior (including faithful tithe giving) were noted by a host pastor in short, handwritten notes on the reverse side of the original letter of recommendation. Writing (November 9, 1959) on behalf of newly baptized (October 28, 1959) bracero Teodoro Juárez, for example, Solana Beach pastor Jesús Rosas (himself a converted bracero-turned-pastor) assured "all the saints" in the Mexico City congregation that his recommendee now "militates as a faithful soldier in the ranks of Christ." Mexico City pastor R. Mendoza's handwritten reply (January 17, 1960), on the margins of the original letter, noted Juárez's faithful attendance up until the day of his departure, "to fill out the terms of his *bracero* contract," as well as the "greetings he carries from us to you, with the supplication of your prayers for our firmness in the faith."[68] Two years earlier, the Solana Beach church received novice deacon Samuel Avalos from Tijuana; in the letter, sending pastor Miguel Venegas noted Avalos's plans to "reside in that place."[69] Avalos's subsequent successful construction career (he was mentored by Solana Beach laymen Eliseo and Luis Ramírez) brought full circle the saga of repatriado Francisco Avalos, Samuel's father.

From Lament to Dance

Pentecostal congregations served, then, as migration trampolines and alternate transnational public squares, erected in the face and wake of xenophobia. They also represented exciting sonic spheres. Migrants who were perennially silenced in (and hounded out of) the U.S. public square filled these alternative squares with sound: testimony, song, and tongues. The sonic sphere expanded with each traveling body and voice. From the beginning, the several hymnal compilation projects gathered up compositions by lay and clerical repatriates, who not only ferried music south of the border but also sent back creations of their own (Fidel García, the Avalos family's rail companion and mentor, is credited with five published compositions).

The unpublished repatriate repertoire was much broader than this. We may also expand the list to include the final compositions by Marcial de La Cruz. Additionally, this analysis must take into account the prolific creativity of the repatriates' spiritual progeny, for example, the eleven published compositions of Maclovio, Miguel, Juana, and Manuel Gaxiola. Maclovio Gaxiola's "Iré si El Va Conmigo" (I Will Go if He Goes with Me) quickly won the hearts of listeners after its debut in convention and congregational settings in Baja and southern California. It was quickly compiled in the Apostolic Assembly's *Consolación* hymnal. It arrived in time to sail along sea routes to the Pacific theater of World War II. [70]

The repatriate repertoire could encompass also the adult compositions of songwriters expelled during childhood, such as U.S.-born Efraím Valverde (over 100 hymns) and Marcelo and Luis Pacheco. Valverde's "Agradecimiento" (Thanksgiving), "Indeleble" (Indelible), and "Decídete" (Decide), in particular, garnered—and still enjoy—wide hemispheric popularity among evangélicos generally. The most striking example of migrating Apostolic music, however, can be seen in the extraordinary story of three young U.S.-born repatriados, Román, Rosario, and Juan Alvarado. The guitar-strumming trio, whose musical career spanned three decades (1950s through 1970s), could stand in as a template for the broader story under discussion, as well as for general twentieth-century Mexican American history.

TABLE 2 Published Repatriado Hymn Compositions

Author	Title	English Translation
Francisco Avalos	Profecía de Jesús	Prophecy of Jesus
Felipe Coronado	Venid a Mí Todos	Come All to Me
Fidel García	Dios al Mundo Amó	God Loved the World
	El Tiempo Está Cerca	The Time Is Near
	Triste en el Huerto	Sad in the Garden
	Somos Soldados de Jesús	We Are Soldiers of Jesus
	Velad y Orad	Watch and Pray
José Ortega	Indefensa Mi Alma te Implora	Defenseless, My Soul Begs You
	Los Caminos de Dios	The Pathways of God
	Hoy Descanso en Jesús	I Rest Today in Jesus
	Divinidad Plena de Jesús	Full Divinity of Jesus
Luis Pacheco	Hay Una Senda	There Is a Path
Reyes Ruelas	Ya No Te Detengas	Detain Yourself No Longer
	Oh, Cuanto Gozo Hay en Mi Alma	Oh, What Joy in My Soul
Gil Valencia	Lucha por Cristo	Fight for Jesus
	Con Amor y Paz que Me De	With Love and Peace He Gives Me
Refugio Varela	El Jefe Celestial	The Celestial Chief
	Verdad Que Cristo Muy Bueno Es	Truly How Good Christ Is
	¿Que Cuenta Le Iremos a Dar?	What Account Shall We Give?

Uprooted Musics: Los Hermanos Alvarado

Pascual and Dolores Alvarado emigrated from northern Mexico early in that country's decade-long revolution. Pascual had fought on the side of Francisco "Pancho" Villa and then Venustiano Carranza. The couple's seven children were born in Texas, Arizona, and California. The parents and maternal grandparents were among the first generation of Apostolic converts in Bakersfield, California. Thus, a tight-knit, sectarian Pentecostal community provided the religious formation for the Alvarado children.[71]

In 1931 or 1932, in spite of her children's U.S. citizenship, Dolores was denied reentry at Ciudad Juárez after a personal trip to Zacatecas. In order to keep the family intact, Pascual forfeited his residency and took their children to Mexico to join their mother. After arriving by rail to Torreón, Coahuila, they slowly made their way, following the railway northward, back to the border. Pascual took welding jobs and Dolores sold tortillas to underwrite the long trek. The trauma of deportation and separation affected her health. An infant son, Juan, was kept alive by the milk of a donated goat. Adolescent daughters Luz and Guadalupe did not survive the stressful experience, dying from malnourishment soon after their arrival in Ciudad Juárez, a stone's throw away from the country of their birth. Upon arrival in Juárez, the family set about two tasks: securing housing and a livelihood and reconnecting with the Apostolic church. A small ranch outside the city limits met the first need. The second was met by fellow repatriates, such as pastor Felipe Coronado. Thus, the transborder networks set in place through the preceding decade by Apostolic leaders and laity served to keep the Alvarado and many other families connected during a period of anomic dislocation.

As they entered their teen years, the Alvarado sons took up guitar playing, soon becoming proficient. As with African American gospel and blues musicians, the venue for performance and the choice of musical genre presented sites of struggle for the artists' souls. Elder brother Román decided early on to dedicate his talents "to the Lord," while Rosario and Juan opted to play in cantinas. When pressed by Román, the two prodigals would agree to accompany him in performance in religious services. The trio's virtuosity soon won them a following in the Apostolic churches of the area. The brothers experienced a hint of things to come when they were invited to perform on a local radio station. Within a few years, Rosario unequivocally joined Román and the church, leaving behind, in classic conversion mode, a womanizing and drinking past. Juan flitted back and forth between sacred and profane venues, waiting two decades to convert. After his conversion, Rosario exchanged his small *requinto* guitar for Román's larger, standard one, reasoning that the move to the simpler strumming instrument would help Rosario resist the tempting cantina memories evoked by the requinto's fancy riffs.

After nearly two decades in Ciudad Juárez, the Alvarado family made their way back to Los Angeles, California. The move exposed the broth-

Hermanos Alvarado LP record cover, 1959.

ers' musical talents to ever-widening evangélico circles, a development that discomfited Apostolic Assembly leadership. A fortuitous encounter with Dale Evans and Laura Harper, wives of famous Hollywood musical cowboys, propelled and broadened the Alvarados' trajectory in ways the singers had never imagined. A 1959 episode bears recounting here.

After assisting two Anglo women (Harper and Evans) with their shopping bags at a downtown market, Pascual Alvarado agreed to accompany them to Hollywood Hills to repeat the favor. While standing in their driveway, he heard music drifting from a rear window (probably played by the Sons of the Pioneers). Pascual boasted to Harper that his sons could sing much better. Intrigued, she took him up on his claim. After an audition, the trio was invited to record in a state-of-the-art studio built by the Hollywood Christian Group. The resulting multiple-volume LP project, managed by Harper, ushered in a long period of expanding fame for the *Hermanos Alvarado* as the hemisphere's mostly widely heard evangélico musical group. Their prominence lasted well after their disbanding in 1973.[72]

While outsider savvy and capital may have provided important impetus to the Alvarados' career, *gringa* imagination and gaze also crippled them at home. Harper's decision to photograph the tejano singers in *jarocho* folk costume (from Veracruz) for the LP covers confirmed their coreligionists' suspicions that the group had become too "*mundano*" (worldly). Yet, as sectarian Apostolic doors closed, others opened, beginning with those of the Concilio Latinoamericano de Iglesias Cristianas (CLADIC), which Román and Juan eventually joined. Thus, sectarian Apostolic leaders unwittingly pushed their movement's music—which already enjoyed great overlap with other confessional repertoires—into even wider spheres. There, the music flourished. And there its provenance became increasingly obscure.

A review of the Alavarado's' discography demonstrates that the core of their music consisted of Apostolic standards of their childhood and youth. Indeed, Román, a prolific composer in his own right, recollected that, no matter the venue, the trio performed "puros cantos apostólicos" (only Apostolic songs), to the delight of non-Apostolic audiences.

Forty-five of the project's fifty-six songs, or eight out of ten, represented Apostolic compositions; approximately twenty-seven of these were authored by Román Alvarado. The LPs also included two original compositions by Guatemalan Alfredo Colom and one each by CLADIC pioneers Eduardo Rodríguez and Refugio Estrada. Only eight of the hymns represented translations, albeit popular ones. While the musical genre remained unquestionably Mexican, the trio's decision to flatten their guitar technique foregrounded the compelling textual content of the songs. Rosario's turn toward simplicity—away from virtuoso riffs—set the mood and aimed the often melancholy lyrics directly to hearts and ears primed for a feeling of melancholic resoluteness. Except for Colom's "Pero Queda Cristo" (But Christ Remains), the first album offered only Apostolic compositions, including repatriate pastor Fidel García's "El Tiempo Está Cerca" (Chapter 3's epigraph and the third track on the first volume).

The appeal of the Alvarados' music in that era seems to have been matched only by that of Alfredo Colom, whose compositions were broadcast through HCJB, the Voice of the Andes, a powerful World Missionary Radio Fellowship station in Quito, Ecuador.[73] The broad dissemination of the Alvarados' music occurred by means of the LP project, several tours sponsored by Harper's organization, and vigorous evangelistic appropriation. In one example recollected by Rosario and confirmed by other sources, Assemblies of God missionary pilot Michael Hines played the Alvarados' music while circling and preaching over distant mountain villages in southern Mexico and Central America.[74] Myriad pirating projects (which persist to this day), and innumerable migrant trajectories, international and domestic, also carried the music far and wide.

That the musical influence of these tejano troubadours extended for long distances is borne out by cursory surveys of YouTube tributes to the Hermanos Alvarado from (now senior) trios in the Andes and elsewhere and by my research in Oaxaca.[75] A veteran Nazarene pastor in that southern Mexican state credited three factors with keeping an earlier generation of evangélicos in southern Mexico "*fiel*" (faithful) in the face of great intolerance in the 1950s and 1960s: *la Biblia* (the Bible), *la oración* (prayer), and "*la música de los Hermanos Alvarado*" (the music of the Alvarado Brothers).[76] In a related vein, convert Imelda Yescas's playing of the Alvarados' rendition of Nellie Rangel's "Responsable," the first cut on their first LP record, over a public address system in her home village of San Juan Yaée, Oaxaca, set off a two-decade chain of events, starting with the formation of the town's first evangélico congregation and finally culminating in the expulsion of over fifty of that Zapoteco mountain community's residents and the destruction of the Apostolic temple in 1996. The community's defense of traditional folkways ("usos y costumbres") and Yescas's dogged claim to constitutional freedoms made the case a cause célèbre in the state and national press. Lost in the reportage, of course, was the catalytic imprint left by the tejano troubadours' long-ago recording of a Chicana Pentecostal composer's song and their rendering of its chorus's opening line's soteriological challenge: "Tú serás responsable de tu alma si hasta hoy no le das tu corazón" (You shall be responsible for your soul if by today you have not given Him your heart). To this day, the Apostolics of San Juan Yaée are referred to by villagers as "los hermanos responsables."[77]

The Hermanos Alvarado never visited Oaxaca, but their music certainly arrived early on, possibly in the luggage of returning braceros, including indigenous Summer Institute of Linguistics converts, or with migrants caught up in *migra* raids, or through converts returning from domestic service jobs in Mexico City.[78] The music of the Hermanos Alvarado, whose familial story epitomized the repatriado and Chicano experience of the midcentury, resonated within a deep cultural and emotive matrix shared by many Latinos and Latin Americans on the move. The bodies moved by emotion also simply moved. With this in mind, we can understand the impact of forced and voluntary movement—linear, cyclical, and circuitous—on Pentecostal musical culture. Lyrically, one-third of original Apostolic hymns reflect these traveling-sojourning motifs, which are then reinforced by the choice of musical genre (*balada, corrido, polka, ranchera,* etc.) and performance conventions.

Subaltern Resilience

The period that began with xenophobic exclusion and anomic confusion concluded with unexpected growth and coherence. The response by subaltern Pentecostals to political and religious marginalization in the early to mid-twentieth century remains an understudied topic for historical and social scientific inquiry. The data clearly press for a rethinking of decades-old notions of societal disengagement, as well as a historicizing of contemporary studies of social and political engagement. The case of repatriated Pentecostals, their converts and coreligionists busily occupied in the interstices between nation-states and hegemonic cultures, helps to fill historical gaps and contest received paradigms; in short, it challenges us to rethink ahistorical and acultural approaches to Pentecostalism and politics (praxis). In order to flesh out these dimensions and before turning to the full musical repertoire of early Latino Pentecostalism, let us consider how the dense periodical record provides glimpses of a vigorous migrating faith.

CHAPTER 5
The Texture of Transnational Apostolicism

Cada cristiano que ama	Every Christian who loves
A su hermano de corazón	his brother from his heart
No ve fronteras, va por	Does not see borders, and goes
La tierra sembrando amor	through the land sowing love
Bienvenidos, seáis hermanos	Be welcomed, Brethren,
En el nombre de Cristo Jesús	in the name of Jesus Christ
Hoy reunidos nos gozamos	We gather today, rejoicing,
Al saber que nos une su amor	united by his love
Bienvenidos, bienvenidos	Welcome, welcome,
En el nombre de Cristo Jesús	in the name of Jesus Christ
Porque sólo Jesús nos da vida	For only Jesus gives us life and
y salud	health [salvation]
Y la gloria al que lleva su cruz	And glory for carrying his cross

As they gathered for conclaves and fellowship, Pentecostals, in their in-imitable fashion, marked such special moments of spiritual and social encounter with music. This was continuous with established Protestant practice. The meticulous record of Mexican Methodist annual conferences is replete with the doxologies and other anthems, along with the formal salutations, that graced such gatherings. But note the new emphases in an emerging hymnody that pulsed in the hearts of a politically disenfranchised and socially subordinated people. "Bienvenidos Seáis, Hermanos" declared that a love-compelled evangelism minimized—*no ve fronteras*—the nation-state's policing prerogatives. This is understandable, in light of the Apostolic repatriado and bracero experience. Also notable is the song's change in rhythm. The graceful 6/8 rhythm of the verses segues quickly into the chorus's bracing 2/4 clip, isolating each verse and chorus of the song for renewed collective singing and focus on the lyrics.[1] The rhythmic segmentation compelled hearers' close attention.

The corpus of welcoming music (to conclaves, to membership, to conversion, etc.) offered migrating bodies rare opportunities to embrace other bodies, hearts, and minds (and to be embraced). The practice of hospitality transformed often heartless and indifferent landscapes into warm soundscapes, familiar ethnoscapes, and invigorating sacroscapes (to borrow Thomas Tweed's notion of religion's imprint on people, places, and social arenas[2]). Our view of these is informed by the texts (periodicals, hymns, and other literature) produced by the Apostolic movement in the mid-twentieth century. Our analysis must be tempered, though, with a critical assessment of intrasubaltern conflict, including tensions between Mexican and Mexican American leaders. This chapter will offer a brief excursus on the "love of many waxing cold" in the period after pioneers relinquished the helm to younger hands. It will conclude with a reading against the grain of mainline Protestant and Catholic appraisals of Pentecostal subterfuge.

Transnational Religious Life: The View from Mexico

Along with the chartering treaty and constitution, the denominations also began to publish official organs, the *Exégeta Apostólico* (first issue, November 1943) in the case of the Iglesia[3] and *La Nube y el Fuego en el Desierto* in the case of the Assembly (circa 1937; note the persistence of the Exodus metaphor). The Assembly's organ was soon rechristened *El Heraldo Apostólico*.

The churches also continued their ambitious hymnal projects. The Assembly's *Consolación* predated the Iglesia's *Himnos de Suprema Alabanza* (1940) by almost a decade. The delegates at the 1934 Iglesia conclave in Torreón sang from the Assembly's *Himnos de Consolación* hymnal.[4] It is noteworthy that the Assembly's hymnal project predated its periodical one by a decade. This underscores the centrality of music for this religious tradition. The hymnals were later often published jointly (by Maclovio Gaxiola, in Mexico City) and even later shared joint copyright permission for each church to publish its hymnal with songs from the counterpart.[5]

The several publications enhanced Apostolicism's mobility and reach. Both the post and luggage carried these religious remittances to places well beyond the reach of ministers and missionaries. Manuel Gaxiola offered the following recollection of the connectional and evangelistic function of the *Exégeta* during the late 1940s:

> For me, my work with *El Exégeta* was like feeling the pulse of the church. I was in touch with pastors and laypersons, men and women some of whom are still alive. The *Exégeta* began to arrive in mysterious ways to people who established contact with the Apostolic

Church. The case I remember with the most satisfaction is that of Bro. Heliodoro Quintero Meza. A copy of the *Exégeta* that somebody sent him arrived to his town perched in the sierra of Jalisco. He read it with great interest, and wrote us ordering a subscription which he renewed for several years; with time he converted to the Gospel.[6]

In a similar vein, Gaxiola also noted that the circulating copies (in Mexico) of the Apostolic Assembly's *La Nube y el Fuego en el Desierto* and *Consolación* hymnal provoked his curiosity about the Iglesia's sister church in the United States.[7]

The periodicals' arrival to unexpected places also helped to usher in the churches' expansion first into Central America and then the Southern Cone. In this latter zone, the unexpected arrival of the *Exégeta* surprised exiled Russian and Polish Apostolics with the realization that their diasporic isolation was over (they were unaware of Spanish-speaking Apostolicism). They welcomed Maclovio Gaxiola's exploratory visit in 1952. This connection prompted the transfer of missionary Leonardo Sepulveda from Nicaragua to Uruguay in 1953. Notably, the South American node translated and sent the *Exégeta* on to homeland pockets in Russia, Poland, and Germany, which then precipitated the arrival to Mexico City of inscrutable letters in Russian and Polish. The circulating religious remittances served, of course, to leverage and intensify the growing interest in foreign missions among Mexican and Mexican American Apostolics.[8]

Editorial notes to readers offer a glimpse of the numerical and geographic circulation of periodicals and other literature. The *Exégeta*'s November 1945 issue announced a circulation goal of 5,000 copies. The following month, the organ reported a monthly circulation of 4,000 and a cumulative one of 75,000 in the first nineteen issues. The August 1957 issue blamed financial difficulties (a perennial complaint) for a reduction in monthly circulation from 3,000 to 2,500 copies. The December issue of that same year revived the circulation goal of 5,000. These numbers can be multiplied several times, of course, to take into account the several readers in a household, congregation, or community. The June 1967 circulation report on the Iglesia's Sunday school quarterly, *El Expositor Bíblico Cristiano*, shows clearly the churches' joint reliance on pedagogical and devotional literature: 8,300 in Mexico and 5,700 in the United States (during the first decade, the *Expositor* was carried as a section of the *Exégeta*).[9]

The View from Mexico

Taking a cue from Andrew Chesnut's study of Pentecostal periodicals in Brazil, this chapter will sift through the Iglesia Apostólica's *Exégeta* periodical. However, in contrast to Chesnut, we will look beyond reports of healing, conversion, and tongues speaking—the usual data for the study of Pentecostal discourse. In other words, as with the repatriado life stories, I propose to read the data against a different, contextual background of migration, borderlands, and quotidian proletarian labor, the things taken for granted.

After a discussion of the beginning period of the periodical, an analysis of an eleven-year run will take us up through a period that encompassed important leadership transitions, namely, in the case of the Apostolic Assembly, the Benjamín Cantú presidency (1950–1963), Antonio Nava's resumption of that office (1963–1966), the golden jubilee year (1966) of the denomination,[10] and Efraím Valverde's inaugural year as president (1967), and, in the case of the Iglesia Apostólica, Felipe Rivas's penultimate and final presidential terms (1954–1958, 1962–1966) and Maclovio Gaxiola's first and second ones (1958–1962, 1966–1970). Externally, of course, national events and developments proceeded apace. Particularly pertinent to Apostolics were the final years of the Bracero program (1957–1964) and the Immigration Reform of 1965 (allowing family reunification and lifting Western Hemisphere restrictions).

Iglesias Hermanas/Sister Churches

The first two years' run of the *Exégeta* (November 1943 to December 1945) reveal a clear transnational optic. The Iglesia's sister Apostolic Assembly received forty-seven mentions in the first nineteen issues, or an average rate of 2.47 mentions per issue. (Often, the mention consisted of an entire article.) The low mention rate (six instances, or a 0.315 rate) of braceros is not surprising, given the newness of the program; the first trainload of guest workers arrived to Stockton, California, in late September 1942.[11] However, if we fold in the twelve mentions of World War II (generally about U.S. Apostolic soldiers) and the twenty concerning repatriado ministers busily at work in the Iglesia, the total (eighty-five) amount to an average rate of direct and indirect mentions of the sister church of 4.58 per issue. (Of course, the mention of the by-now-senior ministers would not have referenced their prior repatriation, as this had receded into the movement's consciousness.)

Out of thirty-four *Exégeta* issues examined in the later period,[12] most mentioned events or issues involving the U.S. Apostolic Assembly or that denomination's leaders, clergy, and members. The ninety-four instances of this pattern yield an average of almost three references per issue, though some issues contained no mention of the Assembly. The greatest number of these (thirty) consisted of notices or announcements concerning national or regional conventions, conferences, and services. Temple dedications, anniversaries, and building projects represented the second highest group (thirteen), reflecting the continued interest and contribution of Apostolics north of the border to the movement's developing infrastructure south of the border. Reports on official summits, retreats, business sessions, and elections involving the two church hierarchies garnered the third highest number (nine), just above that of reports and testimonials concerning conversions among or wrought by returned migrants and repatriates (eight). Reports of personnel and pastoral changes (some cross-border)[13] and deaths in the United States and of progress in the churches' joint missionary programs kept *Exégeta* readers (many of them U.S. based) apprised of developments outside of Mexico and the United States. These, together with announcements about available pedagogical and hymnal materials, represented the remaining categories. Fifteen articles mentioned migratory experience, in concert with the Apostolic Assembly, and often in terms of proselytism.

Borderlands Fellowship

The *Exégeta*'s report on the Baja California district's eleventh convention in late 1956 credited the presence and participation of numerous "brethren from California" with the gathering's success. The 3,000 attendees represented sixty congregations, ranging from Cabo San Lucas at the southern tip of the peninsula to Tijuana, as well as attendees from the United States. The California visitors, led by Assembly president Benjamín Cantú, graced the meetings with music and preaching. The report took special note of the food and hospitality:

> We had the visit of many brethren from California, U.S., who helped with the orchestra and the program of special songs. Our brother

Benjamin Cantú, Presiding Bishop, attended in representation of the Apostolic Assembly of the U.S.A.; he preached on Saturday night, and brought a glorious message of spiritual revival. Several ministers of the Assembly came with him, for which we are very honored and satisfied. The churches from all the state and the southern part of the territory enthusiastically participated in committees for the kitchen and serving tables, and in offerings for the costs of the convention.[14]

Baja California Apostolics surely still savored their memories of the Apostolic Assembly's 1954 General Convention at the Del Mar, California, fairgrounds. The host congregation of neighboring Solana Beach, in addition to organizing kitchen brigades, also charged a hospitality committee with scouring the highway south toward the border for convention-bound pilgrims in distress. One hospitality organizer remembered discreetly waving cross-border visitors through the dining line if they informed him that they could not afford the fifty-cent ticket for meal service (the ticket served for the length of the convention).[15]

Periodic *cultos internacionales* (international services) in the border-zone regions served as occasions for affirming cross-border ties. In late 1957, the *Exégeta* reported on three such events held that year in three regions: Tijuana–Otay, Juárez–El Paso–Las Cruces, and Tamaulipas–Rio Grande Valley. The periodical emphasized the purpose of these meetings and featured a picture of the Las Cruces meeting on the cover page of its October issue:

> Since 1953 Services of International Fellowship have been celebrated in the City of Tijuana, B.C., with the goal of cultivating more closely our Christian fellowship in the ties of God's love which unite us with the brethren who live in the United States. Maclovio Gaxiola preached (Romans 12:1–2 and John 13:34) on the necessity of fulfilling the Lords' commandment, when He said, "A new commandment I give you; that you love one another."[16]

Equally as important for the Tijuana meeting that year was the active participation of the Assembly's *Dorcas* leaders. Isabel Ramírez, national president of the Iglesia's women's auxiliary, offered a detailed report of her meetings with her U.S. counterparts.[17] The following month the magazine reported on the third Confraternidad Internacional for the Chihuahua–western Texas–New Mexico–Colorado region, held in Las Cruces, New

Mexico, on September 21, 1957, and presided over by Assembly president Benjamín Cantú and Iglesia secretary general José Ortega:

> The results of these meetings have been very positive, principally in the forging of ties of friendship, brotherhood and spiritual communion which unite the churches of the Lord in both countries. And as proof of that the attendance of ministers, auxiliary members, and members of the church in general increased.
>
> During the evening, in the closing service, after the several special songs and words from some ministers, the most notable act was the exchange of the flags of Mexico and the United States between our brothers José Ortega and Benjamin Cantú, with meaningful and laudatory words directed to each country, desirous that each other could serve the same God and Christ and saving, through the message of the Gospel, souls for a *better homeland*. Together with this act, the hymn "My Mexico" and finally the hymn "Firmes y Adelante" [Resolute and Forward, or " Onward, Christian Soldiers"] were sung.[18] (emphasis mine)

The article also noted that the gathering's reception, logistics, and program committees were led by a cross-border pastoral team.[19] Importantly, the photograph of Cantú and Ortega exchanging their respective nations' flags behind the pulpit at the Las Cruces celebration passed into the Assembly's documentary record, achieving near iconic status and exemplifying the movement's binational solidarity. In its December issue, the *Exégeta* informed readers of the *Culto de Confraternidad* celebrated on October 25 in Reynosa's (Tamaulipas) Second Church for the "ministers and faithful" of the region, the Rio Grande Valley, and the port city of Tampico.[20]

Pentecostal Pugilism

The *Exégeta*'s descriptions of temple dedications reveal a persistent practice of public music making in both countries and, in the Mexican context, of pugilistic music. The first instance of this appeared in Felipe Rivas's full-page report on the February 4, 1945, dedication of the San Luis Rio Colorado, Sonora, temple:

> A procession entered the temple. At the head the Superintendent of our Church in Mexico, Felipe C. Rivas, accompanied by the Elder of

the work of the Lord in the Peninsula of Baja California, Telésforo Lozano Martínez, followed by other Pastors and Workers of other categories, musicians, children, youth, and the rest of people of God. All singing with great joy the hymn that says: "'Christ is our Chieftain, He takes us into battle.'"[21]

Benjamín Cantú's "Cristo Es Nuestro Jefe," a translation of Carrie E. Breck's 1900 hymn, "Christ Our Mighty Captain" (music by Grant Colfax Tuller, also titled "Forward!"),[22] summoned the faithful to spiritual battle, framing that call with bracing martial music. Other reports of temple dedications and groundbreaking ceremonies in Mexico that included this musical detail in the later *Exégeta* period were offered for Estación Tecolotes, Sonora (January 12, 1957); Ejido Monte Marqueño, near Ojinaga, Chihuahua (February 23, 1957); Villa Aldama, Chihuahua (month unavailable, 1957); Tijuana's Fifth Church (June 23, 1957); Mazatlán, Sinaloa (month unavailable, early 1958); La Dulce Grande, San Luis Potosí (June 8, 1958); and National City, California (March 1966). All the *Exégeta* reports cited the song's number (192) in the Assembly's *Consolación* hymnal, a clear indication of a shared musical repertoire.[23] The song was often coupled with the more solemn but equally martial "Firmes y Adelante" ("Firm and Forward," Spanish reformer Juan Cabrera's translation of "Onward Christian Soldiers").[24] Set against the backdrop of residual intolerance, Cantú's anthem planted a provocative emblem on Catholic turf. This oppositional valence would have been absent, of course, from the English-language original and in the more pluralistic setting of the United States. By dropping Breck's verse about struggle against Satan, Cantú could point to a more general antagonist (hegemonic Catholicism). Also, his two original verses stamped Breck's song with a Oneness imprint.[25]

Pentecostals were not boxing against shadows. Mexico City archbishop Luis Martínez's "Cruzada en Defensa de la Fe Católica," launched as part of the golden anniversary of the coronation of the Virgen de Guadalupe as Patroness of the Americas (1944–1945), culminated a series of bishops' pastoral letters warning about foreign beliefs that were "stealing from Mexicans their dearest treasure, the Catholic faith, which the Very Holy Virgin of Guadalupe brought us four centuries ago." The discursive attacks, together with violent ones across the country, prompted Iglesia de Dios en la República Mexicana leader David Ruesga and other leaders (including Masons) to form the Comité Nacional Evangélico de Defensa in 1948.[26] The Iglesia Apostólica welcomed fellow evangélicos to the field it had already occupied. Every issue of the first two-year run (November 1943 to December 1945) of the *Exégeta* either ran a denunciation of religious intolerance ("clerical terrorism"), a critique of Catholic doctrine, or a report of converted catechists and priests. In its July 1944 issue, the *Exégeta* began a series on the conversion of José L. Sánchez, a priest from the Puebla archdiocese. Sánchez's spellbinding account of defection and evasion of pressure from the Caballeros de Colón (Knights of Columbus) and Catholic Action youth groups drew audiences beyond the Iglesia. In October 1944, Sánchez accompanied Maclovio Gaxiola and other leaders by train to Torreón; the convention's (the one that ratified the treaty and constitution) night programs featured his widely advertised lectures.[27] The provocation came in the wake of an important Eucharistic congress held in June in the cathedral of neighboring Gómez Palacios. That gathering, "How to Prevent the Protestant Work from Growing in Mexico," sought to organize a local chapter of the apologetic Sociedad EVC. Engineer German Herrasti had founded the Sociedad EVC (El Verdardero Catolicismo—The True Catholicism) at the onset of the Cristero War with the blessing of Pope Pius XI and the support (and translated material) of similar European groups and apologetic publishers like the Pía Societá de S. Girolamo of Italy, Bloud et Cie. of France, and the Catholic Truth Society of London. The congress drew several prelates from northern Mexico, including Sonora bishop Juan Negrete. Durango archbishop José María González y Valencia dedicated the Congress to the memory of cristero martyrs. Thus, it was no surprise when the daily *Siglo de Torreón* ran a full two-page story, with graphics, on Durango cristero martyrs Mateo Correa and José de la Parra on the Sunday of the Iglesia's convention (and Sanchez's talks). As noted, several Apostolic Assembly delegates were present at the Iglesia's conclave, for the ratification vote of the unifying treaty and constitution.

Cristero sensibilities persisted in many corners of Mexico and could be provoked at great personal cost. The December 13, 1955, assassination of Guadalajara pastor Benito Peña near Coyutlán de la Barranca, Jalisco ("a martyr of the romanist fanatics"), and the August 3, 1958, one of Villa Hidalgo, Nayarit, pastor Marcos Flores were just two cases of several memorialized in the Iglesia's periodical. Although the latter's death was blamed on his incorruptible leadership of the El Tuchi ejido (he had resigned as pastor upon his election as president of the Comisario Ejidal in February of that year), the *Exégeta* nevertheless counted him as "another victim of the many martyrdoms for noble causes."[28] Pastor José Rodrí-

Christ Our Mighty Captain
(Carrie Breck)

1. Christ, our mighty captain, leads against the foe,
We will never falter when He bids us go;
Tho' His righteous purpose we may never know,
Yet we'll follow all the way.

[Chorus] Forward! forward! 'tis the Lord's command;
Forward! forward! to the promised land;
Forward! forward! let the chorus ring:
We are sure to win with Christ, our king!

2. Let our glorious banner ever be unfurled;
From its mighty stronghold evil shall be hurled;
Christ, our mighty captain, overcomes the world,
And we follow all the way.

3. Fierce the battle rages—but 'twill not be long,
Then triumphant, shall we join the blessed throng,
Joyfully uniting in the victor's song—
If we follow all the way.

4. Satan's fearful onslaughts cannot make us yield;
While we trust in Christ, our buckler and our shield;
Pressing ever on—the Spirit's sword we wield,
And we follow all the way.

guez's report from Mecatán, Nayarit, carried in the April 1963 *Exégeta*, described the return of that locality's Apostolics after a decade of mob-driven exile. Two local peddlers engineered the return of an Apostolic minister. The 1962 conversion of Mecatán's catechist, Patrocinia García, and others precipitated the parish priest's wrath and restoked antipathies:

> The message of salvation continued to be preached with enthusiasm and in March of 1962 the first seven persons were baptized. This grievously wounded the enemy, who mobilized his followers, who

Cristo Es Nuestro Jefe	Christ Is Our Chieftain
(Benjamín Cantú)	(My translation of Cantú lyrics)
Cristo es nuestro jefe; nos lleva a la lid	Christ is our chieftain; he brings us to battle
Y en su santo nombre siempre combatid	And in his holy name you must always fight
Por Su Santa causa debemos luchar	We must fight for his holy cause
Y le seguiremos fiel.	And we shall faithfully follow him.
Adelante! es órden del Señor	Forward! 'tis the Lord's command
Adelante! vamos sin temor	Forward! we go without fear
Adelante! canta ya su grey	Forward! let his host sing
La victoria es cierta con el Rey	Victory is sure with the King
Nuestro estandarte luce por doquier,	Our banner shines everywhere
Con poder y gloria siempre se ha de ver;	Always seen with power and glory;
Cristo nuestro jefe al mundo venció	Christ our chieftain overcame the world;
Y le seguiremos fiel.	And we shall faithfully follow him.
La preciosa lucha larga no será;	The costly struggle shall not be long;
Y a los vencedores nos congregá,	And he shall gather the victorious ones,
Donde cantaremos un himno triunfal;	Where we shall sing a triumphal hymn,
Si hoy le seguiremos fiel.	If we follow him faithfully
Nuestra es la victoria, Jesucristo es Dios	The victory is ours, Jesus Christ is God
Y en su santo nombre vamos sin temor	And in his holy name we go without fear
Nada nos arredre, vamos con valor;	Nothing drives us back, with valor we go
Todos vamos a vencer.	We shall all overcome
Somos bautizados en Cristo Jesús.	We are baptized in Christ Jesus.
Él nos ha salvado muriendo en la cruz;	He has saved us dying on the cross;
Él nos ha sellado con su Espiritú;	He has sealed us with his Spirit;
Y le seguiremos fiel.	And we shall faithfully follow him.

then determined to expel us. One night while we were in service we heard a battle hymn from the street below:

"MARY'S TROOPS, FOLLOW THE BANNER. NONE SHALL FAINT. WE GO TO WAR, WE GO TO WAR." ["Tropas de María." All caps from the original.]

And so it happened. The mob stopped in front of us and began to rant, shouting their demand that we leave the ranch immediately and threatening to remove us at any cost if we did not leave on our own. In response to their demands, we sang a hymn to God and then said a fervent prayer for them, and when we rose from praying, not a single one of them was left.[29]

Although Rodríguez did not include the title of the calming hymn sung by the twenty besieged Apostolics, its juxtaposition with a cristero anthem reminds us, once again, of how the sonic sphere remains imbricated with other ones. In a less dangerous setting, Mecatán's Apostolics could have deployed the *Suprema Alabanza* hymnal's more pugilistic "Carga sobre Roma," a litany that took a decidedly nonecumenical swipe at the majority religion:

A Charge against Rome

We preach the truth, we protest against wrong
We reject the doctrines of error
We cast off invention, which is mere tradition
That invalidates the Word of the Lord

Only Jesus Christ saves
Christ saves the sinner
There is no other Savior, nor other mediator
Only Christ saves and keeps the sinner

We cannot find that we should confess
Sins to a sinful man
He who comes to his God with sincere contrition
Will find that He forgives with love

We ask why they have removed from the law
The second commandment given by God
"A graven image you shall not make:
you shall not bow down to it"
"You shall serve and worship only your God"

We do not want Latin, but just the Gospel
The promises of the blessed Savior
Christ said: "Search the Word of Truth
And you shall find eternal life and salvation"

Poor humanity is exploited
By talk of a purgatory of terror
But we know that Jesus gave his blood on the cross
To cleanse the sinner from all stain

When and where did God say to adore
An image made of wood and metal?
When did He speak of [papal] bulls?
Decreed indulgences?
These cannot be found in the Bible

The musical reprise of Martin Luther's theses surely stiffened evangélico resolve. But even iconoclasm required discretion, especially in cristero
regions. In the 1969 edition of the *Suprema Alabanza* hymnal, the Iglesia
substituted the strident song (No. 192) with Apostolic Assembly leader
Lorenzo Salazar's "Exhortación de Josué," a fetching jazz interpretation of
Joshua's summons to the Hebrews contemplating entry into Canaan. The
softening coincided with Vatican II's recognition of "separated brethren,"
a term understood by Latin American prelates to apply chiefly to historic
Protestant churches and not to Pentecostal *sectas*.

Homecomings and Hospitality

The October 24, 1958, dedication of the new Torreón, Coahuila, temple,
timed to coincide with the Iglesia's twenty-second general convention
in that city, merited special attention in the *Exégeta*, as did the contributions for that construction project by churches and members in the United
States.[30] (Torreón still loomed as the "Jerusalem" of the Iglesia Apostólica.)
Such occasions provided opportunities to acknowledge distant benefactors. In June 1957, the magazine credited José Muñoz of Indio, California,
with contributions to the Villa Aldama temple construction project (the
town of the Iglesia's original "Upper Room").[31] The report on the April 19,
1959, temple dedication for Mexicali's First Church also noted the participation of choirs from Del Mar (Solana Beach) and Otay, California, as well
as the orator, Antonio Nava.[32]

As with any extended family or network, Mexican Apostolics took
great interest in reunions and updates. From the *Exégeta* reportage, it is
evident that temple dedications and anniversaries in northern Mexico
saw the frequent participation of Assembly preachers. Pablo C. García,
pastor in McCamey, Texas, preached at the Ejido Monte Marqueño dedication (February 23, 1957).[33] Juan Castillo, of Dallas, Texas, conducted a
healing campaign in concert with the seventh anniversary of the Ojinaga,
Chihuahua, temple dedication (August 20, 1957); the *Exégeta* reported the
successful healings of "hernias, tumors, the deaf, and the lame."[34] Three

days later, Weslaco, Texas, pastor Amador Carrillo served as the keynote preacher for the seventh anniversary of the temple dedication in Santa Apolonia, Tamaulipas. In October of that year, Pedro Pérez, of Hanover, New Mexico, joined the pastors of Ciudad Juárez's First, Second, and Third Iglesia churches (as well as Eladio Nava, Antonio's brother) in a caravan to the temple dedication in Asunción, Chihuahua:

> On October 26 of the present year, a new temple in Asunción, D.G., Chihuahua was dedicated to the work of the Lord.
>
> The President of the Church authorized the State Supervisor, Bro. Emeterio Reta, to undertake and preside over the act. The local civic authorities also gave the necessary permission to hold the fiesta without any impediment.
>
> A good group of brothers from Juarez city, especially the pastors of the first, second, and third churches (Manuel Esquivel, Jose Mireles, and Apolinar Lopez) attended the fiesta with great enthusiasm. Also in attendance was Bro. Pedro Perez from the church in Hanover, New Mexico, who took the brothers in his truck. Bro. Guillermo Lopez, Ricardo Pampa, Eladio Nava and Juan Valle rode in the other vehicle. All of them are Servants of the Lord.
>
> Bro. Aurelio Alvares, the local pastor, prepared the faithful to give the best reception to the visitors and to attend to them in everything, leaving all very satisfied. We had need of nothing, and there was abundant food.[35]

The tenth anniversary (August 26, 1958) of Ciudad Juárez's First Church's temple dedication saw the homecoming from Delano, California, of Filemón Zaragoza.[36] By this time, the U.S.-born, longtime Juárez resident had assumed the national presidency of the Apostolic Assembly's *Varones* men's auxiliary.[37] An "Hermano Aguirre," identified as one of the earliest members of the Apostolic Assembly (possibly Julian Aguirre Sr., of Stockton, California), accompanied Zaragoza and filmed the event. Two months earlier, the Juárez church had invited coreligionists from across the border to hear the debut of the Estudiantina Asaph. The string ensemble presented a long musical program—including some classical numbers—to great acclaim. The article noted the special musical participation and gifts of newly arrived (May 1958, from Solana Beach, California) El Paso pastor Roberto Ramírez.[38]

The invitations were not unidirectional. In August 1957, Iglesia officials joined their counterparts in officiating at the dedication of the new Apostolic Assembly temple in San Jose, California. The *Exégeta* noted that the construction project had already seen the encouraging visit by José Ortega.[39] Over a decade later, the April 1966 issue of the *Exégeta* carried Bishop Canuto García's invitation to "los hermanos en Mexico" to join the festivities in Weslaco, Texas, at the end of that month, celebrating the Texas district's fiftieth anniversary.[40] Clearly, the transnational networks set in place decades earlier and codified in the mid-1940s had endured and continued to sustain and connect the faithful.

Borderlands Healing and Evangelism

Borderlands Apostolics also relied on each other for healing and evangelism. The documentary evidence seconds Andrew Chesnut's findings concerning healing in early Brazilian Pentecostalism but also allows us to see this feature in the specific zone under study. The second issue of the *Exégeta* (November 1943) led off its six-page chronicle of the Iglesia's twelfth convention in Torreón (December 1943) with a description of the arrival of "multitudes of Christians . . . from different places in the country and even the neighboring states of New Mexico and Texas." The report also noted the remarks by Brawley and San Jose, California, pastors Leandro Montes and Daniel Grijalva. The former was visiting Mexico after a twenty-year absence, the latter for the first time. Montes testified about the healing from a chronic disease (and a paralyzed arm) of a young female relative during one of the convention's night services. Grijalva illustrated his remarks on Mark 16:17–18 by recounting the story of his child's healing from accidental poisoning (through ingestion of ant pesticide) and celebrating the impact of the event on his Italian American neighbors.

As expected, the healing trope surfaced regularly in the testimonial section of the *Exégeta*. The borderlands framing, however, often lent an additional layer of pathos to the accounts, as in this barely edited one (January 1950) by Carmen Meza. After unsuccessfully seeking medical relief from tuberculosis for seventeen months in Ciudad Juárez, Meza withdrew southward to languish in Colonia de Banderas, an isolated border settlement. From that peripheral site he cast hopeful eyes across the border:

> After 13 months of living in that place, my good God, our Lord Jesus Christ, sent our beloved brother in the Faith of the Lord, whose name is Pedro Gutiérrez Aguilera, to whom we know the Lord has given the Gift of praying for the sick in the Name of the Lord Jesus

Christ and these are healed; our brother was in the town of Fabens, Texas, since in that place in those days a Healing campaign was unfolding, from July 28 to 31; I remember clearly that it was already the last day that our brother would be praying for the sick and I had not been able to go partake in such a great blessing; well I should say that I do not have a passport that certifies my passage into that American territory, and finding myself with another brother who was also suffering from a different sickness, we commented on the opportunity to be able to go so that they could pray for us and we lamented greatly my inability to go, but instead I encouraged my brother in the faith that he go that they pray for him, perhaps God would manifest in him; just moments after the afore-mentioned brother and I had separated, I began to feel momentarily, some-thing strange in my body and a great impulse to go running in the mountains glorifying my God and Lord and returning home I felt the same desire, a great joy choked my throat and I wanted to shout with all my strength to the glory of God; a while passed and I began to feel the same thing, at which point I realized that the Lord had blessed me and that what I had received was nothing less than my Healing. . . . This happened between 10 and 12 of the 31st, precisely when brother Pedro Gutiérrez Aguilera was praying for the sick in the town of Fabens. . . . No doubt in those moments some brother who knew about my sickness, asked our brethren to pray for me that I be healed and God had mercy on me, giving me my health.[41]

In May 1957, the *Exégeta* reported on Parker, Arizona, pastor Francisco Ramírez's spontaneous prayers for the sick at the conclusion of a cross-border youth fellowship service in Estaciones Tecolotes, Mexicali. The magazine waxed enthusiastic over the results ("the Lord showed great power in healing"), including the recovery of a wheelchair-bound para-lytic woman who walked out of the church on her own power.[42] In June, *Exégeta* readers were gladdened to read of the March 25 water baptism in General Bravo, Nuevo León, of Benjamín Cantú's sister. The note re-minded readers that the majority of the Apostolic Assembly' president's relatives still lived in that northeastern Mexican town.[43] The May 1958 re-port of March baptisms in Juchipila, Zacatecas, credited Saticoy, Califor-nia, minister Aurelio Salazar with Juchipila's *primicias* (first fruits).[44] One month later, the organ celebrated the progress of the church in Camacho, Zacatecas, in spite of economic crisis and emigration pressures. The article singled out the activity of a returned migrant, "Hermano Cardona." One year later and with a focus farther south, the magazine carried the testimony of Diego Rentería, of Agustín, Jalisco, whose U.S.-based daughter, Josefina, had relied on the post to proselytize her ailing father. She eventually arrived, Bible in hand, to cash in on her remittances:

> For over ten years I suffered from a sickness called arterial pressure, and because of this, what little God had given me I spent on doctors, medicines and herbs. But my sickness grew every day, until a daughter who lives in the United States of America, who is Christian and answers to the name of Josefina Renteria, knowing that I suffered from that sickness, testified to me of the power of Christ, by way of a letter, since she had once suffered greatly from a disease and when she accepted the Lord she was completely healed. . . . She finally made a trip to Agustin, Jalisco, where I lived, to talk to me more about the power of God. And she gave me a Bible, and told me to read it and to look for a place where they preached the Word, that I should go to Guadalajara where there was a temple to which she belonged. [45]

Evangelism continued to be a cross-border affair. In August 1959, the *Exégeta* reported that the *Varones* auxiliary of Nuevo Laredo, Tamaulipas, was sponsoring twice-weekly services and a Sunday school across the border in Laredo, Texas.[46]

The back-and-forth leveraging of bodies and goods continued for many decades. Although the notice of the dedication of the Iglesia temple in Emiliano Zapata, Puebla, appeared after the time frame under study, the coda to *Exégeta* readers north of the border could well have been penned at any moment during the previous decades:

> Pastor Teutle is originally from Santa Ana Acozautla, Puebla. He was reached for the Gospel and baptized in the city of Orange, CA, and as a typical Apostolic, after he understood the truth, he returned to his own to communicate the grace of God which he had received, completing once again the promise of the divine Master, to be able to be his witnesses in our Jerusalem. . . . So if you have encountered Christ and have fully understood the good received, you would do well to move to your hometown or state of origin and communicate the word of God, choosing especially the best cities or towns. Be one more pioneer of the Apostolic Church.[47]

Migration opened conduits for religious influences. Apparently, the Orange, California, Assembly church was sending home more than religiously motivated bodies. One month earlier, the *Exégeta* noted this congregation and pastor Guadalupe Vásquez's material and spiritual assistance in the construction of a temple in Tacuichamona, near Culiacán, Sinaloa. While the Second Iglesia church of Culiacán had initiated the evangelistic project, it counted on that capital city's First Church, as well as on the Iglesia's church in Puerto Peñasco, Sonora, and the Assembly's church in Orange, California, for material assistance (a case of financial remittances rendered symbolic through religious networks).[48]

Borderlands Bereavement

Apostolics also stretched comforting arms across the border. The January 1957 burial in Otay, California, of former Tijuana pastor (1948–1956) Antonio Contreras's mother, Inés, drew ministers from both sides of the border. Felipe Rivas presided over the services. The *Exégeta* noted the deceased's special ministry tending the supply of olive oil for healing ministrations. The same issue announced the February 1 death of Guadalupe Luna, a member of Tijuana's First Church. Luna had managed to cross over to San Ysidro during his final week; he was buried in San Diego.[49] The October 1957 obituary for octogenarian Mexicali minister Marcelo Hernández emphasized his pioneering pedigree: baptism by Antonio Nava in Calexico in 1923 and a ten-year membership there before moving to Mexicali and into the deaconate. Otay pastor Pedro Hermosillo (Arturo's brother) officiated Hernández's funeral, assisted by Tijuana ministers Blas González and Alfonso Mascareño and several ministers from San Diego and Del Mar–Solana Beach.[50]

Foreign Missions

Exégeta readers eagerly awaited news of developments in the two churches' decade-old joint missionary program. The December 1957 issue announced an impending month-long ministerial training institute in Nicaragua for Central American ministers. The Iglesia's José Ortega and Ysidro Pérez were to travel there to join the Assembly's missionaries to the region, Daniel Jauhall and Francisco Gallego, as the institute's faculty.[51] The following month's issue carried news of the region's two national conventions, Nicaragua's and El Salvador's fifth conclaves, and of the attendance at the former of Costa Rican ministers newly encountered by Valentín Nieblas, the Iglesia's missionary to Nicaragua (and repatriate Gil Valencia's nephew).[52] The fortuitous overlap with Billy Graham's Central American evangelistic crusade allowed Ortega, Nieblas, and Pérez to formally join a welcome committee for Graham at the Managua airport on February 2. Ortega's ever-ready camera documented the encounter for prominent display in the *Exégeta*'s March 1958 issue.[53] The interest in Graham would not have surprised readers. The November 1957 issue discussed the evangelist's Latin American tour, reported on his successful recent New York City crusade, called for unity among evangélicos, and exhorted readers to pray for Graham's success in Mexico and elsewhere in the hemisphere.[54]

The Underside of Migration, Culture, and *Caudillismo*

As our survey of the periodical record indicates, Mexican Apostolics clung fast to coreligionists north of the border. Small wonder, then, that they would affectionately refer to the Apostolic Assembly as "our sister church in the United States" ("nuestra hermana iglesia en los Estados Unidos"). But even sisters are wont to quarrel.

While migration facilitated expansion, it also presented significant problems. Maclovio Gaxiola lamented this in his 1962 presidential report to Iglesia ministers gathered in that year's general convention in Torreón.[55] According to the leader, severe drought and low employment trends had intensified emigration pressures in Zacatecas, Durango, and other central and western states. Even ministers were uprooting themselves. Thus, in places like Sierra Mojada, Coahuila, the congregation had practically disappeared, with scant traces besides the temple and a faithful remnant. By contrast, the Chihuahua and Baja California districts were enjoying a ministerial surplus. In view of the depressed countryside and persistent intolerance in rural zones, Gaxiola recommended a new approach. By strategically planting churches in state capitals and larger cities, the Iglesia could ride the crest of internal migration and retain the faithful in the rural–urban flow.[56] It could thus anticipate governmental plans to industrialize zones in such states as Zacatecas, San Luis Potosí, and Aguascalientes. In an echo of an earlier judgment made by Eusebio Joaquín' (apostle Aarón) about Guadalajara, Gaxiola also called for moving the church's headquarters to Mexico City, the "seat of Satan" (a not-so-cryptic reference to the Basilica of Guadalupe).

Gaxiola concluded his presidential remarks by lauding the good relations with the Apostolic Assembly and the United Pentecostal Church, whose representatives had arrived or were about to arrive to Torreón. The fraternal gesture may have glossed over long-simmering tensions, though. Solidarity requires cultivation in order to endure. Even kinfolk disagree and grow distant. The period under study concluded with a tearing and subsequent repairing of the shared ecclesial fabric. The process may have begun as early as 1950 upon Benjamín Cantú's assumption of the Assembly presidency. While Antonio Nava had clung fast to Mexican cultural and linguistic referents, his Texas-raised successor moved in a more bilingual and bicultural universe. Cantú's introduction to Oneness Pentecostalism occurred under the mentorship of Euro-American ministers. (We also cannot discount the long history of tejano chauvinism, a sensibility provoked by Mexican elites.[57]) Finally, the recruitment of Apostolic Assembly youth to United Pentecostal Church Bible colleges, especially Tulsa, Oklahoma, drew some emerging leaders into the orbit of exponents of the narrower soteriological position within the UPC and hence toward sectarian isolation.

Apostolic Assembly ministers and leaders took umbrage at a January 1950 *Exégeta* article authored by Maclovio Gaxiola, the Iglesia's vice president at that time. The one-page report of his tour of Assembly churches in Central and Northern California churches in late December 1949, although laudatory and supportive in the main, did not gloss over such problems as poor local financial administration, uneven (external) holiness standards, cultural introversion, and stunted growth in old congregations limited by colonia (barrio) parameters. He also wondered whether the sister church would not be better served by expanding its reach beyond its narrow ethnic boundaries through English-language ministry.[58] His prescient observations fell on sensitive ears. The Assembly's leadership lodged a formal protest; the matter was taken up at a joint meeting in San Diego in mid-December. The slight was forgiven officially in Phoenix, Arizona, at the Assembly's seventeenth general convention, held at year's end.[59] Gaxiola extended a profuse apology in a January 1951 *Exégeta* article, "Resarcir Holocausto de Paz" (A Peace Offering Amends).[60]

The different national contexts exacerbated the growing divergence. The Iglesia Apostólica began to assert leadership within Mexican Protestantism. Its leanings can be seen in the *Exégeta*'s support of Billy Graham and the Sociedad Bíblica Mexicana, as well as in the periodical's frequent reprints from the global Protestant press; in President Maclovio Gaxiola's endorsement of interdenominational Sunday school and youth congresses in Mexico City; and in *Exégeta* notices about the demise of Francisco E. Estrello, secretary of the Sociedad Bíblica Mexicana, and the installation of Estrello's successor, Daniel López Lara, who spoke at the Iglesia's twenty-third general convention in Torreón in October 1960.[61] Three years later, the *Exégeta* carried an article by López, summoning broad interdenominational support of a Bible distribution and literacy campaign.[62] In fact, Iglesia Apostólica churches had established a strong record by this point. In 1952, they ranked eighth in total contributions among all the country's Protestant churches and ninth in terms of congregations participating in the Sociedad's annual support campaign.[63] In 1945, Maclovio Gaxiola, Leonardo Sepulveda, and Manuel Gaxiola participated, at the invitation of prominent leaders such as Gonzalo Baez Camargo and Federico Heugel, in the fiftieth annual Gran Convención Nacional Evangélica, held in Puebla. The *Exégeta* explained the value of such cooperation: "They makes us feel as one body in Christ, and they encourage us to launch ourselves forward in the winning of many souls who need to know the Lord Jesus as Redeemer."[64] Finally, in the fall of 1967, the *Exegeta* marked the 450th anniversary of Martin Luther's Wittenberg protest and tied the Iglesia's cause to the older project of the Protestant reform.[65]

Against these contrasting backdrops—evangélico convergence in Mexico and sharpening sectarian introversion in the United States—and given the inevitable intraethnic differences, it is not surprising that relations between Iglesia and Assembly leaders wore thin by century's end. What is remarkable is that the patches and stitches held for so long.

Still, cultural and national differences and the dark underside of *caudillismo* continued to tear at comity. Although usually experienced or framed as denominational boundary tussles, the tensions mirrored historical frictions between Mexican Americans and Mexicans, often reflected different class trajectories, and exacerbated personality conflicts between male leaders. The two denominations neared a point of official rupture in 1962. Thus, upon his sudden replacement of Benjamín Cantú in 1963, Antonio Nava pursued reconciliation, an initiative abetted by Felipe Rivas's return to the Iglesia's presidency in 1962 and José Ortega's permanent settlement in the United States in 1964 (he assumed a pastorate in Indio, California). With one final turn at the helm, the veteran leaders recalibrated their de jure ties through a revision of the 1944 treaty and regular consultations. They held a series of four joint board meetings during the final three years (1964–1966) of their respective administrations: in Calexico, California (September 1964); El Paso, Texas (March 1965); Tijuana–San Diego (June–

July 1966); and Phoenix, Arizona (immediately prior to the Apostolic Assembly's general convention in December 1966). At the penultimate meeting, they reaffirmed the second meeting's treaty revision and christened the document *Tratado de Unificación* (Treaty of Unification).

The revised treaty continued to omit mention of relevant immigration law and expanded reciprocal visiting rights to the laity, with the sole proviso of a recent letter of recommendation from the congregation of origin—importantly, this requirement was waived for ministers and members visiting churches in the immediate border zone. At the El Paso meeting, they also agreed to form a joint task force to review constitutional amendments (chiefly term limits for governing board members).[66] A committee completed work on the *Tratado* in August 1966, in time for that year's general conventions. By that point, the leaders had replenished their reservoir of trust. As had become customary, Assembly representatives conducted the ballot counting (as ostensibly neutral referees) for the governing board elections at the Iglesia's convention in Guadalajara, and the Iglesia reciprocated the important task in Phoenix. Rivas summed up the renewed solidarity in a valedictory report to his church's ministers: "In these international meetings, we have seen the intervention of God illuminating us with his Holy Spirit. Thus we have kept ourselves united in faith and doctrine. We should trust in the promises of the Lord: that he will neither leave nor forsake us. I believe that what is missing from the Constitution will be fixed as we have agreed, gradually."[67]

The timing of the rapprochement proved exquisite. In 1966, the Apostolic Assembly's general convention chose Efraím Valverde as presiding bishop. The new leader had been born in the United States (1922) but reared in Mexico—as a repatriated child—and baptized and trained in the Iglesia Apostólica in Tijuana.[68] He served in the Iglesia as pastor and national president of the *Varones* men's auxiliary. In 1957, the charismatic preacher opted to return to the land of his birth, owing to his resentment over limits placed on him by Felipe Rivas and others. Once across the border, he was able to parlay his considerable gifts, including musical ones, into a meteoric rise within the Apostolic Assembly. In 1963, he assumed the bishopric of Northern California and the pastorate in Salinas. When Antonio Nava made clear his wish for retirement at the end of his final term, Valverde seemed the most exciting choice. That choice was soon regretted by Nava and Assembly and Iglesia leaders. The ensuing dispute and schism (1970), however, fall outside the chronological scope of this study.[69]

Despite the fluctuations in official relations between the two denominations throughout the final quarter of the twentieth century, Apostolic Assembly congregations continued to serve as ports of entry for immigrants. As post-1965 waves of migration from Mexico and Central America washed over the U.S. Southwest, Midwest, and Northwest, they stranded human beings in their wake. The newcomers made themselves at home in new harbors. Many Apostolics took advantage of the Immigration Reform and Control Act of 1986 and moved into the naturalization pipeline. For this, many used original letters of recommendation (from Mexico) and other church records (especially tithing reports) to prove long-term residency in the United States. Several Assembly congregations hosted English-language and civics courses, in concert with educational and community agencies, in order to help applicants fulfill naturalization requirements.[70] Other Apostolics arrived too late to qualify and buckled down to await the next window of legal opportunity. As the labor diaspora took a southeastward turn, Apostolic lay members and clergy once again rode its crest and issued calls for denominational support (from the Apostolic Assembly and the Iglesia Apostólica) in Georgia, Tennessee, Florida, and the Carolinas, much like their bracero precursors had done in the Midwest. Still the migratory flow continues and will continue to flow until the economic disparities between the United States and its southern neighbors are equalized. Until such a point in the probably distant future, these refugees from hardship will continue to find safe harbor among the Apostólicos and other aleluyas of the United States. Those who return to their communities of origin will do so along transnational circuits, following patterns set decades earlier by other migrating pilgrims.

Evangélico History Reconsidered

Pentecostalism's centrifugal penchant for division and decentralization has made for recurring or overlapping cycles of revival-sect-church. This renders problematic broad historical and sociological descriptions. The periodic ebullience and chaos of revival and persistent assertions of historical agency, even within institutionalizing wings of the movement, press the Weberian sect-to-church continuum to its limits of utility. Grant Wacker's insistence on the primitivist–pragmatist internal dialectic would seem more helpful. So, too, would greater attention to migration and culture.

We are challenged in the case of Mexican and Chicano Pentecostalism to expand our historiographical toolkit in interdisciplinary and other geographic directions. As the next chapter will argue, we must consider the power and mobility of symbolic goods. Pentecostalism appealed and continues to appeal to restless historical agents; it demonstrates a remarkable ability to ride migration waves and endure and optimize macroevents and trends. In this study of religious practitioners moving throughout "greater Mexico," we have seen how Pentecostalism has succeeded in identifying and filling niches of belief and culture, creative spaces or interstices in which historic Protestantism often moved about clumsily.

When confronted with the challenge of proto-evangélicos voting with their ears and bodies, mainline Protestants often reacted with class-informed disapprobation. J. Merle Davis's (Disciples of Christ) 1940 study of mainline–Pentecostal tensions in Mexico reveals the depth of missionary exasperation over subaltern restiveness:

> A further danger in the social environment to which a small evangelical congregation is exposed is its vulnerability to the proselyting activities of irresponsible Protestant sects. Some of these groups are strangers to comity, and their tactics are extremely difficult for the older churches to meet. They operate in areas where the gospel has been successfully preached and where little groups of enquirers or baptized believers have been gathered but are *neither strongly organized nor regularly shepherded*. This type of proselytism enjoys several advantages over the regular missionary and church activity.
>
> 1. It uses national workers as its missionaries and makes prominent the national appeal of a Mexican movement unattached to foreign missions.
>
> 2. It plays up the advantages of economy of operation. It uses the cottage meeting method, dispenses with appeals for church buildings, funds for pastoral support and the support of a general church body.
>
> 3. It skillfully uses a knowledge of Mexican psychology and customs in all its activities.
>
> This type of proselytism provides a program that gives an outlet for the craving for excitement, for expression, and the release of pent-up emotions among these isolated rural dwellers. It modifies the Anglo-Saxon type of service, with its fixed hours of assembling and closing. It gives far more place to the participation of lay members in the service through hymn singing, impassioned prayer, con-

fession of sins and the congregational discussion, as contrasted with the leadership of the minister. It permits and even encourages loud weeping, groaning, shouting, gesticulating, marching and dancing in the service—"The moving of the Spirit and the gift of tongues." This sort of program is more attractive to an uneducated and emotionally starved people than the conventional type of service and business-like timetable introduced by American missionaries. This process is at work all over Mexico and is disintegrating not a little of the older evangelical work."[71] (emphasis mine)

Davis's lament found ready echo across the border. In that same year, the Board of National Missions of the Presbyterian Church in the U.S.A. complained that autonomous Pentecostals were not only maximizing mainline losses through labor-induced migration but also exacerbating Latino Protestantism's revolving door: "The chances are that many migrating members lost all contact with the Church because not always were there organizations where they went to work. Unfortunately, strange sects have built upon the groundwork of the denominations. They have been unhindered by denominational standards or comity agreements. Regrettably, their work is not constructive, and they lose people rapidly and discredit the cause of Protestantism."[72]

Ironically, Mexican Jesuit Pedro Rivera lodged a critique along many of the same lines as Davis and the Presbyterians, albeit two decades later. Although Rivera directed his fire against recent writings by Protestant missiologists John MacKay and W. Stanley Rycroft and Mexican Protestant journalists Alberto Rembao and Gonzalo Baez-Camargo, Pentecostals served as convenient straw men for his trenchant riposte.[73] After contrasting the inequality in salaries paid to foreign missionaries and national leaders in the mainline churches ("the one lives as lord and the other as servant") with the self-reliance of the autochthonous Pentecostal churches,[74] Rivera tweaked his ostensible antagonists with a proposed analysis of the success of heterodox Protestantism among indigenous Mexicans: "Within the same national territory, the Pentecostals are realizing great progress among the indigenous element. When the occasion demands it a study of this pseudocharismatic Christianity can be done. The mystical rapture and sensual rhythms do not reflect precisely the evangelical purity of which the Protestants boast so much."[75]

Referring to Oscar Lewis's recently published anthropological study of Mexican social misery,[76] Rivera lambasted the ineffectiveness of the by-then-century-old Mexican Protestant project, a project built on sand and lacking the firm foundation of Catholic social doctrine: "Up until now, after one hundred years of Mexican Protestantism, we still have no positive proof of this [social uplift for the masses]. What is more, the Pentecostal communities, with their cultish service and suspicious mystical raptures, with their women jerking in the temple to the penetrating rhythm of tambourines, seem to prove the contrary."[77]

The mainline laments and Rivera's caricature expose—albeit in negative terms—many of the lacunae discussed earlier. Our historical cultural approach, however, flips over the missiological analyses in order to explore the complex underbelly of missionary-convert mentalités and the ability of subaltern agents to transit through such lacunae. I suspect that Pentecostal and Apostolic apologists would unabashedly and ironically affirm many of the written sentiments. Small wonder, then, that a revitalized heterodoxy and heteropraxis would flood over into the carefully (or woefully, depending on the point of view) tended fields of the Catholic and Protestant mainline and encompass such a large turf today. The mainline missionaries' and Jesuit apologist's complaints, however, correctly identified experiential realms where religious migrants were proving most susceptible to Pentecostal charms: corporeality, musicality, and emotion. Although we have frequently glimpsed through this analytic window, we can now climb through it, in order to explore the sonic and lyrical sphere.

CHAPTER 6

Can the Pentecostal Subaltern Sing?

Alabad a Jehovah	Praise the Lord
Naciones todas, pueblos todos	All ye nations, all ye peoples
Alabadle	Praise him
Porque ha engrandecido sobre nosotros	For his merciful kindness is great
Su misericorida	Toward us
Y la verdad de Jehovah	And the truth of the Lord
Es para siempre, aleluya, amen	Endures forever, hallelujah, amen
Y la verdad de Jehovah	And the truth of the Lord
Es para siempre, aleluya, amen	Endures forever, hallelujah, amen

The Hermanos Alvarado's 1959 recording of Marcial de la Cruz's "Aleluya al Señor" (LP volume 4) offers an important clue to the probable authorship of one of Latino and Latin American evangelicalismo's most widely sung choruses (*coritos*). The medley selection leads off with the corito, "Alabad a Jehovah," segues first into the chorus of De la Cruz's "Aleluya al Señor" (the Introduction's epigraph), and then moves into the Spanish-language adaptation of "Joy Like a River" (Yo Tengo un Gozo en Mi Alma). The seamless transitions are helped along by the identical musical and rhythmic frames. The coupling of De la Cruz's chorus with the usually stand-alone corito suggests a tradition distilled during the Alvarado's' childhood in Apostolicism and certainly by the time of the recording, two decades after De la Cruz's demise. The early ubiquity of "Alabad a Jehovah" throughout the Spanish-speaking Americas at once both complicates the definitive attribution of authorship and reminds us of the dynamic social fields that enable the migration of music and that also leave their imprint on that music.

A Mexicanized version of Psalm 117, "Alabad a Jehovah" framed the *Reina y Valera* "Antigua" (1862, 1909/1923) text in toto in a *norteño* genre. The corito demonstrates that, much like their Protestant precursors, Pentecostals valued scriptural literacy. As seen from their life histories, and conference and periodical records, Pentecostals embraced the text and symbolic power of the *Reina y Valera* Bible with all the conviction of the more literate sixteenth-century reformers and the more elite nineteenth-century evangélicos—thus, for example, the strong support of the Iglesia Apostólica for the Bible Society of Mexico. However, the same data remind us that folks can be as much Bible listeners and performers as Bible readers. Much Pentecostal music reflects an intuitive grasp of the higher critics' notion that the scriptures began, after all, as "texts" declared (*declamado*) in communal settings. That declaration was often a musical one. By casting the text in resonant cultural frames, the novel corito tradition embedded evangelicalismo finally into the soil of popular religiosity, much like Martin Luther and John Calvin's musical innovations did for Protestantism in the sixteenth century.

The broad corpus of Pentecostal music includes many nonscriptural songs, of course. It also includes an array of testimonials, Bible stories, vignettes, and even songs about songs. ("Vamos cantando hasta que baje el poder de Dios" [Let us sing until the power of the Lord comes down]). This chapter assays an exploration of that corpus, in order to understand Pentecostalism's continuing musical and corporeal charms.

Early Latino/Latin American Protestant Hymnody

> I stepped over last evening to a chapel opposite my hotel, where one of these congregations was holding service. It was after nine, and the regular meeting had closed. But there stood a group of twenty or so in the upper corner, "going it," like a corner after a revival meeting, in these same songs of Zion. . . . They all put with all their heart and voice, a few sitting about on the benches enjoying the exercise. It was so perfectly Methodistic that I wished to go forward and tell them it seemed just like home.[1]

Methodist Episcopal Church bishop Gilbert Haven's 1875 report on liturgy within the proto-evangélico Iglesia de Jesús surely stirred the hearts and loosened the wallets of potential benefactors in the United States. The hearty anthems sung "lustily" by a Mexico City congregation heralded the dawn of Christian truth after dark centuries of "popery." They also evoked, in their primitive power, painful comparisons with the cooled liturgical passion of Haven's home denomination in the postbellum period.

Expressive (musical) cultural themes were prominently featured in the intelligence gathered and published by missionaries. Haven's account of his three-month missionary exploration of Mexico juxtaposed the cacophonous sounds of Catholic lottery hawkers, beggars, "dancing girls" with guitars and harps, and *zócalo* wind orchestras with the harmonious, "lusty" singing he encountered in the nascent Iglesia de Jesús. Haven's travelogue on the mainland began with a service convened by the American consul in Veracruz:

> "Rock of Ages" and "Jesus, lover of my soul," were sung, and the word spoken from "To you that believe, he is precious." It was the first service the Holy Catholic (not Roman) Church ever held in that city. It was good to be there, as many felt. It seemed as if the day-star was about to arise over this long-darkened soil.
>
> The sound of the vesper bells floats sadly into my ears, as I write close under the towers of the Cortez Cathedral. How long before more Christian bells shall sweetly summon more Christian disciples to a more Christian worship? How long?[2]

Melancholy soon turned into affront as the missionary's sensibilities were assaulted by the sights and sounds of persistent beggars outside the Hotel Diligencias in Orizaba:

> How they whine and grin and show off their horrid rags and sores! What a commentary on Romanism! It breeds these human vermin as naturally as the blankets of its worshippers do the less noisome sort. The more "piety," the more poverty; the more of workless faith, the more of this idle work.[3]

Affront turned into righteous indignation in Mexico City:

> My windows stand open as I write, and the street cries come up into my ears. I suppose this I hear the most frequently is from the lottery-ticket vendors, who stand along the sidewalks, and are the most numerous class of operators in the city. They call the various lotteries the holiest names: Divina Providencia, Virgin of Guadalupe, Purissima Conception, and such like. These lotteries are largely operated by the Church, and are one of its sources of income. The sale of indulgences is another. The right hand and the left rob in the name of God, feeding the poor victims with false hopes of a fortune in this life, and with falser hopes of a fortune, thus acquired, in the life to come.[4]

Haven finally arrived to a recognizable sonic sphere at the Iglesia de Jesús. After noting the horticultural and architectural beauty of the former San Francisco convent, the nearly 400 attendees, and the handful of Americans present, Haven waxed enthusiastic:

> They are dark-colored, Indian in whole or largely, and all sit as pro-
> miscuously as they ought to do in more enlightened congregations.
> They are singing "lustily." John Wesley would have declared that they
> kept that word in his Discipline. They all sing, and sing with all their
> might. I never heard camp-meeting excel them in this heartiness
> and gusto. The words were simple and sweet, and the tunes likewise.
> None of them were familiar till the last one, in which I detected an
> air I had known, and, after a little, found it was, "I'm a pilgrim, I'm a
> stranger."
>
> They sang some four or five times, as often as in an American social
> or prayer meeting.
>
> The bedizened altar furniture was gone, and an open Bible occu-
> pied the place of the idolatrous host. Above it, in a circlet of immor-
> telles in silver letters, was the name of JESUS. The service of song was
> full of Him. The prayers, lessons, and sermon were alike possessed.
>
> It is noticeable, too, as an incident of this movement, that they
> are so full of song. The Roman Catholic Church does not cultivate or
> allow in its services congregational singing. It is as gay of plumage as
> tropical birds, and as songless. A trained choir gives elaborate masses
> and compositions with wonderful power in a few great centres of its
> worship, but its people do not sing. These converts are full of song.[5]

Haven's limited exposure within the walls of the city's cathedrals also limited his judgment. The dissident Catholics-turned-evangélicos had not learned to sing in a vacuum, especially in the absence of Anglo-American tutelage. Rather, the popular spheres of domestic and festive culture were brimming over with musicality. So, too, were the religious sites in the provincial towns and countryside. The MEC bishop was unaware that his Roman Catholic counterparts of the era had banished popular music from the cathedrals in favor of high European musical art forms. Thus, these elite sonic spheres skewed the general picture. Haven may have also failed to listen long enough to profane Mexico.

Haven tempered his enthusiastic approbation of the nascent movement with a word of caution:

> Whatever the ultimate form of this movement, it undoubtedly has
> the right beginning, Jesus Christ himself being the chief corner-

stone. It *needs direction, organization, education*; but, as an outburst against a system which has so long suppressed this vitality, it is divine. The Virgin is not here. The Son of God is alone, as becomes His nature and work. It is a protest against that false mediation and intercession. He has taken the work into His own hands. They sing His praises, they implore His salvation.[6] (emphasis mine)

The missionary strategist got it half right. Converts would indeed learn to sing new versions of the Lord's song in their own and strange lands. But they would also insist, as time passed, on authoring their own version of that song. Such assertions inevitably led to (or reflected) contests over aesthetics, autonomy, and power. Historians seeking to understand the shaping of Latino/Latin American Protestantism must consider the dialectical evolution of its religious musical practice.

The bulk of hymnody from this early period reflected missionaries' preferences.[7] The repertoire contained few surprises and included the hymns of Martin Luther, Isaac Watts, and Charles Wesley.[8] The period of vigorous missionary expansion coincided with the apex of Fanny Crosby (1820–1915) and Ira Sankey's (1840–1908) influence; thus, their music occupied a privileged position in the hymnody of the missions.[9]

An important cadre of Protestant leaders from Mexico, Cuba, and Spain also undertook hymn translation. In the last country, these included Anglican bishop Juan Bautista Cabrera (1837–1916), translator of Martin Luther's "A Mighty Fortress Is Our God," and Pedro Castro, who collaborated in translation and compilation, under the auspices of New York's Tract Society, with Episcopalian Henry Riley. Important Mexican and Mexican American translators included Methodists Vicente Mendoza (1875–1955), Pedro Grado (1862–1923), and Juan N. de los Santos (1876–1944), and Nazarene Honorato Reza (1913–2001). One result of the combined efforts (pre-Reza) was the *Himnario Evangélico*, published in 1893 by the American Tract Society (513 hymns) and drastically revised (348 hymns) as the *Nuevo Himnario Evangélico* in 1914, for use in Methodist, Baptist, Congregational, and Presbyterian churches.[10]

Harvard-trained and Nashville-based Episcopalian Primitivo Rodríguez (from Mexico's Iglesia de Jesús) undertook a significant compilation and redaction project at the behest of Cuban Methodists.[11] The official editor and translator of Spanish-language material for the MECS Board of Missions and Methodist Publishing House,[12] Rodríguez sifted through twenty-seven preexisting Spanish-language hymnals published from 1869 to 1907 to compile his authoritative *Himnario Cristiano* in 1908, one that would "be for the good of Spain and Latin America" and contain more of Charles Wesley's songs than any other hymnal of that time. Rodríguez limited his redaction of Iberian music to the previous forty years, since the earlier hymnody of the peninsula, although attractive in some aspects, was hopelessly mixed with "the leaven of Romanist teachings."[13]

Hearing of the project, Mexican Presbyterians weighed in, lamenting that, while the hymnals then in circulation may have met the needs of prior evangélico work, they were no longer satisfactory from a musical, poetic, literary, or doctrinal standpoint. Their own failure to move quickly on their recent national convention's directives in this area fortuitously allowed for close collaboration with Rodríguez, thereby avoiding the duplication of effort and the inevitable clash between their own competing camps: lyricists versus musicians and musically challenged theologians versus heterodox aesthetes.[14]

Several translators also produced a significant, albeit small, corpus of original compositions. Mendoza and Grado each published modest hymnals, *Himnos Selectos* (1904) and *La Pequeña Colección de Himnos* (1905), respectively, for use in the MEC and MECS churches.[15] Mendoza's later "Jesús Es Mi Rey Soberano" ("Jesus Is My Sovereign King"), composed at the end of a six-year sojourn (1915–21) in southern California, ranks as Latino and Latin American Protestantism's most widely sung hymn and is one of a handful welcomed into mainline English-language hymnody. (Mendoza's subsequent hemispheric trajectory and status eclipsed the notion of the song as a pioneering borderlands and migrant hymn.)

The early compilations did not meet with universal acclaim. In a 1892 response to a query for the *Dictionary of Hymnology*, Congregationalist missionary David Trumbull, of Valparaiso, Chile, noted the "not very satisfactory" quality of the songs in "two or three hymn-books, mostly translations, probably made in Spain."[16] In Spain, the eminent classicist Marcelino Menéndez y Pelayo relegated the heretics' latest poetic attempts to a disdainful footnote at the end of his voluminous survey, *Historia de los Heterodoxos Españoles*. "In general," he sniffed, "the Spanish Protestant muse is one of deplorable and drowsy monotony and insipidity."[17]

Perhaps Menéndez y Pelayo, defender of Spanish Catholic orthodoxy and arbiter of taste in turn-of-the-century Madrid, doubted the muse's authenticity. He may have been onto something. Although the revised *Nuevo Himnario Evangélico* contained an impressive 348 hymns, only about 4 percent (thirteen to fifteen) were original Spanish-language compositions. The situation was not vastly improved in the more revivalistic sectors of the church. As late as 1955, the fourth edition of *Cantos de Alabanza, Pureza y Poder* (Songs of Praise, Purity, and Power), published by the Free Tract Society in Los Angeles, maintained a similar proportion of about 4 percent original Latino composition among its 234 hymns. Surprisingly, the least inclusive hymnal of all was produced under the aegis of the emergent Assemblies of God. Fewer than 2 percent of the 229 hymns in H. C. Ball's *Himnos de Gloria'* (Hymns of Glory) were of original Latino composition. That the most widely disseminated Spanish-language hymnal of the twentieth century bore faint Latino imprint says as much about Anglo-American paternalism as it does about Latino and Latin American dependency.[18] Only Francisco Olazábal's and J. Paul Cragin's *Melodías Evangélicas*, first compiled in 1928 and circulated widely up through the 1960s, offered a significant representation of original Latino compositions, twenty-five out of 165, or 15 percent. Of these, about one-third represented compositions by Apostolic songwriters.[19]

Equally as problematic as the question of original lyric composition were the strict stylistic parameters laid down by missionaries and publishing houses. For example, the 1893 *Himnario Evangélico*'s 513 hymns were indexed to 397 tunes, only twenty-two (or 4 percent) of which may have been set by Spanish and Latin American composers or translators. The parameters widened slightly over the next seven decades. The 1964 hymnal published by the interdenominational Council on Spanish American Work (the comity umbrella for Protestant work among U.S. Latinos) serves as a valuable index for measuring this process; it reflects a consensus among the constituent churches and agencies and coincides with the concluding period under study. It also carried the editorial imprint of veteran Presbyterian missionary George P. Simmonds. Of the 443 total hymns, fifty-nine, or 13 percent, represented original Spanish-language compositions, a notable increase from hymnals of the early twentieth century. The author index (as opposed to translator or musical composer indices) is telling as a reflection of sensibilities; twenty-three Spanish and Latino or Latin American authors were listed. But equally as telling are the complex tune and meter indices; congregations were encouraged to be flexible with unfamiliar songs but to always stay within the parameters of established tunes. The sole song of possible Pentecostal origin, "¿Con Qué Pagaremos?" (With What Shall We Repay?), often performed to a bolero rhythm in Pentecostal circles, was scored in a 3/4 beat by Ethel Winn as a "melodía latino Americana" with anonymous author attribution.[20]

Clearly, missionary Protestantism's musical gifts arrived tightly wrapped in set forms. It would fall to restive Pentecostals to disassemble both content and frame. As they proffered their own compositions and compilations, they could not, of course, avail themselves of tune indices, since these were generally unknown within popular or folk Catholicism, the milieu out of which most Pentecostal converts emerged. What they could rely on to "strangely warm the heart," however, was the familiar fount of chord sequences, melodies, rhythms, and genres of popular musical culture.

The large role assumed by missionaries in hymnal redaction helps to explain the persistent suppression of native musical culture. Later critiques argued that this was accomplished through the imposition of Euro-American ethnocentrism, Greek body–soul dualism, privatized notions of faith and practice, the devaluation of folk culture, and the exclusion of indigenous (Latino) musical styles.[21] Missionaries and their spiritual progeny insisted on strict boundaries for music and liturgy. In a 1928 address to the Baptist State Association of Chihuahua (reprinted in full in the Methodist *Evangelista Mexicano*), a speaker rhapsodized about the centrality of one privileged instrument:

> Music should never be absent from the church. As far as the instruments to be used, in my thinking, it is the organ that should never be absent from the church. Although it may not lend itself to the adornment of music, it is the most appropriate to accompany religious songs. It is not only songs that the organ can accompany; it can also be used to play preludes for the services, which is of utmost importance, as this prepares us better to receive the message. During the offering time something can be played. If not a classical piece, since the organ or organist may not be up to it, then something slow and sweet.[22]

The speaker called for a removal of all melancholy and languidness from hymnody. A missionary need not have been present at the conclave to affirm the concern over propriety. After a half century of tutelage, many evangélicos thoroughly endorsed the value of a liturgy bleached of folk elements. Such a development renders understandable Manuel Gamio's dismissal of the potential for Protestant inroads among Mexican immigrants in the United States. Clearly, though, Gamio failed to listen in on a budding, noisy, and musical revivalism, the very source of concern to guardians of Protestant musical orthodoxy.

Elvira Herrera

The evolution of Latino Protestant music represents a process of continuity as much as discontinuity. This can be seen clearly in the case of Elvira Herrera, a member of one of the few Mexican Methodist families in the California–Mexico border town of Calexico in the early twentieth century. The immigrant family settled in Calexico in the latter part of the 1910s after a three-year stay in the Central Valley town of Fresno, California. Elvira and her younger brother, Luis, finished their high school education in the United States. Both were bilingual.[23] (Elvira was the sole Mexican female high school graduate of her generation in Calexico.)[24] During the same period (1918), the MECS established an outreach to Mexicans and Mexican Americans in this border region. Northern Methodists had arrived one year earlier. MEC Latin American Conference superintendent Vernon McCombs saw Calexico as a "center from which to work godless Lower California," especially Mexicali, "where they assemble in troops in the harlots' houses," and where "the devil has certainly sported undisturbed these decades past."[25] Accordingly, in 1917, McCombs dispatched Tranquilino Gómez from Los Angeles to claim and hold the contested turf on Prohibition's back porch.

The zone's troubled morality notwithstanding, religious musical culture flourished there, at least for the Herreras. With Luis as her accompanist, Elvira translated (or adapted) several English-language hymns into Spanish. Her most popular one was disseminated widely throughout the hemisphere in Spanish-language Protestant hymnals during the twentieth and into the twenty-first centuries. "Es la Oración" (Prayer Is) represented an extremely loose adaptation of F. M. Lehman's 1909 composition "The Royal Telephone," or "Central's Never Busy," which was published in over eighteen Evangelical, Holiness, and Pentecostal hymnals from 1914 to 1949.[26]

What is most striking in this example is Herrera's decision to excise completely any mention of the still-novel appliance, the very title of Lehman's song. Herrera seems to have been purposeful in this symbolic shift.[27] In an era of scarcity and limited technology, her listeners could scarcely identify a luxury appliance that only gringos and wealthy Mexicans owned. (Phone service was not begun in Baja California until 1924; the first direct phone call from the territory to Mexico City was not placed until 1947.)[28] Rather than get lost in the metaphors of American consumerism, better just to have an intimate talk with Jesus instead: Jesus, the

The Royal Telephone
(F. M. Lehman)

1. Central's never busy, always on the line
You may hear from heaven almost any time
'Tis a royal service free for one and all
When you get in trouble give this royal line a call

[Chorus] Telephone to glory, O what joy divine!
I can feel the current moving on the line
Built by God the Father for his loved and own
We may talk to Jesus thro' this royal telephone.

2. There will be no charges, telephone is free
It was built for service, just for you and me
There will be no waiting on this royal line
Telephone to glory always answers just in time

3. Fail to get the answer, Satan's crossed your wire
By some strong delusion or some base desire
Take away obstructions, God is on the throne
And you'll get the answer thro' this royal telephone

4. If your line is "grounded," and connection true
Has been lost with Jesus, tell you what to do
Pray'r and faith and promise mend the broken wire
Till your soul is burning with the Pentecostal fire

5. Carnal combinations cannot get control
Of this line to glory, anchored in the soul
Storm and trial cannot disconnect the line
Held in constant keeping by the Father's hand divine

shepherd, Jesus the Word giver, Jesus who sits on the throne, all metaphors readily understandable in popular religious idioms. The spirit of the message, the direct line to the heart of Jesus, remained intact, helped along by Herrera's aggressive redaction. Also, lifting up Jesus as sole intercessor rather than the telephone as clever metaphor underscored evangélicalismo's pointed Christocentric challenge to popular guadalupanismo.

"Es la Oración" traveled even more widely than its English-language original. Luis del Pilar included it (as No. 1 and with anonymous attribution) in his retrospective compilation of songs of the Disciples of Christ

Es la Oración	Prayer Is
(Elvira Herrera)	(My translation of Herrera lyrics)
Es la oración un medio que el Señor	Prayer is a medium that the Lord
Le dejó a su grey, que anda con temor	Left his flock that walks in the fear (of God)
Viendo su Palabra, en ella tú verás	Looking at His Word you will see
Que la oración te acerca a Cristo más y más	That prayer brings you close to Jesus more and more
¡Oh! Hablar con Cristo, qué felicidad!	Oh, to speak with Jesus, what happiness!
Y contarle todo, todo en verdad	And to tell him everything, everything in truth
Expondiendole tu necesidad	Laying bare all your need
Él te escuchará desde su trono celestial	He will hear you from his celestial throne
Si estás tú triste, ponte en oración	If you are sad, place yourself in prayer
Habla hacia la Gloria con el corazón	Pray toward Glory with your heart
Es un mandamiento que el Señor dejó	This is a commandment that the Lord left
Y tendrás respuesta porque así lo prometió	And you'll receive an answer for so he has promised
¿Estás en espera del Consolador?	Are you tarrying for the Comforter?
Ten fe y paciencia, constancia y amor	Have faith and patience, constancy and love
Y el Señor al ver tu ferviente prez	and the Lord, upon seeing your fervent press(ing)
Cumplirá tu gozo dándote un Pentecostés	Will fulfill your joy giving you a Pentecost
Si no hay respuesta, ora más y más	If there is no answer keep praying on and on
No te desanimes, Cristo no es falaz	Do not be disheartened, Jesus never fails
Siempre a sus promesas, fiel responderá	To his promises he will always hold
Lo que necesites, ésto Él te lo dará	Whatever you may need this he will give you

1930s revival in Puerto Rico.[29] J. P. Cragin's inclusion of it (as No. 40) in the 1933 and 1936 editions of *Melodías Evangélicas* ensured its introduction into the Andes region and points farther south. The hymn continues to circulate throughout the hemisphere. It appeared in the 2000 edition of Mexico's Iglesia Evangélica Independiente's *Himnos de Victoria*.[30] Ironically, Herrera's aggressive reworking not only wrested Lehman's song from its clever metaphor frame but also saved it from obsolescence.

The case of this early twentieth-century gospel hymn distills much of my argument. Clearly, the Herreras were more than prodigal Catholics or restive Methodists. Rather, Elvira was a creative historical agent, bus-ily fashioning an identity in the margin between two societies: Catholic Mexico and Protestant United States. For her, that periphery was a center, a zone in which she moved about comfortably, usually oblivious to the hegemonic centers. In the case of such religious borderlanders, robust agency is especially evident when they are left to their own devices, either by design or neglect. Eventually, for Herrera, Methodism's tentative sup-port system in the Imperial Valley (the MEC reported the Mexican mission in Calexico, California, and surrounding towns without supply in 1918 and 1919), like the telephone metaphor, proved inadequate to her com-munity's needs. She and her family embraced a heterodox Pentecostalism represented in the charismatic ministry of Antonio Nava, who established his transborder base in Calexico in 1921, the same year that the MEC built an impressive parsonage for a Mexican pastor. The case of the Herrera family was not singular. The religious proletariat was voting with its ears as well as its feet, as much enchanted by the cultural musical repertoire as the charisma of tongues-speaking evangelists and healers.

Early Latino Pentecostal Hymnody

In contrast to historic Protestantism's disdainful distancing, Pentecostal hymnody redeemed the fiesta of Mexican and Latino culture. It brightened the previously dark view—held by Protestant missionaries—of popular culture that saw this as hopelessly enmeshed in intractable pathologies of alcoholism and unbridled machismo. Pentecostals returned popular musi-cal culture to the sacred place of ritual, performance, and spectacle. They forged a new sonic universe that replaced the earlier popular Catholic visual world of saints, candles, gilded altars, and paintings—stimuli that had been erased by iconoclastic Protestantism—with intense sonic and sensory stimulation. Against mainline missionary censure, Pentecostals reintroduced a measure of the carnivalesque (laughter, weeping, body movement, profane instruments, feasts, etc.) into liturgical space and time.[31] This emotive liberation also required a percussive and repetitive frame to extend and intensify the corporeal experience. The new corito tradition allowed for this, as these could be repeated or strung along in thematic medleys for any length of time needed. These floating musical and lyrical units traveled even more freely than hymns. Their first compila-tion was undertaken by J. P. Cragin (an indication of an already established tradition). The early *Melodías Evangélicas* hymnal included seventy-three coritos along with 140 hymns. The Iglesia Apostólica's *Suprema Alabanza* hymnal followed suit with this supplemental compilation practice. Such traces evidence a boom in original Spanish-language music.

We can see hints of the approaching boom by reviewing once again Bernardo Hernández's minutes of the 1925 convention of the Iglesia de la Fé Apostólica Pentecostés. We should keep in mind that the IFAP's inaugural conclave was contemporaneous with the above-referenced Baptist address in Chihuahua championing the organ's "appropriateness" and with anthropologist Manuel Gamio's study dismissing Protestantism's appeal to Mexican immigrants owing to its "lack of color and artistic impression." According to Hernández, the ministers opened their first meetings with the hymns "Ama el Pastor Sus Ovejas" ("As the Shepherd Loves His Sheep," a translation of "Dear to the Heart of the Shepherd"); "Cerca, Mas Cerca, Oh Dios de Ti" ("Near, Nearer, Oh God, to Thee," translation of "Nearer, Still Nearer"); and "Jesús, Yo He Prometido" (translation of "Oh, Jesus, I Have Promised"). Hernández's meticulous record listed sixteen of the hymns sung by the conventioneers. All but four were taken from Spanish-language Protestant hymnals—the inherited hymnody. Importantly, Hernández also highlighted the debut of several compositions by Marcial de la Cruz and his daughter Beatriz.[32]

As noted, De la Cruz's music resonated throughout wider evangélico circles. The Chihuahua City-based *Evangelista Mexicano* made special mention of him in its report on the third meeting of the newly established interdenominational Convención Evangélica Mexicana del Estado de Arizona, held June 4–7, 1930, in Phoenix. The over 600 attendees from the state's Baptist, Presbyterian, Methodist, Nazarene, and Pentecostal churches were greeted by Governor John Phillips (a Methodist) and were regaled during the services, including an outdoor one, by church choirs and three bands. Correspondent E. P. Muñoz noted that the *banda típica* was directed by the "active and pious brother Marcial de la Cruz, an apostolic minister."[33] The report underscored not only De la Cruz's prominence—or notoriety, given his heterodox Oneness position—but also his identification in the minds of readers with a folkloric musical ensemble tradition.[34]

Also as noted, the Great Depression, which initially threatened Apostolicism's viability, in fact fostered its cultural fecundity. Set against the grim backdrop of economic recession and political persecution, Apostolic hymnody expanded into such a large corpus that the first compilation effort in the early 1930s, the much-referenced *Himnos de Consolación*, gathered more than 200 hymns, the vast majority original compositions. The later compilation effort in Mexico, *Himnos de Suprema Alabanza*,[35] gathered more than 160 hymns; again, the majority were organic to the movement. Even after accounting for a significant overlap, the overall number of published original hymns by 1941 can be conservatively estimated at 300 (we can double this to account for nonpublished hymns). This creativity throws into sharp relief the stark situation in the mainline churches. Apostolics were certainly grateful to inherit Protestantism's translated hymnody but judged it inadequate in style and problematic in doctrinal content. Trinitarian doxologies, in particular, according to one recollection, often caused Apostolics to choke, as they followed and pronounced the songs' requisite rhymes.[36]

Apostolic hymn writers matched perennial poetic tropes (e.g., pilgrimage) with popular musical genres (e.g., polka or *vals*) to produce a familiar sensory experience. They composed songs for ritual occasions (e.g., child dedications, water and Spirit baptisms, initiations, birthdays, communion services, marriages, partings, welcomings, offerings, and death), thereby binding popular music and religious ritual. The affective reconciliation found ready reception. As noted, beginning in the late nineteenth century, Mexican Catholicism had experienced a revival of high art and cathedral choral music. This development once again pushed folk music and instruments out of that country's principal sanctuaries and relegated them to village churches and the external performance spaces of pilgrimages and fiestas.[37] The situation for Mexican American Catholics under the tutelage of a Baltimore-based hierarchy bent on "Americanizing" the culturally and theologically recalcitrant "bad Catholics" of the Southwest seemed even bleaker.[38]

Form mattered as much as content in Pentecostal hymnody. Composers appropriated most of the available popular Mexican musical idioms and instruments: from *polka* to *ranchera* to *corrido* to *vals* to *huapango* to *marcial* to *canción romántica* to *bolero*—all, apparently, except *cha-cha-cha* and *danzón*, which were probably considered too irredeemably wedded to the carnal dance floor. Yet even the exclusion of the last cannot be maintained strictly, given the bolero's derivation from the *danzón*, *conga*, and *contradanza*, the first two demonstrating clear Afro-Cuban roots and the third Afro-Cuban adaptations.[39] Although introduced into Mexico (Yucatán) and Central America through marimba bands in the nineteenth century, bolero's wider dissemination occurred via radio broadcasts in the 1930s by Mexico City's powerful XEW radio station and by means of the virtuoso interpretation of the genre by guitar *tríos* such as Los Panchos, Las Calaveras, and Los Diamantes.[40] Almost simultaneously, the bolero's slightly syncopated 2/4 rhythm (eight beats with the third left out) crowded out its Andalusian cousin progenitor and was applied to Mexican regional repertoires and to Pentecostal hymnody. The genre reinforced the mystical eroticism of such songs as "Qué Lindo Es Mi Cristo" (How Lovely Is My Christ), whose verses speak of being cradled in Christ's arms and the chorus of receiving Christ's loving caresses.[41]

The musical poetry that emanated from the fields and orchards where many of the songwriters labored had to pierce through borderlands dust. The proletarian work site itself often inspired compositions, as in the case of Filemón Zaragoza's tender *vals*, "Mi Plegaria" (My Plea). The melancholy melody and lyrics were impressed upon him as he toiled in the cotton fields outside of El Paso in 1940. Zaragoza took the epiphany as an answer to a long-standing prayer he had often breathed in envy of other church members' facility in hymn composition. The Ciudad Juárez resident stooped to trace the lyrics in the dirt and returned to the spot throughout the workday to commit the words to memory. Upon returning across the border to Juárez after the day's stint, and before going home to wash the dirt off his weary body, he dashed to the church to find paper and pencil.[42] The song was heartily received in the region's churches and beyond. It helped to smooth Zaragoza's ascent into national leadership of the Apostolic Assembly's *Varones* men's auxiliary after his settlement in Delano, California, in 1951. The poignant datum about musical epiphany in the cotton borderlands has escaped, of course, labor and economic studies of the region. The song persists seven decades later in nostalgic YouTube tributes, although often in norteño form, a result of popular consumption and practice.[43]

Pentecostal composers freely appropriated metaphors drawn from ancient scriptural and modern tropes: for example, "Trigo Soy" (I Am [as] Wheat), "Vamos Todos a la Siembra" (Let's All Go to the Sowing), "El Sembrador" (The Sower), "Rosa de Sarón" (Rose of Sharon), "Como la Primavera" (As the Springtime), and "El Tren del Evangelio" (The Gospel Train). Maternity's emotive well watered numerous elegies, such as "Mi Madre Oraba por Mí" (My Mother Prayed for Me). The bitter fruit of poverty, lamented in Roberto Hernández's "Contigo Viviré" ("Contigo viviré / Y ya nunca sufriré / Tú eres refugio del pobre / Por eso a ti alabaré"

[With you I shall live / And suffer no more / You are the refuge of the poor / This is why I shall praise you]), fed scathing prophetic commentary like that in the chorus and third verse of Marcial de la Cruz's "Profecia de Habacuc" (Habakuk's Prophecy), a retrospective denunciation of global conflicts like World War I:

> Knowledge has increased
> Daniel prophesied of this,
> And the men of this world,
> Wish to know everything.
> There is great confusion,
> Desiring to heap up
> Goods for this world.
> They shall carry nothing with them.

> With infernal war machines
> They have wished to exterminate,
> The most powerful nations,
> Fighting by land and sea.
> And also from the skies,
> Wreaking great destruction;
> Felling homes,
> Destroying the nation.

Composers wrapped heroic biblical passages in corrido and *décima* ballad forms, a practice useful for improved biblical literacy. Ancient Christian hagiography came in for similar treatment. One notable example of this innovation can be seen in Jorge and Ramón López's corrido rendering of Benjamín Cantú's 1944 "Persecuciones a los Cristianos," a poem about martyrs in the Roman Coliseum. The Hermanos López added the balladeer's obligatory introduction—"Hermanos, voy a contarles . . . allá en el siglo primero" ("Brethren, I am going to tell you . . . way back in the first century")—and dutifully applied metric (e.g., octosyllabic lines) and other lyric conventions of the genre to Cantú's hagiographic portrait.[44] The duo's (original) final verse ratcheted up the stakes for contemporaries in Mexico: the example of early martyrs steeled believers against Catholic intolerance. The irony of the exhortation, against a backdrop of residual *cristerismo* deploying the same rhetoric about martyrdom at the hand of the modern-day embodiments of Nero (i.e., presidents Plutarco Calles and Lázaro Cardenas), merits noting:

1. Her/ma/nos, /voy /a /con/ tar/les	Brothers, I am going to tell you
Las /mu/chas /per/se/cu/cio/nes	Of the many persecutions
De /los /pri/me/ros /cris/tia/nos	That the early Christians
Que /pa/de/cie/ron /por /Cris/to	Suffered for Christ
A/llá /en /el /si/glo /pri/me/ro	Back in the first century
Cuan/do /cre/cí/a /el /cris/tia/ nis/mo	When Christianity first grew
Es/ta/ba /en /su /a/po/ge/o	Paganism was in its apogee
En /Ro/ma /el /pa/ga/nis/mo	in Rome
[Chorus] De Juan Bautista y en adelante	From John the Baptist forward
Los mensajeros relatan	So the messengers tell us
Al reino se hace la fuerza	The Kingdom (of God) suffers violence
Los valientes lo arrebatan	And the violent take it by force
9. En aquel tiempo pasado	In that time in the past
Con sincera abnegación	With sincere abnegation
Sufrieron nuestros hermanos	Our brothers suffered
Buscando su salvación	Seeking their salvation
No es raro que en estos días	It is not rare in these days
Tengamos persecuciones	For us to suffer persecution
Y debemos con hombría	We should therefore with courage
Disponer los corazones	Prepare our hearts

Although we have followed the musical pathways of one important variant of Pentecostalism, we would do well to listen in on other soundscapes. Juan Lugo, Puerto Rico's "Apostle of Pentecost," found a ready musical collaborator in Juan Concepción.[45] Concepción's *Ecos de vida: Selección especial de himnos y canciones espirituales por compositores hispanos* (note the explicit "by Hispanic composers") gathered 160 hymns, sixty-nine of these of Concepción's authorship. The Nuyurican composer wielded metaphors as adeptly as his Apostolic counterparts. His compositions "El Tren de la Vida" (The Train of Life), "En Avión con Cristo" (On the Plane with Jesus), and "Mi Barca" (My Boat) reference travel technologies familiar to island-locked Puerto Ricans and their countrymen moving along migration circuits to the U.S. mainland. Francisco Olazábal's Concilio Latinoamericano de Iglesias Cristianas spawned an indigenous hymnody as well. In the wake of J. Paul Cragin's assumption of the original *Melodías Evangé-*

licas copyright, Felipe Gutierrez added an additional one hundred mostly original Spanish-language compositions to the CLADIC corpus in his 1944 compilation, *Nuevo Himnario de Melodías Evangélicas Selectas*.[46]

The desperate financial straits of mainline sponsors also hampered attempts to contain newly assertive cultural nationalisms. In the case of the Disciples of Christ, the recall of missionaries from Puerto Rico coincided with a successful move for independence by islanders. The ensuing revival and emergence of an indigenous, proto-Pentecostal hymnody so transformed the *Discípulos* musical culture that longtime Mexico-based Disciples missionary Frederic Huegel, on a trip to the island in 1951, complained that his hosts had carried their liturgy beyond the point of recognition.[47] By contrast, the long-term control of Anglos over Mexican Disciples in Texas resulted in scant liturgical innovation. Historian Daisy Machado ascribed the general stagnation of Latino Disciples work in Texas to racist indifference.[48] By contrast, the Puerto Rican Disciples' robust hymnody prefigured an assumption of key hemispheric and ecumenical leadership in theological and historical fields later in the twentieth century. This outsized projection of *Discípulos* influence evidenced, of course, Puerto Ricans' unique brokering role as U.S. citizens and Latin Americans.

Ethnomusicological Issues in Latino Pentecostal Music

The careful reader (and listener) will have noted the similarities with the parallel emergence of black gospel music in this period; indeed, Latino Pentecostalism's early musical shoots drew from African American nutrients. Within the field of Latino Protestantism, as in that of black Protestantism, the aesthetic tensions revolved around three issues: autonomy, cultural memory, and orality. Concerning the first, according to ethnomusicologist Mellonee Burnim, the autonomous space of the invisible church incubated the slave spirituals: "Whether in the ravine, field or living quarters, African-American slaves fiercely guarded their privacy, not merely out of a fear of reprisal, but out of their collective desire to express themselves in a way that was uniquely meaningful to them."[49] In addition, Burnim noted the psychological benefit of later gospel music—the spirituals' progeny—for folks who had left land and kin behind in the Great Migration. Chicago-based gospel pioneer Mahalia Jackson's recollection served to illustrate Burnim's point: "Gospel music in those days of the early 1930s was really taking wing. It was the kind of music colored people had left behind them down South and they liked it because it was just like a letter from home."[50] As historian Wallace Best has demonstrated in the case of southern migrants in Chicago, the ability of Baptist and Holiness/Pentecostal churches to capture and express such sentiments translated into greater numerical success vis-à-vis the more urbanized African Methodist Episcopal churches that disdained southern folkways.[51]

Burnim also underscored early gospel's rare use of scored music to buttress her argument about the orality of expressive religious culture.[52] Similarly, while Apostolic performers and congregations sought avidly to preserve and pass along the lyrics of new compositions, often collecting them in ringed binders, the lack of scoring strengthened a dependence on oral tradition to ensure the songs' melodic survival.

The Pentecostal proletariat also democratized liturgy, creating a communitarian performance space for any lay member, singly or in groups, to express or declaim musical and poetic creations. Thus, two of the same processual dynamics observed by Burnim in black gospel seem to apply to its Latino counterpart: transformation of personae and transformation of space.[53] To extend Burnim's analysis, the framing of individual performance by testimonial or scripture declamation, the invocation of integrity (soloists often asked for prayer in order to be able to "sing with complete liberty" ["Oren por mí para que la pueda cantar con toda libertad"]), and the affirmation of "anointing" through congregational response all worked in tandem to sanctify the performer and performance space.

The process of transformation also applied to instruments and musical genres. As noted, the guitar and kindred instruments emerged as markers of a new liturgical space, a zone replete, as one observer remarked, with transgressive significance: "The (Disciples) revival of '33 redeemed the guitar. This was not well received in devotional circles. Folks thought it too romantic, forgetting that the Gospel itself is a romance."[54] Photos of Marcial de la Cruz and other early Latino Pentecostal musicians captured the ubiquitous instrument (previously disdained as profane—and erotic—by mainline missionaries and their converts), which according to pioneer Nava was often the only instrument available to the proletarian Pentecostals: "La guitarra ... p'al pobre ... la guitarra" ("The guitar ... for the poor ... the guitar").[55] The guitar and banjo were also included in ensembles of wind, string, and percussive instruments, such as the *bajo sexto* and the *tololoche*—two favorites in *tejano conjunto* style. Freed of the libidinal stain of profane venues, the sanctified instruments evoked deep-seated affects embedded in the heart and memory of popular musical culture.

Viewed through a cultural lens, these religious *bricoleurs* busily as-

Phoenix, Arizona, Apostolic *Orquestra*, 1928. Front row, left to right: Eugenio Martínez, Bernardo Lerma, Juan Briseño, Juan Vásquez, Rosario Lerma; Back row, left to right: Clemente Bracamonte, Julian Bracamonte, Santos Bracamonte, Tereso Gamboa. (Note: in 1985, Rosario Lerma musically scored Marcial de La Cruz's music.) Photo courtesy of Benjamín Ortega; José Ortega Photograph Collection.

sembled a new set of shared meanings, ideas, feelings, concepts, and symbols—in other words, like the first *Himnos de Consolación*, a new assemblage of text. The embrace of Protestantism's more enthusiastic variant allowed them to stretch Protestantism's aesthetic web. That weakened web—rent in places by revolution, economic depression, repatriation, massive migration, and missionary mismanagement—could not, ultimately, contain creative impulses. Early Pentecostals selected strands from weakened hegemonic cultural systems (whether Protestant or Catholic) and wove these together with entirely new ones and in different patterns, in order to create a familiar religious cultural home and way station.

Perhaps more than any other song, Benjamín Cantú's "El Predicador Pionero" (The Pioneer Preacher) epitomized the creative reassembly process. The medley, whose principal melody was taken from "The Battle Hymn of the Republic," wove that tune and new lyrics (all the verses and the first and last choruses) with the melody and lyrics of choruses of long-standing evangélico standards: "There Is Power in the Blood" ("Wonder Working Power"), "Beautiful Words of Life," and "Leaning on the Everlasting Arms." Importantly, Cantú's creative reworking emptied the iconic Civil War anthem entirely of its nationalistic messianism and replaced this with a hagiography fit for a Methodist circuit rider or repatriate preachers like Francisco Avalos and Ignacio Mariscal. The finished product represented more than a patchwork. The blended tapestry provided a musical burial shroud for deceased clergy. The hymn's performance—often by *Dorcas* choirs—at clergy burials throughout several decades lent it a solemnity and ensured its special status in funeral liturgy—like that accorded to "Más Allá del Sol" (Beyond the Sun). In other words, "El Pionero Predicador" worked.

El Pionero Predicador	*The Pioneer Preacher*
[Tune: "Battle Hymn"]	
1. Cantaré una hermosa historia	I shall sing a beautiful story
del pionero predicador	of the pioneer preacher
Que llevaba el mensaje	Who carried the message
con constancia y con amor	with constancy and love
Yendo a pie por valles, bosques,	Going on foot through valleys,
predicando con fervor	forests, preaching with fervor
Y diciéndole a las gentes	And telling the people
de Jesús el Salvador	of Jesus the Savior
[Chorus] ///Gloria, gloria, aleluya///	///Glory, glory, hallelujah///
A nuestro Salvador	To our Savior
2. Siempre fiel y tezonero	Always faithful and hardworking
por la obra del Señor	for the work of the Lord
Y aunque hiciera frío o lluvia,	Even in cold or rain,
o fuera intenso el calor	or in intense heat
Llegaba por las aldeas	He would arrive in villages
deseoso de predicar	desiring to preach
Y con la voz de un monarca	And with the voice of a monarch
les empezaba a cantar	he would start to sing
[tune: "Power in the Blood"]	
[Chorus] Hay poder, poder, sin igual poder	There is power, power, unequalled power
En Jesús quien murió	In Jesus who died

Hay poder, poder, sin igual	There is power, power, unequalled
poder	power
En la sangre que Él vertió	In the blood He shed

[tune: "Battle Hymn"]

3. Decía del Cordero Santo	He would speak of the Holy Lamb
que del mundo quitará	who will take away
Toda mancha de pecado	Each stain of sin
del que se arrepentirá	from him who repents
Son palabras tan preciosas	They are such precious words
que en el mundo nunca habrá	that the world will never have
Una canción tan hermosa	So beautiful a song
que el mortal escuchará	for mortals to hear

[tune: "Wonderful Words of Life"]

[Chorus] O, cantádmelas otra vez	O, sing them to me once again
Bellas palabras de vida	Beautiful words of life
Son de luz y vida, son sostén	They are light and life, sustenance
y guía	and guide
//Que bellas son, que	//How lovely they are, how lovely
bellas son	they are
Bellas palabras de vida//	Beautiful words of life//

[tune: "Battle Hymn"]

4. Como pobre peregrino	Like a poor pilgrim
que de paso en marcha va	passing through
Sin mundanas pretenciones	Without worldly pretensions
sino sólo el predicar	save preaching
Unos vieron el progreso	Some saw the progress
de la obra del Señor	of the work of the Lord
Otros se fueron con Cristo	Others went with Christ
en medio del gran batallar	in the middle of the great battle

[tune: "Leaning on the Everlasting Arms"]

[Chorus] Libre, salvo, del pecado	Free, saved, from sin
y de temor	and fear
Libre, salvo, en los brazos de	Free, saved, in the arms of
mi Salvador	my Savior

[tune: "Battle Hymn"]

| 5. Ya su Biblia está en la mesa, | His Bible is now on the table, |
| su sombrero a la pared | his hat on the wall |

Su calzado ya descansa	His shoes are at rest
pues su carrera acabó	as his race is finished
Ahora ya está en el cielo	He is now in heaven
en una hermosa convención	at a beautiful convention
Y la Iglesia le veremos	And the Church will see him
en la gran resurrección	in the great resurrection
[Final Chorus] ///Gloria, gloria, aleluya///	///Glory, glory, hallelujah///
A nuestro Salvador	To our Savior

Again, note that choruses 2–4 are lifted from Spanish-language translations of well-known evangelical hymns of the period.[56] Cantú's reliance on this musical fount made for ready performance and memorization. The same familiarity may not have accrued, however, to the "Battle Hymn," especially for Latin Americans. The first introduction of the song into Spanish-language hymnody via the 1893 *Himnario Evangélico* consisted only of the chorus's melody, strung out over five verses. "¡Gloria a Ti, Jesús Divino!" addressed Jesus in the second-person voice for all but the final verse.[57] While *tejano* Methodists (Cantú spent his childhood and adolescent as one) were probably familiar with Julia Ward Howe's original song, the full melody was not introduced to Latin American evangélicos until J. P. Cragin offered a faithful translation, "El Himno de la Batalla de la República," in *Melodías Evangélicas*, about the time of Cantú's conversion to Pentecostalism. The tardy reception of Cragin's song left it scant time to embed itself in the evangélico mind and heart. Thus, Cantú could mold it to his needs, without fear of offending patriotic sensibilities; indeed, his radical adaptation rendered it inoffensive to Mexicans' nationalistic sensibilities.

In a sense, Cantú's composition resembles the products of today's border *maquiladoras*. However, unlike these factories, his process did not adhere faithfully to assembly design instructions sent from a distant headquarters office. Also, the products of religious cultural bricolage must prove their utility in consumption. In the case of "El Pionero Predicador," Apostolics consumed Cantú's musical product with solemn gusto.

Apostolic "Nightsong"

The carving out of liturgical performance spaces in a territory where colonized and migratory brown bodies had been exploited and criminalized suggests an oppositional liminality akin to that of the *isicathamiya* "Nightsong" performances studied by Veit Erlmann in Cape Town.[58] As in apartheid South Africa, borderlands Pentecostal worship and music seem to represent a space for the "recomposition of a fragmented social universe" and hence "an assertion of power."

To be sure, Erlmann noted the ambiguity of such symbolic action, given the seemingly insurmountable dividing lines between the social and economic center and periphery, between the grim here and now and the imagined egalitarian social order. Yet the macroeconomic and political context could not quench completely the sensory and ideological experience of music, rhythm, movement, and tongues speaking. While the proletarian Pentecostal body may have been pulled in several directions by globalizing capitalism—at once a consuming body and a laboring and producing body—it remained, nevertheless, *one* body, a body not merely shaped by domination and fevered by disease (many early Pentecostal composers suffered from blindness, tuberculosis, pneumonia, and similar poverty-indexing conditions) but a body inhabited by a historical agent—like Filemón Zaragoza—searching for meaning and belonging. Like "Nightsong," the hymns and ballads of noncitizens imagined an alternative construction of power relations over and against an inequitable social order. While avoiding officialdom's gaze, these shadowy denizens of the nation-state proclaimed a transcendental citizenship through the lyrics of Juan Concepción's "La Biblia Es la Bandera" (see Chapter 4), layering on a valence never intended by the composer (as a Puerto Rican, Concepción's legal status was not ambiguous after 1917). Thus, spaces of home, family, and nation were reconstructed in and through the performance frame of Pentecostal worship. The body in motion was both the site and agent of aesthetic experience. The singing body affirmed in performance by other emoting bodies signified idealized community. Pentecostal hymnody and performance represented spatial strategies enacted and formalized within the context of mutual support and prophetic articulation of an aesthetics of power directed to the outside world. They articulated "a utopian space in which a possibility, by definition miraculous in nature, [is] affirmed by religious stories" and "ethical protest opposed to statutory fact, to ostensibly natural order."[59] Over time, this articulation acquired sharper tones.

Although it dates from a more recent time period than the one under study (it references the amnesty provisions of the approaching 1986 Immigration Reform and Control Act), the complexity of borderlands Pentecostal life can be seen in the lyrics of a corrido ballad by mariachi composer Ramón "El Solitario" González. Like other corrido protagonists, the hero retrospectively relates a succession of events and lamentable circumstances that propel cross-border movement in search of well-being but haunted by regret.[60] The ethical ambivalence over the matter of undocumented crossing and residency contrasts with the celebration of divine encounter in the wake of homesickness and disappointment with the fabled "American Dream." In this "illegal" gospel song, the prodigal son acquires heroic status as a converted migrant poised to return home to share his good news with kin. The lyrics' melancholy and yearning are reinforced by the *banda* style: an accompanying tuba and other instrumental accoutrements of the norteño genre.

The Undocumented Ones

I left my country hoping to find
A life different from my past one
And I slipped into the American Union [U.S.]
Without a passport I arrived undocumented
Eager to obtain citizenship
I looked immediately for work
And since amnesty was just around the corner
I obtained documents, though all was false
I'd been told there was no hunger in this land
And that money could be had in abundance
For this reason I abandoned my parents
To end the poverty in which I lived
And now I find myself alone in a strange land
And I confess to you that sometimes I have cried
When I remember my very dear loved ones
Only my God out of pure love has consoled me
To you, Lord, who keeps the abandoned one
I ask that your grace never leave me
If in other times I offended you in my arrogance
Repentant, today I ask for your pardon

The other day at nighttime I went searching
For someone to tell me about God
Across from the corner there was a church
My heart invited me to step inside
I heard the message where the preacher spoke

Of a country that Christ had prepared
With no hungers, pains nor sadness
That was the land of which I had always dreamed
Hopeful, I converted to the gospel
And I hope to share it one day with my parents
When I return to my land I hope to see them
And to tell them about Jesus Christ and his love

Although we come to this land seeking money
The gospel of Jesus has saved us
I came out ahead, and I'll never be ashamed
Of this, the story of the undocumented ones

The purposeful return of a converted migrant, rendered in musical verse, reminds us of the many narratives of early Pentecostal growth and of the catalytic power of religious remittances. The song communicates in familiar sonic terms many of the themes we encountered in Urías Rodríguez's testimony carried in the *Exégeta* of May 1957. Like the Mexican Revolution, the Pentecostal one has been memorialized in song.

Sentimiento

In his study of Kaluli "sound and sentiment" in the Papua New Guinea rain forest, ethnomusicologist Steven Feld described how the sonic environment of bird sounds and waterfalls were part and parcel of Kaluli musical cultural practice, often serving as overarching metaphors.[61] As noted, Pentecostal music contains similar contextually formed metaphors. For Feld, such cultural constructions have as their aim symbolic persuasion. In his discussion of "songs that move men to tears," Feld examined the way that Kaluli *gisalo* performance was tailored to evoke an uncontrollable weeping response, first among women and then among men. Virtuosity is measured by the success of such social and emotional evocation in performance. Pentecostals expressed it differently—"anointing," "Holy Spirit presence," and "singing with complete liberty," to name three common expressions— but I think many of the same features apply. In fact, Apostolics insisted on weeping, even if it meant slowing down an author's original upbeat arrangement, as in the case of Lorenzo Salazar's "Fuente de Misericordia" (Fount of Mercy):[62]

Fuente de Misericordia	Fount of Mercy
1. Dios con su poder afirmó los cielos y la tierra	With his power God established the heavens and earth,
Y a las estrellas vistió de claridad	And he clothed the stars with brightness
Y la expansión, obra de Sus manos, habla doquiera	And the vast expanse, work of His hands, speaks throughout;
Mas el milagro más grande del mundo fue el sacrificio de Jesús allá en la cruz.	But the greatest miracle of all was Jesus' sacrifice on the cross
[Chorus] Oh, manantial, fuente de misericordia!	[Chorus] Oh, wellspring, font of mercy!
Sol de justicia es Tu compasión.	Your compassion is the sun of justice.
Vida eterna es la ofrenda de Tu gloria,	Your glory offers life eternal,
Dulce esperanza que llena el corazón.	sweet hope that fills the heart
2. Incontables son las riquezas de su alabanza,	Countless are the riches of His praise,
Casa de Dios, feliz hogar e intensa luz	House of God, happy dwelling, full of light;
Indecibles son los misterios que hay en lontananza;	Unspeakable are the distant mysteries,
Mas el milagro más grande del mundo Fue el sacrificio de Jesús allá en la cruz.	But the greatest miracle of all was Jesus' sacrifice on the cross
3. Roca de salud es la Ley de su tierna clemencia	His law of tender mercy is our rock of salvation
Con Su poder sostiene al mundo en su lugar	Its power holds the world in its place
Muy sublimes son las virtudes de su gran potencia	Very sublime are the virtues of his great power
Mas el milagro más grande del mundo Fue el sacrificio de Jesús allá en la cruz.	But the greatest miracle of all was Jesus' sacrifice on the cross
4. Cuan sublimes son las palabras de su fortaleza	How sublime are the words of his might
Puso en las puertas el perdón, por su bondad	His mercy stained the portals with forgiveness

Manto de salud puso sobre la naturaleza	He cloaked nature with goodness;
Mas el milagro más grande del mundo	But the greatest miracle of all was
Fue el sacrificio de Jesús allá en la cruz.	Jesus' sacrifice on the cross

Salazar, the heir to De la Cruz's prolific songwriting legacy, originally set the tune to a boogie-woogie rhythm, a style that he, a member of the bilingual World War II Zoot Suit generation, clearly relished.[63] Over time and with broad diffusion, however, the tempo was slowed considerably and the hymn stylistically infused with sweet melancholy; the faithful insisted on weeping. Thus, an urban Chicano song and text were rendered "habitable through mutation"[64] by a religious community still anchored to Mexican musical cultural referents. Such affective displays among teetotaling adult males were particularly striking, since they countered literary critic Octavio Paz's notion that only through drunkenness are Mexican males allowed to remove their stoic masks.[65] The collective creation of music, then, allowed Apostolics to reshape the original musical frame and excavate deeper veins of meaning below the lyrics.

Intergenerational Legacies

Like Salazar, Elvira and Luis Herrera, and Daniel Morales, the agents of cultural change were often youthful musicians. Take, for example, Manuel Chabiel's big band, which was based in Tulare, California, debuted at the first Apostolic *Esfuerzo Juvenil* (a term borrowed from Presbyterians) conference in Otay, California, in 1934, and traveled to the Texas Rio Grande Valley a decade later. The band members included the saxophonist's daughters and sons. (Before migrating to California's Central Valley, Chabiel played in an African American big band in Phoenix, Arizona.) Lorenzo Salazar's boogie-woogie gospel career prefigured that of Los Bienaventurados (The Beatitudes), a Solana Beach musical ensemble. Formed in 1965 to "attract and inspire young people away from sin and perdition," the wind and electronic string ensemble crooned an Apostolic and Evangelical repertoire and sported a look and sound similar to rhythm-and-blues and Chicano groups of the era; this earned them the uncomfortable moniker "Los Beatles Apostólicos." The Bienaventurados, in turn, inspired Los Heraldos, an electronic band that fused the East Los Angeles and Tijuana sound into a considerable repertoire (quickly taken up by youth choirs).[66] The melody of the verses of composer Arnulfo Espinosa's "Cuando Llega el Final" (When the End Comes) matches exactly that of the contemporaneous secular hit song "I'm in Love with an Angel." Not surprisingly, the switch from acoustic to electronic instruments invited censure from coreligionists. Although beyond the scope of this study, the list of innovators could be expanded to include today's Rojo, a binational rock ensemble composed of children and grandchildren of Apostolic musicians—and innovators—of yesteryear: Benjamin Espinosa of Culiacan, Sinaloa and Eliezer Moreno of Tucson, Arizona. (Several of the youthful musicians have also recorded mariachi tributes to their progenitors.) The musical bridge has, thus, spanned generations as much as it has cultures and borders.

"Alabaré a Mi Señor": Contemporary Popular Catholic Music

The emergence by century's end of a majority Pentecostal movement within Latino and Latin American Protestantism and the Charismatic Renewal within Roman Catholicism, evidence a Pentecostalization of Christianity, especially in terms of liturgy and music. The contemporary religious musical culture of Latino and Latin American Catholics holds intriguing clues about the wandering nature of music and the porosity of confessional boundaries. Catholics, too, perform their own type of bricolage, for example, combining Marian devotion with borrowings from early aleluya musical culture and even switching gender in coritos (e.g., from "Yo tengo un amigo que me ama . . . su nombre es Jesús" to "Yo tengo una amiga que me ama . . . su nombre es María"). Pentecostal music now reverberates in rural mountain pilgrimages, as well as in urban spaces such as Mexico City's Basilica of the Virgin of Guadalupe. By the time Vatican II opened the windows of the Mass to vernacular languages and sounds, the Pentecostal siblings and cousins of Catholics had prepared an inviting repertoire. For example, Asambleas de Dios composer Juan Romero reported hearing his "Visión Pastoral," a slow, moving retelling of the lost sheep story (akin to the English-language "Ninety and Nine"), emanating out of a Catholic church in the Dominican Republic during his missionary travels in that country (the date is not clear). A Charismatic Renewal priest recognized the author's name upon Romero's self-introduction.[67] This researcher heard Romero's song and various Pentecostal coritos during a cristero martyr canonization pilgrimage from Las Cruces to Cuquío in Jalisco (May 21, 2000). The 1989 Spanish-language Catholic hymnal *Flor y Canto* includes, among others, old, upbeat Pentecostal standards such as "Una Mirada de Fe" ("A Glimpse of Faith"), "Alabaré" ("I Will Praise"), and "La Mañana Gloriosa" ("The Glorious Morning").[68] Other examples of popular borrowings include "No Hay Dios Tan Grande como Tú" (There Is No God Greater than You) and the melancholy but hopeful funeral standard "Mas Allá del Sol" (Beyond the Sun). Edwin Aponte's discussion of coritos as "religious symbols in Hispanic Protestant popular religion" can, thus, be expanded to include their resonance in popular Latino Catholic religiosity.[69]

Migrating Music

The difficulty in tracing precisely the origin and dissemination of most Latino Pentecostal hymns and coritos suggests that they ride in the luggage and in the hearts of a mobile religious proletariat. Gastón Espinosa has traced the Pentecostal–Catholic Charismatic connection through Glenn and Marilynn Kramer, ex–Assemblies of God missionaries to Columbia who converted to Catholicism in 1972 and provided key leadership in the Catholic Charismatic movement through their Los Angeles–based Charisma in Missions.[70] Edward Cleary has argued for multiple and overlapping origins, for example, among Brazilian Baptists in the late 1950s and among liberationist priests in Bolivia.[71] Scant attention, however, has been paid to the broader impact of regular, quotidian contact over decades between Catholics and their aleluya relatives and neighbors. Most Pentecostals, after all, with the exception of the Luz del Mundo, do not inhabit sectarian enclaves. The ubiquity of decades-old Pentecostal coritos in the musical repertoire of Catholics—of all stripes—denotes a long-standing permeation across confessional boundaries. The overlapping soundscapes hint at overlapping sacroscapes. Our mapping of these, including at those points where the overlap brings friction, must attend carefully to the musical texts of subaltern religiosity.

Can the Pentecostal Subaltern Speak?

//Alabaré, alabaré	//I shall praise, I shall praise
Alabaré a mi Señor//	I shall praise my Lord//
Juan vió el número de los redimidos	John saw the number of the redeemed
Todos alababan al Señor	They all were praising the Lord
Unos cantaban, otros oraban	Some were singing, others praying
Pero todos alababan al Señor	But all were praising the Lord

Few coritos traveled the *Américas* as widely (and early on) as "Alabaré a Mi Señor." While possibly emanating out of the black–brown Pentecostal borderlands, the chorus, of anonymous authorship, did not remain tethered there but rather drifted over later into general evangélico and Catholic spheres. It heralds John the Divine's vision of a heavenly cacophony-turned-symphony, one in which the "poor, rough" Indian of Azusa Street finally would be given a deeper hearing. But that is a question for eschatology and theology. In terms of history, we are challenged to ponder the meaning of the pioneer's speech acts, the power of others to redact these, and the insistence of other subalterns to have their say. This social and cultural history of borderlands and transnational Pentecostalism has explored, among other things, the very circuits and processes that carried "Alabaré a Mi Señor" far and wide. The circuits left sonic traces to guide hopeful travelers along the way. Although we have been denied the full story of Azusa's subaltern Mexican, we can recover, through careful acoustical and archival sleuthing, many similar ones in the ensuing decades, including that of Urías Rodríguez (Introduction). The youthful prodigal would have encountered this corito in 1955 as he flitted through the Baja California borderlands and felt drawn to the warmth of Pentecostal worship and hospitality in Tijuana and Colonia Zaragoza. Importantly, that welcoming zone had been prepared by enterprising Pentecostals—repatriados and others—who maximized the opportunities that geographical, political, and religious liminality presented. Institutional Catholicism developed late in the region; the dioceses of Tijuana and Mexicali were established in 1964 and 1966, respectively. Except for Baptists, the thin Protestant (main)line likewise awaited in vain the timely arrival of reinforcements. (Methodism was strengthened later by the migration of believers from central Mexico.[1]) Meanwhile, Pentecostalism filled the gap, built impressive earthworks, and sallied forth to capture more territory.

This retelling of United States (and Mexican) religious history, then, presses against perspectival limitations and notions of center and periphery. It also recalibrates disciplinary tools, in order to more precisely survey soundscapes and sacroscapes. Finally, it offers a longer historical context—Pentecostalism's early and middle time periods—for the comparative study of patterns and processes of current pneumatic renewal.

I return now to the theoretical grounding for *Migrating Faith*'s sociocultural historical approach. I will follow this with a critical rethinking of Pentecostal societal engagement, a discussion of proto-evangélico genealogies and mobility, and a return to the question about the Pentecostal subaltern voice.

Musical Culture, Habitus, and Practice

As seen from Mexican and Central American Apostolics' embrace of Puerto Rican Juan Concepción's "La Biblia es la Bandera" and from Caribbean and Latin American Pentecostals' embrace of Elvira Herrera's "Es la Oración," a song can acquire multiple and intensified layers of valence, once embedded in different hearts and bodies and performed in different social settings. The appropriation of Abundio López's "La Nube de Fuego" (C. Austin Miles's "The Cloud and Fire") to protest the expulsion of Nellie Laidlaw from Santiago's Methodist church in 1909 (Chapter 2) represents an example of shifting meanings. Two decades after that episode, the song was sung by expelled members of the Methodist Church in Lota, when they left to form the Misión Wesleyana Nacional. A century later, it remains part of the core historic hymnody of Chilean Pentecostalism, as seen in YouTube clips of its performance by choirs of the Iglesia Metodista Pentecostal and by congregations of the Ejército Evangélico de Chile.[2] It is doubtful that C. Austin Miles meant for his composition to signal schism and sectarian triumphalism.

Miguel Mansillas and Luis Orellana have explored deeply, through their study of early periodicals and movement folklore, the emotive contours of Pentecostal life on the Chilean street, the *canuto* identity disdained by Chilean Catholic society (much like the aleluya one of Mexican and Mexican American society) and recovered and celebrated in Pentecostal music and memory.[3] Mansillas has probed the affective and lyrical dimensions of subaltern life, in order to understand how canuto culture faced and interpreted disease, death, and persecution. In both canuto and aleluya culture, the guitar emerged early on as a marker of a new musical aesthetic. In contrast to mainline missionaries' (and their native progeny's) disdain for the instrument, owing to its evocative shape and profane use, Pentecostals found it the ideal companion for travel and public evangelism around the farmworker campfire and on the street corner. The performance field made possible the inclusion of other popular instruments, especially percussive ones. Popular instrumentation led inevitably to popular musical frames. As a result, even closely translated standards from the missionary repertoire could wander off and be captured in *chileno*, *peruano*, *colombiano*, *caribeño*, or *mexicano* musical frames.

These processes of creative adaption and consumption both support and interrogate Pierre Bourdieu's notion of habitus. For the French sociologist, aesthetic taste is enmeshed in an overarching web that determines, by class location, the preferences and behavior of all social actors, who consciously and unconsciously adopt things as they are. The ideology of natural taste then "naturalizes real differences, converting differences in the mode of acquisition of culture into differences of nature."[4] Family history, socioeconomic location and circumstances, and the concomitant socialization generally lock into place dispositions, preferences, and practices. The bourgeoisie, the artisan, and the village shopkeeper behave according to an inscribed and ascribed cultural script.

It was precisely this rigidity that theorist Michel de Certeau critiqued in *The Practice of Everyday Life* (1984). Rather than the relative immobility of conditioned subjects, de Certeau posited their ability to implement creative tactics of sly resistance and clever reappropriation that short-circuit or subvert "institutional stage directions" or "strategies" imposed by more powerful actors and systems.[5] De Certeau's discussion of a force field between "strategies" and "tactics" would seem to apply to the behavior of Anglo-American missionaries and their Latino progeny. For de Certeau, hegemonic strategy represents

> the calculus of force-relationships which becomes possible when a subject of will and power (a proprietor, an enterprise, a city, a scientific institution [I would add a missionary or a missionary enterprise] can be isolated from an "environment." A strategy assumes a place

that can be circumscribed as *proper* and thus serve as the basis for generating relations with an exterior distinct from it (competitors, adversaries, "clienteles," "targets," or "objects" of research).[6]

Once isolated and set in place, the dominant force seeks to manage relations with "an exteriority composed of targets or threats (customers or competitors, enemies, etc.)." Such a process represents the triumph of place over time and the mastery of places through sight, through "panoptic practices" that control and include (totalize) objects.[7]

The opposing calculus represented by the "tactic," however, ignores the "proper" and the "borderline" demarcated by hegemonic strategy. Indeed, the tactic has no space to call its own or operate from. It is best characterized as a guerrilla force, weaving in and out of the field and snatching opportunities to impose its own time on the hegemonic other's space. De Certeau offers the example of a housewife calculating her options at the supermarket and making a series of decisions on the fly. I would argue that such decisions, made over time and articulated every now and then by strong assertions of preference ("This store carries the wrong kind of chili powder! I'll have my sister-in-law bring some from Tijuana next time"), provide glimpses of such tactics. The dismissal and circumvention of the market's available stock, and the purposeful commissioning of a relative's travel to fetch alternatives from a resource-filled borderlands, offers a metaphor for Latino popular religious musical practice.

In sum, Mexican and Mexican American Pentecostals resembled their Mesoamerican predecessors undergoing colonization. In de Certeau's analysis, the Nahuas (Aztecs)

often *made of* the rituals, representations, and laws imposed upon them something quite different from what their conquerors had in mind; they subverted them not by rejecting or altering them, but by using them with respect to ends and references foreign to the system they had no choice but to accept. They were *other* within the very colonization that outwardly assimilated them; their use of the dominant social order deflected its power, which they lacked the means to challenge; they escaped it without leaving it. The strength of their difference lay in procedures of "consumption." To a lesser degree, a similar ambiguity creeps into our societies through the use made by the "common people" of the culture disseminated and imposed by the "elites" producing the language.[8]

In line with de Certeau, I argue that the subjects of this study demonstrated considerable agency in their construction of a Pentecostal identity. Their musical cultural practice is but one example of this. Beyond de Certeau's description of the "dispersed, tactical, and makeshift creativity of groups or individuals already caught in the nets of 'discipline,'" [9] these subaltern actors purposefully set up meaningful alternatives, with powerful imaginaries that now cast long nostalgic shadows. They rejected some elements of hegemonic systems (e.g., hymn tune indices), altered others, and fashioned wholly original ones. These were not merely brown Protestants. Evangelicalismo's flexibility in the face of this creativity has helped to determine the relative strength of its several streams. At 150 years, modern Latino Protestantism as a viable project is a relatively young social phenomenon (the 1602 *Reina y Valera* Bible notwithstanding). The newness of certain cultural practices suggests that, at the front end, the habitus of Latino religious musical practice had not yet fully calcified into stratified, let alone essentialized, categories by the time pneumatic revivalism began to shape it into new forms.

Rethinking Opiate "Lite"

Like several recent analyses of Latin American Pentecostalism, this one interrogates the ideological premises evident in the dismissive swipes taken in some earlier social scientific studies. These are worth revisiting, in order to measure the field's shifting markers. A few examples suffice here: Lalive d'Epinay's seminal 1968 study of Chilean Pentecostals; Abelino Martínez's and Jaime Valverde's 1989 and 1990 studies of *sectas* (the term is deployed in both Weberian and pejorative senses) in Nicaragua and Costa Rica, respectively; and Leslie Gill's 1994 study of indigenous (Aymara) female domestic workers in La Paz, Bolivia.[10] All four studies concluded that the religious enthusiasts were, in d'Epinay's famous phrase, on social strike (*huelga social*), hopelessly disengaged in their sectarian enclaves from meaningful societal commitment, or, worse, passive dupes available for right-wing manipulation.[11] Given the political exigencies of Allende's Chile and the Sandinista's' Nicaragua, the false consciousness of revivalistic religion seemed, at worst, a result of Central Intelligence Agency machinations and, at best, the narcoticizing effects of opiate "lite." The grim diagnosis was even extrapolated northward and presumed to apply to the U.S. Latino Protestant experience.[12]

The limited success of liberation projects—theological and political—prompted a reframing of the questions (and answers) posited by d'Epinay and others. Several anthropological studies situated themselves in different and specific locales and from these points of particularity challenged the sociologists' universalizing description by offering more in-depth analyses of conversion dynamics at the ground level of gender, race, and indigenous identity. Elizabeth Brusco described Colombian women's promotion of conversion as "female collective action" aimed at the "reformation of machismo" (the term I appropriated in the Preface). John Burdick found that black Pentecostal women implicitly and explicitly upended the oppressive racial aesthetic hierarchy of Brazilian society by means of a countercultural redefinition of female beauty. Rosalva Hernández uncovered multiple identities among the borderlands (Chiapas–Guatemala) Mayan Mam, many of whom credited the Presbyterian Church with providing linguistic and cultural sanctuaries during earlier times of governmental cultural oppression.[13] Hernández's conclusion coincided with Carlos Garma's earlier argument that Pentecostalism had provided Totonaca Indians in central Mexico with leveraging resources against monopolistic mestizo *caciques* (political strongmen) and indigenous shamans.[14] Hernández and Garma's findings preceded anthropologist Peter Cahn's sanguine assessment (2003) of general religious tolerance and equilibrium wrought by migration and globalization in Tzintzuntzan, the heavily Purepecha town in Michoacán whose customs were studied decades earlier by anthropologist George Foster.[15]

In tandem with this cultural anthropological work, historian Virginia Garrard-Burnett demonstrated how Pentecostal congregations in the devastated countryside provided indigenous Guatemalan women with space for important personal reconstruction in the midst of the calamitous social destruction of civil war.[16] Further to the south, sociologist Waldo Cesar and theologian Richard Shaull reached a similar conclusion—about "the reconstruction of human life beginning at the most basic level" in an atomizing age—in their 2000 study of Brazilian Pentecostals.[17] While Shaull felt pressed to rethink his prior liberationist paradigm in the case of Brazil's Igreja Universal do Reino de Deus, Dutch researcher Frans Kamsteeg applied his smoothly to a minority stream of Chilean Pentecostalism, countering the d'Epinay thesis about *huelga social*.[18]

By the turn of the century, Garrard-Burnett and anthropologist David Stoll had recast the debate in an important anthology that moved beyond the earlier political acquiescence–liberation binary. *Rethinking Protestant-*

ism in Latin America appeared in the same time period as the survey by David Martin (mentioned in the Introduction), whose predilection for rational choice theory propelled his larger global study of Pentecostal success. Rational choice theory also undergirded sociologist Andrew Chestnut's 2003 analysis of Pentecostal growth in Latin America, which built on his earlier study (1997) of Pentecostalism's thaumaturgical charms in Brazil.[19]

To be sure, the allure of politics loomed large at century's end. Peruvian theologian Darío López, for example, traced a transition from pilgrims to power brokers among Peruvian Pentecostals. Their flirtation with confessional parties and support of Alberto Fujimori during his 1990 election ended in feelings of betrayal.[20] The failed experiments in confessional parties were attributed, in part, to the electoral ambivalence of Pentecostal laity. Similarly, the several experiences with political engagement by Latin American Pentecostals—from endorsement of military coups and juntas (Chile and Guatemala) to evangélico political parties and legislative caucuses (Peru, Argentina, Colombia, and Brazil)—have left a decidedly mixed record.[21]

Mexican anthropologist Patricia Fortuny Loret de Mola was one of the first to explore the intersection of Mexican Pentecostalism and migration in her groundbreaking studies of the Luz del Mundo. She argued that the transnational vision, centralized authority, and required pilgrimage to the church's seat in Guadalajara kept migrants in Houston and other U.S. sites tethered to their homeland.[22] Similarly, Carlos Garma's in-depth study of Pentecostalism in Mexico City's Iztapalapa *delegación* (borough) examined such variables as gender and domestic migration in his exploration of a religious ecosystem characterized by what he termed "religious mobility."[23] Finally, Leah Sarat's recent ethnography of Otomí townspeople in the state of Hidalgo and their coreligionists in Phoenix, Arizona (members of the Iglesia Cristiana Independiente Pentecostés), has offered the first full treatment of Pentecostalism as resource for transnationally tied ethnic communities.[24]

Clearly, the study of Latin American Pentecostalisms has moved beyond d'Epinay's grim thesis. Timothy Steigenga's political surveys of Central American Pentecostals and Charismatics, however, caution against a full pendulum swing in the other direction. Focusing on religious practices rather than affiliations, Steigenga points to a persistent ambivalence on the question of democratic potential or acquiescence.[25] Still, much of the recent scholarship remains historically unframed. *Migrating Faith* seeks to tug these analyses back to earlier periods, in order to more fully understand the innovations and processes unfolding in later ones. It also ties the analyses to Pentecostalism in Latin America's northernmost nation, Latino USA.

The imprecise extrapolation to U.S. Latinos of findings drawn from the several studies of Latin American Pentecostals has been owing, in part, to the limited role of religious variables, especially those related to Pentecostal faith and practice, in political and other social scientific studies of U.S. Latinos. Early survey instruments were designed to capture traditional dimensions of political and social behavior (e.g., party affiliation, voting record, and religious affiliation) but not religiously motivated quotidian behavior. I have argued elsewhere about the minimal utility of the religious data gleaned in the groundbreaking 1992 Latino National Political Survey and its follow-up Latino Political Ethnography Project.[26] These two studies' focus on the political behaviors and attitudes of U.S. citizens glossed over the complex web of relationships that tie many of these to permanent, temporary, and undocumented immigrants. Such relationships have been the hallmark of Pentecostal churches throughout the twentieth century. Such relationships emerged front and center during the wave of migrant protests against onerous proposed federal legislation in 2006. Here, closer attention to the dimensions of what Renato Rosaldo and others call "cultural citizenship," including that religious cultural one shaped in the Latino church and pew over generations, can help us understand the impact of these on the public square. While the 2006 follow-up Latino National Survey expanded notions of civic participation to include that exercised by noncitizen legal residents, the analytical yield on Pentecostals has remained minimal.[27] Furthermore, researchers have assumed that the frequency of church attendance or operative typologies of religious ascription—versus, say, more quotidian activities in the pew, the home, or work site—represent the most telling markers of religious identity and religiosity.

The several studies by the Hispanic Church in American Public Life project and the Pew Hispanic Center ("Changing Faiths: Latinos and the Transformation of American Religion," 2007) augur a shift toward a more nuanced and expansive view of civic engagement.[28] The Pew study's dense snapshot captures Latinos' deep impact on U.S. Christianity, Protestant and Catholic, an impact with an outsized pneumatic or "renewalist" imprint. Its otherwise nuanced collation of survey data concerning religious and political affiliation, electoral choices, and hot-button issues fails ultimately, however, to factor in the agency of undocumented Latino Christians. Yet several tantalizing clues concerning their presence can be found embedded in the data. For example, the significantly higher rate of Evangelical respondents (vs. Catholic and mainline Protestant ones) who said that their churches helped members in need with employment, financial problems, and housing hints at informal networks tending to disenfranchised populations, which would be consonant, as we have seen, with long-standing Latino Pentecostal practice (Catholics could turn to church agencies).[29] That long-standing practice remains absent, of course, from this ahistorical snapshot. Also, the flip side of the extrapolation problem noted above means that these U.S.-sited studies, drawn from the sociology of U.S. Protestantism, draw confessional boundaries too brightly. A more transnational approach would allow for typological porosity and nuanced ascription. Finally, a response of Pentecostal converts and Catholic Charismatics in the Pew Study to the query about their conversion process resonates, albeit unintentionally, with the previous chapter's argument. Sixty-one percent of Evangelicals who were formerly Catholic viewed the Mass as "unexciting" (36 percent left the church because of this). And 65 percent of Charismatic Catholics reported that the Masses they attended included occasional, frequent, or constant ("always") "displays of excitement and enthusiasm such as raising hands, clapping, shouting or jumping."[30] Such motor movements accompany, of course, Pentecostal-like music, a phenomenon about which "Changing Faiths" remains, lamentably, silent.

Historical Evangélicalismo, Mobility, and Religious Remittances

In the early to mid-nineteenth century, liberal Mexican priests, Masons, and others conspired to introduce thousands of Bibles (first Catholic and then Protestant ones) into Mexico. An organic evangelicalismo was strengthened as a result. In the late nineteenth century, missionary strategists overwhelmed a nascent dissident religious movement in Mexico and the U.S. Southwest with superior resources, laid down much of the infrastructure of early Mexican Protestantism, and sought to construct a Spanish-speaking semblance of themselves. There was not enough time for this, however; the middle and aspiring middle classes also proved too small. Macroevents such as the Mexican Revolution and the U.S. Great Depression intervened, pushing out missionaries, stymieing projects, and leaving, for brief but critical interludes, the field to intrepid returned migrants and their coreligionists. The inflow of revivalism carried the evangélico stream over and far beyond the well-laid banks of the mainline project, often in heterodox directions. The overflow also muddled eddies in popular Catholicism.

The circuits and templates set in place by subaltern agents in the early to mid-twentieth century prefigured and facilitated the explosive growth of Pentecostalism and the mutation of Latino and Latin American Protestantism in the late twentieth century. The shift has troubled several researchers, especially Jean-Pierre Bastian, from whom I borrow the biological metaphor of mutation. Bastian lamented the abandonment of a liberal dissident project that championed democratic impulses for a hyperpietistic one that replicates the caudillismo (strongman chieftaincy) of Latin American machista cultures and the magical features of popular Catholicism.[31] Whether benign or not, that mutation occurred in part owing to the musical cultural seeds carried and planted by these agents. Clearly, such agency remains outside the control of missionary and elite strategists as well as academic analysts.

Can the Pentecostal Subaltern Speak?

This book began by noting the unfortunate redactions in early Pentecostalism and interpretations of early Pentecostal history. It has sought to understand the processes whereby the silenced subaltern worked around or in spite of these to articulate a view of a more abundant life. The appropriation of Gayatri Spivak's provocative question about the subaltern speaking is not gratuitous; I borrow it with some trepidation. In her seminal essay, the noted literary critic offered a dismal appraisal of ostensibly solidary representations of peripheral people, especially women, by privileged postcolonial intellectuals. She directed her critique to the work of the Indian subcontinent-based Subaltern Studies group; it also resonated in the parallel musings of earnest Latin Americanist and feminist guilds. The caution over naive complicity with modern global capitalism, epistemology, and essentializing typologies is well taken. *Migrating Faith* shares Spivak's concern to differentiate between two modes of representation: "speaking about" versus "speaking for." But what, then, do we do with the babbling Pentecostal subaltern? With the "wordless talk by a [black] sister" derided in the Los Angeles *Daily Times*'s first report of the Azusa Street Revival? With the discourse of the "poor, rough" Mexican Indian of Azusa Street? *Migrating Faith* argues that American religious historians can no longer beg the absent archive. The guild stands in need of other disciplinary instruments, in order to begin to probe the semiotics of a socially embedded glossolalia and xenolalia that protested both Jim Crow and the Enlightenment. Perhaps, then, it can break through the impasse over origins and progenitors. But it must also emancipate itself from epistemic boundaries set by nation-states and powerful knowledge production systems. There is much historical data to recover and historiographical method and ideology to revisit here. In the case of Azusa's muted Mesoamerican subaltern, we can at least measure the muting and think about its cost. His presence and participation summon us beyond the black–white binary and even critical race theory. Just as we cannot discuss Latino Catholic identity and experience without taking into account the spillover of church–state, cristero, and folk healing influences from Mexico, so the expanded history of Pentecostalism in the U.S. Southwest and Midwest must account for contemporaneous phenomena and circular flows from south of the border. A decade after that loquacious outburst at Azusa, Manuel Gamio decried that the majority of Mexico's indigenous population "does not know how, cannot, or lacks the means to express what they feel."[32] Perhaps Franz Boas's celebrated student can be forgiven, as his storied career was just taking shape in Mexico City in 1906. (We cannot be as indulgent about his acoustic myopia in the late 1920s.) His visionary 1916 *Forjando Patria* (Forging Nation) chartered that country's nascent anthropology and *indianismo/indigenismo* program of the twentieth century. By century's end, however, the indigenous subaltern had wrested away the guild's agenda from the course set by Gamio and others and had spoken back. Similarly, it is clear from our vantage point at the turn of the twenty-first century that the tiny cloud of pneumatic revival first heralded at Azusa Street in 1906 by a "poor, rough" " indigenous Mexican migrant prefigured later torrential downpours in *las Américas*. The unique and fluctuating contours of the revival are finally coming into view. Can the Pentecostal subaltern speak? Clearly, s/he has and continues to do so, to speak and sing. A more pertinent question may be: "Who has ears to hear?"

APPENDIX *Hermanos Alvarado Discography, Volumes 1–5*

Title	English Title	Composer/Translator	Translated?
VOL. 1			
Responsable	Responsible	Nellie Rangel	
El Trigo	The Wheat	Román Alvarado [L. Morales]	
El Tiempo Está Cerca	The Time Is Near	Fidel García	Yes
Un Testimonio	A Testimony	Román Alvarado	
Pero Queda Cristo	But Christ Remains	Alfredo Colom	
Siguiendo Yo a Cristo	I Am Following Jesus	Román Alvarado	
El Mundo Conocerá	The World Shall Know	Román Alvarado	
Un Día Estaremos con el Señor	One Day We Will Be with the Lord	Román Alvarado	
Un Lema	A Theme	Román Alvarado	
Este Mundo Infiel	This Unfaithful World	R. B. Sesma	
No Tienes Excusa	You Have No Excuse	Lita Alvarez	
VOL. 2			
Dame Sabiduria	Give Me Wisdom	Vicente Moreno Reyes	
En la Cruz	At the Cross	Pedro Grado Valdés	Yes
Yo Sigo a Cristo	I Follow Christ	Román Alvarado	
Pecador, Ven al Dulce Jesús	Sinner, Come to the Sweet Jesus	Juan B. Cabrera	Yes
En las Letras de un Papel	In the Letters of a Sheet	Román Alvarado	
Vagué Yo sin Jesús [El es mi Todo Aquí]	I Wandered without Jesus [He's Everything to Me]	Manuel Baca Garcia	Yes
Petición de una Madre	A Mother's Request	Lorenzo Salazar [Román Alvarado]	
Oh, Ven sin Tardar	Oh, Come without Delay	E. A. Hunt [Oh, Why Not Tonight?]	Yes
En Tren Llegará	The Train Shall Arrive	Román Alvarado	

Title	English Title	Composer/Translator	Translated?
VOL. 3			
Mi Doctor Dios Conoce Todo	God My Physician Knows All	Román Alvarado	
Una Petición	A Request	Román Alvarado	
Hay una Senda	There Is a Path	Luis Pacheco [Tomas Estrada]	
Miraron un Cajón	They Watched a Box (TV)	Román Alvarado	
Mensaje a la Iglesia	Message to the Church	Anonymous [Suprema Alabanza]	
El Prisionero	The Prisoner	Román Alvarado	
Al Amanecer [Toma Tiempo para Orar]	At Dawn [Take Time to Pray]	Anonymous [Suprema Alabanza / Consolación]	
Un Día Nuevo	A New Day	Román Alvarado	
El Criticón	The Critic	Román Alvarado	
VOL. 4			
La Luz	The Light	Román Alvarado	
Ten Compasión	Have Compassion (on You)	Román Alvarado	
Una Llamada al Cielo	A Call to Heaven	Román Alvarado	
La Trompeta Final	The Final Trumpet	Román Alvarado	
Ven a El, Pecador	Come to Him, Sinner [Leave It There]	Guadalupe T. Mendoza	Yes
Medley: Alabad a Jehová / Aleluya al Señor / Gozo en mi Alma	Praise the Lord / Hallelujah to the Lord / Joy in my Soul	Anonymous / Marcial de la Cruz / Anonymous	
Dos Sendas	Two Paths	Anonymous [Apostolic]	
Canta Mi Alma	My Soul Sings	Anonymous [Apostolic]	
Llanto de Gratitud	Cry of Gratitude	Anonymous [Apostolic]	
El Tiempo de Pruebas	The Time of Trials	Eduardo Rodríguez	
Más Allá del Sol	Beyond the Sun	Refugio Estrada [Emiliano Ponce]	

Title	English Title	Composer/Translator	Translated?
VOL. 5			
Mundo de Falsedad	World of Falsehood	Baldemar Rodríguez	
Llevar la Cruz de Cristo	Taking the Cross of Christ	Lorenzo Salazar	
Mi Bendito Salvador	My Blessed Savior	Román Alvarado	
Mi Jornada	My Journey	Román Alvarado	
Por una Senda	Along a Pathway	E. Louise Jeter [Take up Your Cross]	Yes
Para Qué Pecar	Why [Should I] Sin?	Alfredo Colom	
Verdad, Verdad	In Truth	Francisco Llorente	
Llévame	Take Me	Román Alvarado	
Mi Ultima Jornada	My Last Journey	Johnson Oatman [The Last Mile of the Way]	Yes
Cuando en Pruebas	When in Trials	Román Alvarado	
Ahora Soy Feliz	I Am Happy Now	[Román Alvarado]	
Fiel Siervo Sigue [Sigue Adelante]	Keep on, Faithful Servant	Anonymous [Suprema Alabanza]	
Tu Todo en el Altar	Is Your All on the Altar?	J. P. Cragin	Yes
Recuerdo para Tí	A Memory for You	[Román Alvarado]	
Seguiré a Mi Jesús	I Will Follow My Jesus	L. Vega	
Decídete	Decide	Efraím Valverde	

NOTES

Introduction

1. Verse 2: "Jesus has promised many dwelling places / Of which he promised to prepare / Leaving these ones forever in forgetfulness / We shall never remember them"; Verse 3: "It is said that peace shall abound for a thousand years / For those who have received free salvation / His song shall always say he was triumphant / That he was delivered from eternal perdition"; Verse 4: "A white gown, and crown and palm branch / One by one shall receive in the end / The eternal life that God gives the soul / This promise shall never fail." The full Spanish and English-language lyrics, scored music (when available), and recordings (when available) of this and the other songs discussed in *Migrating Faith* can be viewed and heard at migratingfaithmusic. com.

2. José Ortega, *Memorias*, 279–80.

3. Registro Civil, Municipio de Tijuana, Baja California, 7 July 1935.

4. The Pew Forum's 2006 global survey estimated that "renewalists" represented one-quarter of the world's two billion Christians. "Spirit and Power: A 10-Country Survey of Pentecostals," Pew Forum on Religion and Public Life, October 2006, http://pewforum.org/surveys/pentecostal/.

5. Spivak, "Can the Subaltern Speak?"

6. *The Apostolic Faith* (Los Angeles), September 1906, 3.

7. Ibid., 2.

8. A San Juan de los Lagos, Jalisco, native, Andrés Ornelas, migrated northward during the Revolution and worked in Miami, Arizona. His encounter with the Book of Proverbs proved catalytic in his subsequent conversion to *evangelicalismo* and foundational to the later narrative of his leadership of a branch of Mexican Pentecostalism. He returned to Mexico in 1921 and joined the Methodist Church in Pachuca, Hidalgo (northwest of Mexico City). One year later, he and Raymundo Nieto, a returned migrant from Kansas, founded the Iglesia Pentecostés Independiente; Ornelas assumed the pastorate fully in 1927. Soon thereafter, the congregation affiliated with Swedish missionary Axel Anderson's Filadelfia Church in Mexico City. In 1941, however, Ornelas disavowed all missionary connections. After several permutations and mergers, the church assumed the name Iglesia Cristiana Independiente Pentecostés. Raymundo Ramírez, *Bodas de oro*.

9. Xenolalia is considered the ability to speak miraculously in a foreign language, a gift claimed by early Pentecostal missionaries. Glossolalia, the more common phenomenon, refers to Spirit speech in nonhuman or angelic language.

10. *The Apostolic Faith* (Los Angeles), November 1906, 1.

11. Almaguer, *Racial Faultlines*.

12. *Exégeta*, May 1957, 8–9.

13. I suggest the term "Apostolicism" to encompass this cultural and doctrinal tributary of non-Trinitarian Pentecostalism, both for sake of leaner nomenclature and to reflect the more common self-designation (*"apostólico"* or "Apostolic") by practitioners.

14. Martin, *Pentecostalism: The World Their Parish*; Martin, *Tongues of Fire*.

15. "Pentecostalism is the Christian equivalent of Islamic revivalism, and as such part of the awakening self-consciousness of the 'rest' of our global society. But it operates in a completely different mode, following the logic of a fissiparous pluralism, not of a 'fortress Islam' militantly engaged in a unity of people and faith." Martin, *Pentecostalism: The World Their Parish*, 167.

16. Währisch-Otto, *The Missionary Self-Perception*.

17. "The color line was washed away in the blood." Eyewitness journalist-evangelist-historian Frank Bartleman Jr. penned the provocative reference to W. E. B. Du Bois's prescient line about a racialized twentieth-century America. Bartleman, *Azusa Street*, 54; Du Bois, "The Souls of Black Folk," vii.

18. Robert Mapes Anderson, *Vision of the Disinherited*.

19. Wacker, *Heaven Below*.

20. Poloma, *Assemblies of God at the Crossroads*.

21. Robert Mapes Anderson relied heavily (this is evident in his footnotes) on anthropologist Felicitas Goodman's early theoretical work on the psycholinguistic dimensions of glossolalia among Mayan Apostolics in Yucatán, Mexico. According to Goodman, socially deprived practitioners accessed a universal linguistic substratum known as tongues-speak. Thus, a pioneering anthropological study of indigenous Mexican Pentecostals informed—indeed was constitutive to—a seminal historical study of U.S. Pentecostals, a fact largely ignored in the historiography of Pentecostalism. Goodman, *Speaking in Tongues*; Goodman, "Disturbances in the Apostolic Church." Goodman later offered a retrospective ethnographic appraisal—through a feminist lens—of her Yucatán project. Goodman, *Maya Apocalypse*.

22. Dayton, "The Limits of Evangelicalism"; Dayton, *The Theological Roots of Pentecostalism*; Spittler, "Are Pentecostals and Charismatics Fundamentalists?"; Allan Anderson, *Introduction to Pentecostalism*.

23. Pew Hispanic Center, "Changing Faiths."

24. "Censo de Población y Vivienda, 2010," Instituto Nacional de Información Estadística y Geográfica de México. The other non-Catholic Christian category, "Bíblicos Diferentes de Evangélicos," was composed of 661,878 Seventh-Day Adventists, 314,932 Latter-day Saints, and 1,561,086 Jehovah's Witnesses.

25. Valenzuela, "Loosening the Nailed Hand," 273–74.

26. Julio C. García Blanco, "Estadísticas y crecimiento de la IAFCJ," in Torres, *Cien años de Pentecostés*, 429–60.

27. Ismael Martín del Campo, "Apostolic Assembly of the Faith in Christ Jesus," in Martínez and Scott, *Los Evangélicos*, 51–75.

28. The 8 December 2014 death of Luz del Mundo apostle Samuel Joaquin in Guadalajara and the question of succession after his fifty years of leadership received front-page treatment in the regional and national dailies and other press outlets, including mention of formal visits of condolences paid by the Jalisco governor and

Guadalajara mayor. Press sources and academics echoed uncritically the church's reported membership of five million adherents in Mexico and abroad. Nevertheless, the hospitality challenge faced by a city expecting over 150,000 bereaving pilgrims speaks to the Luz del Mundo's remarkable prominence in Mexican political life. See http://m.eluniversal.com.mx/notas/estados/2014/muere-lider-espiritual-de-la-iglesia-de-la-luz-del-mundo-97077.html; http://www.noticiasmvs.com/#!/emisiones/primera-emision-con-carmen-aristegui/esperan-asistencia-de-300-mil-fieles-por-muerte-del-lider-de-la-luz-del-mundo-renee-de-la-torre-274.html (10 December 2014).

29. I use the term "template" not in a prospective sense but rather as a retrospective understanding of similar and repetitive patterns in different time periods.

30. Dolan and Hinojosa, *Mexican Americans and the Catholic Church*; Dolan and Vidal, *Puerto Rican and Cuban Catholics in the U.S.*; Dolan and Figueroa Deck, *Hispanic Catholic Culture in the U.S.*; Matovina, *Tejano Religion and Ethnicity*; Matovina, *Guadalupe and Her Faithful*; Matovina and Wiebe-Estrella, *Horizons of the Sacred*; Matovina and Poyo, *¡Presente!*; Pulido, *Sacred World of the Penitentes*; Badillo, *Latinos and the New Immigrant Church*; Treviño, *The Church in the Barrio*; Medina, *Las Hermanas*; Griswold del Castillo and García, *César Chávez*.

31. Atkins-Vásquez, *Hispanic Presbyterians in Southern California*; Barton, *Hispanic Methodists, Presbyterians, and Baptists in Texas*; Brackenridge and García-Treto, *Iglesia Presbiteriana*; Maldonado, *Protestantes/Protestants*; Maldonado and Barton, *Hispanic Christianity within Mainline Protestant Traditions*; Rodríguez, *La primera evangelización norteamericana en Puerto Rico*; Machado, *Of Borders and Margins*; Silva, *Protestantismo y política en Puerto Rico*; Martínez-Fernández, *Protestantism and Political Conflict in the Nineteenth-Century Hispanic Caribbean*; Juan F. Martínez, *Sea la Luz*; Walker, *Protestantism in the Sangre de Cristos*; Juan F. Martínez and Scott, *Los Evangélicos*. Juan Martinez and Lindy Scott's anthology includes several chapters on Pentecostal churches. Arlene Sánchez Walsh's discussion of Latino Pentecostalism's first two decades, with her focus on the Assemblies of God flagship training school in California, the Berean Bible Institute (later Latin American Bible Institute), on the one end, and her analysis of contemporary Evangelical youth identity, on the other end, bracket most of the period studied in *Migrating Faith*. Sánchez Walsh, *Latino Pentecostal Identity*. Gaston Espinosa's recent overview overlaps chronologically with part of the *Migrating Faith* story but follows the more orthodox Trinitarian streams of Mexican American and Puerto Rican Pentecostalism. Espinosa, *Latino Pentecostals*.

32. Busto, *King Tiger*.

33. The moniker was applied to Chicano movement leaders César Chávez, Rodolfo "Corky" González, José Angel Gutiérrez, and Reies Tijerina by Matt Meier and Feliciano Rivera. Meier and Rivera, *The Chicanos*.

34. Peter Nabakov provided the fullest account of the raid. Nabakov, *Tijerina and the Courthouse Raid*.

35. Acuña, *Occupied America: The Chicano's Struggle toward Liberation*; Acuña, *Occupied America: A History of Chicanos*.

36. Ginzburg, *The Cheese and the Worms*.

37. Tijerina participated in the 1968 Peoples' March on Washington, D.C.

38. Luis León's recent oeuvre restores the historiographical balance on labor activist César Chávez as a public prophet. León, *The Political Spirituality of Cesar Chavez*.

39. Gamio, *Mexican Immigration to the United States*; Gamio, *The Mexican Immigrant*.

40. "Appendix I: Guide for Field-Workers Used in Connection with This Study," in Gamio, *Mexican Immigration to the United States*, 197–203.

41. Gamio, *The Mexican Immigrant*, 223.

42. Gamio, *Mexican Immigration to the United States*, 117.

43. Ibid., 84. The 2002 Spanish-language edition of the life history volume included the fuller set of songs and credited Luis Recinos with its compilation. Gamio, *El inmigrante mexicano*, 571–635. Recinos was also the Gamio team member who interviewed journalist Márquez. Ibid., 179.

44. Manuel Gamio Collection, Reel 2. See discussion of Francisco Olazábal in Chapter 1. The church was probably the Presbyterian one identified by researcher Robert C. Jones, the English translator of *The Mexican Immigrant*, in his unpublished 1928 sketch, "The Religious Life of the Mexican in Chicago," included (in Spanish translation) in Patricia Arias and Jorge Durand's remarkable edition of Gamio contemporary Robert Redfield's field journal. Arias and Durand, *Mexicanos en Chicago*, 53–54, 166.

45. Saldivar, *Border Matters*.

46. See Gastón Espinosa's discussion of the trajectory (from confessional-theological to religious studies). Espinosa, "History and Theory in the Study of Mexican American Religions," in Espinosa and García, *Mexican American Religion*, 17–56. Explicit religious studies appointments remain notably absent in most Latino studies departments and programs.

47. George Sánchez, *Becoming Mexican American*, 3–4, 14, 274.

48. "Brisas del campo: De Los Angeles, Cal.," *El Evangelista Mexicano*, 23 April 1928, 124; "Brisas del campo: De Los Angeles, Cal.," *El Evangelista Mexicano*, August 1928, 249.

49. See Luis León's phenomenological synthesis of popular religiosity spanning indigenous, Catholic, and Pentecostal traditions. León, *La Llorona's Children*.

50. Romo, *History of a Barrio*; Montejano, *Anglos and Mexicans in the Making of Texas*. See chapter 7, "The Sacred and the Profane," in George Sánchez, *Becoming Mexican American*, 151–70; Griswold del Castillo and Garcia, *César Chávez*.

51. Levy, Ross, and Levy, *Cesar Chavez*, 115–16.

52. Ibid., 120–21.

53. Cross, *The Burned-over District*.

54. Anzaldúa, *Borderlands/La Frontera*.

55. Mora, *Border Dilemmas*; Valerio-Jiménez, *River of Hope*.

56. Truett, *Fugitive Landscapes*, 9.

57. Ibid., 8.

58. Vélez-Ibáñez, *Border Visions*.

59. Ahlstrom, *A Religious History of the American People*.

60. Tweed, *Retelling U.S. Religious History*; Tweed, *Crossing and Dwelling*.

61. Busto, *King Tiger*, 13.

62. Ibid., 14.

63. Hale, *Mexican Liberalism*; Canclini, *Diego Thomson*; Juan F. Martínez, "The Bible in *Neomejicano* Protestant Folklore," 21–26.

64. Bastian, *Los disidentes*; Baldwin, *Protestants and the Mexican Revolution*.

65. The Southern Methodist periodical *El Evangelista Mexicano* began publication in January 1879 amid a debate with the Iglesia de Jesús over the latter's vaunted nationalism; the Iglesia de Jesús traced its lineage to the Padres Constitucionalistas, an organic nationalist Catholic schism encouraged by liberal president Benito Juárez.

66. Massey and Parrado, "Migradollars"; Daniel Ramírez, "¿Creencias migrantes o peligro transgénico?"

67. The introduction of religious dissidence in San Juan Yaée, a Zapoteco village in Oaxaca's Sierra Juárez, occurred by means of transgressive new music—*tejano* gospel music, to be precise. Over time, the evangélico growth precipitated strong reaction in defense of traditional folkways (*usos y costumbres*). The case unfolded in the period beyond this study's chronological scope but involved Apostolic music from the period under study. Daniel Ramírez, "Usos y costumbres (¿y mañas?)."

68. My notion parallels and offers a historical, inter-Latino and interregional comparison with sociologist Peggy Levitt's discussion of social remittances in U.S.–Dominican transnationalism. Levitt, "Social Remittances"; Levitt," *The Transnational Villagers*; Levitt, *God Needs No Passport*. Levitt's study of social remittances and cultural diffusion within Dominican migration led Helen Ebaugh and Janet Chafetz to coin the term "religiously relevant resources," to describe the flow of resources to Houston immigrant congregations from congregations in their home countries. Ebaugh and Chafetz, *Religion across Borders*.

69. The Mexican Migration Project is based at Princeton University and the Universidad de Guadalajara. http://mmp.opr.princeton.edu/.

70. Durand, *Más allá de la línea*. See especially chapter 7, "Patrones culturales y migración."

71. Massey, Alarcón, Durand, and González, *Return to Aztlán*.

72. Durand, *Más allá de la línea*; Massey and Parrado, "Migradollars"; Massey and Singer, "The Social Process of Undocumented Border Crossing."

73. Durand and Massey, *Miracles on the Border*.

74. Linde, *Life Stories*.

Chapter 1

1. Verse 3: "The time of affliction, of affliction nears / When there will no longer be room / But now the Savior / Has come to save his people."

2. Cragin, *Melodías evangélicas* (1933), no. 45; Hargrave, *Rayos de Esperanza*.

3. Antonio Nava interview.

4. Griswold del Castillo, *The Los Angeles Barrio*, 161–70.

5. Historian Cecil Robeck has offered the thickest description of the Azusa Street Revival's multicultural features and unfolding events and relies on Arthur Osterberg's recollections to buttress this point about the first Spirit baptisms at the Azusa Street locale. Robeck, *The Azusa Street Mission and Revival*, 72–73, 196; Osterberg,

"I Was There." See also Arthur Osterberg's transcribed oral history in Espinosa, *William J. Seymour*, 343–45.

6. The Los Angeles *Daily Times* (18 April 1906) described a congregation of "colored people and a sprinkling of whites" in the paper's first account of the revival. The story's headlines—"Weird Babble of Tongues. New Sect of Fanatics is Breaking Loose. Wild Scene Last Night on Azusa Street. Gurgle of Wordless Talk by a Sister"—primed readers for racialized caricature:

> Breathing strange utterances and mouthing a creed which it would seem no sane mortal could understand, the newest religious sect has started in Los Angeles. Meetings are held in a tumble-down shack on Azusa Street, near San Pedro Street, and devotees of the weird doctrine practice the most fanatical rites, preach the wildest theories and work themselves into a state of mad excitement in their peculiar zeal. Colored people and a sprinkling of whites compose the congregation, and night is made hideous in the neighborhood by the howling of the worshippers who spend hours swaying forth and back in a nerve-racking attitude of prayer and supplication. They claim to have "the gift of tongues," and to be able to comprehend the babble.

7. *The Apostolic Faith* (Los Angeles), September 1906, 1.

8. *The Apostolic Faith* (Los Angeles), October 1906, 4. The editors' clumsy Spanish orthography is also worth noting.

9. *The Apostolic Faith* (Los Angeles), November 1906, 4; *The Apostolic Faith* (Los Angeles), December 1906, 4; Robeck, *The Azusa Street Mission and Revival*, 189, 196–98.

10. Juan Navarro, naturalized in 1871, appears as a "laborer" in the household of prominent Los Angeles developer and attorney Charles J. Ellis in the 1880 census. He is similarly listed in the 1898 city directory. The city's 1906–1907 international directory lists him as a "laborer." I acknowledge here the assiduous research efforts of Herminia "Minnie" Martínez, who has supplied me with binders of the relevant naturalization and other documents for Juan Navarro, Francisco Llorente, and others. (Material in author's files.)

11. A consensus on the significance of the Azusa Street Revival's interracial character and on African American evangelist William J. Seymour's status as co-progenitor of twentieth-century Pentecostalism (vs. Charles Parham of Topeka, Kansas, and Houston, Texas) continues to elude historians. Creech, "Visions of Glory"; Goff, *Fields White unto Harvest*; Nelson, "For Such a Time as This"; Walter Hollenweger, "The Black Roots of Pentecostalism," in Allan H. Anderson and Hollenweger, *Pentecostals after a Century*, 33–44; Blumhofer and Wacker, "Who Edited the Azusa Mission's *Apostolic Faith*?"; Callahan, "Fleshly Manifestations"; Daniel Ramírez, "Beyond Racial Incommensurability in American Revivalism."

12. Bartleman, *Azusa Street*, 58–59. Bartleman's sentiments are best understood when juxtaposed with his recollection of the revival's initial harmony: "We had no 'respect of persons.' The rich and educated were the same as the poor and ignorant. . . . We only recognized God. All were equal. No flesh might glory in His presence. . . . Those were Holy Ghost meetings, led of the Lord. It had to start in poor surroundings, to keep out the selfish, human element. All came down in humility

together, at His feet. . . . The rafters were low, the tall must come down. By the time they got to 'Azusa' they were humbled, ready for the blessing. The fodder was thus placed for the lambs, not for the giraffes. All could reach it." Ibid., 58–59.

13. Cantú, Ortega, Cota, and Rangel, *Historia de la Asamblea Apostólica*, 6.

14. Ibid., 6.

15. The 1912 Los Angeles city directory lists a Spanish Apostolic Faith Mission at 627 Alpine, pastored by Reverend G. Valenzuela, and the Star of Bethlehem (Spanish) Mission at 1514 St. James. Juan Navarro is listed separately as pastor of the Star of Bethlehem Mission.

16. Robert Mapes Anderson, *Vision of the Disinherited*, 113.

17. Espinosa, "Borderland Religion," 190–93.

18. Antonio Nava, *Autobiografía*, 1 (translation mine). For the following chapters, unless otherwise noted, the English translations of original Spanish-language materials will be mine.

19. Ibid., 2.

20. Ibid., 2.

21. "He saw himself once again in the military compound on a review day. They were lined up by height as was the rule, and suddenly the General appeared in gala dress, although not in the requisite army uniform, but in an immaculate whiteness, with boots shining as though of gold, and with a shining sword at his hip. Looking over all of them, he suddenly fixed his gaze on him, and unsheathing his shining and brilliant sword, he nudged him forward, pushing him with the sword, thereby indicating to me that I was not in my correct place; forcing me to occupy the spot immediately in front of me and, with a new nudge, the next position, and so on repeatedly up to the head of the formation; at which point he sheathed his sword and left. Upon relating this to Saulo and Silas, this caused them to comprehend with a wider vision the work of God, whereupon Saulo said to Silas: 'Do you know what is happening? God has left us in order to raise him up.'" Rentería, *La Luz del Mundo*, 32–33.

22. I suggest a notion similar to Arjun Appadurai's idea of "global ethnoscape," a term he coined to refer to the Hindu Indian diaspora. Appadurai, *Modernity at Large*.

23. Colonia Zaragoza was formalized as an *agrarista* (agrarian reform) settlement on expropriated land in 1925, partially in response to xenophobic (anti-Chinese) agitation led by Oaxaca native Filiberto Crespo. Contreras Mora, *El movimiento agrario*, 123. Bonifaz de Hernández, Gil Durán, and Miranda Polanco, "La frontera en la actualidad," 140.

24. José Ortega, *Memorias*, 281. Antonio Nava convert Ursula Gutiérrez had recently moved, first to Mexicali, Baja California, and then to the more tolerant terrain of Calexico, California, from Santa Rosalía after the death there of her husband Pablo. His clandestine Bible reading in the mine's caves provoked clerical and communal censure. Anticipating his demise from an infected wound (caused by a projectile thrown by fellow miners), Gutiérrez instructed his wife, "Today you bury me; tomorrow you take the family north [to the United States] and search for the Gospel." Moses Gutiérrez, *In My Father's House Are Many Mansions*, 59.

25. Robeck, *The Azusa Street Mission and Revival*, 197.

26. Vernon McCombs, "Spanish Work," "Spanish and Portuguese District," and "Latin American Mission," *MEC Journal of the Southern California Annual Conference*, 1912–21.

27. Robeck, "Evangelization, or Proselytism of Hispanics?," 6; Robeck, *The Azusa Street Mission and Revival*, 196–98. Gastón Espinosa's report of Abundio López's prior Presbyterian membership does not preclude López's movement within Holiness circles (his *Apostolic Faith* testimonial is trenchant with Wesleyan language) and reinforces the notion of proto-evangelicalismo. Espinosa, *Latino Pentecostals in America*, 285.

28. *The Apostolic Faith* (Los Angeles), October 1906, 1.

29. Domínguez, *Norteamérica y las Antillas*.

30. "The Mexican Work: Ricardo, TX," *Evangel*, 31 July 1915, 1.

31. "A Mexican Pastor's Testimony," *Evangel*, 6 January 1917, 16.

32. "Brother Lopez Makes His Report," *Evangel*, 2 June 1917, 13.

33. This does not represent a zero-sum equation; Pentecostal growth did not necessarily entail Methodist declension. Methodism rebounded and prospered in southern California in the ensuing decades, projecting a significant social and institutional presence, helped in part by the arrival of prominent leaders from revolutionary Mexico, such as Vicente Mendoza, Ecuario Sein, a liberal leader from San Luis Potosí, and Miguel Narro. Mendoza, Methodism's gifted hymn translator and composer, shored up the Latin American Mission's Sunday school program throughout the region. Sein headed up the area's first Mexican Protestant ministers' association; his son was the first Mexican to enroll in the University of Southern California (and later in Drew University, New Jersey). Narros's daughter Rosa, aided by fellow deaconess Ida Birkemeier, rescued the tottering outpost in Calexico–Mexicali, drawing official interest and favor in the territorial capital of Baja California. *Journal of the Latin American Mission*, 2nd session, June 23–25, 1921, 24–25; *Journal of the Latin American Mission*, 3rd session, February 9–10, 1922. Holland, *The Religious Dimension in Hispanic Los Angeles*, 240–89.

34. Antonio Nava, *Autobiografía*, 7; Antonio Nava sermon, "Es Tiempo de Milagros," (sermon preached at the Apostolic Assembly, Hayward, Calif., 1985, audiocassette recording in author's possession). Nava's written and spoken recollections reflect contemporaneous developments in Mexico. For a critical treatment of the Knights of Columbus and Catholic resistance to the restrictive anticlerical measures of the Plutarco Calles government, especially its belated (1926) enforcement of the 1917 constitution, see Matute, *Historia de la revolución mexicana*, 287. The polemics often took poetic form. Manuel Gamio's research team discovered a martial anti-Catholic parody of the Mexican national anthem, penned by Tucson Baptist pastor M.A. Urbina. "Parodia del Himno Nacional Mexicano hecha por los mexicanos protestantes," in Manuel Gamio, *El inmigrante mexicano* [2002], 614–17. The item and text were not included in the 1931 English edition of *The Mexican Immigrant*.

35. Ewart, *The Phenomenon of Pentecost*, 94–144; Fred Foster, *Their Story: 20th Century Pentecostals*, 88–122; Reed, "*In Jesus' Name*." Douglas Jacobsen has systematized the theological ideas of Oneness pioneers Garfield T. Haywood (African American),

Andrew Urshan (Persian American), and Robert C. Lawson (African American). Jacobsen, *Thinking in the Spirit*. For a nuanced historical study of early Oneness Pentecostal theology and soteriology (mostly white), see Fudge, *Christianity without the Cross*, 43–74.

36. See my discussion of this in Daniel Ramírez, "A Historian's Response."

37. Alice Luce, "Mexican Work along the Border," *Evangel*, 15 June 1918.

38. Given the continued military tumult in northeastern Mexico, the U.S. consul in Monterrey ordered Luce and Sunshine Marshall's exit from Mexico. Florence Murcutt, a Jewish convert and medical doctor who worked with them in Monterrey, was charged with espionage and prevented from reentering Mexico after a sudden trip to San Antonio, Texas. "Historia de los primeros años de las Asambleas de Dios latinas: El principio," cap. 1, *La Luz Apostólica*, March 1966, 6. Mexican resentment over the prolonged punitive expedition against Francisco Villa, violent labor agitation against U.S. oil companies in the port city of Tampico, Tamaulipas, and Yaqui revolts in Sonora caused the U.S. secretary of state Robert Lansing to issue forceful directives for evacuation to consular representatives and other officials. "Consul Dickenson to Secretary of State," San Luis Potosí, 29 December 1916; "Secretary of State to Consul Dickenson," Washington, D.C., 2 January 1917; "Collection of Customs Cobb to Secretary of State," El Paso, 31 January 1917, *Foreign Relations of the United States*, 1019–30.

39. Alice Luce, "Mexican Work in California," *Evangel*, 20 April 1918, 11.

40. Alice Luce, "License Application," 1920, Flower Pentecostal Heritage Center, Springfield, Mo. Luce's response to question number 20 of the application is telling: "Do you yourself or any native evangelists with you hold or teach any doctrine contrary to the Fundamentals of the General Council?: No—God forbid."

41. "The Missionary Department," *Evangel*, 1 November 1919, 23.

42. "Historia de los primeros años de las Asambleas de Dios latinas: el principio," cap. 1, *La Luz Apostólica*, March 1966, 2.

43. "Reports from the Field," *Evangel*, 3 May 1919, 14.

44. "The Missionary Department," *Evangel*, 27 December 1919, 12.

45. Cantú, Ortega, Cota, and Rangel, *Historia de la Asamblea Apostólica*, 9. The Disciples' official history blamed the closing of once-promising churches in the California Imperial Valley on the absence of leadership and finances: "Churches were once alive and seemingly prospering at Niland, Seeley, Imperial and Calexico. Appeals were made by each of these churches for assistance at various times, but all of them faded out of the picture and in some instances property was sold to other religious bodies. The congregation at Calexico was a Negro church. After a long struggle the church disbanded; the property was sold by the State Society in 1924 to a Spanish-speaking church." Cole, *The Christian Churches (Disciples of Christ) of Southern California*, 164.

46. Herrera interview.

47. Alice Luce, "Mexican Work in California," *Evangel*, 1 September 1923.

48. "Report of the Pentecostal Mexican Work in Texas, New Mexico, Colorado, Arizona, and Old Mexico," *Evangel*, 1 November 1919, 22.

49. McGee, "Pioneers of Pentecost," 5–6, 12–16.

50. "Historia de los primeros años de las Asambleas de Dios latinas," cap. 3, *La Luz Apostólica*, May 1966, 3.

51. J. W. Welch, "Report of Trip through Texas," *Evangel*, 12 June 1920, 10–11.

52. H. C. Ball, "A Call for More Laborers for the Mexican Work," *Evangel*, 24 March 1917, 13.

53. "Observaciones del Hno. Bazan sobre esta historia," *La Luz Apostólica*, April 1966, 12.

54. "Mexican Work in California," *Evangel*, 20 April 1918, 11.

55. "Mexican Work along Border," *Evangel*, 15 June 1918; *Evangel*, 28 December 1918, 7.

56. Olazábal credited a sympathetic group of "Apostolic Faith sisters" with lending him use of their building during a lean financial period. These were probably African American leaders of the Apostolic Faith Training Home. Francisco Olazábal, "Datos biográficos de la obra pentecostal en El Paso, Texas," *El Mensajero Cristiano*, April 1923, 5, 9.

57. "The Mexican Work at El Paso," *Evangel*, 30 September 1922, 13.

58. "A Bible School for the Mexican Workers," *Evangel*, 6 January 1923, 13.

59. The school in San Diego, California, later adopted the same name, Latin American Bible Institute, and was moved to La Puente, near Los Angeles, California, in 1940. For a thoughtful appraisal of Luce and the California LABI, see Sánchez Walsh, *Latino Pentecostal Identity*, chapter 2; and Sánchez Walsh, "Workers for the Harvest," 54–79.

60. "Historia de los primeros años de las Asambleas de Dios latinas," cap. 4, *La Luz Apostólica*, June 1966, 3.

61. Ibid.; Guillén, *La historia del Concilio Latino Americano*, 79–91. Demetrio and Nellie Bazán soon returned to the AG and Ball's mentorship. Bazán, "Historia de los primeros 50 años de las Asambleas de Dios," *La Luz Apostólica*, November 1967, 7; Gohr, "A Dedicated Ministry among Hispanics," 7–9, 17.

62. Guillén, *La historia del Concilio Latino Americano*, 90. For an assessment of the "pious paternalism" of H. C. Ball and Alice Luce, especially toward Francisco Olazábal, see Espinosa, "Borderland Religion," 141–83.

63. "¡De estas cositas debe estar llena la independencia!" Francisco Olazábal, "Remitido," *El Evangelista Mexicano*, 1 August 1908. The intra-Protestant debate—argued chiefly on the MECS side by Guadalajara-based ex-Catholic priest Antonio Valiente y Pozo—was carried in the biweekly issues of the *Evangelista Mexicano* running from 1 August to 15 October 1908. The periodical declared a unilateral truce ("La Ultima Palabra") in that last issue.

64. "Another confirmation of this underlying desire among the Latin Americans for national evangelical Churches is found in Mexico. A movement of independence from foreigners and missionary support was begun by preachers who had been previously employed by mission Boards, some of them from the United States, but most of them Mexicans. They refused to have anything to do with mission Boards, identifying them with a foreign invasion. They appealed particularly to the patriotism of the people, and naturally to their prejudices. At one time in the Mexican

churches in San Antonio, Texas, there was such a strong movement that the denominational churches were practically depopulated, and all the Mexicans came together in an immense 'Iglesia Evangélica Independiente.' This movement grew very rapidly for a while. The pastors received no stated salary. It was largely wrecked on the financial rock, though there are still some strong congregations existing and doing good work. While it seemed to the missionaries that the whole movement was selfish, yet its great temporary success showed the strong appeal nationalism makes and the tendency among all the people to unite in a national Church which refuses to recognize the differences which exist in the United States." "The Report of Commission VIII on Cooperation and the Promotion of Unity," in *Christian Work in Latin America*, 3:66–67. Notably, of the eight commissions established for the Panama conclave (a U.S.-led response to the 1910 World Missionary Conference in Edinburgh, Scotland), only one (Literature) was chaired by a Latin American, Mexican Methodist educator Andrés Osuna.

65. Guillén, *La historia del Concilio Latino Americana*, 118.

66. Espinosa, "Francisco Olazabal: Charisma, Power, and Faith Healing," in Goff and Wacker, *Portraits of a Generation*, 192–93.

67. Gastón Espinosa listed at least eight Latino Pentecostal denominations in the United States and Puerto Rico that derive directly from Olazábal's ministry and six others it affected (including Latino jurisdictions within white Pentecostal denominations). Ibid., Espinosa, 403. See also Espinosa, "God Made a Miracle in My Life," 121–38; Espinosa, "Latino Pentecostal Healing in the North American Borderlands," 129–49.

68. Abundio López finished his ministerial career in CLADIC. Espinosa, "Borderland Religion," 122.

69. Espinosa, *Latino Pentecostals in America*, 233–54.

70. De la Luz García, *El movimiento pentecostal en México*.

71. Historian Deyssi de la Luz García noted David Ruesga's inconsistent approach to his erstwhile U.S. denominational partners, initially embracing them in formal agreements and then, in reaction to what he perceived to be underhanded paternalism, decrying to the federal government the subterfuge of foreigners. Ibid., 155–89.

72. Nava included white and black leaders in this judgment. Antonio Nava interview.

73. For an uncritical account of the tutelage, see De León, *The Silent Pentecostals*. On Luce as a strategic pedagogue and her imprint on AG missions, see Everett B. Wilson and Ruth M. Wilson, "Alice Luce: A Visionary Victorian," in Goff and Wacker, *Portraits of a Generation*, 159–76.

74. The PAW's 1919–1920 ministerial roster listed two Latino ministers from California: Albino Jiménez of Los Angeles and Manuel Sánchez of Oakland, as well as African American Emanuel Walker, a participant in charter Apostolic conclaves in California and Mexico. "Minute Book and Ministerial Record of the General Assembly of the Pentecostal Assemblies of the World, 1919 and 1920," appendix in Tyson, *The Early Pentecostal Revival*, 293–315. Walker and Jiménez were listed on the roster of attendees at the 1925 convention of the Iglesia de la Fe Apostólica Pentecostés, held in San Bernardino, California, Walker as pastor in Yuma, Arizona, and Jiménez

as pastor/evangelist in Chino, California (along with Chino pastor Margarito Vargas). The 1926 IFAP roster listed only Vargas as pastor in Chino.

75. "Delphine Llorenti Death Certificate," County of Alameda, 21 May 1925. Antonio Nava, *Autobiografía*, 7–8.

76. Bernardo Hernández, *Estatutos acordados en la 1ra. convención mexicana*.

77. Ibid., 4.

78. Ibid., 5.

79. Ibid., 8.

80. Ibid., 8.

81. Bernardo Hernández, *Catequista del Concilio Apostólico Cristiano del Pentecostés*.

82. Dayton, *Theological Roots*. Sammy Alfaro has posited pneumatic Christology as a common ground for Latino Pentecostal Trinitarian–Oneness dialogue. Alfaro, *Divino Compañero*.

83. Hernández, *Estatutos*, 8.

84. José Ortega, *Memorias*, 64–65.

85. Ibid., 64.

86. Facsimile copies in Cantú, Ortega, Cota, and Rangel, *Historia de la Asamblea Apostólica*, n.p.

87. José Ortega, *Memorias*, 49. Ortega's volume includes a photographic reproduction of Nicolasa García's license certificate, dated 15 January 1939.

88. On borderlands healers Teresa de Caborca and el Niño Fidencio, see Luis León, *La Llorona's Children*.

89. The Mexicali and Colonia Zaragoza (Baja California) cases are archived as "Encarnación Meza-Mexicali," Archivo General de la Nación, 2/344 (30)/5, Caja 21, Exp. 5.

90. Abelardo Rodríguez to Secretario de Gobernación, 9 March 1928, ibid.

91. Secretaría de Gobernación to Governor Aberlado Rodríguez, 24 March 1928, ibid.

92. Pedro Ceniceros et al., "Petition," 1 July 1928, ibid. Note this contemporaneous mention of the "aleluya" moniker.

93. Encarnación Meza et al. to Secretario de Gobernación, 16 April 1929, ibid.

94. Ramón V. Santoyo letter to Secretario de Gobernación, 23 June 1931, ibid.

95. Carlos Trejo Lerdo de Tejada and Ramón V. Santoyo letter to Secretario de Gobernación, 16 July 1931, ibid.

96. Antonio Nava interview; Herrera interview.

97. Bundy, "G. T. Haywood: Religion for Urban Realities," in Goff and Wacker, *Portraits of a Generation*, 237–53; Tyson, *The Early Pentecostal Revival*, 241–53.

98. José Ortega interview.

99. For a study of such Gramscian strategies, see Peña, *The Texas-Mexican Conjunto*.

100. H. S. Ball, "The Work Prospers on the Mexican Border," *Evangel*, 8 July 1922, 13.

101. *Evangel*, 30 September 30 1922, 13. Both Blaisdell and Howard were married to Mexican American evangelists-pastors. Blaisdell later headed the AG work in Central America. Chinese immigrants established important beachheads in Mexico's northern border towns, especially Mexicali, where the MEC Latin American Mis-

sion established a viable congregation. On Chinese migration and repatriation, see Roberto Chao Romero, *The Chinese in Mexico*.

102. I borrow the term from the historian Herbert Bolton, whose magisterial biography of Eusebio Kino, the Italian-born pioneer of Jesuit missions in Sonora and Arizona, carried this suggestive title. Bolton, *Rim of Christendom*.

Chapter 2

1. Hall, Mack, and Miles, *The Service of Praise*, No. 16.

2. "La Nube del Fuego" appears (as No. 4) in the 1933 edition of Paul Cragin's *Melodías Evangélicas*, attributed to Abundio López. Hymnal redaction often indicates a prior long-standing oral tradition.

3. Methodist Episcopal Church missionary Buell C. Campbell reported from his newly assigned Valparaiso station on Nellie Laidlaw's prior "dissolute life and propensity to getting drunk" and the broad Protestant concern over matters in the Santiago MEC. "Buell C. Campbell Letter to Homer C. Stuntz," 25 July 1910, United Methodist Archives.

4. *Chile Evangélico*, 19 November 1909, 2. Quoted in Rasmussen and Helland, *La Iglesia Metodista Pentecostal*, 74.

5. Mansilla, *La cruz y la esperanza*, 42–43. The song was revived to mark the centennial celebrations of Chilean Pentecostalism in 2009. http://www.youtube.com/watch?v=5BlWRuGYOBY (21 April, 2014).

6. Maclovio Gaxiola, *Historia de la Iglesia Apostólica*; Manuel J. Gaxiola, *La serpiente y paloma*; Kenneth Gill, *Toward a Contextualized Theology*. Maclovio Gaxiola secured an interview with Nicolasa García during a March 1944 visit to Westmoreland, California, and published forthwith the information on the Iglesia Apostólica's origins (along with a photo of Romana Valenzuela and her husband) in the church's new periodical. Maclovio Gaxiola, "Mensajeros de Paz y Amor," *Exégeta*, 1 July 1944, 3.

7. Cumberland, *Mexican Revolution*.

8. González, Ramos, and Pérez, *La batalla de Torreón*.

9. Samuel López, *Historia de la Iglesia Apostólica*.

10. Guzmán attended the 1924 Concilio Interdenominacional Mexicano de Iglesias Cristianas convention in San Antonio, Texas, renewing his earlier friendship with Francisco Olazábal. Guillén, *La historia del Concilio Latino Americano*, 302–5.

11. "Historia de los primeros años de las Asambleas de Dios latinas: El principio," cap. 1, *La Luz Apostólica*, March 1966, 2; Stock, "George S. Montgomery," 12–14, 20. Manuel Gaxiola documented the irruption of an isolated revival in 1907 in Tecupeto, Sonora. The revival, whose catalyst may have been more a case of a circulating Bible than missionary evangelism, endured for eleven years. Several adherents later joined the Asambleas de Dios and Iglesia de Dios (Evangelio Completo). Manuel J. Gaxiola, *La serpiente y la paloma*, 145–46. George Blaisdell reported on his encounter with the Tecupeto group in late 1922 and lamented the lack of personnel: "The work looks prosperous here in Agua Prieta. We met Brother Escarcega here and he tells me that they have finished their chapel in Tacupeto, Mexico, with the exception of whitening it on the inside, all of which means an advance in the work. Hallelujah!

The great lack here is workers—consecrated men and women. Three big states and only four workers, counting my wife [Francisca], who is the equal of a man. The wives of the other workers have several little ones." *Evangel*, 30 September 1922, 13.

12. "Historia de los primeros años de las Asambleas de Dios latinas," cap. 3, *La Luz Apostólica*, May 1966, 3.

13. Ibid., 11.

14. De Certeau, *Practice of Everyday Life*.

15. Manuel J. Gaxiola, *La serpiente y la paloma*, 149.

16. Kenneth Gill, *Toward a Contextualized Theology*, 47; Manuel J. Gaxiola, *La serpiente y la paloma*, 151.

17. Maclovio Gaxiola, "Mensajeros de Paz y Amor," *Exégeta*, 1 July 1944, 3. Manuel Gaxiola claimed that Carbajal de Valenzuela traveled between Chihuahua and Los Angeles, California, more than once from 1914 to 1916. Manuel J. Gaxiola, *La serpiente y la paloma*, 149. Kenneth Gill agreed with this, citing his 1979 interview with the aged Pánfila Guevara. Kenneth Gill, *Toward a Contextualized Theology*, 49.

18. Manuel J. Gaxiola, *La serpiente y la paloma*, 151.

19. Manuel and Maclovio Gaxiola identified this as Congregationalist, José Ortega as Methodist. Ibid., 142–143; Maclovio Gaxiola, "Mensajeros de Paz y Amor," *Exégeta*, 1 July 1944, 3; José Ortega, *Memorias*, 61. The ambiguity reinforces the notion of a proto-evangélico identity. Villa Aldama first appeared as a preaching point ("to be supplied") of the MECS Mexican Northwest Mission Conference in 1890. Baquiero, *La Conferencia Annual Fronteriza*, 13. The MECS Mission Board reported periodic visits in 1906 and 1907 to Villa Aldama by missionaries Samuel E. Kilgore and Lemuel B. Newberry from their Chihuahua City base, as well as plans to prepare students of that city's Colegio Palmore to take up mission work in Aldama and other outlying towns. The 1906 report also mentioned that the Congregationalists had abandoned several localities in the area, owing to the lack of funds. "Mexico Mission Conferences," *Foreign Missions Board Annual Report*, MECS, 1906, 92; "Northwest Mexican Mission Conference," *Foreign Missions Board Annual Report*, MECS, 1907, 97. Nevertheless, the American Board of Commissioners for Foreign Missions maintained a strong institutional presence—through the Iglesia Trinidad and Instituto Chihuahuense—in Chihuahua City through the end of the decade.

20. Kenneth Gill, *Toward a Contextualized Theology*, 45–46. Under the proposed comity arrangement, the American Board of Commissioners for Foreign Missions and the Methodist MECS Foreign Missions Board would trade responsibility for Chihuahua and Guadalajara. "Conference of Missionaries and Mission Boards Working in Mexico," Cincinnati, Ohio, 30 June–1 July 1914, appendix D of "The Report of Commission VIII on Cooperation and the Promotion of Unity," *Christian Work in Latin America*, 3:111–20. On Mexican Protestant nationalism and residual resentment toward the "Plan de Asesinato" (a play on words), see Young, "The Cincinnati Plan."

21. The Edinburgh conclave excluded Latin America from its scope, owing to the sensibilities of high church Anglicans who were reticent to label long-standing Catholic territories as lands in need of Christian missions. By the time the CCLA had consolidated, a second and third generation of Latin American and Latino

leaders, many trained in Protestant schools and institutes, had begun to assume national and hemispheric leadership. Their expanding influence was on display at the congresses convened by the CCLA and in their steady literary and theological production in denominational periodicals and interdenominational journals. Inman, *Evangelicals at Havana*. The gentlemanly pursuit of Pan-Americanism could not fully mask, however, the policy's alignment with U.S. geopolitical imperatives and the power imbalance favoring missionary structures. Historian Arturo Piedra overlaid the chronologies and argued that many missionaries were, at best, naively complicit in their support of U.S. expansionism (e.g., the acquisition of Puerto Rico, Cuba, and the Philippines in 1898 and of the Panama Canal territory in 1904). Others, such as Warren Candler, were more forthright. In the wake of the Spanish American War, the Southern Methodist bishop challenged the churches to send "the preacher and teacher" to build on the exemplary work of the soldier and marine. Piedra, *Evangelización protestante en América Latina*, 163–218.

22. Bishop Henry C. Morrison convened a meeting of all the MECS's Mexico missionaries and workers to discuss the comity arrangements in preparation for the denomination's General Conference in Cincinnati, Ohio. None of the thirteen attendees at this, the second MECS all-Mexico strategy meeting, were Mexican. The first such MECS meeting—called by Bishop Joseph S. Key and also without Mexican clergy present—was held in 1896 in San Luis Potosí. "Mexican Border Mission Conference," *Board of Missions Annual Report*, MECS, 1914, 189; Baquiero, *La Conferencia Anual Fronteriza*, 15. A proto-comity plan put forth in 1896 by MEC (northern) bishop John W. Butler was rejected by the Mexican preachers. Ruiz, *Hombres nuevos*, 63.

23. *Christian Work in Latin America*, 3:24.

24. "Papal Lands: Mission to Mexico," *ABCFM The One Hundred and Eighth Annual Report, 1918*, 198–202.

25. "El Movimiento en Pro de Un Gran Avivamiento Nacional," "Gran Convención Nacional de San Luis Potosí," "La Cruzada para el Despertamiento Religioso," *El Evangelista Mexicano*, 15 September 1908, 141–42.

26. Ibid.

27. The school reported an enrollment of 522 in 1906 and 512 in 1913. "Mexico Mission Conferences," *Board of Missions Annual Report*, MECS, 1914, 93; "Secretaries Reports," *Board of Missions Annual Report*, MECS, 1914, 19.

28. The American congregation proved too mercurial to anchor Methodism in Chihuahua. Missionary Lemuel B. Newberry was listed as pastor of Chihuahua City's American congregation from 1906 to 1910; E. T. Campbell was pastor in 1911; however, this congregation remained absent from reports beginning in 1912—again, probably the result of the tumult. Campbell relocated to El Paso, Texas, and soon thereafter to the East Oklahoma Conference.

29. "The Secretary of State to Certain American Consuls," Washington, D.C., 11 September 1915, *Foreign Relations of the United States*, 837.

30. Bastian, *Los disidentes*, 281.

31. "Central Mexico Conference," *Board of Missions Annual Report*, MECS, 1915, 212. Historian Ramiro Jaimes argues that the relative silence concerning revolutionary

events up through 1912 in the northern MEC's *Abogado Cristiano* periodical demonstrates a bifurcation in Methodist responses to the Revolution. While missionaries fretted over the end of Porfirio Díaz's regime, several Mexican MEC preachers, including José Rumbia, Andrés Mota, Benigno Zenteno, and José Trinidad Ruiz, sparked revolutionary agitation in central Mexico. The role played by evangélicos in the Revolution was largely a matter of personal initiative. Jaimes Martínez, "El metodismo ante la Revolución." A young Pascual Orozco subordinate, Alberto Rembao, also Congregationalist, was spirited to the United States after being wounded in combat; he later served as a prominent hemispheric leader and editor of the literary periodical, *Nueva Democracia.*

32. Baquiero, *La Conferencia Anual Fronteriza*, 11.

33. Ibid., 17.

34. "Northwest Mexican Mission Conference," *Board of Missions Annual Report*, MECS, 1907, 97.

35. "Mexico Mission Conferences," *Board of Missions Annual Report*, MECS, 1906, 92–93.

36. "Mexican Border Mission Conference," *Board of Missions Annual Report*, MECS, 1915, 195.

37. *Actas de la XIX Conferencia Anual Central de México de la Iglesia Metodista del Sur de México.*

38. The English Mexican family of clergy included Juan's brother Francisco and nephew Santos. Juan's father Santiago (James) served as a longtime missionary to Mexico (he married Juana Gómez, a member of one of the country's pioneer evangélico families with a martyrdom legacy). "El Rev. Francisco Pascoe," and "Cae otro siervo fiel," *El Evangelista Mexicano*, 15 December 1928, 374, 380–81.

39. "Mexican Border Mission Conference," *Board of Missions Annual Report*, MECS, 1914, 192.

40. "Northwest Mexican Mission Conference," *Board of Missions Annual Report*, MECS, 1913, 182; "Mexican Border Conference," *Board of Missions Annual Report*, MECS, 1917, 159.

41. Manuel J. Gaxiola, *La serpiente y la paloma*, 150.

42. The recovery of Rubén Ortega's post-Chihuahua trajectory argues against a zero-sum approach for the study of religious conversion. His story's eclipse in Apostolic history may reflect a need for apologists always to present Pentecostalism as supersessive to a waning Methodism. In fact, Methodism's heyday extended further into the twentieth century. Ortega's thirty-year career with the Texas Tuberculosis Association and his pursuit of studies under the agency's auspices at the University of Michigan remind us of Methodism's capacious vocation to permeate other spheres of human activity. The data on Ortega's later trajectory were taken from an oral history left by his son Abel, a World War II veteran. Abel Ortega interview. Rubén Ortega's later reputation as a persuasive ("spiritual anointing") and eager evangelist ("always ready to present God's messages") is evident from reports of his sermons for the Wesleyan Institute's weeklong seminar held in June 1930 at the Trinidad church in San Antonio, Texas. The "selfless servant of God" attracted a full house over five nights. José Alva, "Ecos del Instituto Bíblico," *El Evangelista Mexicano*,

1 July 1930, 588; P. G. Verduzco, "Instituto Bíblico de la Misión Mexicana de Texas," *El Evangelista Mexicano*, 8 July 1930, 596.

43. José Ortega, *Memorias*, 229–30.

44. Ibid., 63.

45. Ibid., 226.

46. The 1933 Iglesia Apostólica convention, held in Torreón, wrestled with the question of disciplining Rosa Flores, of Monterrey, for laying hands on the sick for healing. Evangelist Ricardo Belmonte argued for a softer approach than the excommunication meted out by Monterrey pastor Encarnación Rangel. The ministers agreed that the female healer, who had moved to Saltillo, Coahuila, should be placed on probation for one year, during which time she was to show due deference to ordained ministers. The minutes also recognized a minority opinion in favor of women's healing gifts and laying of hands. The general issue had been raised initially at the 1932 convention by Felipe Rivas. That gathering had also agreed with Catarino Ortiz that women should avoid quoting scripture while testifying or presenting prayer requests in the church, as this would amount to a type of preaching. Ortega, "Actas de las convenciones generales," 7–9, Manuel J. Gaxiola Collection.

47. *Exégeta*, April–June 1975, 3, 12–13.

48. Cantú, Ortega, Cota, and Rangel, *Historia de la Asamblea Apostólica*, 27.

49. Pedro Nava and Manuel Sánchez, two of Isabel Sánchez's converts, later helped to consolidate the Apostolic church in San Francisco, California, begun in 1916 by Guadalupe Dominguez and pastored by Francisco Llorente. José Ortega, *Memorias*, 154, 172; Daniel Nava interview. The 1926 IFAP convention roster listed Pedro Nava as San Francisco pastor. Bernardo Hernández, *Catequista*, 22.

50. Gamio, *The Mexican Immigrant*, 223.

51. Gamio, "El problema religioso en México," 11–12.

52. Gamio Collection, Reel 2. Researcher team notes identified "Galvan" as Manuel R. Márquez, a correspondent for the San Antonio, Texas, newspaper, *La Prensa*. After extensive travel throughout the Southwest, the binational journalist had based himself in San Antonio for an extended period (four years at the time of the undated interview) of writing for and raising *La Prensa* subscriptions. His observations, thus, reflected his experiences in Arizona, New Mexico, and Texas, as well as his native Chihuahua, where he served as a correspondent for the *Prensa Asociada Pro-Patria de México* and represented several Mexico City newspapers.

53. Stewart and fellow missionary David Buchanan's exit, according to the CMA, "was rendered necessary by a radical change in the religious views of these missionaries, owing to their difference of conviction on questions relating to Restorationism and the future life." *Fifteenth Annual Report*, CMA, 1911–12, 26.

54. Joseph Stewart's ten years in and out of southern California (up to 1922) coincided with the emergence of Apostolicism in that region. The possible connections between Stewart and Buchanan, who resided in San Diego, and early Apostolics are unclear. The possible overlap also includes several existential parallels. Forced out of institutional missionary structures due to his heterodoxy and out of the nation-state (i.e., the United States) for his alien status, Stewart endured hospitalization in Patton State Hospital, located in San Bernardino, California (an

instance of state discipline of the heterodox subject); the death of his wife, Genevieve; and loss of their children to her parents' custody in Indiana during that time.

55. José Ortega, *Memorias*, 68.

56. Tomasita Cantú, *Una auténtica pionera*, 22–36.

57. In a commemorative edition dedicated to Felipe Rivas, the *Exégeta* credited the formative influence of the "biblical wisdom of Methodism . . . and the example, dignity and preaching passion of its ministers" over the church's recently deceased (8 January 1986) patriarch. *Exégeta*, n.d. 1986, 11.

58. "García Barragán, Marcelino," in *Diccionario de la Rrevolución Mexicana en Jalisco*, 106–7.

59. Rentería Solís, *La Luz del Mundo*, 71–72.

60. For a hagiographic biography of García, see Castañeda Jiménez, *Marcelino García Barragán*. The army's violent suppression of student protests in 1968 tarnished García's legacy.

61. Historian Jason Dormady's comparative study of three restorationist groups in postrevolutionary Mexico (the other two are Catholic inspired) highlights the Luz del Mundo's unique ability to "burrow . . . deeply into the structure of the state." Dormady, *Primitive Revolution*, 19–62.

62. Amatulli, *Religión, política y anticatolicismo*.

63. Instituto Nacional de Información Estadística y Geográfica de México, "Censo de Población y Vivienda, 2000 y 2010."

64. In 2005, the Luz del Mundo Church claimed 1.5 million members in Mexico and five million worldwide. http://www.ldmbethel.org/historia_es.html. The 2000 census counted a more modest national membership of 69,254 over the age of five years, and the 2010 one 188,326. Instituto Nacional de Información Estadística y Geográfica de México, Censo de Población y Vivienda, 2000 and 2010. Some Luz del Mundo census respondents may have opted to identify under "Otras Evangélicas." For critical studies of the Luz del Mundo, see De la Torre, *Los hijos de la luz*; Masferrer Kan, *La Luz del Mundo*; Morán Quiroz, *Alternativa religiosa en Guadalajara*.

65. Antonio Nava, *Autobiografía*, 11.

66. Marital ties also enhanced or complicated ecclesial ones. José Ortega married Esther Rivas, Felipe's sister, in 1933. Felipe Rivas, in turn, was brother-in-law to Francisco Borrego through Rivas's 1928 marriage to María Borrego.

67. The rebellions of Generals José Gonzalo Escobar (Torreón) and Marcelo Caraveo (Chihuahua) were soon suppressed by General Juan Andreu Almazán and represented the consolidating regime's final intramilitary convulsions. "Andreu Almazán, Juan," "Caraveo, Marcelo," and "Escobar, José Gonzalo," in Camp, *Mexican Political Biographies*, 14, 37–38, 76–77. See Marcosson, *Turbulent Years*, 189, for the *Saturday Evening Post* writer's recollection.

68. Antonio Nava, *Autobiografía*, 13.

69. José Ortega, *Memorias*, 88.

70. Cantú, Ortega, Cota, and Rangel, *Historia de la Asamblea Apostólica*, 28.

71. José Ortega, *Memorias*, 88.

72. Cantú, Ortega, Cota, and Rangel, *Historia de la Asamblea Apostólica*, 24. Such receptions (and departures) engendered appropriate hymnody and liturgy, a pat-

tern seen, for example, in José Ortega's poignant descriptions of his 29 October 1929 farewell service from Calexico, California. José Ortega, *Memorias*, 92. Ortega also recalled the hymn sung at the Calexico railroad station during Antonio Nava's 1928 departure: "Dios Os Guarda en Su Santo Amor" (God Keep You in His Holy Love, a translation of "God Be with You," from H. C. Ball's *Himnos de Gloria*). Ortega, *Memorias*, 87.

73. After their expulsion in 1916 from the Assemblies of God, black and white Oneness ministers began to organize in several small ecclesial bodies. By 1918, the oldest of these, the Pentecostal Assemblies of the World (founded a half decade earlier on the U.S. West Coast), had attracted the majority of the dissidents. G. T. Haywood shared prominent leadership with several Euro-American leaders such as E. W. Doak, Daniel Opperman, Howard Goss (a Charles Parham disciple), Frank Ewart, and Andrew Urshan. In 1923, after a fractious half decade of interracial tensions, the majority of the white ministers withdrew to form separate groups, several of which merged later in 1945 as the United Pentecostal Church. Fred Foster, *Their Story: 20th-Century Pentecostals*, 101–52; Tyson, *Early Pentecostal Revival*, 169–314; French, *Our God Is One*, 85–114. In 1931, the PAW reincorporated elements of white Oneness Pentecostalism through a merger with the Apostolic Church of Jesus Christ; the merged group assumed the name Pentecostal Assemblies of Jesus Christ. The reconstitution of the Pentecostal Assemblies of the World in 1937 as a predominantly African American denomination under the original PAW charter signaled the end of U.S. Pentecostalism's interracial experiment, at least at the level of polity. French, *Our God Is One*, 79–80. The 1930 break with the PAW may not have been as clean and consensual as official Apostolic Assembly history has presented it or as Nava recalled it ("a sad, gentlemanly goodbye"). Antonio Nava interview. As late as 1945, several prominent dissident (by this time independent) ministers claimed to operate under the aegis of the PAW as its "Spanish Department": Guadalupe Lara (Los Angeles, California), pastor general; Ramón González (Thermal, California), secretario general; Sotero Carranza (Coachella, California), anciano ejecutivo; Bautista Castro (Palm City, California), anciano de distrito; and Heriberto Soto (Palm City, California), secretario de distrito. Soto relinquished the group's affiliation after Castro's death when their following was received into fellowship that year by the Iglesia Apostólica in Tijuana, Mexico. "Libro de Registro de la Iglesia de Tijuana, B.C., Mexico," 1945 (copy in author's files), cited in Samuel López, *Historia de la Iglesia Apostólica*, 26–27, 43. The continued PAW affiliation may have been more a means for the dissidents to leverage status in their local sphere of action than a meaningful search for or recovery of interracial communion.

Chapter 3

1. The information and quotations in this chapter concerning Francisco Avalos are drawn from the unpublished memoirs of José Avalos Orozco, Francisco Avalos's younger brother. José Avalos, "Historia de la Iglesia Apostólica," 39.

2. The other two songs were Marcial de la Cruz's "La Anunciación" (The Annunciation) and J. F. Vásquez's "¿Por Cual Camino Vas?" (Which Road Are You On?).

Filiberto López, in Uriarte, *Memoria*, anexo 2. The Apostolic testimonial template often included the mention of music and even hymn numbers. The reference to the De la Cruz song as "el 19 de Consolación," indicates the early diffusion of the U.S. Apostolic Assembly's new hymnal (see Chapters 5 and 6).

3. Grebler, *Mexican Immigration*.

4. Hoffman, *Unwanted Mexican Americans*.

5. Balderrama and Rodríguez, *Decade of Betrayal*, 121–22.

6. http://www.census.gov/apsd/wepeople/we-2r.pdf.

7. "In the United States he learns better methods of cultivation, how to use modern tools and industrial machinery, to construct roads and transform raw materials into manufactured objects. This effective and invaluable experience which the immigrants cannot obtain in Mexico will effectively contribute to national reconstruction when they return permanently to their own country." Gamio, "Observations."

8. Alanís Enciso, *El valle bajo del Río Bravo*.

9. Cota interview; José Ortega, *Memorias*, 201, 253.

10. Cantú, Ortega, Cota, and Rangel, *Historia de la Asamblea Apostólica*, 9; José Ortega, *Memorias*, 249. The Iglesia de la Fe Apostólica Pentecostés 1925 roster listed Antonio Arias as pastor-evangelist in San Francisco, California. The year of departure to Baja California and length of stay there before his final return to Verdura (now León Fonseca), Sinaloa, remain unclear. Manuel Gaxiola proffered an earlier commissioning (at the hands of Antonio Nava and Miguel García) and departure date for Tiburcio Santos: July 1925. Manuel J. Gaxiola, *La serpiente y la paloma*, 192–93.

11. José Ortega, Memorias, 21–25, 91–100.

12. José Ortega's extraordinary documentary memoir identifies Montellano and Cerros as assistants to pioneer Miguel García in Westmoreland, California, in a 1926 photo of that church's ministers. José Ortega, *Memorias*, 79.

13. Ibid., 159–60.

14. Ibid., 229–30.

15. Uriarte, *Memoria*, 27–29, anexo 2.

16. Felipe Gaxiola, *Mi Tío Maclovio*.

17. Rocha Zapata, *Nuestros ancestros espirituales*, 86.

18. On the cristero tradition and war, see Meyer, *La Cristiada*; and Moisés González Navarro, *Masones y cristeros en Jalisco*. A survey of (post–Cristero War) twentieth-century church–state relations is provided in Blancarte, *Historia de la Iglesia Católica*.

19. Ortega, "Actas de las convenciones generales," 24–25, Manuel J. Gaxiola Collection.

20. Mariscal, "Buen Siervo y Fiel: La Vida de Ignacio Mariscal," *Exégeta*, September–November 1972, 4–10. The common recourse to commissioning visions can be seen in the report of Indio, California, pastor Jesús Torres receiving divine instructions to hasten to Calexico, California (a ninety-mile trip), to "baptize my servant whom I have prepared." Mariscal's hosts had accompanied him to Calexico upon the convert's request for water baptism, only to find that Antonio Nava was away on a trip. Torres arrived at that precise moment and inquired after a divinely designated baptismal candidate. José Ortega, *Memorias*, 305–6.

21. Ibid., 307.

22. Mariscal, "Buen Siervo y Fiel: La Vida de Ignacio Mariscal," *Exégeta*, September–November 1972, 6.

23. Ortega, "Actas de las convenciones generales," Manuel J. Gaxiola Collection.

24. Mariscal, "Buen Siervo y Fiel: La Vida de Ignacio Mariscal," *Exégeta*, September–November 1972, 6.

25. The Quebrada Honda congregation also received regular supervisory visits from Guadalupe García and José Ortega. Montes interview.

26. Pérez, *Memorias*, 11.

27. Ibid., 26.

28. According to Luciano and Graciela Montes, the woman's name was Rosalva Rodríguez (Ysidro Pérez remembered her as Rosaura Rios). Montes interview.

29. Pérez, *Memorias*, 11. The orthodox warnings against patripassianism and modalism would have coincided with and referred to Apostolic pioneer Epifanio Cota's active evangelization in the California San Fernando and Ventura Valley towns of Saticoy, El Rio, Oxnard, Santa Paula, North Hollywood, Pacoima, and Van Nuys during 1928–1929. José Ortega, *Memorias*, 263.

30. Pérez, *Memorias*, 35–39.

31. Ibid., 39.

32. Ibid., 40–50.

33. A Montemorelos, Nuevo León, native (b. 1911), Leonardo Sepulveda converted in 1934 in González, California (Antonio Nava officiated his water baptism), entered into ministry the following year, and moved to Torreón in 1940. He was named to succeed José Ortega as Torreón pastor at the Iglesia's convention in December of that year. After a half decade, he was summoned to serve in Mexico City. In 1949, he left for a ten-year stint as the Iglesia and Assembly's first missionary to Central America and the Southern Cone. He returned to the United States in 1961 and secured legal residency in 1962 (with the Assembly's vigorous support), in time for his election as vice president at the Assembly's convention at year's end in Phoenix, Arizona. Maclovio Gaxiola, *Historia de la Iglesia Apostólica*, 54, 56–58; Cantú, Ortega, Cota, and Rangel, *Historia de la Asamblea Apostólica*, 41, 45–48; José Ortega, *Memorias*, 176–82.

34. Pérez, *Memorias*, 51–52.

35. José Ortega, *Memorias*, 210; Pérez, *Memorias*, 64; Pérez, "Sigamos Adelante," in *Hacia la meta* (1948), 13–14; *Hacia la meta* (1966).

36. Pérez later led ITAI as rector (1962–1966). Pérez, *Memorias*, 96–106. The inclusion of English in ITAI's early curriculum speaks to the Iglesia's transnational vision and ties to the U.S. Apostolic Assembly. Several ITAI students, such as World War II veteran Luis Aspeytia of Solana Beach, California, were originally members of the U.S. Apostolic Assembly or later transferred their ministry to the Iglesia's sister denomination. ITAI's 1948 yearbook carried nineteen paid full-page church advertisements. U.S. Apostolic Assembly congregations sponsored seven of these (six California congregations: Delano, Calexico, Salinas, Bakersfield, Los Angeles, and Merced; and the Arizona congregation of Parker), and three United Pentecostal Church Bible institutes purchased half-page recruitment advertisements (in Spanish). By contrast, the 1966 yearbook carried no advertisements from Apostolic As-

sembly churches or UPC institutes; it listed two U.S. students. This change reflected institutional developments in the Apostolic Assembly, namely, the 1966 founding of its own Colegio Bíblico Apostólico Nacional (CBAN). On Aspeytia, see Pérez, *Memorias*, 56.

37. In 1946, UPC general superintendent Howard Goss and youth auxiliary president Eldridge Lewis attended the Iglesia Apostólica and Apostolic Assembly general conventions in Torreón and Riverside, California, respectively The leaders of the newly merged (as of September 1945) Euro-American flagship denomination were surprised to discover a flourishing parallel movement among Mexican Americans and Mexicans. Apostolic leaders reciprocated the visits by attending the UPC's general conference in Dallas, Texas, in October 1947. Antonio Nava, Arturo Hermosillo, Epifanio Cota, Daniel Grijalva, and recently returned World War II veteran Daniel Morales represented the Apostolic Assembly, and Felipe Rivas, José Ortega, and Maclovio and Manuel Gaxiola represented the Iglesia Apostólica. Cantú, Ortega, Cota, and Rangel, *Historia de la Asamblea Apostólica*, 35–37. Thereafter, Goss and others invited several promising students to study in UPC bible schools in St. Paul, Minnesota, Tupelo, Mississippi, and Tulsa, Oklahoma. At least ten young men (several of these returned veterans with GI bill support) and women took up the offer, including Antonio Nava's daughter Bernice, Daniel Morales, Eleazar Rodríguez (later founder of CBAN), Lorenzo and Juan Salazar, Pablo Mejía, David Palma, Ysidro Pérez, and Manuel Gaxiola. For Pérez's recollection of the invitation to him and Manuel Gaxiola, see Pérez, *Memorias*, 58–60.

38. José Avalos, "Historia de la Iglesia Apostólica," 23.

39. Ibid., 28.

40. Ibid., 31.

41. Ibid., 32.

42. Ibid., 34.

43. On the Mexican government's uneven success in incorporating repatriates into its ambitious agricultural development plans for regions such as the Mexicali Valley, see Walsh, "Demobilizing the Revolution."

44. José Avalos, "Historia de la Iglesia Apostólica," 38.

45. Lucas Lucio interview, quoted in Balderrama and Rodríguez, *Decade of Betrayal*, 124–25.

6. Maclovio Gaxiola, *Historia de la Iglesia Apostólica*, 186, 198–200; José Ortega, *Memorias*, 247–49.

47. An early 1920s convert to Protestantism, Gándara spent three years in Guadalajara in order to escape cristero persecution in Nayarit. Gándara, "Mi Testimonio," *Exegeta*, July 1948, 10–11. The hymn, by Marcial de la Cruz, "Oh Señor, Que No Se Pierda Ni Uno" (Oh Lord, Let Not Even One Be Lost), would have represented a new acoustic and aesthetic experience for Gándara. Verse 1: "For a long time I have asked / That you bring to the fold / All the creatures / You wish to redeem / Give them understanding / Do not let them suffer / The strong, hard punishment / That is coming."

48. Ortega, "Actas de la convenciones generales," 35–41, 49–59, Manuel J. Gaxiola

Collection. The official disposition is evident in an October 1937 reply by Nayarit governor Francisco Parra to president Lázaro Cárdenas (1934–1940) advising against approval of the petition by Francisco, Secundino, Isidro, and José Avalos, Francisco Gándara, and others, for permission to build a temple in Santiago, Ixcuintla. Parra claimed that the disuse of existing (probably Catholic) churches obviated the need for new ones ("sea [whether] evangélico o católico"). "Gobernador Francisco Parra to Secretario de Gobernación," 18 October 1937, and "Francisco Avalos *et al.* to Secretario de Gobernación," 4 September 1937, Archivo General de la Nación, (15)27874, Caja 16, Expediente 7, Fondo Gobernación.

49. Manuel J. Gaxiola, *La serpiente y la paloma*, 220–23.

50. José Avalos was named first bishop of the newly formed Nayarit district in 1959. *Exegeta*, 15 March 1959, 3.

51. José Ortega, *Memorias*, 237.

52. See anthropologist Federico Besserer's multilayered cultural mapping of a transnational labor diaspora anchored in the San Pedro Mixtepec municipality of the state of Oaxaca. Besserer, *Topografías transnacionales*.

53. José Avalos Orozco, "Historia de la Iglesia Apostólica." The interdenominational periodical *El Mundo Cristiano* reported that cristero mobs in Ameca and Tlajomulco, Jalisco, and Tepic, Nayarit, gathered in the belief that the government was about to hand over nationalized Catholic temples to Protestant control. *El Mundo Cristiano*, 12 August 1926.

54. In 1933, the Iglesia Episcopal Mexicana (the reconstituted Iglesia de Jesús) and its Catholic antagonists barraged President Abelardo Rodríguez with contesting claims to several vacant Catholic temples. Moisés González, *Masones y cristeros en Jalisco*, 55–56.

55. We can glean these biographical data—and a sense of the family's role in the Guadalajara congregation—from the obituary of Lorenzo Varela's daughter (a *repatriada*), Teresa, printed in the Iglesia's periodical in March 1957. "In Memoriam," *Exégeta*, 30 March 1957, 9.

56. Maclovio Gaxiola, *Historia de la Iglesia Apostólica*, 37; José Ortega, *Memorias*, 243.

57. E-mail communication from Ruth Varela Figueroa to author, 7 July 2004.

58. José Ortega, *Memorias*, 243–47.

59. Figueroa e-mail; José Ortega, *Memorias*, 244–47.

60. Rentería, *La Luz del Mundo*, 90.

61. Ibid., 108.

62. José Ortega, *Memorias*, 244.

63. Manuel J. Gaxiola, *La serpiente y la paloma*, 206.

64. "Taking advantage of the discontent of a prominent member who separated from our ranks, whom they recruited so that he would provide the money for the paperwork and help them with other arrangements with the authorities." José Ortega, *Memorias*, 244; Maclovio Gaxiola, *Historia de la Iglesia Apostólica*, 61.

65. The Guadalajara case is compiled in the Archivo General de la Nación, under Serie de Generalidades de Cultos Religiosos 340, Caja 48, Expediente 16, Fondo

Gobernación. The dossier's petitions, missives, and directives span the period from 1 October 1948 to 31 May 1955. The several cited in this discussion are taken from the dossier.

66. Both cases are compiled in "Ejido la Palma, Tepic, Nayarit," (15)5, Archivo General de la Nación, Caja 16, Expediente 5, Fondo Gobernación.

67. José Ortega, *Memorias*, 225.

68. Buriel interview.

Chapter 4

1. Manuel J. Gaxiola, *La serpiente y la paloma*, 212–13.

2. Maclovio Gaxiola, *Historia de la Iglesia Apostólica*, 36–37; Cantú, Ortega, Cota, and Rangel, *Historia de la Asamblea Apostólica*, 28; Manuel J. Gaxiola, *La serpiente y la paloma*, 212–13; José Ortega, *Memorias*, 104–5. Notably, official and unofficial Iglesia Apostólica and Apostolic Assembly histories characterized the 1932 conclave as the Iglesia's inaugural one. José Ortega's later memoirs help correct this erasure and shed light on the abortive 1931 meeting. The institutional redaction testifies to the heated chaos of early Apostolicism in Mexico.

3. José Ortega, *Memorias*, 114.

4. A decade before, Alice Luce reported on the delayed arrival of George Blaisdell and others to the AG's second regional "Mexican work" convention in Los Angeles, California, in May 1923: "It was a great sorrow to us all that Brother Blaisdell and his party from Sonora, Mexico, who had planned to be with us before the dedication, were detained in the desert through the breakdown of the auto truck in which they were traveling, and did not reach us until a few days later. We hope, however, that they will be able to remain and help us during the summer in this needy field." Alice Luce, "Mexican Work in California," *Evangel*, 1 September 1923.

5. Carrillo interview. The Eduardo and Gabriela Curiel family immigrated in 1926 and 1927 from Magdalena, Jalisco, to Farmersville, California. Eduardo's disappointment at clerical turpitude in Jalisco led him to welcome friendship with Apostolics in Central California. Their gift of a New Testament incurred the displeasure of a visiting priest in Dinuba, California, where the family had relocated. The incident cemented Curiel's evangélico leanings and fired his acquisition of literacy through scripture study. The Curiels joined the Methodist church pastored by Mardoqueo García, until their Apostolic friends tracked them down. Beginning with their baptism in early 1933, Eduardo, Gabriela, and young Mary Lou (a public school teacher had rechristened María Luisa) embedded themselves into the growing network of Pentecostal farmworkers in the Central California valley towns of Sanger, Selma, Dinuba, Cutler, Farmersville, and Tulare, among others. In 1935, Mary Lou married Ramón Carrillo, son of a family converted by Pedro Banderas. Banderas, "Memorias."

6. José Ortega, *Memorias*, 115.

7. Verse 2: "When death comes and carries a loved one to rest / I ask myself, Why is it that others live out their years following evil?" Chorus: "But in the beyond, I see my prize / In the great beyond where He is / And although I may suffer struggles and trials here / I know my prize is certain." Lerma, *Marcial de la Cruz*, 73–74.

8. One year after his 1922 baptism in Selma, California, at the hands of Abel Estrada, Pedro Banderas began evangelizing the neighboring towns of Tulare, Shafter, Wasco, Cutler, Porterville, and Farmersville. Besides the Carrillo family, Banderas also counted among his converts the Gregorio Préndez (Shafter) and Julian Aguirre (San Jose) families, who would prove key to growth in Central and Northern California. He oversaw the construction of the Tulare temple in 1926. In 1928, he turned over responsibilities to Epifanio Cota and Jesús Valdez and left for Half Moon Bay, California, to work in the pea harvest. His first converts were Puerto Rican farmworkers, followed by peach harvesters in San Jose, California, where he established the first Apostolic congregation and dedicated a temple in July 1931. By the end of that year, he was dispatched to aid Felipe Coronado in New Mexico. He separated from the Apostolic Assembly in 1934 and continued to serve independent churches in San Jose and the San Mateo peninsula, several of which later rejoined the denomination. José Ortega, *Memorias*, 151–57; Banderas, *Memorias*.

9. José Ortega, *Memorias*, 115. The trio also celebrated services in Calexico, California; Rivas administered baptism there to Telésforo Lozano, future bishop of Baja California. Maclovio Gaxiola, *Historia de la Iglesia Apostólica*, 40. Lozano's son José pioneered Apostolicism in Washington, D.C., in 1971.

10. Manuel J. Gaxiola, *La serpiente y la paloma*, 242.

11. Ortega continued: "He loved and still loves the work of the Lord in Mexico and has considered it to be the same as that of the Assembly in the United States, for the simple reason that we believe in the same Christ and we have the same doctrine. At the time that I am writing of this episode (April 1993), Bro. Nava has turned 100 years of age, and his feeling toward the work of God in Mexico is the same." José Ortega, *Memorias*, 115.

12. The Mexico City work began to consolidate in 1941–1942 with the arrival from California and Arizona of ministers Segismundo Zamudio, Quirino Canseco, and Manuel Ruvalcaba (the first two were from San Bernardino, the last from Phoenix). Ibid., 209. Manuel J. Gaxiola, *La serpiente y la paloma*, 232. These joined converts baptized earlier by Mazatlán, Sinaloa, pastor Simón García, along with Apostolics from Los Angeles, California, and Torreón (e.g., Ana Zúñiga, in whose home the first congregation met). Manuel J. Gaxiola, "Cincuenta Años Después," 15. Maclovio Gaxiola's arrival in 1941 and the beginning of a temple construction project also helped to buttress the Iglesia's presence in the nation's capital. Maclovio Gaxiola, *Historia de la Iglesia Apostólica*, 44–45.

13. José Ortega, *Memorias*, 117.

14. Ortega, "Actas de las convenciones generales," 11–19, Manuel J. Gaxiola Collection. Coronado's efforts were rewarded a decade later with the dedication of the Ciudad Juárez temple. "Noticias de la obra de Dios," *Exégeta*, November 1943, 11.

15. Ortega, "Actas de las convenciones generales," Manuel J. Gaxiola Collection.

16. Ortega's ubiquitous camera documented Lara and Castro's presence at the 1937 conclave. José Ortega, *Memorias*, 366.

17. Ibid., 137.

18. "Alianza Internacional Concertada entre los Representantes de la Iglesia Apostólica en Estados Unidos de Norte America y Mexico," in *Constitución de la Asamblea*

Apostólica (1945), 22. Each clause (nos. 1–4 were buttressed by scriptural citations) reiterated the theme: (1) a common constitution; (2) an Apostolic form of polity in each country; (3) reciprocal rights of hospitality and visiting protocols; (4) mutual intervention (by invitation) in internal matters, verification of general conventions, dissemination of literature and hymnals, and financial assistance for temple construction; (5) mutual official and personal correspondence; (6) periodic publishing of progress reports; and (7) periodic official visits.

19. Tercer Punto, "Alianza Internacional," in *Constitución de la Asamblea Apostólica* (1945), 23–24.

20. "When a member of the Board of Directors shall leave a vacancy, due to death, or having left the country, or having failed the Word of God." Capítulo II, "Organización," in *Constitución de la Asamblea Apostólica* (1945), 32–33. The 1950 revision of the constitution made the point clearer, "or having left the country to reside definitively." Punto 17, "Doctrina y Credo de la Iglesia Apostólica de la Fe en Cristo Jesús," Artículo 9, Capítulo II, *Constitución de la Asamblea Apostólica* (1951), 21.

21. "The present accords shall not be altered without the consent of both parties and can be changed only in a special meeting of the Elders convened by either one of the two delegations." Nota, "Alianza Internacional," *Constitución de la Asamblea Apostólica* (1945), 25. "The present Constitution shall be changed or reformed only in a General Convention; however, in such case the representatives of the Iglesia Apostólica de la Fe en Cristo Jesús, from all the countries that have accepted it [i.e., the constitution] as a fundamental principle, shall be present." Capítulo III, "Convenciones y Acuerdos," *Constitución de la Asamblea Apostólica* (1945), 36.

22. "The baptism of the Holy Spirit is a special Gift that in the era of Grace, our Lord Jesus Christ promised to his Church, and this is a seal for the day of redemption. (2 Cor. 5:5; Eph. 1:13,14). The Holy Spirit is also the faithful guide that leads the Church, aids her, and consoles throughout the sufferings that she undergoes in the world. (John 14:16–18). Individually, each member of the Church should be filled with the Holy Spirit, and thus should seek this from God by faith, from the moment that he/she gives himself/herself over to Him to serve Him. (Luke 11:13; James 1:17). The evidence that a brother receives that power is when he speaks in new tongues. (Mark 16:17; Acts 2:4; 1 Cor. 14:2). No brother can be initiated into the ministerial career without having had the experience of infilling of the Holy Spirit. (Acts 6:3). Our Lord did not permit his apostles to preach after his death, until they were filled with the Holy Spirit. (Luke 24:49; Acts 1:8) Thus, the Ministers of the Apostolic Church should fulfill this requirement without fail. (1 Cor. 2:11,12)." "Reglamentación para la práctica de los puntos doctrinales," Capítulo XI, *Constitución de la Asamblea Apostólica* (1945), 75–76. The soteriological controversy over the "full plan of salvation" consumed white Oneness Pentecostals a year later during the merger of the Pentecostal Church, Incorporated (PCI), and the Pentecostal Assemblies of Jesus Christ. The 1945 charter of the UPC acknowledged and bridged the tension between the two positions (the more ambiguous one was held by PCI leader Howard Goss, a Charles Parham disciple) by means of a conciliatory caveat to "keep the unity of the Spirit until we all come into the unity of the faith." Foster, *Their Story: 20th-Century Pentecostals*, 148; Fudge, *Christianity without the Cross*, 75–199.

23. *Constitución de la Asamblea Apostólica* (1945), 104–12.

24. José Ortega, *Memorias*, 137.

25. Antonio Nava baptized Marcelo Hernández in Calexico, California, in 1923. After a decade, Hernández moved to Mexicali, Baja California, and entered the ministry, serving there until his death in 1957. "Defunciones," *Exégeta*, 30 October 1957, 8. José Ortega listed Cayetano Torres as one of the first pastors of San Pedro de las Colonias and Miguel Alvarez as one of the first evangelists in Francisco I. Madero, towns near Torreón, Coahuila. José Ortega, *Memorias*, 200. As discussed previously, Carrillo was a 1924 convert of Pedro Banderas.

26. The Avalos family's rail companion had returned to the United States by 1933. José Ortega captured him in a photo of ministers at the 1933 Apostolic Assembly convention in Tulare, California. José Ortega, *Memorias*, 114. He resumed the Corona, California, pastorate in 1937. Mendoza, "Memoria," n.d., Manuel Vizcarra Collection. The Iglesia Apostólica's 1939 convention minutes reported a $37.60 offering sent in by Fidel García for temple construction projects in Mexico, along with similar contributions from Central California: pastor Jesús Valdez ($75.00) and the Delano church ($82.50). The Bakersfield church pastored by Torreón native Juan Rodríguez sent a $30 gift to underwrite convention costs. Ortega, "Actas de las convenciones generales," 50–53, Manuel J. Gaxiola Collection.

27. On the Pérez–Rodríguez friendship, see Pérez, *Memorias*, 37–39. On the Corrales family conversion, see "Sección de Testimonios," *Exégeta*, 30 November 1957, 8. In another example of real and fictive kinship ties, young Ernesto Cantú, a Nuevo León native, lent his signature in Torreón, as did his uncle Benjamín in Los Angeles, California. A college graduate in Nuevo León, Ernesto Cantú was baptized by José Ortega in Mission, Texas, in 1942 and took up youth work first in Monterrey and later in the Texas Rio Grande Valley. After his full ordination (October 1945), he moved to Los Angeles, where he assumed the first presidency of the Assembly's newly formed youth auxiliary, Mensajeros de Paz (Messengers of Peace), and the longtime editorship of the denomination's official organ, *El Heraldo Apostólico*. "Biografía: Rev. Ernesto Sada Cantú" in Cantú, Ortega, Cota, and Rangel, *Historia de la Asamblea Apostólica*, n.p.

28. Portes Gil, "Globalization from Below"; Guarnizo and Smith, *Transnationalism from Below*.

29. Given their similar class location, Trinitarian Pentecostals were as vulnerable as Apostolics, although they could count on important connectional resources. Alice Luce reported on the deportation of a Latin American Bible Institute (San Diego, California) graduate who had been stopped at an immigration checkpoint in Santa Ana on his way to assume a pastorate in Tulare. Lacking the documentation (in a period when it was rarely required), the hapless preacher found himself in Mexicali facing "deep poverty and great opposition from false teachers" (probably Apostolics). His success in the border city augured well for the Assemblies' continued growth in Mexico (100 congregations in 1940) and Southern and Central California, where the Latin-American District Council counted sixteen congregations. Luce's lament attests to the continued strength of Oneness heterodoxy in the region. Also, her estimate of the number of Mexicans repatriated during the decade

(1.5 million out of three million) coincides with scholars' highest estimates. The article's opening mirrors the teleology evident in Apostolic repatriado narratives: "'Perhaps the Lord wants me to go and work for Him in Mexico, and His plans are always best,' said a young Spanish Christian to Miss Alice E. Luce, secretary-treasurer of the California Spanish American work." Luce, "Arrested-Jailed-Deported to the Glory of God!," *The King's Trumpet*, 1 March, 1940.

30. "Prólogo," *Constitución de la Asamblea Apostólica* (1945), 18.

31. Punto 17, "Doctrina y Credo de la Iglesia Apostólica de la Fe en Cristo Jesús," Capítulo XI, *Constitución de la Asamblea Apostólica* (1951), 74.

32. See Paul Alexander, *Peace to War.*

33. *Exégeta*, May 1944, 2.

34. "Testimonio de un soldado cristiano," *Exégeta*, September 1944, 14–15.

35. *Exégeta*, February 1945, 4.

36. *Exégeta*, August 1945, 18.

37. "Noticias de la obra de Dios," *Exégeta*, March 1945, 14.

38. *Exégeta*, November 1945, 16.

39. Galarza, *Farm Workers and Agri-Business in California*, 32; Galarza, *Merchants of Labor.*

40. Samora, *Los Mojados*, 46. Ernesto Galarza and Julian Samora's findings of widespread abuse influenced the decision by the U.S. Congress to terminate the bracero program in 1964.

41. Gerald López, "Undocumented Mexican Migration," 654.

42. "Cuantos Braceros Saldrán de Cada Provincia," *El Siglo de Torreón*, 1 April 1944, 5; "Los Braceros de Durango Lanzan un Manifiesto Acerca de su Situación," *El Siglo de Torreón*, 28 June 1944, 2; "Ayuda a los Braceros de Durango," *El Siglo de Torreón*, 1 July 1944, 2; "Se solucionó el Caso de Braceros," *El Siglo de Torreón* 28 October 1956, 4.

43. U.S. Congress, 8 USC §1324, 1952.

44. Samora, *Los Mojados*, 46.

45. Samuel López, *Historia de la Iglesia Apostólica*, 54, 67.

46. Manuel J. Gaxiola, "Cincuenta Años Después," 8. Manuel Gaxiola reported that donated calves and wartime ration coupons served to nourish the conventioneers.

47. José Ortega, *Memorias*, 170. Ortega placed the 1940 convention in Phoenix, Cantú, et al., in Los Angeles. Cantú, Ortega, Cota, and Rangel, *Historia de la Asamblea Apostólica*, 32.

48. Manuel J. Gaxiola, "Cincuenta Años Después," 11–12.

49. In one humorous recounting, the newly arrived Prado family (from Juchipila, Zacatecas) sought to escape their Tijuana landlord Miguel Valverde's persistent proselytism, which always included his guitar rendition of Ruelas's song. Their next moves of residence, however, placed them immediately next to other Apostolic households, including that of Luis and Felicitas Pacheco, Miguel's parents-in-law and fellow repatriados. The pesky song would drift over into the Prado home during Miguel's family visits. The inevitable invitations to supper and fellowship led to conversion. Son Victoriano Prado's progeny later included members of the Apostolic Assembly governing board. Samuel Valverde, "Apostolic Families' Migration, Message and Song," 10–11, 14.

50. Information about the Solana Beach, California, bracero outreach was obtained from Eliseo Ramírez. Ramírez interview. Mesilla, Zacatecas, pastor Amado Martínez's letter of recommendation for Rafael Casas provided the Solana Beach bracero convert with an important bona fide for his return to the place of his conversion ("with the goal of securing a labor contract") and for his stopover in the border city of San Luis Rio Colorado, Sonora, where, according to a handwritten marginal note by pastor Anselmo Reyes, his "presence gladdened" his hosts. "Amado Martinez Letter of Recommendation for Rafael Casas Macías," 7 September 1957 (in author's files). In 1958, the Solana Beach church formally commissioned Casas to evangelize in his home state. M. N. Astorga, "Dando Hijos para que Sirvan en Su Viña," *Heraldo Apostólico*, March–April 1959, 14. Casas later served as bishop of Zacatecas, Aguascalientes, and San Luis Potosí. Casas interview.

51. Religious intolerance abetted by local authorities in Mesillas prompted Zacatecas bishop Manuel Pérez to appeal in person to Governor Francisco E. García. *Exégeta*, 15 September 1957, 16.

52. McGavran, Huegel, and Taylor, *Church Growth in Mexico*, 58. On bracero evangelism, principally by Southern Baptists, see Taylor, *God's Messengers to Mexico's Masses*. Taylor juxtaposed Baptist conversion imperatives with mainline social ministries, clearly favoring the former. He ignored the more intimate outreach by proletarian Pentecostals.

53. *Journal of the Conferencia Anual Mexicana del Suroeste*, 9–12 October 1941, Del Rio, Tex.

54. *Journal of the Conferencia Anual Mexicana del Suroeste*, 8–11 June 1943, Kerrville, Tex.

55. "Superintendents' Reports," *Journal of the Conferencia Anual Mexicana del Suroeste*, 9–12 October 1941, Del Rio, Tex.

56. Tejano Methodists joined their counterparts in the Latin American Provisional Conference of California and Arizona in 1945 to petition for a theological program at Southern Methodist University's Perkins School of Theology. IMM bishop Guerra also weighed in in favor of the change. *Journal of the Conferencia Anual Mexicana del Suroeste*, 3–5 July 1945, El Paso, Tex.

57. Hermina Hernández, a native of Linares, Nuevo León, immigrated as a teenager to Texas in 1918. She married Conrado Anaya in 1925. Anaya "Eulogy," n.d., 1990 (copy in author's files).

58. Cantú, Ortega, Cota, and Rangel, *Historia de la Asamblea Apostólica*, 40. The Iglesia's Manuel Gaxiola had already anticipated the summons, while studying at the Pentecostal Bible Institute in Tupelo, Mississippi; he performed the first baptisms in Chicago, Illinois, in 1946. Manuel J. Gaxiola, "Tiempos de cambio," 2.

59. Salazar, ["History of the Apostolic Assembly"], 32.

60. José Ortega, *Memorias*, 167.

61. Martha A. Vizcarra, "Historia de la Asamblea Apostólica. Distrito Norte de California," Manuel J. Vizcarra Collection.

62. José Ortega interview.

63. Samora, *Los Mojados*, 96–97.

64. Cantú interview.

65. Concepción, *Ecos de vida*, no. 4; *Himnario de suprema alabanza a Jesús* (1969), no. 190; *Himnos de consolación*, 4th ed. (1980), no. 296; *Himnario de suprema alabanza, aumentada* (n.d.), no. 33.

66. The breakdown of letters by year is as follows: 1952 (3), 1953 (2), 1954 (2), 1956 (5), 1957 (5), 1958 (11), 1959 (15), 1960 (5), 1961 (15), 1962 (3), 1963 (7), 1964 (1), and 1965 (2) (in author's files).

67. The letters were issued by Iglesia Apostólica pastors in Mexico City and Mexicali and received and filed in the East Palo Alto Apostolic Assembly Church. TLS, 12 May 1991 and 26 May 1991 (in author's files).

68. "Jesús Rosas to Todos Los Santos," TLS, 9 November 1959 (in author's files).

69. "Miguel Venegas to Sr. Jesús Rosas," TLS, 26 October, 1958 (in author's files).

70. Eliseo Ramírez reported epiphanic recall of Gaxiola's song while nervously picking his way over corpses on a jungle path (in near view of an enemy battalion across a mountain gorge) in Mindanao, Philippines. Ramírez interview. The slow minor chords of the verses resolve into a major chord for the transition into the chorus and thus undergird the movement from a graphic description of resolute pilgrimage (e.g., the pilgrim's bleeding heels) and tearful, joyful arrival to Calvary. The bleeding feet reference both reflects the compositional setting—Gaxiola was evangelizing in the Sierra Madre on foot at the time—and evokes sentiments and sanguinary images intrinsic to popular (i.e., Catholic) Mexican piety. Verse 3: "If you lead me I will always follow you / Even though my heel begins to bleed / I must arrive with your heavy cross / To Calvary where I shall weep with joy"; Chorus: "Along the lonely and sad path / I will follow you, Jesus / Waiting for your hand / To guide me always in the light / Even along the difficult hill / That you climbed with your cross / In the most bitter trials / I will hope in you, Jesus."

71. Information on the family biography and Hermanos Alavardo's career was gathered in a series of interviews with Rosario, Juan, and Román Alvarado in San Jose and Whittier, California, from 30 July 1999 to 29 December 2000 (audiocassette).

72. The stylized story is reconstructed, of course, in the Alvarado interviews.

73. For example, "América Será para Cristo" (America Will Be for Christ, a country-by-country prediction of hemispheric salvation), "Pero Queda Cristo" (But Christ Remains), and "¿Para Que Pecar?" (Why [Should I] Sin?). Colom credited an independent Apostolic Salvadoran evangelist, José María Alvarez, in Nueva Santa Rosa, Guatemala, with his renewed conversion in 1942. Colom, *Música en su alma*, 11–12. Quito-based missionary Robert Savage was instrumental in fostering the composer's prominence by means of radio promotion, tours, and musical scoring and hymnal compilation. See "Alfredo Colom M.," in *Celebremos su gloria*, no. 94. Colom's important career awaits critical treatment.

74. Jeter de Walker, *Siembra y cosecha*, 57, 146, 166. Hines was a member of a pioneering Pentecostal missionary family. Christopher and Ines Hines arrived in Guatemala in 1912. Ibid., 119–20.

75. "Trio los Hermanos Ramos: Alabad a Jehovah," http://www.youtube.com/watch?v=MAtOCmNhO4c (8 September 2013); "Trio Los Trigales Recordando a los Hermanos Alvarado," http://www.youtube.com/watch?v=wLLzeHyYiOI (8 September 2013). YouTube uploads of the Hermanos Alvarado's music offer re-

markable discursive sites for general evangélico nostalgia about deceased parents and grandparents (and laments about contemporary worship music). To take one example, the upload of the iconic (and now ecumenical) funeral song "Más Allá del Sol" (Beyond the Sun) attracted 663,369 views and 201 comments from all points of the Latin American migratory compass (including Spain and North Africa): http://www.youtube.com/watch?v=D9i3_H4zMV4 (21 April 2014). A cursory survey of five uploaded Alvarado recordings ("Mas Allá del Sol," "Petición de una Madre," "Un Testimonio," "El Tren del Evangelio," and "Trigo Soy,"), one compilation ("Mini Concierto de los Hermanos Alvarado"), and a video marking Juan Alvarado's September 2006 passing ("Murió el Último Cantante de los Hermanos Alvarado") reveals a total number of 2,482,078 views and 889 comments: "Petición de una Madre," http://www.youtube.com/watch?v=huHfBSpJuwQ; "Un Testimonio," http://www.youtube.com/watch?v=eh4CYDuiLlA&list=RDrgGEV5W3nMU; "El Tren del Evangelio," http://www.youtube.com/watch?v=8Datt51Fijg&list=RDrgGEV5W3nMU; "Trigo Soy," http://www.youtube.com/watch?v=FZuhRO6pUx8&list=RDrgGEV5W3nMU; "Mini Concierto de los Hermanos Alvarado," http://www.youtube.com/watch?v=U7_e6V1CFmM; "Murió el Último Cantate de los Hermanos Alvarado," http://www.youtube.com/watch?v=SIzA_22v9Ts (all 21 April 2014).

76. Hernández interview.

77. Daniel Ramírez, "Usos y costumbres (¿y mañas?)."

78. The Bracero program carried Oaxacan Zapoteco-speaking converts of the Summer Institute of Linguistics as far away as Arkansas in 1950. Wallace, *Two Thousand Tongues to Go*, 132–33.

Chapter 5

1. Verse 1: "May all the servants of Jesus Christ receive today / The welcome from their brethren in the Lord"; Verse 3: "Joyfully join all the songs with sweet voice / With reverence, as you are in the presence of God"; Verse 4: "Very soon, united, the chosen shall go to God / And there in heaven, they shall have their prize for their labor." Note the third verse's reference to prepared musical performances (usually by women's, men's, and youth auxiliary choirs) in conclaves and services.

2. Tweed, *Crossing and Dwelling*, 61.

3. Manuel J. Gaxiola, "Cincuenta Años Después," 12. José Ortega and Simón García proposed to launch the organ as "El Mensajero Apostólico" in 1935. Manuel J. Gaxiola, *La serpiente y la paloma*, 244.

4. Ortega, "Actas de las convenciones generales," 16, Manuel J. Gaxiola Collection.

5. The July 1948 issue of the *Exégeta* announced the availability of both the Assembly's *Consolación* hymnal and the sixth edition of the Iglesia's *Suprema Alabanza*. *Exégeta*, July 1948, 16. The stock of hymnals suffered constant depletion. The May 1944 issue reminded readers in a small note about the new, third edition of the *Suprema Alabanza* hymnal. *Exégeta*, 1 May 1944, 2. The combined November–December issue of that year carried a full-page advertisement on the back cover announcing the edition's stock depletion and the beginning of a fourth edition (four years after the hymnal's launch). *Exégeta*, 1 November 1944, 32. Over a decade later the *Exégeta*

advised readers that the stock of *Suprema Alabanza* was depleted ("agotados"), while copies of *Consolación* could be ordered from the church's publishing house, Librería Latinoamericana, at five pesos apiece. *Exégeta*, 31 July 1958, 15.

6. Manuel J. Gaxiola, "Cincuenta Años Después," 17.

7. Manuel J. Gaxiola, "Tiempos de Cambio," 1.

8. *Exégeta*, July 1948, 4, 15; February 1950, 2.

9. *Exégeta*, June 1967, 9.

10. Antonio Nava commissioned the Apostolic Assembly's first official history, the much-referenced 1966 work by Ernesto Cantú et al. The denomination set Nava's baptismal year (1916) as the beginning point for the Assembly's Jubilee anniversary. The reverence for the pioneer caudillo, of course, leaned the narrative (and dating) of origins toward his coherent leadership but also eclipsed the constitutive work of many others, like Juan Navarro, Francisco Llorente, and Marcial de la Cruz.

11. Mitchell, *They Saved the Crops.*

12. The issues included all months from January 1957 to December 1958 (except for July 1957; November and December 1958 were combined into a single issue); March, May, June, and August 1959; January and March 1962; January, July, and November–December (combined into a single issue) 1963; April 1966; January, June, and October–November 1967 (combined into a single issue).

13. Mexicali (Baja California) Second Church pastor Silvestre Peña's transfer to Calexico, California, was noted in the "Noticias" section of the March 1957 issue: "Silvestre Peña arranged his immigration in order to live in the United States, and he is now passing over to take charge of the small congregation in Calexico, Calif." *Exégeta*, 30 March 1957, 12. Efraím Valverde's similar transfer—marked by a formal dismissal sermon preached by a San Diego, California, pastor—nearly nine months later merited mention in the January 1958 issue. *Exégeta*, 31 January 1958, 14.

14. "De la XI Convención en Baja California," *Exégeta*, 30 January 1957, 15.

15. Ramírez interview.

16. *Exégeta*, 30 October 1957, 1.

17. These included San Joaquin Valley residents Esther Valdez and Anita Quiroz, and immigrant María Fraijo, the *Dorcas*'s longtime president. *Exégeta*, 30 October 1957, 7.

18. *Exégeta*, 30 November 1957, 14.

19. Eutimio Rios of Las Cruces, New Mexico; Emeteria Reta of Chihuahua, Chihuahua; and Manuel Esquivel and Felipe Coronado of Ciudad Juárez, Chihuahua.

20. *Exégeta*, 31 December 1957, 18.

21. *Exégeta*, March 1945, 9. Rivas noted another Apostolic liturgical custom for such events: the antiphonal recitation and singing of Psalm 136 (the individual declamation of each verse's first half was followed by a congregational musical rendition of "Porque para Siempre Es Su Misericordia" [For His Mercy Endures Forever]). This feature was also reported in the March 1944 issue's report on the 7 February dedication of the expanded Tijuana temple. *Exégeta*, March 1944, 9, 14.

22. Shepard, *Gloria: A Hymnal for Use in Sunday Schools*, no. 218.

23. *Exégeta*, 30 March 1957, 15; 30 April 1957, 15; 30 June 1957, 11; 15 September 1957, 14; 30 April 1958, 10; 31 July 1958, 13; 1 April 1966, 12.

24. Juan B. Cabrera (1837–1916), Spain's sole ordained Protestant bishop of his era, translated several Protestant standards. *Celebremos su gloria*, 539, 554.

25. The song also served a similar public function in Chilean Pentecostalism, marking *canuto* (the equivalent of the Mexican aleluya epithet) turf in predominantly Catholic settings. The difference in lyrics, however, prompts a question of translator and author. While the Apostolic version emphasizes baptism in Jesus's Name and Oneness theology, the Chilean one does not include Cantú's two verses, and adds a nationalistic: "Chile para Cristo, Cristo para él / Nuestras peticiones siempre han de ser / Y la gran victoria nuestro Dios dará / Y le seguiremos fiel" (Chile for Christ, Christ for Chile / So should our prayers always be / And the great victory our God will give / And we shall follow Him, faithful). In Chile, the song also served a performative function, similar to that of Abundio López's "La Nube de Fuego," in moments of schism (Chapter 2). It marked the 1925 birth of an early scission of the Iglesia Metodista Pentecostal, the Iglesia Evangélica de los Hermanos (IEH). Dissenters sang it as they exited the IMP temple in Santiago. Orellana, *El fuego y la nieve*, 96–98. Chilean musicologist Cristián Guerra argues for the possible authorship (at least of the verse about Chile) by Genaro Ríos, a converted circus musician and founder of the Ejército Evangélico de Chile (the product of another IMP schism). Guerra Rojas, "La música en el movimiento pentecostal de Chile." The puzzle over date and authorship reminds us of the messy migration of music. The IEH episode occurred three years before Genaro's 1928 conversion. Benjamín Cantú had moved in Methodist orbits since childhood; thus, it is not implausible that his version—or at least an early version of it—may have traveled to South America by 1925. The variance also reminds us of the importance of in situ performance. "Cristo es Nuestro Jefe" later served an even more public function in Chile, gracing national *evangélico Te Deum* services in the flagship IMP Jotabeche cathedral in Santiago (with the nation's presidents, political, and military leaders present) and resurfacing in the large Pentecostal centenary services in 2009.

26. De la Luz García, *El movimiento pentecostal en México*, 191–222.

27. *Exégeta*, November 1944, 14.

28. *Exégeta*, June, 1957, 7; "Fallecimientos," *Exégeta*, October 1958, 6.

29. *Exégeta*, April 1963, 5.

30. *Exégeta*, November–December 1958, 4, 16.

31. *Exégeta*, 30 June 1957, 11.

32. *Exégeta*, 15 June 1957, 3.

33. *Exégeta*, 30 April 1957, 15.

34. *Exégeta*, 30 October 1957, 12, 15.

35. "Nuevo Templo en . . . ," *Exégeta*, 31 December 1957, 19.

36. *Exégeta*, 31 October 1958, 14–15.

37. Filemón Zaragoza was born in Denver, Colorado, in 1919, and taken to Romita, Guanajuato, in 1927 by his father, who then abandoned the family. Zaragoza made his way to the border in adulthood, settling in Ciudad Juárez, Chihuahua, in 1939 among relatives, several of whom were Apostolic. After a decade of cross-border work in cotton work and flour mills (in El Paso, Texas)—interrupted by U.S. naval

service from 1943 to 1945—he moved to Delano, California, in 1951. Zaragoza interview.

38. *Exégeta*, 31 July 1957, 7; *Heraldo Apostólico*, July 1987, 7.

39. *Exégeta*, 30 November 1957, 13.

40. *Exégeta*, April 1966, 8.

41. *Exégeta*, January 1950, 3–4. The writing shows a level of literacy well below that of the editors', proof of its utility as a pristine (unredacted) discursive datum.

42. *Exégeta*, 30 May 1957, 14.

43. *Exégeta*, 30 June 1957, 14.

44. *Exégeta*, 31 May 1957, 14.

45. "Testimonio," *Exégeta*, 31 January 1958, 11.

46. *Exégeta*, 15 August 1959, 5.

47. *Exégeta*, July–August 1983, 7.

48. *Exégeta*, May–June 1983, 14–15.

49. "Defunciones," *Exégeta*, 30 April 1957, 11–12.

50. "Defunciones," *Exégeta*, 30 October 1957, 8.

51. *Exégeta*, 1 December 1957, 11–12.

52. *Exégeta*, 31 January 1958, 6.

53. *Exégeta*, 31 March 1958, 10.

54. "Billy Graham vendrá a Mexico," *Exégeta*, 30 November 1957, 16. U.S. Apostolics were equally as interested in foreign missions. The December 1955 issue of the Assembly's *Heraldo Apostólico* displayed a bold caption, "Gran Convención Apostólica en Managua, Nicaragua," under a front-page photo of ministers and dignitaries gathered at that country's conclave. The issue also heralded the 19 December homecoming of Lorenzo Salazar. A photo of the Assembly's young missionary was superimposed over a map of Nicaragua and surrounded by five images of his robust Harley-Davidson motorcycle. *Heraldo Apostólico*, December 1955, 9.

55. Maclovio Gaxiola, "Informe de Obispo Presidente," 26 October 1962.

56. Maclovio Gaxiola noted that the Iglesia lacked congregations in the following states' capitals: Zacatecas, Tlaxcala, Puebla, Colima, Hidalgo (Pachuca), Mexico (Toluca), Guerrero (Chilpancingo), Morelos (Cuernavaca), Veracruz (Jalapa), Tabasco (Villahermosa), Campeche (Mérida), Quintana Roo (Chetumal), Michoacán (Morelia), and Guanajuato (León). Maclovio Gaxiola, "Informe de Obispo Presidente," 26 October 1962, 6, 16–17. Gaxiola reported 766 congregations (363 churches plus 403 evangelism points) and 19,609 church members.

57. Sociologist Pablo Vila has noted that the complex, hybrid experiences of border Latinos can reinforce borders as well as disassemble them; thus, tejanos often view themselves oppositionally to both Mexicans and Anglos. Vila, *Crossing Borders*. Anthony Mora noted a similar symbiosis between proximate communities in southern New Mexico. Mora, *Border Dilemmas*, 258–70.

58. Maclovio Gaxiola, "Panorámica de la Iglesia Estadounidense," *Exégeta*, January 1950, 15.

59. Salazar, ["History of the Apostolic Assembly"], 28.

60. *Exégeta*, January 1951, 4–5.

61. "Progreso Evangélico en América Latina," *Exégeta*, 15 June 1959, 5, 7; *Exégeta*, 15 January 1960, 7; *Exégeta*, 15 November 1959, 2.

62. Daniel López Lara, "Todas las iglesias evangélicas en la cruzada bíblica 1963," "*Exégeta*, July 1963, 8.

63. *Informe anual de la Agencia Bíblica en México correspondiente a 1952*. Manuel Gaxiola later served as president of the Sociedad Bíblica de México (SBM) and as a board member of the United Bible Societies, the SBM's hemispheric counterpart.

64. *Exégeta*, October 1945, 16.

65. "La Reforma, sus causas y sus resultados," *Exégeta*, October–November 1967, 8.

66. Felipe Rivas, "Informe del Obispo," *Exégeta*, January 1967, 5–6; Maclovio Gaxiola, "Escalando una cima," *Exégeta*, January 1967, 12; Maclovio Gaxiola , "Informe del Obispo Presidente," *Exégeta*, June 1967, 3.

67. Felipe Rivas, "Informe del Obispo," *Exégeta*, January 1967, 6.

68. Efraím Valverde's paternal grandfather, Refugio, an immigrant from Durango and longtime California resident, led his extended family, including married sons and their U.S.-born children, from Fresno, California, to the Tijuana–San Ysidro border area in 1932 in response to repatriation pressures and opportunities (offers of settlement assistance from the Mexican government). The relocation resulted in contact with the nascent Apostolic movement and in the conversion of Refugio and many Valverde and Pacheco family members, most of whom, like Refugio, had adopted a Baptist identity in the United States. Efraím Valverde, *Recuerdo, Señor*, 19–40. Refugio's confessional shift was prompted by fellow repatriate Apolinar Alemán, who had converted in 1934 in the Otay–San Diego church (his family arrived to Tijuana from California's San Fernando Valley via Brawley, California, in 1929). Jesús Arballo, Tijuana's pioneer evangelist, also aided in the recruitment of this important Baptist clan. Alemán interview. Samuel López, *Historia de la Iglesia Apostólica*, 19.

69. For a brief account of the schism, see Daniel Ramírez, "Antonio Castañeda Nava: Charisma, Culture, and *Caudillismo*," in Goff and Wacker, *Portraits of a Generation*, 304–5. For a discussion of the Valverde schism's unexpected outcome in the Oaxacan homeland and diaspora, see chapter 7 in Daniel Ramírez, "Migrating Faith."

70. The Assembly's periodical offered information and contacts concerning the amnesty provisions of the previous year's Immigration Reform and Control Act. *Heraldo Apostólico*, July 1987, 13.

71. Davis, *The Economic Basis of the Evangelical Church in Mexico*, 31–32, quoted in Kenneth Gill, *Toward a Contextualized Theology*, 107–8. Gill conjectured that the missionary critique was aimed squarely at the Iglesia Apostólica.

72. Board of National Missions of the Presbyterian Church in the U.S.A., *Seventeenth Annual Report* (1940), 69.

73. MacKay, *The Other Spanish Christ*; Rycroft, *Religion and Faith in Latin America*; Rembao, " *Pneuma*"; "Baez-Camargo, "Mexico: Concerns of the Protestant Minority."

74. Rivera, *Instituciones protestantes en México*, 97.

75. Ibid., 114.

76. Lewis, *The Children of Sanchez*.

77. Rivera, *Instituciones protestantes en México*, 125.

Chapter 6

1. Haven, *Mexico: Our Next-Door Neighbor*, 95–96.
2. Ibid., 52–54.
3. Ibid., 69–70.
4. Ibid., 91.
5. Ibid., 92–94.
6. Ibid., 93–94.
7. U.S. Protestantism's top five hymns, ranked by frequency of publication ("All Hail the Power of Jesus' Name," "Jesus, Lover of My Soul," "Am I a Soldier of the Cross," "Alas, and Did My Savior Bleed," and "How Firm a Foundation"), were carried over into Spanish-language hymnals. For a study of publication frequency in 175 U.S. Protestant hymnals, see Marini, "American Protestant Hymns Project"; Marini, "From Classical to Modern"; Marini, "Hymnody as History." On the nexus between hymnody and foreign missions, see Schneider, "Jesus Shall Reign."
8. The Wesleyan revival in England and First and Second Great Awakenings in the United States had wrested Reform Protestant liturgy loose from the strictures of lined Psalms, the only acceptable form of congregational song in Puritan New England. Dickinson, *Music in the History of the Western Church*.
9. For Sankey's collaboration with evangelist Dwight L. Moody and composer Fanny Crosby and his significance as "gospel song's" chief composer/compiler/publisher/ promoter/popularizer, see Wilhoit, "'Sing Me a Sankey.'"
10. *Himnario evangélico para el uso de todas las iglesias* (1893); *Nuevo himnario evangélico para el uso de la iglesias evangélicas* (1914).
11. "Cuba Mission," *Annual Report of the Board of Foreign Missions*, MECS, 1907, 193.
12. Primitivo Rodríguez's translations of John Wesley's theological corpus were used extensively in ministerial training curricula. He also created and redacted the MECS's Sunday school Spanish-language curriculum. Upon his death in 1909, the denominational eulogy boasted that "two-thirds of the Protestant Sunday School children in Mexico are using our literature; in fact, through Mr. Rodríguez's skill and industry our Church has been brought to the front rank in the matter of Spanish literature, and in that respect is steadily widening its influence." "Rev. P. A. Rodríguez," *Annual Report of the Board of Foreign Missions*, MECS, 1909, 122–23; see also Nañez, *History of the Rio Grande Conference*, 56–57.
13. Primitivo Rodríguez, *Himnario cristiano para uso de las iglesias evangélicas*, iv–vii. Of the twenty-seven hymnals, sixteen had been compiled or published by missionaries and native leaders in Spain, three in Mexico, three in New York, and one each in Nashville, Philadelphia, Buenos Aires, London, and Laredo. The MECS Board of Missions offered a capacious posthumous tribute to Rodríguez's opus: "His last and in his own estimation, his greatest work . . . . as perhaps the very best hymnal in the Spanish language [which] has met with a most favorable reception among Protestants in all Spanish-speaking countries . . . is being used by other denominations . . . and was exhausted in a short time after its appearance." "Rev. P. A. Rodríguez," *Annual Report of the Board of Foreign Missions*, MECS, 1909, 122.
14. The remarkable gesture of denominational humility was noted by the editors

of the MECS *Evangelista Mexicano*, which reprinted the Presbyterian's *El Faro* (The Lighthouse) article in full. "Himnología," *El Evangelista Mexicano*, 1 April 1907.

15. Mendoza, *Himnos selectos*; Grado, *Pequeña colección de himnos*.

16. Stevenson, "Missions, Foreign," 740.

17. Menéndez y Pelayo, *Historia de los heterodoxos españoles*, 455.

18. According to Alice Luce, at least 115,000 copies of *Himnos de Gloria* were sold in the first decade of publication. Alice Luce, "The Latin-American Pentecostal Work," *Evangel*, 25 June 1927, 6.

19. By 1933, Cragin assumed the copyright for *Melodías Evangélicas* but eventually credited collaborators Francisco Olazábal, Benjamin N. Cortez, Antonio Gamboa, Manuel Baca García, Eliseo Chavira, Eduardo R. Rodríguez, and Patricio López. "Prefacio," in Cragin, *Melodías evangélicas* (1965, 1970 editions). The "Dedicatorio" section of the 1933–1936 and 1955 editions omitted this important detail concerning CLADIC collaborators.

20. *Himnario para el Departamento de Música y Adoración del Concilio para la Obra Hispano Americana.* The Council's 1950 hymnal for youth included no Latino composers. *Himnos de aspiración* (1950).

21. Lockwood, "Recent Developments in U.S. Hispanic and Latin American Protestant Church Music," 16. United Methodism's 1996 *Mil Voces para Celebrar* faced squarely the Lockwood critique. Raquel Mora Martinez, "Mil Voces Para Celebrar." An equally remarkable ecumenical compilation project, with significantly greater Pentecostal content than *Mil Voces*, appeared three years earlier under Mennonite auspices. The second edition of the Iglesia de Dios en Cristo, Menonita's *Alabanzas Favoritas*, with 232 hymns, represented a scoring and expansion of the original *Alabanzas Favoritas*, compiled in 1954 by Mennonites in Chihuahua, Mexico. For a discussion of hymnody contestation between Brazilian Baptists and missionaries, see Spann, "A Tale of Two Hymnals."

22. *El Evangelista Mexicano*, 1 May 1928, 136–37.

23. Herrera interview.

24. Gutiérrez interview.

25. Vernon McCombs, "Spanish and Portuguese District," *Journal of the Southern California Annual Conference*, MEC, 1917.

26. Letter from Mary L. VanDyke (The Hymn Society) to author, 28 October 1998. Lehman's song also entered into the folk music repertoire in Appalachia, the Caribbean, and New Orleans.

27. McDannell, *Material Christianity*.

28. Rubén and Manuel Barbachano's Compañía Eléctrica Fronteriza, founded in 1914, won the federal concession for telegraph, phone, and power service in 1924. Bonifaz de Hernández, Gil Durán, and Miranda Polanco, "La frontera en la actualidad," 89, 356. Prior to this, territorial officials had to cross over into California to communicate with their superiors in Mexico City.

29. Del Pilar, *Himnos de "El Avivamiento."*

30. Parra Herrera, Huerta de Parra, and Rodríguez Camara, *Himnos de victoria*, no. 338.

31. I borrow here from Mikhail Bakhtin, who argued that the medieval festivals

and carnivals in the works of Rabelais "always [represented] an essential, meaningful philosophical content" in uneasy tension with official church-sanctioned feasts. Bakhtin, *Rabelais and His World*, 8–9.

32. Bernardo Hernández, *Estatutos acordados en la 1ra. convención mexicana.*

33. "La Convención Evangélica Mexicana del Estado de Arizona," *Evangelista Mexicano*, 1 July 1930, 584–85.

34. According to Manuel Peña, the *orquestra típica* tradition, "the ultimate symbol of nationalism . . . found strong support among the Mexicans of the Southwest. In an Anglo society in which they were not yet accepted as full-fledged citizens, musical expressions like the *típica* gave these Americans of Mexican descent a feeling of 'cultural citizenship,' even if it was, to the displeasure of many Americans, that of a foreign country." Peña, *The Mexican American Orquestra*, 80–86.

35. Maclovio Gaxiola listed a first edition published in Guamuchil, Sinaloa, in 1941, a second in Hermosillo, Sonora, in 1942, and a third in Mexico City, 1943. Maclovio Gaxiola, *Historia de la Iglesia Apostólica*, 47.

36. Reta interview. Emeterio Reta's 1950 "Hasta El Fin Lucharé" (I Will Fight to the End), a musicalization of Paul's valedictory words to Timothy (2 Timothy 4:7–8), emanated out of his Torreón–Chihuahua axis and traveled widely. The Spanish-language Mennonite hymnal included a musically scored version of the song in its 1993 edition, an indication of the song's widespread popularity. Iglesia de Dios en Cristo, Menonita, *Alabanzas favoritas*, no. 126. Current YouTube recordings list it by its original title and its first line, "Al Señor Yo Le Quiero Servir" (I Wish to Serve the Lord)," and demonstrate its longevity and nostalgic power. http://www.youtube.com/watch?v=tozavlK2DTQ (30 April 2014).

37. Campos, *El folklore y la música mexicana*, 191–96.

38. Dolan and Deck, *Hispanic Catholic Culture in the U.S.*; Dolan and Hinojosa, *Mexican Americans and the Catholic Church.*

39. Kahl, "Bolero."

40. Af Geijerstam, *Popular Music in Mexico*, 77.

41. Cardoza, "Qué Lindo Es Mi Cristo."

42. Zaragoza interview.

43. Tony Saucedo, "Mis Plegarias," http://www.youtube.com/watch?v=VMtvccuc820 (30 April 2014).

44. Benjamín Cantú, "Persecuciones a los cristianos," *Exégeta*, July 1944. The twin López brothers, blinded at age fifteen, were entrusted to José Ortega by the captain of the Salvation Army in Monterrey, Nuevo León, whereupon Ortega introduced them to the Iglesia Apostólica's 1950 convention in Torreón. They toured Iglesia and Assembly churches during the following decade and a half. José Ortega, *Memorias*, 220–22.

45. Juan Lugo separated definitively from the AG after a long period of alternatingly eager and ambivalent collaboration. On Lugo and the eclipse of his ministry due to morals accusations, see Espinosa, "Borderland Religion," 184–224.

46. Felipe Gutiérrez, *Nuevo himnario de melodías evangélicas selectas.* CLADIC leaders accused Cragin of copyright theft.

47. Huegel, *Apóstol de la cruz*, 273–74.

48. Machado, *Of Borders and Margins*.

49. Burnim, "Conflict and Controversy in Black Religious Music," 83. See also Burnim, "Functional Dimensions of Gospel Music Performance"; and Burnim and Maultsby, "From Backwoods to City Streets."

50. Mahalia Jackson (with Evan Wylie), *Movin' on Up* (New York: Hawthorne, 1966), 60, quoted in Burnim, "Conflict and Controversy in Black Religious Music," 90.

51. Best, *Passionately Human*.

52. Burnim, "Conflict and Controversy in Black Religious Music," 93.

53. Burnim, "The Performance of Black Gospel Music."

54. Florentino Santana, "Address to the Annual Assembly of the Iglesia Discipulos de Cristo en Puerto Rico, Bayamón, Puerto Rico, February 19, 1983." Quoted in Del Pilar, *Himnos de "El Avivamiento."*

55. Antonio Nava interview.

56. Chorus 4 represents a loose adaptation of the English original: "Leaning, leaning, safe and secure from all alarm / Leaning, leaning, leaning on the everlasting arms."

57. Verse 1: "Glory to you, Jesus! / Glory to you, Jesus! / Glory to you, Jesus! / Beloved Savior"; Verse 2: "You loved me with tenderness / You loved me with tenderness / You loved me with tenderness / Beloved Savior"; Verse 5: "Have courage, Christian courage / Christ is your best friend / He shall take you with him / Jesus is your Lord." *Himnario evangélico*, no. 89.

58. Erlmann, *Nightsong*.

59. De Certeau, *Practice of Everyday Life*, 16.

60. Music researcher Gustavo López compiled 407 migrant songs in his 1995 survey of popular musical recordings in western Mexico. The vast majority dealt with the bracero and *mojado* (wetback) experiences and were performed within *norteño* musical genres. López Castro, *El Río Bravo es charco*.

61. Feld, *Sound and Sentiment*.

62. Salazar, *Himnario cantar de los cantares*.

63. Lorenzo Salazar's impressive career—from national youth leader to missionary to Nicaragua to pastor to presiding bishop—casts a contrasting light on Methodist reactions to the notorious Zoot Suit riots of 1943, conflicts sparked by sailors invading Los Angeles barrios in order to strip Mexican American youth of their trademark wear. In the wake of the troubles, MEC Board of Missions and Church Extension head W. W. Reid prepared a reassuring note for church bulletins: "Commenting on recent zoot-suit difficulties in Los Angeles and vicinity, Superintendent Vernon M. McCombs of the Methodist Latin American Conference in the southwest, says that no 'pachuco' (prankster) has come from among the thousands of boys and young men connected with the Mexican Protestant missions and churches on the Pacific coast." W. W. Reid, "No Zoot-Suiters in Mission Centers," 21 July 1943, Vernon McCombs Correspondence, United Methodist Archives.

64. De Certeau, *Practice of Everyday Life*, xxi.

65. Paz, *Labyrinth of Solitude*.

66. On the "East LA Sound," see Loza, *Barrio Rhythm*.

67. Romero, *No vale tres manies*, 108.

68. Alstott, *Flor y canto*.

69. Aponte, "Coritos as Active Symbol."

70. Espinosa, "The Impact of Pluralism."

71. Cleary, *The Rise of Charismatic Catholicism in Latin America*.

Conclusion

1. Jaimes, "La paradoja neopentecostal."

2. http://www.youtube.com/watch?v=S-308Dv7O3k (21 April 2014).

3. Mansillas, *La cruz y la esperanza*; Orellana, *El fuego y la nieve*.

4. Bourdieu, *Distinction*, 68. For a fuller discussion of habitus, see Bourdieu, *Outline of a Theory of Practice*.

5. De Certeau, *Practice of Everyday Life*, 58.

6. Ibid., xix.

7. Ibid., 36. Such a power arrangement relegates subordinated rationalities and discourses to the level of what Michel Foucault calls "subordinated knowledges." Foucault, *Power/Knowledge*, 81–133.

8. De Certeau, *Practice of Everyday Life*, xiii.

9. Ibid., xiv–xv.

10. D'Epinay, *Haven of the Masses*; Willems, *Followers of the New Faith*; Abelino Martínez, *Las sectas en Nicaragua*; Jaime Valverde, *Las sectas en Costa Rica*; Leslie Gill, *Precarious Dependencies*.

11. D'Epinay's theory of "huelga social" followed in the tradition of Max Weber's "relative deprivation," which sociologists, in turn, developed to encompass economic, social, and psychic dimensions. See Max Weber, "The Social Psychology of the World Religions," in *From Max Weber*; and Glock, *The Role of Deprivation*.

12. Orozco, *Republican Protestantism in Aztlán*.

13. Brusco, *The Reformation of Machismo*; Burdick, *Blessed Anastacia*; Hernández Castillo, *La otra frontera*.

14. Garma Navarro, *Protestantismo en una comunidad totonaca*.

15. Cahn, *All Religions Are Good in Tzinzuntzan*; George M. Foster, *Tzintzuntzan*.

16. Garrard-Burnett, *Protestantism in Guatemala*. Garrard-Burnett, like David Stoll, carefully demarcated important social and ideological differences between Pentecostals and Charismatics, especially in the case of dictator Efraín Ríos Montt (1982–1983), a military convert to the Church of the Word/Gospel Outreach in Eureka, California, who enjoyed support from key leaders of the U.S. religious Right. Garrard-Burnett, *Terror in the Land of the Holy Spirit*; Stoll, *Is Latin America Turning Protestant?*

17. Shaull and Cesar, *Pentecostalism and the Future of the Christian Churches*, 116. See also the several chapters authored by Latin American scholars in Boudewijnse, Droogers, and Kamsteeg, *Algo más que opio*; and Benjamín Gutiérrez, *En la fuerza del espíritu*.

18. Kamsteeg, *Prophetic Pentecostalism in Chile*. The several oral histories of Pentecostal pastors (spanning the Allende–Pinochet years) compiled by Eduardo Valen-

cia and others also invite a critical interrogation of the d'Epinayan thesis. Valencia, *En tierra extraña*.

19. Garrard-Burnett and Stoll, *Rethinking Protestantism in Latin America*; Chesnut, *Competitive Spirits*; Chesnut, *Born Again in Brazil*. Sociologist Donald Miller and others provided strong impetus to the comparative global study of "renewalist" (Pentecostal, Charismatic, and Neo-Pentecostal) Christianity's civic and political dimensions, through the Templeton-funded Pentecostal and Charismatic Research Initiative. ccrc.usc.edu/initiatives/pcri; see also Miller and Yamamori, *Global Pentecostalism*.

20. Darío López, *La seducción del poder*.

21. Cepeda, *Clientelismo y fe*; O'Neill, *City of God*.

22. Patricia Fortuny, "The *Santa Cena* of the *Luz del Mundo* Church," in Ebaugh and Chafetz, *Religion across Borders*, 15–51. The church later decentralized and virtualized its annual Lord's Supper pilgrimage in the wake of several tragic bus accidents involving poor pilgrims from throughout Mexico and the intensified border vigilance by U.S. authorities that hampered the safe return of undocumented church members to the United States after the *Santa Cena* in Guadalajara.

23. Garma, *Buscando el espíritu*.

24. Sarat, *Fire in the Canyon*. Leah Sarat's consultants drew on migratory experience and transnational connections to, among other civic engagements, sustain the innovative, cautionary Caminata Nocturna, a border-crossing simulation set in an ecotourism park. While noting that El Alberto residents inserted themselves relatively late into the post-1970s migration wave, Sarat carefully notes the importance of an older bracero history in neighboring communities and of a sui generis evangélico one in central Mexico, including the foundational translation work of the Summer Institute of Linguistics.

25. Steigenga, *The Political Implications of Pentecostalized Religion*; Steigenga, "The Politics of Pentecostalized Religion: Conversion as Pentecostalization in Guatemala," in Steigenga and Cleary, *Conversion of a Continent*, 256–80.

26. Daniel Ramírez, "Public Lives in American Hispanic Churches: Expanding the Paradigm," in Espinosa, Elizondo, and Miranda, *Latino Religions and Civic Activism*, 177–95; De la Garza et al., *Latino Voices*; De la Garza, Menchaca, and DeSipio, *Barrio Ballots*.

27. Fraga et al., *Latino Lives in America*. The 2006 Latino National Survey instrument offered nine options for respondents' religious tradition: Catholic, Assemblies of God, Southern Baptist, Pentecostal, Other Protestant, Mormon, Jewish, Don't Identify, Jehovah's Witness, and Other. http://www.icpsr.umich.edu/icpsrweb/ICPSR/studies/20862.

28. Rudiger V. Busto, "'In the Outer Boundaries': Pentecostalism, Politics, and Reies López Tijerina's Civic Activism," in Espinosa, Elizondo, and Miranda, *Latino Religions and Civic Activism*, 65–76; Elizabeth D. Ríos, "'The Ladies Are Warriors': Latina Pentecostalism and Faith-Based Activism in New York City," in Espinosa, Elizondo, and Miranda, *Latino Religions and Civic Activism*, 197–217; and Daniel Ramírez, "Public Lives in American Hispanic Churches."

29. Evangelicals (including Pentecostals) offered a 74, 82, and 67 percent affirma-

tive response rate, versus a Catholic 52, 58, and 45 one when queried whether their church or house of worship helped members in need with finding a job, financial problems, and finding housing. "Religious Practices and Belief," in Pew Hispanic Center, "Changing Faiths," 23.

30. Ibid., 44, 35.

31. Bastian, *La mutación religiosa de América Latina*.

32. Gamio, *Forjando Patria*, 178.

BIBLIOGRAPHY

Archives and Research Collections

Berkeley, Calif.
   University of California at Berkeley, Bancroft Library
      Manuel Gamio Collection
Madison, N.J.
   United Methodist Archives and History Center
México, D.F.
   Archivo General de la Nación
      Fondo Gobernación
Pasadena, Calif.
   David Allan Hubbard Library, Fuller Theological Seminary
      Manuel J. Gaxiola Collection
      Manuel J. Vizcarra Collection
Springfield, Mo.
   Flower Pentecostal Heritage Center

Government Report

Instituto Nacional de Información Estadística y Geográfica de México.
   "Población de 5 años y más por entidad federativa, sexo y religión, y su
   distribución según grupos quinquenales de edad. Censo de Población y
   Vivienda, 2000 y 2010." México, D.F.: INEGI. www.inegi.gob.mx.

Interviews

Alemán, Apolinar. Interview by author, 11 October 1992, Oceano, Calif.
   Videorecording.
Alvarado, Rosario, Juan Alvarado, and Rosario Alvarado. Interviews by author, 5
   August 1999 to 29 December 2000, San Jose and Whittier, Calif. Audiocassette.
Buriel, Jesse. Interview by author, 3 July 1991, San Diego. Notes.
Cantú, Benjamín. Interview by author, 19 September 1994, Los Angeles.
   Videorecording.
Carrillo, Mary Lou. Interview with author, 5 July 1993, Visalia, Calif.
   Videorecording.
Casas, Jacobo. Phone interview with author, 7 September 2013. Notes.
Cota, Isaac. Interview by author, 4 July 1991, San Diego. Notes.
Gaxiola, Manuel. Interview by author, 7 August 2003, México, D.F. Notes.

Gutiérrez, Moses, Sr. Interview by author, 19 July 1999, National City, Calif. Audiocassette.

Hernández, José. Interview by author, 20 May 2002, Oaxaca City. Notes.

Herrera, Luis. Interview by author, 16 September 1994, Los Angeles. Videorecording.

Montes, Luciano, and Graciela Montes. Interview by author, 31 October 2004, Phoenix, Ariz. Notes.

Nava, Antonio. Interview by author, 25 March 1994, Union City, Calif. Videorecording.

Nava, Daniel. Phone interview by author, 30 October 2004. Notes.

Ortega, Abel. Interview by Joanne Sanchez, 29 March 2001, San Antonio, Tex. (U.S. Latino and Latina World War II Oral History Project/Oral History Project—Voces, University of Texas Libraries). http://www.lib.utexas.edu/voces/.

Ortega, José. Interview by author, 10 July 1991, San Diego. Videorecording.

Ramírez, Eliseo. Interview by author, 5 January 2000, Encinitas, Calif. Audiocassette.

Reta, Emeterio. Interview by author, 25 March 1994, Union City, Calif. Videorecording.

Rodríguez, John C. Phone interviews by author, 8 October 1998 and 17 February 2005. Notes.

Rodríguez, Johnny. Interview by author, 30 September 1991, Solana Beach, Calif. Notes.

Zaragoza, Filemon, and Priscilla Castro de Zaragoza. Interview by author, 12 July 2000, Otay, Calif. Audiocassette.

Unpublished Papers

Avalos Orozco, José. "Historia de la Iglesia Apostólica de la Fe en Cristo Jesús en el Estado de Nayarit, República Mexicana." n.d. (Made available to author by Absalón Avalos).

Banderas, Pedro. "Memorias." 23 July 1966 (unpaginated, copy in author's files).

Gaxiola Gaxiola, Manuel J. "Cincuenta Años Después." México, D.F., n.d.

———. "Tiempos de cambio: Breve análisis histórico-teológico de la relación entre la Asamblea Apostólica de los Estados Unidos y la Iglesia Apostólica de México." México, D.F., n.d.

Gaxiola López, Maclovio. "Informe del Obispo Presidente." 26 October 1962. Torreón, Coahuila (copy in author's files).

Ramírez, Daniel. "Beyond Racial Incommensurability in American Revivalism." In Proceedings of the 31st Annual Assembly of the Society for Pentecostal Studies, Lakeland, Fla., March 2002.

Robeck, Cecil M., Jr. "Evangelization, or Proselytism of Hispanics? A Pentecostal Perspective." Fuller Theological Seminary, Pasadena, Calif., 1996.

Salazar, Lorenzo. ["History of the Apostolic Assembly"]. n.d. (untitled essay, copy in author's files).

Valverde, Samuel. "Apostolic Families' Migration, Message and Song: A Brief Review of the Valverde/Pacheco Family Migration Cycles and Evangelization in the United States and Mexico." McCormick Theological Seminary, Chicago, 2013.

Walsh, Casey. "Demobilizing the Revolution: Migration, Repatriation and Colonization in Mexico, 1911–1940." Paper presented to the Center for Comparative Immigration Studies, University of California, San Diego, November 2000.

Dissertations and Thesis Projects

Callahan, Leslie D. "Fleshly Manifestations: Charles Fox Parham's Quest for the Sanctified Body." Ph.D. diss., Princeton University, 2002.

Espinosa, Gastón. "Borderland Religion: Los Angeles and the Origins of the Latino Pentecostal Movement in the U.S., Mexico, and Puerto Rico, 1900–1945." Ph.D. diss., University of California, Santa Barbara, 1999.

Hernández Hernández, Alberto. "Transformaciones sociales y cambio religioso en la frontera norte de México." Ph.D. diss., Universidad Complutense de Madrid, 2004.

Jaimes Martínez, Ramiro. "La paradoja neopentecostal. Una expresión del cambio religioso fronterizo en Tijuana, Baja California." Ph.D. diss., Colegio de la Frontera Norte, 2007.

Lockwood, Manuel. "Recent Developments in U.S. Hispanic and Latin American Protestant Church Music." D.Min. project, Claremont School of Theology, 1981.

Nelson, J. D. "For Such a Time as This: The Story of Bishop William J. Seymour and the Azusa Street Revival. A Study of Pentecostal/Charismatic Roots." Ph.D. diss., University of Birmingham, 1981.

Ramírez, Daniel. "Migrating Faith: A Social and Cultural History of Pentecostalism in the U.S.–Mexico Borderlands." Ph.D. diss., Duke University, 2005.

Valenzuela, María Eugenia. "Loosening the Nailed Hand: A Critical Analysis of the Pentecostal Movement in Mexico." Ph.D. diss., University of Regina, 1999.

Young, Daniel J. "The Cincinnati Plan and the National Presbyterian Church of Mexico: A Brief Study of Relations between American Mission Boards and Mexican Protestant Churches during the Mexican Revolution." MA thesis, University of Texas at El Paso, 2006.

Newspapers and Church Periodicals, Reports, and Yearbooks

Actas de la XIX Conferencia Anual Central de México de la Iglesia Metodista del Sur de México. San Luis Potosí: Imprenta del Colegio Wesleyano, 1904.

Apostolic Faith (Los Angeles)

Daily News (Los Angeles)

El Evangelista Mexicano

El Exégeta Apostólico

El Heraldo Apostólico

El Mensajero Cristiano

El Mundo Cristiano

El Siglo de Torreón (Torreón, Coahuila)

Fifteenth Annual Report, New Constitution and Principles, 1911–1912. Boone, Iowa: Christian Missionary Alliance, 1912.

Foreign Missions Board Annual Reports, 1906–1918. Methodist Episcopal Church, South.

Hacia la meta: Anuario del Instituto Teológico Apostólico Internacional. México, D.F., 1948.

Hacia la meta: Anuario del Instituto Teológico Apostólico Internacional. Tepic, Nayarit, 1966.

Journal of the Conferencia Annual Mexicana del Suroeste, 1941, 1943, 1945. El Paso, Tex.

Journal of the Latin American Mission of the Methodist Episcopal Church, 1921, 1922. Gardena, Calif., Spanish American Institute Press.

Journal of the Southern California Annual Conference, 1912–1921. Methodist Episcopal Church.

The King's Trumpet

La Luz Apostólica

One Hundred and Eighth Annual Report of the American Board of Commissioners for Foreign Missions, 1918. Boston: American Board of Commissioners for Foreign Missions, 1919.

Pentecostal Evangel

Hymnals and Song Collections

Alstott, Owen, ed. *Flor y canto*. Portland: Oregon Catholic Press, 1989.

Celebremos su gloria. Dallas: Libros Alianza, 1992.

Concepción, Juan, ed. *Ecos de vida. Selección especial de himnos y canciones espirituales por compositores hispanos*. Brooklyn, N.Y.: Editorial Ebenezer, n.d.

Cragin, J. Paul, ed. *Melodías evangélicas. Nuevos cantos y coros de despertamiento cristiano*. Los Angeles: J. Paul Cragin, 1933, 1936, 1955, 1970.

Gaxiola, Maclovio, ed. *Himnos de suprema alabanza a Jesús*, 2nd. ed. Hermosillo, Sonora: 1942.

Grado, Pedro, ed. *Pequeña colección de himnos*. Laredo, Tex.: n.p., 1905.

Gutiérrez, Felipe, ed. *Nuevo himnario de melodías evangélicas selectas*, 1st. ed. Brownsville, Tex.: Latin American Council of Christian Churches, 1944.

Hall, J. Lincoln, Irvin H. Mack, and C. Austin Miles, eds. *The Service of Praise: A Collection of Appropriate Songs for Use in Sunday Schools*. Philadelphia: Hall-Mack, 1900.

Hargrave, Vessie D. *Rayos de Esperanza*. San Antonio: Editorial Evangélica, 1952.

Himnario de suprema alabanza a Jesús. 6th ed. Guadalajara: Iglesia Apostólica de la Fe en Cristo Jesús, 1996.

Himnario de suprema alabanza, aumentada. 2nd ed. Managua: Iglesia Apostólica
de la Fe en Cristo Jesús, n.d.
Himnario evangélico para el uso de todas las iglesias. New York: American Tract
Society, 1893.
*Himnario para el Departamento de Música y Adoración del Concilio para la Obra
Hispano Americana.* Los Angeles: Concilio Interdenominacional para la Obra
Hispana en los Estados Unidos, 1964.
Himnos de aspiración. Los Angeles: Concilio Interdenominacional para la Obra
Hispana en los Estados Unidos, 1950.
Himnos de consolación. 6th ed. Los Angeles: Apostolic Assembly of the Faith in
Christ Jesus, 1980.
Iglesia de Dios en Cristo, Menonita. *Alabanzas favoritas.* 2nd ed. Moundridge,
Kans.: Gospel Publishers, 1993.
Lerma, Rosario V. *Marcial de la Cruz: Himnos del pasado.* Pasadena, Calif.: Rosario V.
Lerma, 1985.
Mendoza, Vicente, ed. *Himnos selectos.* México, D.F.: Vicente Mendoza, 1904.
*Nuevo himnario evangélico para el uso de la iglesias evangélicas de habla española en todo
el mundo.* New York: American Tract Society, 1914.
Parra Herrera, Santos, Josefina Huerta de Parra, and Cesar Rodríguez Camara, eds.
Himnos de victoria. México, D.F.: Iglesia Evangélica Independiente, 2000.
Rodríguez, Primitivo A. *Himnario cristiano para uso de las iglesias evangélicas.*
Nashville: Smith and Lamar, 1908.
Salazar, Lorenzo E. *Himnario cantar de los cantares.* Los Angeles: Apostolic
Assembly of the Faith in Christ Jesus, 1980.
Shepard, Benjamin, ed. *Gloria: A Hymnal for Use in Sunday Schools, Young People's
Societies, and Devotional Meetings.* New York: A. S. Barnes, 1916.
Songs of Joy and Gladness. Boston: McDonald, Gill, 1885.

Journal Articles

Aponte, Edwin. "Coritos as Active Symbol in Latino Protestant Popular Religión."
Journal of Hispanic/Latino Theology 2, no. 3 (1995): 57–66.
Blumhofer, Edith, and Grant Wacker. "Who Edited the Azusa Mission's *Apostolic
Faith*?" *Assemblies of God Heritage* (Summer 2002): 15–21.
Burnim, Mellonee. "Functional Dimensions of Gospel Music Performance."
Western Journal of Black Studies 12, no. 2 (1988): 112–21.
———. "The Performance of Black Gospel Music as Transformation." *Concilium:
International Review of Theology* 2, Special Issue: "Music and the Experience of
God" (March–April 1989): 52–61.
Creech, Joel. "Visions of Glory: The Place of the Azusa Street Revival in
Pentecostal History." *Church History* 65 (1996): 405–24.
Espinosa, Gastón. "The Impact of Pluralism on Trends in Latin American and U.S.
Latino Religions and Society." *Perspectivas* 7 (Fall 2003): 9–55.
Gamio, Manuel. "El problema religioso en México." *La Nueva Democracia* (April
1920): 11–12.

————. "Observations on Mexican Immigration into the United States." *Pacific Affairs* 8 (August 1929): 463–69.

Garma Navarro, Carlos. "Los estudios antropológicos sobre el protestantismo en México." *Iztapalapa* 15 (1988): 53–66.

Gohr, Glenn. "A Dedicated Ministry among Hispanics: Demetrio and Nellie Bazán." *Assemblies of God Heritage* (Fall 1989): 7–9.

González, Jorge. "The Reina-Valera Bible: From Dream to Reality." *Apuntes* 1 (Winter 1981): 10–15.

Guerra Rojas, Cristián. "La música en el movimiento pentecostal de Chile (1909–1926): El aporte de Willis Collins Hoover y de Genaro Ríos Campos." Santiago: Centro de Documentación Evangélico Protestante Sendas, 2008.

Jaimes Martínez, Ramiro. "El metodismo ante la Revolución: *El Abogado Cristiano* y el levantamiento maderista." *Estudios de Historia Moderna y Contemporánea de México* 43 (January–June 2012): 69–103.

Kinder, Gordon A. "Religious Literature as an Offensive Weapon: Cipriano de Valera's Part in England's War with Spain." *Sixteenth Century Journal* 19, no. 2 (1988): 223–35.

Levitt, Peggy. "Social Remittances: Migration Driven, Local-Level Forms of Cultural Diffusion." *International Migration Review* 32 (1998): 926–48.

López, Gerald. "Undocumented Mexican Migration: In Search of a Just Immigration Law and Policy." *UCLA Law Review* 28, no. 4 (1981): 615–714.

Marini, Stephen. "Hymnody as History: Early Evangelical Hymns and the Recovery of American Popular Religion." *Church History* 71 (2002): 273–306.

Martínez, Juan F. "The Bible in *Neomejicano* Protestant Folklore during the 19th Century." *Apuntes* 17, no. 1 (1997): 21–26.

Martinez, Raquel Mora. "Mil Voces Para Celebrar—Himnario Metodista." *The Hymn* 49, no. 2 (1998): 25–29.

Massey, Douglas S., and Emilio Parrado. "Migradollars: The Remittances and Savings of Mexican Migrants to the United States." *Population Research and Policy Review* 13 (1994): 3–30.

Massey, Douglas S., and Audrey Singer. "The Social Process of Undocumented Border Crossing among Mexican Migrants." *International Migration Review* 32, no. 3 (1998): 561–92.

McGee, Gary B. "Pioneers of Pentecost: Alice E. Luce and Henry C. Ball." *Assemblies of God Heritage* (Summer 1985): 5–6.

Osterberg, Arthur. "I Was There." *Full Gospel Business Men's Fellowship International Voice* (May 1966).

Ramírez, Daniel. "Creencias migrantes o peligro transgénico? Reconsiderando el pluralismo religioso y el flujo cultural en circuitos de diáspora." *Estudios Migratorios Latinoamericanos* 17, no. 52 (2003): 681–709.

————. "A Historian's Response to the Trinitarian-Oneness Pentecostal Dialogue." *Pneuma* 30, no. 2 (2008): 245–54.

Sánchez Walsh, Arlene. "Workers for the Harvest: The Latin American Bible Institutes and the Institutionalization of the Latino Pentecostal Identity." *ACHTUS: Journal of Hispanic/Latino Theology* 8, no. 1 (2000): 54–79.

Spann, E. Edward. "A Tale of Two Hymnals: The Brazilian Baptist *Cantor Cristão* (1891) and *Hinário Para o Culto Cristão* (1991)." *The Hymn* 43, no. 2 (1992): 15–21.

Stock, Jennifer. "George S. Montgomery: Businessman for the Gospel." *Assemblies of God Heritage* (Summer 1989): 12–14.

Wilhoit, Mel R. "'Sing Me a Sankey': Ira D. Sankey and Congregational Song." *The Hymn* 24, no. 1 (1991): 13–18.

Books, Book Chapters, and Reports

Acuña, Rodolfo. *Occupied America: The Chicano's Struggle toward Liberation*. San Francisco: Canfield Press, 1972.

———. *Occupied America: A History of Chicanos*. 2nd ed. New York: Harper and Row, 1988.

Af Geijerstam, Claes. *Popular Music in Mexico*. Albuquerque: University of New Mexico Press, 1976.

Ahlstrom, Sidney E. *A Religious History of the American People*. New Haven, Conn.: Yale University Press, 1972.

Alanís Enciso, Fernando Saúl. *El valle bajo del Río Bravo, Tamaulipas, en la década de 1930. El desarrollo regional en la posrevolución a partir de la irrigación, la migración interna y los repatriados de Estados Unidos*. Ciudad Victoria, Tamaulipas: El Colegio de Tamaulipas, 2003.

Alexander, Paul. *Peace to War: Shifting Allegiances in the Assemblies of God*. Scottdale, Penn.: Herald Press, 2009.

Alfaro, Sammy. *Divino Compañero: Toward a Hispanic Pentecostal Christology*. Eugene, Ore.: Wipf and Stock, 2010.

Almaguer, Tomás. *Racial Faultlines: The Historical Origins of White Supremacy in California*. Berkeley: University of California Press, 1994.

Amatulli Valente, Flaviano. *Religión, política y anticatolicismo. La extraña mezcla de la Iglesia La Luz del Mundo*. México, D.F.: Comisión Episcopal para la Doctrina de la Fe and Apóstoles de la Palabra, 1989.

Anderson, Allan. *Introduction to Pentecostalism: Global Charismatic Christianity*. Cambridge: Cambridge University Press, 2004.

Anderson, Allan H., and Walter J. Hollenweger, eds. *Pentecostals after a Century: Global Perspectives on a Movement in Transition*. Sheffield: Sheffield Academic Press, 1999.

Anderson, Robert Mapes. *Vision of the Disinherited: The Making of Modern Pentecostalism*. New York: Oxford University Press, 1979.

Anzaldúa, Gloria. *Borderlands/La Frontera: The New Mestiza*. 3rd ed. San Francisco: Aunt Lute Books, 1991.

Appadurai, Arjun. *Modernity at Large: Cultural Dimensions of Globalization*. Minneapolis: University of Minnesota Press, 1996.

Arias, Patricia, and Jorge Durand. *Mexicanos en Chicago. Diario de campo de Robert Redfield, 1924–1925. Investigación y edición*. Guadalajara: Universidad de Guadalajara, 2008.

Atkins-Vásquez, Jane. *Hispanic Presbyterians in Southern California: One Hundred Years of Ministry.* Los Angeles: Synod of Southern California and Hawaii, 1988.

Badillo, David. *Latinos and the New Immigrant Church.* Baltimore: John Hopkins University Press, 2006.

Baez-Camargo, Gonzalo. "Mexico: Concerns of the Protestant Minority." In *Concerns of a Continent,* edited by James W. Hoffman, 81–99. New York: Friendship Press, 1958.

Bakhtin, Mikhail. *Rabelais and His World.* Translated by Hélène Iswolsky. Bloomington: Indiana University Press, 1984.

Balderrama, Francisco E., and Raymond Rodríguez. *Decade of Betrayal: Mexican Repatriation in the 1930s.* Albuquerque: University of New Mexico Press, 1995.

Baldwin, Deborah J. *Protestants and the Mexican Revolution: Missionaries, Ministers, and Social Change.* Urbana: University of Illinois Press, 1990.

Baquiero, Oscar G. *La Conferencia Anual Fronteriza. Síntesis histórica.* México, D.F.: Dirección de Literatura y Comunicaciones de la Iglesia Metodista de México, 1990.

Bartleman, Frank, Jr. *Azusa Street: The Roots of Modern-Day Pentecost,* edited by Vinson Synan. Plainfield, N.J.: Logos International, 1980. Original: *How "Pentecost" Came to Los Angeles—How It Was in the Beginning.* Los Angeles: privately printed, 1925.

Barton, Paul. *Hispanic Methodists, Presbyterians, and Baptists in Texas.* Austin: University of Texas, 2006.

Bastian, Jean-Pierre. *La mutación religiosa de América Latina. Para una sociología del cambio social en la modernidad periférica.* México, D.F.: Fondo de Cultura Económica, 1997.

———. *Los disidentes. Sociedades protestantes y revolución en México, 1872–1911.* México, D.F.: El Colegio de México, 1989.

Besserer, Federico. *Topografías transnacionales. Hacia una geografía de la vida transnacional.* México, D.F.: Universidad Autónoma Metropolitana-Iztalapa, 2004.

Best, Wallace. *Passionately Human, No Less Divine: Religion and Culture in Black Chicago, 1915–1952.* Princeton, N.J.: Princeton University Press, 2005.

Blancarte, Roberto. *Historia de la Iglesia Católica en México.* México, D.F.: Fondo de Cultura Económica, 1992.

Blumhofer, Edith, and Mark A. Noll, eds. *Singing the Lord's Song in a Strange Land: American Protestant Hymnody.* Tuscaloosa: University of Alabama Press, 2004.

Bolton, Herbert E. *Rim of Christendom: A Biography of Eusebio Francisco Kino, Pacific Coast Pioneer.* San Francisco: Macmillan, 1936.

Bonifaz de Hernández, Rosalía, Ileana Gil Durán, and Rafael Miranda Polanco. "La frontera en la actualidad. De 1945 a nuestros días, Baja California." In *Visión histórica de la frontera norte de México.* Vol. 3, edited by David Piñera Ramírez. Mexicali: Universidad Autónoma de Baja California, 1987.

Boudewijnse, Barbara, André Droogers, and Frans Kamsteeg, eds. *Algo más que opio. Una lectura antropológica del pentecostalismo latinoamericano y caribeño.* San José, Costa Rica: Departamento Ecuménico de Investigaciones, 1991.

──── . *More than Opium: An Anthropological Approach to Latin American and Caribbean Pentecostal Praxis*. Lanham, Md.: Scarecrow Press, 1998.

Bourdieu, Pierre. *Distinction: A Social Critique of the Judgment of Taste*. Cambridge, Mass.: Harvard University Press, 1984.

──── . *Outline of a Theory of Practice*. New York: Cambridge University Press, 1977.

Brackenridge, R. Douglas, and Francisco O. García-Treto. *Iglesia Presbiteriana: A History of Presbyterians and Mexican Americans in the Southwest*. 2nd. ed. San Antonio: Trinity University Press, 1987.

Brusco, Elizabeth. *The Reformation of Machismo: Evangelical Conversion in Colombia*. Austin: University of Texas Press, 1995.

Burdick, John. *Blessed Anastacia: Women, Race and Popular Christianity in Brazil*. New York: Routledge, 1998.

Burgess, Stanley, and Gary B. McGee, eds. *Dictionary of Pentecostal and Charismatic Movements*. Grand Rapids, Mich.: Zondervan, 1988.

Burnim, Mellonee. "Conflict and Controversy in Black Religious Music." In *African-American Religion: Research Problems and Resources for the 1990s*, edited by Victor N. Smythe and Howard Dodson, 82–97. New York: Schomberg Center for Research in Black Culture, 1992.

Burnim, Mellonee V., and Portia K. Maultsby. "From Backwoods to City Streets: The Afro-American Musical Journey." In *Expressively Black*, edited by Geneva Gay and Willie L. Baber, 109–36. New York: Praeger Press, 1987.

Busto, Rudy. *King Tiger: The Religious Vision of Reies López Tijerina*. Albuquerque: University of New Mexico Press, 2005.

Butler, Matthew. *Popular Piety and Political Identity in Mexico's Cristero Rebellion: Michoacán, 1927–29*. Oxford: British Academy, 2004.

Cahn, Peter S. *All Religions Are Good in Tzintzuntzan: Evangelicals in Catholic Mexico*. Austin: University of Texas Press, 2003.

Camp, Roderic Ai. *Mexican Political Biographies, 1884–1935*. Austin: University of Texas Press, 1991.

Campos, Rubén. *El folklore y la música mexicana. Investigación acerca de la cultura musical en México, 1525–1925*. México, D.F.: Secretaría de Educación Pública, 1928.

Canclini, Arnoldo. *Diego Thomson. Apóstol de la enseñanza y distribución de la Biblia en América Latina y España*. Buenos Aires: Asociación Sociedad Bíblica Argentina, 1987.

Cantú, Ernesto S., José A. Ortega, Issac Cota, and Phillip Rangel. *Historia de la Asamblea Apostólica de la Fe en Cristo Jesús*. Mentone, Calif.: Sal's Printing Service, 1966.

Cantú, Tomasita Saénz. *Una auténtica pionera*. Rosemead, Calif.: Prentiz Printing Press, 1992.

Cardoza Orlandi, Carlos F. "Qué Lindo Es Mi Cristo: The Erotic Jesus/Christ in the Caribbean, Latin American, and Latino/a Protestant Christian Music." In *Jesus in the Hispanic Community: Images of Christ from Theology to Popular Religion*, edited by Harold J. Recinos and Hugo Magallanes, 157–70. Louisville: Westminster John Knox Press, 2009.

Castañeda Jiménez, Héctor F. *Marcelino García Barragán. Una vida al servicio de México*. Guadalajara: Gobierno del Estado de Jalisco, 1987.

Cepeda van Houten, Alvaro. *Clientelismo y fe. Dinámicas políticas del pentecostalismo en Colombia*. Bogotá: Editorial Bonaventuriana, 2007.

Chesnut, Andrew R. *Born Again in Brazil: The Pentecostal Boom and the Pathogens of Poverty*. New Brunswick, N.J.: Rutgers University Press, 1997.

———. *Competitive Spirits: Latin America's New Religious Economy*. Oxford: Oxford University Press, 2003.

Christian Work in Latin America. Vol. 3. New York: Committee on Cooperation in Latin America/Missionary Education Movement, 1917.

Cleary, Edward L. *The Rise of Charismatic Catholicism in Latin America*. Gainesville: University Press of Florida, 2011.

Cole, Clifford A. *The Christian Churches (Disciples of Christ) of Southern California: A History*. St. Louis: by the author, 1959.

Colom Maldonado, Alfredo. *Música en su alma. Autobiografía de Alfredo Colom M.* Guatemala: Ediciones SABER, 1985.

Constitución de la Asamblea Apostólica de la Fe en Cristo Jesús. México, D.F.: Maclovio Gaxiola López, 1945.

Constitución de la Asamblea Apostólica de la Fe en Cristo Jesús. México, D.F.: Maclovio Gaxiola López, 1951.

Contreras Mora, Francisco. *El movimiento agrario en el Territorio Norte de Baja California*. Mexicali: n.p., 1987.

Cox, Harvey. *The Rise of Pentecostal Spirituality and the Reshaping of Religion in the Twenty-First Century*. Reading, Mass.: Addison-Wesley, 1995.

Cross, Whitney R. *The Burned-over District: The Social and Intellectual History of Enthusiastic Religion in Western New York, 1880–1850*. Ithaca, N.Y.: Cornell University Press, 1950.

Cumberland, Charles C. *Mexican Revolution: The Constitutionalist Years*. Austin: University of Texas Press, 1972.

Dayton, Donald W. "The Limits of Evangelicalism: The Pentecostal Tradition." In *The Variety of American Evangelicalism*, edited by Donald W. Dayton and Robert K. Johnston, 36–56. Knoxville: University of Tennessee Press, 1991.

———. *The Theological Roots of Pentecostalism*. Peabody, Mass.: Hendrikson Publishers, 1987.

D'Epinay, Lalive. *Haven of the Masses: A Study of the Pentecostal Movement in Chile*. London: Lutterworth Press, 1969.

De Certeau, Michel. *The Practice of Everyday Life*. Berkeley: University of California Press, 1984.

De la Garza, Rodolfo O., Louis DeSipio, F. Chris Garcia, John Garcia, and Angelo Falcon. *Latino Voices: Mexican, Puerto Rican, and Cuban Perspectives on American Politics*. Boulder, Colo.: Westview Press, 1992.

De la Garza, Rodolfo O., Martha Menchaca, and Louis DeSipio, eds. *Barrio Ballots: Latino Politics in the 1990 Elections*. Boulder, Colo.: Westview Press, 1993.

De la Luz García, Deyssi Jael. *El movimiento pentecostal en México. La Iglesia de Dios, 1926–1948*. México, D.F.: Editorial Letra Ausente, 2010.

De la Peña, Moisés T. *El pueblo y su tierra. Mito y realidad de la reforma agraria en México*. México, D.F.: Cuadernos Americanos, 1964.

De la Torre, Renée. *Los hijos de la luz. Discurso, identidad y poder en la Luz del Mundo*. Guadalajara: Universidad de Guadalajara, 2000.

De León, Victor. *The Silent Pentecostals: A Biographical History of the Pentecostal Movement among the Hispanics in the Twentieth Century*. Taylors, S.C.: Faith Printing Company, 1979.

Del Pilar, Luis F. *Himnos de "El Avivamiento."* 2nd ed. Bayamón, P.R.: Impresos Quintana, 1983.

Diccionario de la revolución mexicana en Jalisco. Guadalajara: Mario Aldana Rendón, 1997.

Dickinson, Edward. *Music in the History of the Western Church*. New York: Charles Scribner's Sons, 1902. Reprint: New York: Greenwood Press, 1969.

Dolan, Jay P., and Allan Figueroa Deck, eds. *Hispanic Catholic Culture in the U.S.: Issues and Concerns*. Notre Dame, Ind.: University of Notre Dame Press, 1994.

Dolan, Jay P., and Gilberto M. Hinojosa, eds. *Mexican Americans and the Catholic Church, 1900–1965*. Notre Dame, Ind.: University of Notre Dame Press, 1994.

Dolan, Jay P., and Jaime R. Vidal, eds. *Puerto Rican and Cuban Catholics in the U.S., 1900–1965*. Notre Dame, Ind.: University of Notre Dame Press, 1994.

Domínguez, Roberto. *Norteamérica y Las Antillas*. Vol. 1 of *Pioneros de Pentecostés en el mundo de habla hispana*. Bayamón, P.R.: by the author, 1971.

Dormady, Jason. *Primitive Revolution: Restorationist Religion and the Idea of the Mexican Revolution, 1940–1968*. Albuquerque: University of New Mexico Press, 2001.

Du Bois, W. E. B. *The Souls of Black Folks*. Chicago: A. C. McClurg, 1903.

Durand, Jorge. *Más allá de la línea. Patrones migratorios entre México y Estados Unidos*. México, D.F.: Consejo Nacional para la Cultura y las Artes, 1994.

Durand, Jorge, and Douglas S. Massey. *Miracles on the Border: Retablos of Mexican Migrants to the United States*. Tucson: University of Arizona Press, 1995.

Durkheim, Emile. *Suicide: A Study in Sociology*. London: Routledge, 1970.

Ebaugh, Helen Rose, and Janet Saltzman Chafetz, eds. *Religion across Borders: Transnational Immigrant Networks*. Walnut Creek, Calif.: Altamira Press, 2002.

Erlmann, Veit. *Nightsong: Performance, Power, and Practice in South Africa*. Chicago: University of Chicago Press, 1996.

Espinosa, Gastón. "'God Made a Miracle in My Life': Latino Pentecostal Healing in the Borderlands." In *Religion and Healing in America*, edited by Linda L. Barnes and Susan Starr Sered, 121–38. New York: Oxford University Press, 2001.

———. "Latino Pentecostal Healing in the North American Borderlands." In *Global Pentecostal and Charismatic Healing*, edited by Candy Gunther Brown, 129–49. Oxford: Oxford University Press, 2011.

———. *Latino Pentecostals in America: Faith and Politics in Action*. Cambridge, Mass.: Harvard University Press, 2014.

———. *William J. Seymour and the Origins of Global Pentecostalism: A Biography and Documentary History*. Durham, N.C.: Duke University Press, 2014.

Espinosa, Gastón, Virgilio Elizondo, and Jesse Miranda, eds. *Latino Religions and Civic Activism in the United States*. Oxford: Oxford University Press, 2005.

Espinosa, Gastón, and Mario T. García, eds. *Mexican American Religions: Spirituality, Activism, and Culture.* Durham, N.C.: Duke University Press, 2008.

Ewart, Frank. *The Phenomenon of Pentecost.* Houston: Herald Publishing House, 1947.

Feld, Steven. *Sound and Sentiment: Birds, Weeping, Poetics, and Song in Kaluli Expression.* 2nd. ed. Philadelphia: University of Pennsylvania Press, 1990.

Foreign Relations of the United States, 1917. Washington, D.C.: Government Printing Office, 1926.

Foster, Fred. *Their Story: 20th Century Pentecostals.* Hazelwood, Mo.: Word Aflame Press, 1983. Reprint and revision of *Think It Not Strange.* St. Louis, Mo.: Pentecostal Publishing House, 1965.

Foster, George M. *Tzintzuntzan: Mexican Peasants in a Changing World.* Boston: Little, Brown, 1967.

Foucault, Michel. *Power/Knowledge: Selected Interviews and Other Writings, 1972–1977.* Edited by Colin Gordon. New York: Pantheon Books, 1980.

Fraga, Luis R., John A. Garcia, Rodney E. Hero, Michael Jones-Correa, Valerie Martínez-Ebers, and Gary M. Segura. *Latino Lives in America: Making It Home.* Philadelphia: Temple University Press, 2010.

French, Talmadge L. *Our God Is One: The Story of Oneness Pentecostals.* Indianapolis: Voice and Vision Publications, 1999.

Fudge, Thomas A. *Christianity without the Cross: A History of Salvation in Oneness Pentecostalism.* Parkland, Fla.: Universal Publishers, 2003.

Galarza, Ernesto. *Farm Workers and Agri-Business in California, 1947–1960.* Notre Dame, Ind.: University of Notre Dame Press, 1977.

———. *Merchants of Labor: The Mexican Bracero Story.* Santa Barbara: McNally & Loftin, West, 1964.

Gamio, Manuel. *El inmigrante mexicano: La historia de su vida, Entrevistas completas, 1926–1927.* Edited by Devra Weber, Roberto Melville, and Juan Vicente Palerm. México, D.F.: Centro de Investigaciones y Estudios Superiores en Antropología Social, 2002.

———. *Forjando Patria.* 4th ed. México, D.F.: Editorial Porrúa, 1992.

———. *The Mexican Immigrant: His Life Story.* Chicago: University of Chicago Press, 1931.

———. *Mexican Immigration to the United States: A Study of Human Migration and Adjustment.* Chicago: University of Chicago Press, 1930.

Garma Navarro, Carlos. *Buscando el espíritu. Pentecostalismo en Iztapalapa y la Ciudad de Mexico.* México, D.F.: Universidad Autónoma Metropolitana, Iztapalapa, 2004.

———. *Protestantismo en una comunidad totonaca de Puebla.* México, D.F.: Instituto Nacional Indigenista, 1987.

Garrard-Burnett, Virginia. *Protestantism in Guatemala: Living in the New Jerusalem.* Austin: University of Texas Press, 1998.

———. *Terror in the Land of the Holy Spirit: Guatemala under General Efraín Ríos Montt, 1982–1983.* Oxford: Oxford University Press, 2010.

Garrard-Burnett, Virginia, and David Stoll, eds. *Rethinking Protestantism in Latin America*. Philadelphia: Temple University Press, 1993.

Gaxiola Gaxiola, J. Felipe. *Mi Tío Maclovio*. Tijuana: Publicaciones Apostólicas, 1972.

Gaxiola Gaxiola, Manuel J. *La serpiente y la paloma. Análisis del crecimiento de la Iglesia Apostólica*. 2nd ed. México, D.F.: by the author, 1994.

Gaxiola López, Maclovio. *Historia de la Iglesia Apostólica de la Fe en Cristo Jesús*. México, D.F.: by the author, 1964.

Gill, Kenneth. *Toward a Contextualized Theology for the Third World: The Emergence and Development of Jesus' Name Pentecostalism in Mexico*. Frankfurt: Peter Lang, 1994.

Gill, Lesley. *Precarious Dependencies: Gender, Class, and Domestic Service in Bolivia*. New York: Columbia University Press, 1994.

Ginzburg, Carlo. *The Cheese and the Worms: The Cosmos of a Sixteenth-Century Miller*. Translated by John Tedeschi and Anne Tedeschi. Baltimore: John Hopkins University Press, 1980.

Glock, Charles Y. *The Role of Deprivation in the Origins and Evolution of Religious Groups*. Berkeley: University of California Press, 1958.

Goff, James R., Jr. *Fields White unto Harvest: Charles F. Parham and the Missionary Origins of Pentecostalism*. Fayetteville: University of Arkansas Press, 1988.

Goff, James R., Jr., and Grant Wacker, eds. *Portraits of a Generation: Early Pentecostal Leaders*. Fayetteville: University of Arkansas Press, 2002.

González Garza, R., P. Ramos Romero, and J. Pérez Rul. *La batalla de Torreón*. El Paso: El Paso Printing Co., 1914.

González Navarro, Moisés. *Masones y cristeros en Jalisco*. México, D.F.: El Colegio de México, 2000.

Goodman, Felicitas D. "Disturbances in the Apostolic Church: A Trance-Based Upheaval in Yucatan." In *Trance, Healing, and Hallucination: Three Field Studies in Religious Experience*, edited by Felicitas D. Goodman, Jeannette H. Henney, and Esther Pressel, 227–380. New York: Wiley Interscience, 1974.

———. *Maya Apocalypse: Seventeen Years with the Women of a Yucatan Village*. Bloomington: University of Indiana Press, 2001.

———. *Speaking in Tongues: A Cross-Cultural Study of Glossolalia*. Chicago: University of Chicago Press, 1972.

Grebler, Leo. *Mexican Immigration to the United States: The Record and Its Implications*. Mexican American Study Project Advance Report 2. Westwood, Calif.: UCLA Graduate School of Business Administration, 1966.

Griswold del Castillo, Richard. *The Los Angeles Barrio: 1850–1890*. Berkeley: University of California Press, 1979.

Griswold del Castillo, Richard, and Richard A. García. *Cesar Chavez: A Triumph of Spirit*. Norman: University of Oklahoma Press, 1995.

Guarnizo, Luis, and Michael P. Smith, eds. *Transnationalism from Below: Comparative Urban and Community Research*. Vol. 6. Rutgers, N.J.: Transaction Publishers, 1998.

Guillén, Miguel. *La historia del Concilio Latino Americano de Iglesias Cristianas.* Brownsville, Tex.: Latin American Council of Christian Churches, 1982.

Gutiérrez, Benjamín F., ed. *En la fuerza del espíritu. Los pentecostales en América Latina: Un desafío a las iglesias históricas.* Guatemala: Centro Evangélico Latinoamericano de Estudios Pastorales, 1995.

Gutiérrez, Benjamín F., and Dennis A. Smith, eds. *In the Power of the Spirit: The Pentecostal Challenge to Historic Churches in Latin America.* Louisville: Presbyterian Church (U.S.A.) Worldwide Ministries Division, 1996.

Gutiérrez, Moses, Jr. *In My Father's House Are Many Mansions: A Testimonial.* Los Angeles: by the author, 2014.

Hale, Charles. *Mexican Liberalism in the Age of Mora, 1821–1853.* New Haven, Conn.: Yale University Press, 1968.

Haven, Gilbert. *Mexico: Our Next-Door Neighbor.* New York: Harper and Bros., 1875.

Hernández, Bernardo. *Catequista del Concilio Apostólico Cristiano del Pentecostés.* Los Angeles: Bernardo Hernández, 1927.

———. *Estatutos acordados en la 1ra. convención mexicana de la Iglesia de la Fe Apostólica Pentecostés.* Los Angeles: Bernardo Hernández, 1926.

Hernández Castillo, Rosalva Aída. *Histories and Stories from Chiapas: Border Identities in Southern Mexico.* Austin: University of Texas Press, 2001.

———. *La otra frontera. Identidades múltiples en el Chiapas poscolonial.* México, D.F.: Centro de Investigaciones y Estudios Superiores de Antropología Social, 2001.

Hoffman, Abraham. *Unwanted Mexican Americans in the Great Depression: Repatriation Pressures, 1929–1939.* Tucson: University of Arizona Press, 1974.

Holland, Clifton. *The Religious Dimension in Hispanic Los Angeles: A Protestant Case Study.* South Pasadena, Calif.: William Carey Library, 1974.

Hollenweger, Walter J. *Pentecostalism: Origins and Developments Worldwide.* Peabody, Mass.: Hendrickson Publishers, 1997.

Huegel, Juan E. *Apóstol de la cruz: La vida y labor misionera de Federico J. Huegel.* México, D.F.: Ediciones Transformación, 1995.

Informe anual de la Agencia Bíblica en México correspondiente a 1952. México, D.F.: Agencia Bíblica en México, 1952.

Inman, Samuel Guy. *Evangelicals at Havana.* New York: Committee on Cooperation in Latin America, 1929.

Jacobsen, Douglas. *Thinking in the Spirit: Theologies of the Early Pentecostal Movement.* Bloomington: Indiana University Press, 2003.

Jeter de Walker, Luisa. *Siembra y cosecha. Reseña histórica de las Asambleas de Dios de México y Centroamérica.* Deerfield, Fla.: Editorial Vida, 1990.

Kahl, Willi. "Bolero." In *The New Grove Dictionary of Music and Musicians,* edited by Stanley Sadie, 870–71. London: Macmillan, 1980.

Kamsteeg, Frans H. *Prophetic Pentecostalism in Chile: A Case Study on Religion and Development Policy.* Lanham, Md.: Scarecrow Press, 1998.

León, Luis. *La Llorona's Children: Religion, Life, and Death in the U.S.-Mexican Borderlands.* Berkeley: University of California Press, 2004.

———. *The Political Spirituality of Cesar Chavez: Crossing Religious Borders.* Berkeley: University of California Press, 2014.

Levitt, Peggy. *God Needs No Passport: Immigrants and the Changing American Religious Landscape.* New York: New Press, 2007.

———. *The Transnational Villagers.* Berkeley: University of California Press, 2001.

Levy, Jacques E., Fred Ross, and Jacqueline Levy. *Cesar Chavez: Autobiography of La Causa.* Minneapolis: University of Minnesota Press, 2007. Original edition: New York: Norton, 1975.

Lewis, Oscar. *The Children of Sanchez.* New York: Random House, 1961.

Linde, Charlotte. *Life Stories: The Creation of Coherence.* New York: Oxford University Press, 1993.

López Castro, Gustavo, ed. *El Río Bravo es charco. Cancionero del migrante.* Zamora, Michoacán: El Colegio de Michoacán, 1995.

López Cortés, Eliseo. *Ultimo cielo en la cruz. Cambio sociocultural y estructuras de poder en Los Altos de Jalisco.* Zapopan: El Colegio de Jalisco, 1999.

López Rodríguez, Darío. *La seducción del poder. Los evangélicos y la política en el Perú de los noventa.* Lima: Instituto de Ciencias Políticas, Investigación y Promoción del Desarrollo Nueva Humanidad, 2004.

López Torres, Samuel. *Historia de la Iglesia Apostólica de la Fe en Cristo Jesús en Tijuana, 1927–1997.* Tijuana, B.C.: by the author, 1998.

Loza, Steven. *Barrio Rhythm: Mexican American Music in Los Angeles.* Urbana: University of Illinois Press, 1993.

Machado, Daisy. *Of Borders and Margins: Hispanic Disciples in Texas, 1888–1945.* New York: American Academy of Religion, 2003.

MacKay, John A. *The Other Spanish Christ: A Study in the Spiritual History of Spain and South America.* New York: Macmillan, 1932.

Maldonado, David, ed. *Protestantes/Protestants: Hispanic Christianity within Mainline Traditions.* Nashville: Abingdon Press, 1999.

Maldonado, David, Jr., and Paul Barton. *Hispanic Christianity within Mainline Protestant Traditions: A Bibliography.* Decatur, Ga.: Asociación para la Educación Teológica Hispana, 1998.

Mansilla, Miguel Angel. *La cruz y la esperanza. La cultura del pentecostalismo chileno en la primera mitad del siglo XX.* Santiago: Editorial Universidad Bolivariana, 2009.

Marcosson, Issac Frederick. *Turbulent Years.* New York: Dodd, Mead, 1938.

Marini, Stephen. "American Protestant Hymns Project: A Ranked List of Most Frequently Printed Hymns, 1737–1960." In *Wonderful Words of Life: Hymns in American Protestant History and Theology*, edited by Richard Mouw and Mark A. Noll, 251–64. Grand Rapids, Mich.: Eerdmans, 2004

———. "From Classical to Modern: Hymnody and the Development of American Evangelicalism, 1737–1970." In *Singing the Lord's Song in a Strange Land: Hymnody in the History of North American Protestantism*, edited by Edith L. Blumhofer and Mark A. Noll, 1–38. Tuscaloosa: University of Alabama Press, 2004.

Martin, David. *Pentecostalism: The World Their Parish.* Oxford: Blackwell, 2002.

————. *Tongues of Fire: The Explosion of Protestantism in Latin America.* Oxford: Blackwell, 1990.

Martínez, Abelino. *Las sectas en Nicaragua. Oferta y demanda de salvación.* San José, Costa Rica: Editorial Departamento Ecuménico de Investigaciones, 1989.

Martínez, Juan F. *Sea la Luz: The Making of Mexican Protestantism in the American Southwest, 1829–1900.* Denton: University of North Texas Press, 2006.

Martínez, Juan F., and Lindy Scott, eds. *Iglesias peregrinas en busca de identidad. Cuadros del protestantismo latino en Estados Unidos.* Buenos Aires: Ediciones Kairos, 2004.

————. *Los Evangélicos: Portraits of Latino Protestantism in the United States.* Eugene, Ore.: Wipf and Stock, 2009.

Martínez-Fernández, Luis. *Protestantism and Political Conflict in the Nineteenth-Century Hispanic Caribbean.* New Brunswick, N.J.: Rutgers University Press, 2002.

Masferrer Kan, Elio, ed. *La Luz del Mundo. Un análisis multidisciplinario de la controversia religiosa que ha impactado a nuestro país.* México, D.F.: Revista Académica para el Estudio de las Religiones, 1997.

Massey, Douglas S., Rafael Alarcón, Jorge Durand, and Humberto González. *Return to Aztlán: The Social Process of International Migration from Western Mexico.* Berkeley: University of California Press, 1987.

Matovina, Timothy M. *Guadalupe and Her Faithful: Latino Catholics in San Antonio, from Colonial Origins to the Present.* Baltimore: John Hopkins University Press, 2005.

————. *Tejano Religion and Ethnicity: San Antonio, 1821–1860.* Austin: University of Texas Press, 1995.

Matovina, Timothy M., and Gerald E. Poyo, eds. *¡Presente!: U.S. Latino Catholics from Colonial Origins to the Present.* Maryknoll, N.Y.: Orbis Books, 2000.

Matovina, Timothy M., and Gary Wiebe-Estrella, eds. *Horizons of the Sacred: Mexican Traditions in U.S. Catholicism.* Ithaca, N.Y.: Cornell University Press, 2002.

Matute, Alvaro, ed. *Historia de la revolución mexicana.* México, D.F.: El Colegio de México, 1977.

McDannell, Colleen. *Material Christianity: Religion and Popular Culture in America.* New Haven, Conn.: Yale University Press, 1995.

McGavran, Donald, John Huegel, and Jack Taylor. *Church Growth in Mexico.* Grand Rapids, Mich.: Eerdmans, 1963.

Medina, Lara. *Las Hermanas: Chicana/Latina Religious-Political Activism in the U.S. Catholic Church.* Philadelphia: Temple University Press, 2004.

Meier, Matt, and Feliciano Rivera. *The Chicanos: A History of Mexican Americans.* New York: Hill and Wang, 1972.

Menéndez y Pelayo, Marcelino. *Historia de los heterodoxos españoles.* 2nd ed., revised. Vol. 4. Madrid: Librería General de Victoriano Suárez, 1911–1932.

Meyer, Jean. *La Cristiada: The Mexican People between Church and State, 1926–1929.* Translated by Richard Southern. Cambridge: Cambridge University Press, 1976.

Miller, Donald, and Tetsunao Yamamori. *Global Pentecostalism: The New Face of Christian Social Engagement*. Berkeley: University of California Press, 2007.

Mitchell, Don. *They Saved the Crops: Labor, Landscape, and the Struggle over Industrial Farming in Bracero-Era California*. Athens: University of Georgia Press, 2012.

Montejano, David. *Anglos and Mexicans in the Making of Texas, 1836–1986*. Austin: University of Texas Press, 1987.

Mora, Anthony. *Border Dilemmas: Racial and National Uncertainties in New Mexico, 1848–1912*. Durham, N.C.: Duke University Press, 2011.

Morán Quiroz, Luis Rodolfo. *Alternativa religiosa en Guadalajara. Una aproximación al estudio de las iglesias evangélicas*. Guadalajara: Universidad de Guadalajara, 1990.

Nabakov, Peter. *Tijerina and the Courthouse Raid*. Albuquerque: University of New Mexico Press, 1969.

Nañez, Alfredo. *History of the Rio Grande Conference of the United Methodist Church*. Dallas: Bridwell Library, Southern Methodist University, 1980.

Nava, Antonio. *Autobiografía del Hermano Antonio Castañeda Nava*. Rancho Cucamonga, Calif.: Apostolic Assembly of the Faith in Christ Jesus, 1994.

O'Neill, Kevin Lewis. *City of God: Christian Citizenship in Postwar Guatemala*. Berkeley: University of California Press, 2010.

Orellana Uturbia, Luis. *El fuego y la nieve. Historia del movimiento pentecostal en Chile, 1909–1932*. 2nd ed. Concepción: Centro Evangélico de Estudios Pentecostales, 2008.

Orozco, E. C. *Republican Protestantism in Aztlán: The Encounter between Mexicanism and Anglo-Saxon Humanism in the United States Southwest*. Glendale, Calif.: Petereins Press, 1980.

Ortega, José. *Mis memorias en la Iglesia y la Asamblea Apostólica de la Fe en Cristo Jesús*. Indio, Calif.: by the author, 1998.

Paz, Octavio. *The Labyrinth of Solitude: Life and Thought in Mexico*. Translated by Lysander Kemp. New York: Grove Press, 1961.

Peña, Manuel. *The Mexican American Orquestra*. Austin: University of Texas Press, 1999.

———. *The Texas-Mexican Conjunto: History of a Working-Class Music*. Austin: University of Texas Press, 1985.

Pérez, Isidro. *Memorias de un pastor*. Guadalajara: by the author, 1992.

Pew Hispanic Center. "Changing Faiths: Latinos and the Transformation of American Religion, 2007," www.pewhispanic.org/files/reports/75.pdf.

Piedra, Arturo. *Evangelización protestante en América Latina. Análisis de las razones que justificaron y promovieron la expansión protestante, 1830–1960*. Quito: Consejo Latinoamericano de Iglesias Cristianas, 2000.

Poloma, Margaret M. *The Assemblies of God at the Crossroads: Charisma and Institutional Dilemmas*. Knoxville: University of Tennessee Press, 1989.

Portes Gil, Andrés. "Globalization from Below: The Rise of Transnational Communities." In *Latin America in the World Economy*, edited by W. P. Smith and R. P. Korczenwicz, 151–68. Westport, Conn.: Greenwood Press, 1996.

Pulido, Alberto L. *The Sacred World of the Penitentes*. Washington, D.C.: Smithsonian Institution Press, 2000.

Ramírez, Daniel. "Usos y costumbres (¿y mañas?): Cambio religioso y cultural en Oaxaca." In *Religión y culturas contemporáneas*, edited by Antonio Higuera, 77–94. Aguascalientes: Universidad Autónoma de Aguascalientes, 2011.

Ramírez, Raymundo. *Bodas de oro. Movimiento de la Iglesia Cristiana Independiente Pentecostés*. Pachuca, Hidalgo: Libro Histórico, 1972.

Rangel, Nellie. *Historia de la Confederación Nacional de Sociedades Feminiles "Dorcas": Asamblea Apostólica, 1916–1984*. Los Angeles: Apostolic Assembly, 1984.

Rasmussen Schick, Alice and Dean Helland Talbert. *La Iglesia Metodista Pentecostal. Ayer y hoy*. Vol. 1. Santiago: Dean Helland T., 1987.

Reed, David. *"In Jesus' Name": The History and Beliefs of Oneness Pentecostals*. Blandford Forum, England: Deo Publishing, 2008.

Rembao, Alberto. *Pneuma. Los fundamentos teológicos de la cultura*. México, D.F.: Casa Unida de Publicaciones, 1957.

Rentería Solís, René. *La Luz del Mundo. Historia de la iglesia cristiana. Vida y obra del apóstol Aarón Joaquín*. Bogotá: Iglesia La Luz del Mundo, 1997.

Rivera R., Roberto. *Instituciones protestantes en México*. México, D.F.: Editorial Jus, 1962.

Robeck, Cecil. *The Azusa Street Mission and Revival: The Birth of the Global Pentecostal Movement*. Nashville: Nelson, 2006.

Rocha Zapata, Julio César. *Nuestros ancestros espirituales. Breve historia de la Iglesia Apostólica de la Fe en Cristo Jesús de Nicaragua*. Managua: Editorial El Renacimiento, 1999.

Rodríguez, Daniel R. *La primera evangelización norteamericana en Puerto Rico, 1898–1930*. México, D.F.: Ediciones Borinquen, 1986.

Romero, Juan. *No vale tres manies. Memorias de Juan Romero*. Deerfield, Fla.: Editorial Vida, 1994.

Romero, Roberto Chao. *The Chinese in Mexico, 1882–1940*. Tucson: University of Arizona Press, 2010.

Romo, Richard. *History of a Barrio: East Los Angeles*. Austin: University of Texas Press, 1983.

Ruiz Guerra, Rubén. *Hombres nuevos. Metodismo y modernización en México, 1873–1930*. México, D.F.: Centro de Comunicación Cultural CUPSA, 1992.

Rycroft, W. Stanley. *Religion and Faith in Latin America*. Philadelphia: Westminster Press, 1958.

Saldivar, José David. *Border Matters: Remapping American Cultural Studies*. Berkeley: University of California Press, 1997.

Samora, Julian. *Los Mojados: The Wetback Story*. Notre Dame, Ind.: University of Notre Dame Press, 1971.

Sánchez, George. *Becoming Mexican American: Ethnicity, Culture, and Identity in Chicano Los Angeles, 1900–1945*. New York: Oxford University Press, 1993.

Sánchez Walsh, Arlene M. *Latino Pentecostal Identity: Evangelical Faith, Self, and Society*. New York: Columbia University Press, 2003.

Sarat, Leah. *Fire in the Canyon: Religion, Migration, and the Mexican Dream*. New York: New York University Press, 2013.

Schneider, Robert A. "Jesus Shall Reign: Hymns and Foreign Mission, 1800–1870." In *Wonderful Words of Life: Hymns in American Protestant History and Theology*, edited by Richard Mouw and Mark A. Noll, 69–95. Grand Rapids, Mich.: Eerdmans, 2004.

Shaull, Richard, and Waldo Cesar. *Pentecostalism and the Future of the Christian Churches: Promises, Limitations, Challenges*. Grand Rapids, Mich.: Eerdmans, 2000.

Silva Gotay, Samuel. *Protestantismo y política en Puerto Rico, 1898–1930*. San Juan: Universidad de Puerto Rico, 1997.

Spittler, Russell. "Are Pentecostals and Charismatics Fundamentalists? A Review of American Uses of These Categories." In *Charismatic Christianity as a Global Culture*, edited by Karla Poewe, 103–16. Columbia: University of South Carolina Press, 1994.

Spivak, Gayatri. "Can the Subaltern Speak?" In *Marxism and the Interpretation of Culture*, edited by Cary Nelson and Lawrence Grossberg, 66–111. Urbana: University of Illinois Press, 1988.

Steigenga, Timothy J. *The Political Implications of Pentecostalized Religion in Costa Rica and Guatemala*. Lanham, Md.: Lexington Books, 2001.

Steigenga, Timothy J., and Edward L. Cleary, eds. *Conversion of a Continent: Contemporary Religious Change in Latin America*. New Brunswick, N.J.: Rutgers University Press, 2007.

Stevenson, W. R. "Missions, Foreign." In *A Dictionary of Hymnology*, edited by John Julian, 740. New York: Charles Scribner's Sons, 1892.

Stoll, David. *Is Latin America Turning Protestant? The Politics of Evangelical Growth*. Berkeley: University of California Press, 1990.

Taylor, Jack. *God's Messengers to Mexico's Masses: A Study of the Religious Significance of the Braceros*. Eugene, Ore.: Institute of Church Growth, 1962.

Torres Alvarado, Domingo, ed. *Cien años de Pentecostés desde la vivencia de la Iglesia Apostólica*. Zapopan, Jalisco: Iglesia Apostólica de la Fe en Cristo Jesús, 2014.

Treviño, Roberto. *The Church in the Barrio: Mexican-American Ethno-Catholicism in Houston*. Chapel Hill: University of North Carolina Press, 2006.

Truett, Samuel. *Fugitive Landscapes: The Forgotten History of the U.S.-Mexico Borderlands*. New Haven, Conn.: Yale University Press, 2006.

Tweed, Thomas A. *Crossing and Dwelling: A Theory of Religion*. Cambridge, Mass.: Harvard University Press, 2006.

———, ed. *Retelling U.S. Religious History*. Berkeley: University of California Press, 1997.

Tyson, James L. *The Early Pentecostal Revival: History of Twentieth-Century Pentecostals and the Pentecostal Assemblies of the World, 1901–30*. Hazelwood, Mo.: Word Aflame Press, 1992.

Uriarte, Tito. *Memoria. Hermano Tito Uriarte Armenta*. Culiacán, Sinaloa: by the author, 2001.

Valencia, Eduardo. *En tierra extraña. Itinerario del pueblo pentecostal chileno.* Santiago: Amerinda, 1988.

Valerio-Jiménez, Omar S. *River of Hope: Forging Identity and Nation in the Rio Grande Borderlands.* Durham, N.C.: Duke University Press, 2013.

Valverde, Efraím. *Recuerdo, Señor. Autobiografía del Pastor Efraím Valverde, Sr.* Salinas, Calif.: Publicaciones Maranata, 2002.

Valverde, Jaime. *Las sectas en Costa Rica. Pentecostalismo y conflicto social.* San José, Costa Rica: Editorial Departamento Ecuménico de Investigaciones, 1990.

Vélez-Ibáñez, Carlos. *Border Visions: Mexican Cultures of the Southwest.* Tucson: University of Arizona Press, 1996.

Vila, Pablo. *Crossing Borders, Reinforcing Borders: Social Categories, Metaphors, and Narrative Identities on the U.S.-Mexico Frontier.* Austin, University of Texas Press, 2000.

Wacker, Grant. *Heaven Below: Early Pentecostals and American Culture.* Cambridge, Mass.: Harvard University Press, 2001.

Währisch-Otto, Claudia. *The Missionary Self-Perception of Pentecostal/Charismatic Church Leaders from the Global South in Europe: Bringing back the Gospel.* Leiden, the Netherlands: Brill, 2009.

Walker, Randi J. *Protestantism in the Sangre de Cristos, 1850–1920.* Albuquerque: University of New Mexico Press, 1991.

Wallace, Ethel E. *Two Thousand Tongues to Go: The Story of the Wycliffe Bible Translators.* New York: Harper and Bros., 1959.

Weber, Max. *From Max Weber: Essays in Social Theory.* Edited by H. Gerth and C. W. Mills. London: Routledge, 1970.

Willems, Emilio. *Followers of the New Faith: Culture Change and the Rise of Protestantism in Brazil and Chile.* Nashville: Vanderbilt University Press, 1967.

INDEX

African American influences, 11, 14, 33–35, 56–59, 231 (n. 73)
Agrarismo, 15, 91, 92, 219 (n. 23); anti-agrarismo, 86
Ahlstrom, Sidney, 26
Alabanzas favoritas (hymnal, 1954, 1993), 249 (n. 21)
Aleluya, as epithet and culture, 7, 14, 27, 55, 72–73, 198–99
Alemán, Apolinar, 247 (n. 68)
Alemán, Valdes, Miguel, 108
Alvarado, Hermanos (Román, Rosario, and Juan), 16, 134–39, 167; discography of, 138, 209–11
American Board of Commissioners for Foreign Missions (ABCFM), 66, 226 (nn. 19, 20)
Anaya, Conrado and Herminia, 129
Anderson, Axel, 5, 213 (n. 8)
Anderson, Robert, 10–11, 36, 38–39, 60
Anticlericalism, 15, 48, 54–56, 90–91, 220 (n. 34), 235 (n. 48)
Anzaldúa, Gloria, 23–24
Aponte, Edwin, 196
Apostolicism, as movement, 8, 12–13, 14–15, 25, 43, 60, 65, 65, 72, 105, 120–21, 229 (n. 54); definition of, 214 (n. 13)
Appadurai, Arjun, 219 (n. 22)
Arballo, Jesús, 63, 247 (n. 68)
Archivo General de la Nación, 14
Assemblies of God (AG), 14, 18, 41, 43–49, 58–59, 64, 75, 138, 173, 196, 224 (n. 101), 225 (n. 11), 231 (n. 73), 239 (n. 29), 253 (n. 27)
Avalos, Francisco, 84–85, 97–104, 105, 106, 120, 134, 187
Avalos, Isidro, 98–101, 103, 104, 120

Avalos, José, 85, 97–102, 104
Avalos, Samuel, 133–34
Avalos, Secundino, 84–85, 97, 99, 101–4
Avila Camacho, Manuel, 108
Azusa Street Revival, 2–6, 14, 34–35, 40, 43, 60, 61, 62, 63, 72, 110, 197, 206–7; as contested origin myth, 218 (n. 11)

Badillo, David, 25
Baez-Camargo, Gonzalo, 161
Balderrama, Francisco, and Raymond Rodríguez, 86, 102
Ball, H. C., 44, 45–47, 49, 57, 58, 64, 70, 173
Banderas, Pedro, 115, 236 (n. 5), 237 (n. 8)
Bartleman, Frank, 35, 43, 214 (n. 17), 218 (n. 12)
Bastian, Jean-Pierre, 206
Bazán, Demetrio, 46, 222 (n. 61)
Best, Wallace, 185
Bienaventurados, Los (musical group), 194
Boas, Franz, 18, 207
Bolero, 180–81
Borderlands, 197; theory, 23–26
Borrego, Francisco, 74–76, 79, 106, 113
Bourdieu, Pierre, 199
Bracero evangelism, 15–16, 125–30
Bracero program, 15–16, 123–24, 144
Braceros, 16, 117, 127–30, 132–34, 144, 163, 251 (n. 60), 253 (n. 24)
Bricolage, bricoleurs, 16, 185–86, 189, 195
Bridegroom's Songs (hymnal), 56
Brusco, Elizabeth, 202

World Missions Conference (Edinburgh, 1910), 66, 223 (n. 64), 226 (n. 21)

World War II, 11, 86, 96, 122–23, 134, 144, 194, 228 (n. 42)

Worldwide Pentecostal Camp Meeting (Arroyo Seco, 1913), 42–43

Xenophobia, 1, 2, 14, 15, 83–86, 112, 116, 121, 134, 140

Yescas, Imelda, 139

Zapata, Emiliano, 38, 63
Zapata, María, 109
Zapoteco, 139
Zaragoza, Filemón, 154, 190, 245 (n. 37); "Mi Plegaria," 181

Made in the USA
Middletown, DE
23 July 2018